THE O'LEARY SER

Microsoft®
Excel 2000

Introductory Edition

Timothy J. O'Leary
Arizona State University

Linda I. O'Leary

Irwin
McGraw-Hill

Boston   Burr Ridge, IL   Dubuque, IA   Madison, WI   New York
San Francisco   St. Louis   Bangkok   Bogotá   Caracas   Lisbon
London   Madrid   Mexico City   Milan   New Delhi   Seoul
Singapore   Sydney   Taipei   Toronto

McGraw-Hill Higher Education

*A Division of The **McGraw-Hill** Companies*

MICROSOFT® EXCEL 2000, INTRODUCTORY EDITION

This book is printed on acid-free paper.

domestic   6 7 8 9 0 QPD/QPD 9 0 9 8 7 6 5 4 3 2 1
international 6 7 8 9 0 QPD/QPD 9 0 9 8 7 6 5 4 3 2 1

ISBN 0-07-233739-7

Vice president/Editor-in-chief: *Michael W. Junior*
Publisher: *David Brake*
Sponsoring editor: *Trisha O'Shea*
Senior marketing manager: *Jodi McPherson*
Senior project manager: *Beth Cigler*
Manager, new book production: *Melonie Salvati*
Freelance design coordinator: *Gino Cieslik*
Cover design: *Francis Owens*
Supplement coordinator: *Marc Mattson*
Compositor: *Rogondino & Associates*
Typeface: *11/13 Century Book*
Printer: *Quebecor World Dubuque*

Library of Congress Catalog Card Number 99-65258

INTERNATIONAL EDITION ISBN 0-07-116813-3
Copyright © 2000, Exclusive rights by The McGraw-Hill Companies, Inc.
for manufacture and export.
This book cannot be re-exported from the country to which it is consigned
by McGraw-Hill.
The International Edition is not available in North America.

http://www.mhhe.com

THE O'LEARY SERIES

Microsoft® Excel 2000

Introductory Edition

Timothy J. O'Leary
Arizona State University

Linda I. O'Leary

At McGraw-Hill Higher Education, we publish instructional materials targeted at the higher education market. In an effort to expand the tools of higher learning, we publish texts, lab manuals, study guides, testing materials, software, and multimedia products.

At **Irwin/McGraw-Hill** (a division of McGraw-Hill Higher Education), we realize that technology has created and will continue to create new mediums for professors and students to use in managing resources and communicating information with one another. We strive to provide the most flexible and complete teaching and learning tools available as well as offer solutions to the changing world of teaching and learning.

Irwin/McGraw-Hill **is dedicated to providing the tools for today's instructors and students to successfully navigate the world of Information Technology.**

- **Seminar series**–Irwin/McGraw-Hill's Technology Connection seminar series offered across the country every year demonstrates the latest technology products and encourages collaboration among teaching professionals.

- **Osborne/McGraw-Hill**–This division of The McGraw-Hill Companies is known for its best-selling Internet titles *Harley Hahn's Internet & Web Yellow Pages* and the *Internet Complete Reference*. Osborne offers an additional resource for certification and has strategic publishing relationships with corporations such as Corel Corporation and America Online. For more information visit Osborne at **www.osborne.com**.

- **Digital solutions**–Irwin/McGraw-Hill is committed to publishing digital solutions. Taking your course online doesn't have to be a solitary venture, nor does it have to be a difficult one. We offer several solutions that will allow you to enjoy all the benefits of having course material online. For more information visit **www.mhhe.com/solutions/index.mhtml**.

- **Packaging options**–For more about our discount options, contact your local Irwin/McGraw-Hill Sales representative at 1-800-338-3987 or visit our Web site at **www.mhhe.com/it**.

Preface

Goals/Philosophy

The goal of **The O'Leary Series** is to give students a basic understanding of computing concepts and to build the skills necessary to ensure that information technology is an advantage in whatever path they choose in life. Because we believe that students learn better and retain more information when concepts are reinforced visually, we feature a unique visual orientation coupled with our trademark "learn by doing" approach.

Approach

The O'Leary Series is the true *step-by-step way to develop computer application skills*. The new Microsoft Office 2000 design emphasizes the step-by-step instructions with full screen captures that illustrate the results of each step performed. Each Tutorial (chapter) follows the "learn by doing" approach in combining conceptual coverage with detailed, software-specific instructions. A running case study that is featured in each tutorial highlights the real-world capabilities of each of the software applications and leads students step by step from problem to solution.

APPROVED COURSEWARE

APPROVED MICROSOFT COURSEWARE

Use of the Microsoft Office User Specialist Approved Courseware Logo on this product signifies that it has been independently reviewed and approved in compliance with the following standards: Acceptable coverage of all content related to the Microsoft Office Exam entitled Microsoft Excel 2000 and sufficient performance-based exercises that closely apply to all required content, based on sampling of text. For further information on Microsoft's MOUS certification program, please visit Microsoft's Web site at http://www.microsoft.com/office/train_cert/.

About the Book

The O'Leary Series offers 2 *levels* of instruction: Brief and Introductory. Each level builds upon the previous level.

■ **Brief**—This level covers the basics of an application and contains two to three chapters.

■ **Introductory**—This level includes the material in the Brief textbook plus two to three additional chapters. The Introductory text prepares students for the *Microsoft Office User Specialist Exam (MOUS Certification)*.

Each text features:

- **Common Office 2000 Features**–This section provides a review of several basic procedures and Windows features. Students will also learn about many of the features that are common to all Microsoft Office 2000 applications.

- **Overview**–The Overview contains a "Before You Begin" section which presents both students and professors with all the information they need to know before starting the tutorials, including hardware and software settings. The Overview appears at the beginning of each lab manual and describes (1) what the program is, (2) what the program can do, (3) generic terms the program uses, and (4) the Case Study to be presented.

- **Working Together sections**–These sections provide the same hands-on visual approach found in the tutorials to the integration and new collaboration features of Office 2000.

- **Glossary**–The Glossary appears at the end of each text and defines all key terms that appear in boldface type throughout the tutorials and in the end-of-tutorial Key Terms lists.

- **Index**–The Index appears at the end of each text and provides a quick reference to find specific concepts or terms in the text.

Introductory Edition

- -

The Introductory Edition is divided into six tutorials, followed by two Working Together sections.

Tutorial 1: Your first project is to develop a forecast for the café for the first quarter. You will learn to enter numbers, perform calculations, copy data, label rows and columns, and format entries in a spreadsheet using Excel 2000.

Tutorial 2: After creating the first quarter forecast for the Downtown Internet Café, you have decided to chart the sales data to make it easier to see the trends and growth patterns. You also want to see what effect a strong advertising promotion of the new café features will have on the forecast sales data.

Tutorial 3: You have been asked to revise the workbook to include forecasts for the second, third, and fourth quarters. Additionally, the owner wants you to create a composite worksheet that shows the entire year's forecast and to change the data to achieve a 5 percent profit margin in the second quarter.

Working Together: Your analysis of sales data for the first quarter has shown a steady increase in total sales. Evan, the café owner, has asked you for a copy of the forecast that shows the growth in Internet sales if a strong sales promotion is mounted. You will include the worksheet and chart data in a memo to the owner.

Tutorial 4: As you continue to work on the financial forecast for the Downtown Internet Café, you will use the Solver tool to achieve a quarterly profit margin of 6½ %. Additionally, you will create three different scenarios that will show the best, worst, and most likely scenarios for the annual forecast. Once the annual forecast for 2001 is complete, Evan wants you to use the same procedure to create the forecast for 2002. You will use the 2001 annual forecast worksheet to create a template for the next year's forecast and then you will use the template to create the first quarter forecast for that year.

Tutorial 5: Evan is considering the purchase of a new espresso/cappuccino machine and would like you to evaluate several different loan options. You will create a loan analysis spreadsheet that incorporates Excel's PMT function, macros, and data table feature. Next, Evan would like you to develop a spreadsheet to calculate and record customer Bonus Dollars. You will create an electronic form that uses the IF and Index functions to calculate and record customer Bonus Dollars.

Tutorial 6: You will create a separate worksheet database that contains the Café customers' contact information. You will also generate several reports from the database that summarize the monthly connection times to keep track of the computer usage at the Café, analyze seasonal trends, and plan marketing campaigns. In addition, you will create a data map based on the information in the worksheet database that will illustrate the diversity of the Café clientele by highlighting their home states on a U.S. map.

Working Together 2: To make it easier for the Café employees to enter the customer connection time information in one worksheet and customer contact information into another, you will create a hyperlink between them. Also, Evan has requested a copy of the pivot chart sheet and five-year forecast. You will e-mail the pivot chart sheet to him and embed the five-year forecast with the scenarios in a memo. Additionally, Evan has asked you to convert the data map sheet to a Web page so he can see if it would be a good candidate to add to the Café Web site.

Each tutorial features:

- **Step-by-step instructions**—Each tutorial consists of step-by-step instructions along with accompanying screen captures. The screen captures represent how the student's screen should appear after completing a specific step.

- **Competencies**—Listed at the beginning of each tutorial, the Competencies describe what skills will be mastered upon completion of the tutorial.

- **Concept Overview**—Located at the start of each tutorial, the Concept Overviews provide a brief introduction to the concepts to be presented.

- **Concept boxes**—Tied into the Concept Overviews, the Concept boxes appear throughout the tutorial and provide clear, concise

EXCEL 2000

explanations of the concepts under discussion, which makes them a valuable study aid.

- **Marginal notes**—Appearing throughout the tutorial, marginal notes provide helpful hints, suggestions, troubleshooting advice, and alternative methods of completing tasks.

- **Case study**—The running case study carried throughout each tutorial and is based on real use of software in a business setting.

- **End-of-tutorial material**—At the end of each tutorial the following is provided:

  Concept Summary—This two-page spread presents a visual summary of the concepts presented in the tutorial and can be used as a study aid for students.

  Key Terms—This page-referenced list is a useful study aid for students.

  Matching/Multiple Choice/True False Questions

  Command Summary—The Command Summary includes keyboard and toolbar shortcuts.

  Screen Identifications—These exercises ask students to demonstrate their understanding of the applications by identifying screen features.

  Discussion Questions—These questions are designed to stimulate in-class discussion.

  Hands-On Practice Exercises—These detailed exercises of increasing difficulty ask students to create Office documents based on the skills learned in the tutorial.

  On Your Own—These problems of increasing difficulty ask students to employ more creativity and independence in creating Office documents based on new case scenarios.

Acknowledgments

The new edition of the Microsoft Office 2000 has been made possible only through the enthusiasm and dedication of a great team of people. Because the team spans the country, literally from coast to coast, we have utilized every means of working together including conference calls, FAX, e-mail, and document collaboration . . . we have truly tested the team approach and it works!

Leading the team from Irwin/McGraw-Hill is Trisha O'Shea, Sponsoring Editor. Her renewed commitment, direction, and support has infused the team with the excitement of a new project.

The production staff is headed by Beth Cigler, Senior Project Manager whose planning and attention to detail has made it possible for us to successfully meet a very challenging schedule. Members of the production team include: Gino Cieslik and Francis Owens, art and design, Pat Rogondino, layout; Susan Defosset, Betsy Blumenthal, and Joan Paterson, copy editing. While all have contributed immensely, I would particularly like to thank Pat and Susan . . . team members for many past editions whom I can always depend on to do a great job. My thanks also go to the project Marketing Manager, Jodi McPherson, for her enthusiastic promotion of this edition.

Finally, I am particularly grateful to a small but very dedicated group of people who helped me develop the manuscript. My deepest appreciation is to my co-author, consultant, and lifelong partner, Tim, for his help and support while I have been working on this edition. Colleen Hayes who has been assisting me from the beginning, continues to be my right arm, taking on more responsibility with each edition. Susan Demar and Carol Dean have also helped on the last several editions and continue to provide excellent developmental and technical support. New to the project this year are Bill Barth, Kathi Duggan, and Steve Willis, who have provided technical expertise and youthful perspective.

Reviewers

We would also like to thank the reviewers for their insightful input and criticism. Their feedback has helped to make this edition even stronger.

Josephine A. Braneky, *New York City Technical College*
Robert Breshears, *Maryville University*

Gary Buterbaugh, *Indiana University of Pennsylvania*
Mitchell M. Charkiewicz, *Bay Path College*
Seth Hock, *Columbus State Community College*
Katherine S. Hoppe, *Wake Forest University*
Lisa Miller, *University of Central Oklahoma*
Anne Nelson, *High Point University*
Judy Tate, *Tarrant County Junior College*
Dottie Sunio, *Leeward Community College*
Charles Walker, *Harding University*
Mark E. Workman, *Blinn College*

Additionally, each semester I hear from students at Arizona State University who are enrolled in the Introduction to Computers course. They constantly provide great feedback from a student's perspective . . . I thank you all.

Finally, I would like to thank Keri Howard, Manager for the Coffee Plantation, for her evaluation and input into the Downtown Internet Café case study.

Features of This Text

Concept Boxes identify the most important concepts in each Tutorial.

Concept ⑤ Automatic Grammar Check

The automatic grammar-checking feature advises you of incorrect grammar as you create and edit a document, and proposes possible corrections. If Word detects grammatical errors in subject-verb agreements, verb forms, capitalization, or commonly confused words, to name a few, they are identified with a wavy green line. You can correct the grammatical error by editing it or you can display a suggested correction. Not all grammatical errors identified by Word are actual errors. Use discretion when correcting the errors. Grammar checking does not occur until after you enter punctuation or end a line.

suggested correction

2 ■ Right-click on Announcing four to display the Grammar shortcut menu.

Your screen should be similar to Figure 1–10.

related menu options

Grammar shortcut menu

Tables provide quick summaries of toolbar buttons, key terms, and procedures for specific tasks.

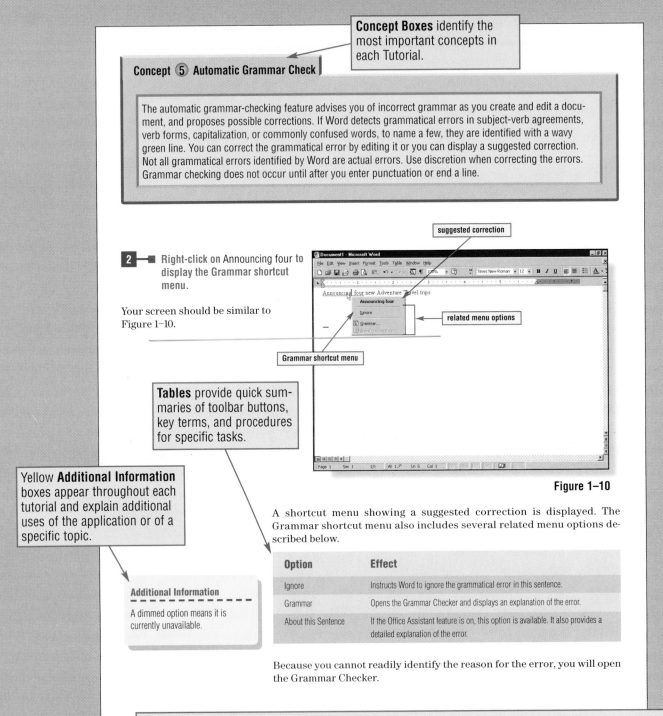

Figure 1–10

Yellow **Additional Information** boxes appear throughout each tutorial and explain additional uses of the application or of a specific topic.

A shortcut menu showing a suggested correction is displayed. The Grammar shortcut menu also includes several related menu options described below.

Additional Information

A dimmed option means it is currently unavailable.

Option	Effect
Ignore	Instructs Word to ignore the grammatical error in this sentence.
Grammar	Opens the Grammar Checker and displays an explanation of the error.
About this Sentence	If the Office Assistant feature is on, this option is available. It also provides a detailed explanation of the error.

Because you cannot readily identify the reason for the error, you will open the Grammar Checker.

Other Features

Real World Case—Each O'Leary Lab Manual provides students with a fictitious running case study. This case study provides students with the real-world capabilities for each software application. Each tutorial builds upon the gained knowledge of the previous tutorial with a single case study running throughout each Lab Manual.

End-of-Chapter Material—Each tutorial ends with a visual **Concept Summary**. This two-page spread presents a concept summary of the concepts presented in the tutorial and can be used as a study aid for

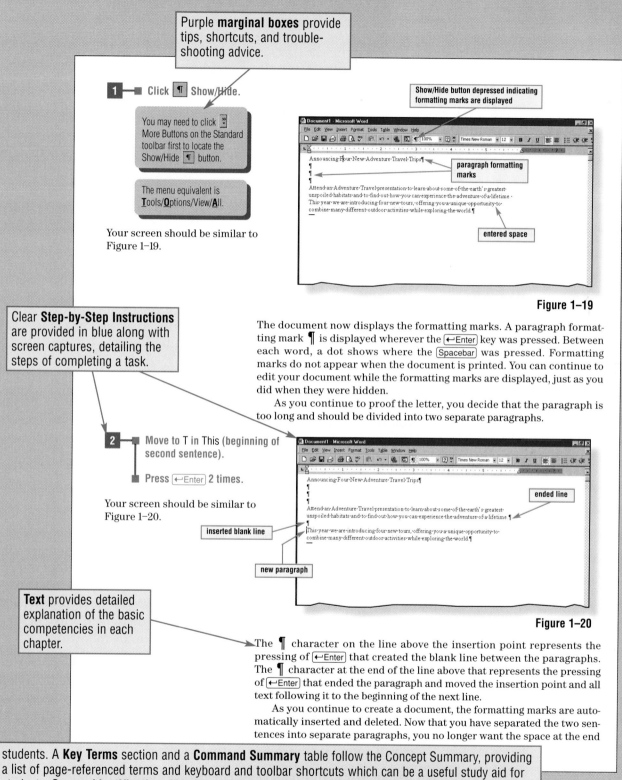

Purple **marginal boxes** provide tips, shortcuts, and trouble-shooting advice.

1 ■ Click ¶ Show/Hide.

You may need to click More Buttons on the Standard toolbar first to locate the Show/Hide ¶ button.

The menu equivalent is **T**ools/**O**ptions/View/**A**ll.

Your screen should be similar to Figure 1–19.

Show/Hide button depressed indicating formatting marks are displayed

paragraph formatting marks

entered space

Announcing·Four·New·Adventure·Travel·Trips¶

Attend·an·Adventure·Travel·presentation·to·learn·about·some·of·the·earth's·greatest·unspoiled·habitats·and·to·find·out·how·you·can·experience·the·adventure·of·a·lifetime·This·year·we·are·introducing·four·new·tours,·offering·you·a·unique·opportunity·to·combine·many·different·outdoor·activities·while·exploring·the·world.¶

Figure 1–19

The document now displays the formatting marks. A paragraph formatting mark ¶ is displayed wherever the ←Enter key was pressed. Between each word, a dot shows where the Spacebar was pressed. Formatting marks do not appear when the document is printed. You can continue to edit your document while the formatting marks are displayed, just as you did when they were hidden.

As you continue to proof the letter, you decide that the paragraph is too long and should be divided into two separate paragraphs.

Clear **Step-by-Step Instructions** are provided in blue along with screen captures, detailing the steps of completing a task.

2 ■ Move to T in This (beginning of second sentence).

■ Press ←Enter 2 times.

Your screen should be similar to Figure 1–20.

inserted blank line

new paragraph

ended line

Announcing·New·Adventure·Travel·Trips¶

Attend·an·Adventure·Travel·presentation·to·learn·about·some·of·the·earth's·greatest·unspoiled·habitats·and·to·find·out·how·you·can·experience·the·adventure·of·a·lifetime·¶
This·year·we·are·introducing·four·new·tours,·offering·you·a·unique·opportunity·to·combine·many·different·outdoor·activities·while·exploring·the·world¶

Figure 1–20

Text provides detailed explanation of the basic competencies in each chapter.

The ¶ character on the line above the insertion point represents the pressing of ←Enter that created the blank line between the paragraphs. The ¶ character at the end of the line above that represents the pressing of ←Enter that ended the paragraph and moved the insertion point and all text following it to the beginning of the next line.

As you continue to create a document, the formatting marks are automatically inserted and deleted. Now that you have separated the two sentences into separate paragraphs, you no longer want the space at the end

students. A **Key Terms** section and a **Command Summary** table follow the Concept Summary, providing a list of page-referenced terms and keyboard and toolbar shortcuts which can be a useful study aid for students. **Screen Identification**, **Matching**, **Multiple Choice**, and **True False Questions** provide additional reinforcement to the tutorial material. **Discussion Questions**, **Hands-on Practice Exercises**, and **On Your Own Exercises** develop critical thinking skills and offer step-by-step practice. These exercises have a rating system from Easy to Difficult and test the student's ability to apply the knowledge they have gained in each tutorial. Each O'Leary Lab Manual provides at least two **On the Web** exercises where students are asked to use the Web to solve a particular problem.

Teaching Resources

The following is a list of supplemental material that can be used to help teach this course.

Skills Assessment

Irwin/McGraw-Hill offers two innovative systems that can be used with The O'Leary Series, ATLAS and SimNet, which take skills assessment testing beyond the basics with pre- and post-assessment capability.

- **ATLAS (Active Testing and Learning Assessment Software)**—ATLAS is our **live** in-the-application skills assessment tool. ATLAS allows students to perform tasks while working *live* within the Microsoft applications environment. ATLAS is web-enabled and can be customized to meet the needs of your course. ATLAS is available for Office 2000.

- **SimNet (Simulated Network Assessment Product)**—SimNet permits you to test the actual software skills students learn about Microsoft Office applications in a simulated environment. SimNet is web-enabled and is available for Office 97 and Office 2000.

Instructor's Resource Kits

Instructor's Resource Kits provide professors with all of the ancillary material needed to teach a course. Irwin/McGraw-Hill is committed to providing instructors with the most effective instructional resources available. Many of these resources are available at our Information Technology Supersite, found at **www.mhhe.com/it**. Our Instructor's Resource Kits are available on CD-ROM and contain the following:

- **Diploma by Brownstone**—Diploma is the most flexible, powerful, and easy to use computerized testing system available in higher education. The Diploma system allows professors to create an exam as a printed version, as a LAN-based Online version, or as an Internet version. Diploma also includes grade book features, which automate the entire testing process.

- **Instructor's Manual**—The Instructor's Manual includes solutions to all lessons and end of the unit material, teaching tips and strategies, and additional exercises.

- **Student Data Files**—Students must have student data files in order to complete practice and test sessions. The instructor and students using this text in classes are granted the right to post student data files on any network or stand-alone computer, or to distribute the files on individual diskettes. The student data files may be downloaded from our IT Supersite at **www.mhhe.com/it**.

- **Series Web site**—Available at **www.mhhe.com/cit/oleary**.

Digital Solutions

- **Pageout Lite**—This software is designed for you if you're just beginning to explore Web site options. Pageout Lite will help you to easily post your own material online. You may choose one of three templates, type in your material, and Pageout Lite will instantly convert it to HTML.

- **Pageout**—Pageout is our Course Web Site Development Center. Pageout offers a syllabus page, Web site address, Online Learning Center content, online exercises and quizzes, gradebook, discussion board, an area for students to build their own Web pages, plus all features of Pageout Lite. For more information please visit the Pageout Web site at **www.mhla.net/pageout**.

- **OLC/Series Web Sites**—Online Learning Centers (OLCs)/series sites are accessible through our Supersite at **www.mhhe.com/it**. Our Online Learning Centers/series sites provide pedagogical features and supplements for our titles online. Students can point and click their way to key terms, learning objectives, chapter overviews, PowerPoint slides, exercises, and Web links.

- **The McGraw-Hill Learning Architecture (MHLA)**—MHLA is a complete course delivery system. MHLA gives professors ownership in the way digital content is presented to the class through online quizzing, student collaboration, course administration, and content management. For a walk-through of MHLA, visit the MHLA Web site at **www.mhla.net**.

Packaging Options

For more about our discount options, contact your local Irwin/McGraw-Hill sales representative at 1-800-338-3987 or visit our Web site at **www.mhhe.com/it**.

EXCEL 2000

Contents

Introducing Common Office 2000 Features

This section will review several basic procedures and Windows features. In addition, you will learn about many of the features that are common to all Microsoft Office 2000 applications. Although Excel 2000 will be used to demonstrate how the features work, only common features will be addressed. The features that are specific to each application will be introduced individually in each tutorial.

Turning on the Computer

If necessary, follow the procedure below to turn on your computer.

1

Do not have any disks in the drives when you start the computer.

- **Turn on the power switch.** The power switch is commonly located on the back or right side of your computer. It may also be a button that you push on the front of your computer.

- **If necessary, turn your monitor on and adjust the contrast and brightness.** Generally, the button to turn on the monitor is located on the front of the monitor. Use the dials (generally located in the panel on the front of the monitor) to adjust the monitor.

Press [Tab ⇤] to move to the next box.

- **If you are on a network, you may be asked to enter your User Name and Password. Type the required information in the boxes. When you are done, press** [← Enter].

The Windows program is loaded into the main memory of your computer and the Windows desktop is displayed.

Your screen should be similar to Figure 1.

Figure 1

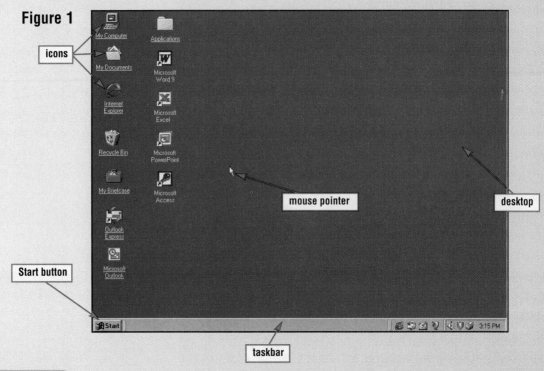

The **desktop** is the opening screen for Windows and is the place where you begin your work using the computer. Figure 1 shows the Windows 98 desktop. If you are using Windows 95, your screen will look slightly different. Small pictures, called **icons**, represent the objects on the desktop. Your desktop will probably display many different icons than those shown here. At the bottom of the desktop screen is the **taskbar**. It contains buttons that are used to access programs and features. The **Start button** on the left end of the taskbar is used to start a program, open a document, get help, find information, and change system settings.

> If a Welcome box is displayed, click ☒ (in the upper right corner of the box) to close it.

> If you are already familiar with using a mouse, skip to the section Loading an Office Application.

Using a Mouse

The arrow-shaped symbol on your screen is the **mouse pointer**. It is used to interact with objects on the screen and is controlled by the hardware device called a **mouse** that is attached to your computer.

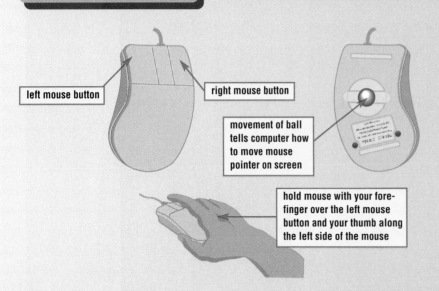

The mouse pointer changes shape on the screen depending on what it is pointing to. Some of the most common shapes are shown in the table below.

Pointer Shape	Meaning
⬉	Normal select
👆	Link select
⧗	Busy
⊘	Area is not available

If your system has a stick, ball or touch pad, the buttons are located adjacent to the device.

On top of the mouse are two or three buttons that are used to choose items on the screen. The mouse actions and descriptions are shown in the table below.

Action	Description
Point	Move the mouse so the mouse pointer is positioned on the item you want to use.
Click	Press and release a mouse button. The left mouse button is the primary button that is used for most tasks.
Double-click	Quickly press and release the left mouse button twice.
Drag	Move the mouse while holding down a mouse button.

Throughout the labs, "click" means to use the left mouse button. If the right mouse button is to be used, the directions will tell you to right-click on the item.

1 Move the mouse in all directions (up, down, left, and right) and note the movement of the mouse pointer.

■ Point to 🖳 My Computer ►

Your screen should be similar to Figure 2.

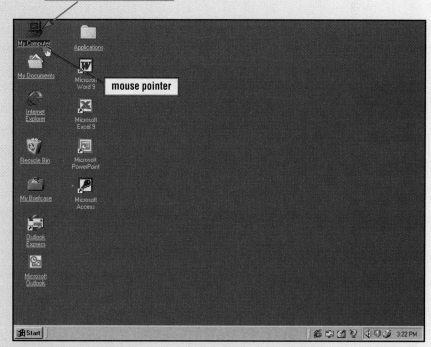

Figure 2

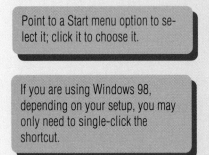

The pointer on the screen moved in the direction you moved the mouse and currently appears as a 🖑. The icon appears highlighted, indicating it is the selected item and ready to be used. A **ScreenTip** box containing a brief description of the item you are pointing to may be displayed.

Starting an Office Application

There are several ways to start an Office application. One is to use the Start/New Office Document command and select the type of document you want to create. Another is to use Start/Documents and select the document name from the list of recently used documents. This starts the associated application and opens the selected document at the same time. The two most common ways to start an Office 2000 application are by choosing the application name from the Start menu or by clicking a desktop shortcut for the program if it is available.

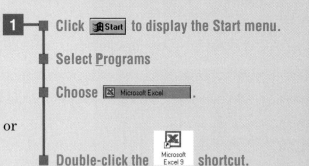

1 ■ Click ▣Start to display the Start menu.

■ Select **P**rograms

■ Choose 🅧 Microsoft Excel .

or

■ Double-click the [Microsoft Excel 9] shortcut.

After a few moments, the Excel application window is displayed, and your screen should be similar to Figure 3.

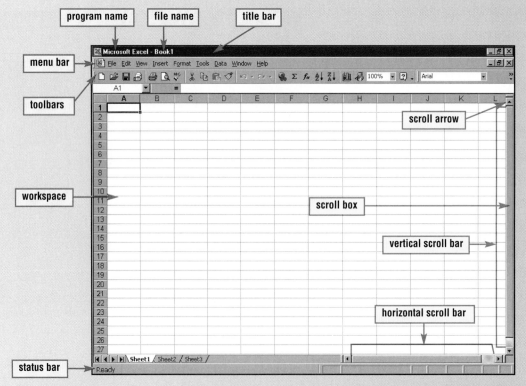

Figure 3

Basic Windows Features

As you can see, many of the features in the Excel window are the same as in other Windows applications. Among those features is a title bar, a menu bar, toolbars, a document window, scroll bars, and mouse compatibility. You can move and size Office application windows, select commands, use Help, and switch between files and programs, just as you can in Windows. The common user interface makes learning and using new applications much easier.

TITLE BAR

The Excel window title bar displays the program name, Microsoft Excel, followed by the file name Book1, the default name of the file displayed in the window. The left end of the title bar contains the Excel application window ⬛ Control-menu icon, and the right end displays the ⬛ Minimize, ⬛ Restore, and ⬛ Close buttons. They perform the same functions and operate in the same way as in Windows 95 and Windows 98.

1 — If necessary, click ⬛ in the title bar to maximize the application window.

MENU BAR

The **menu bar** below the title bar displays the Excel program menu, which consists of nine menus. The right end displays the workbook window Minimize, Restore, and Close buttons. As you use the Office applications, you will see that the menu bar contains many of the same menus, such as File, Edit, and Help. You will also see several menus that are specific to each application. You will learn about using the menus in the next section.

TOOLBARS

The **toolbar** located below the menu bar contains buttons that are mouse shortcuts for many of the menu items. Commonly, the Office applications will display two toolbars when the application is first opened: Standard and Formatting. They may appear together on one row, or on separate rows. You will learn about using the toolbars shortly.

WORKSPACE

The **workspace** is the large center area of the Excel application window where workbook files are displayed in open windows. Currently, there is one open workbook window, which is maximized and occupies the entire area.

STATUS BAR

The **status bar** at the bottom of the window displays location information and the status of different settings as they are used. Different information is displayed in the status bar for different applications.

SCROLL BARS

A **scroll bar** is used with a mouse to bring additional lines of information into view in a window. It consists of **scroll arrows** and a **scroll box**.

Clicking the scroll arrows moves the information in the direction of the arrows, allowing new information to be displayed in the workspace. You can also move to a general location within the area by dragging the scroll box up or down the scroll bar. The location of the scroll box on the scroll bar indicates your relative position within the area of available information. Scroll bars can run vertically along the right side or horizontally along the bottom of a window. The vertical scroll bar is used to move vertically, and the horizontal scroll bar moves horizontally in the space.

Using Office 2000 Features

MENUS

A **menu** is one of many methods you can use to tell a program what you want it to do. When opened, a menu displays a list of commands. Most menus appear in a menu bar. Other menus pop up when you right-click (click the right mouse button) on an item. This type of menu is called a **shortcut menu**.

1 ■ **Click File to open the File menu.**

Your screen should be similar to Figure 4.

menu command

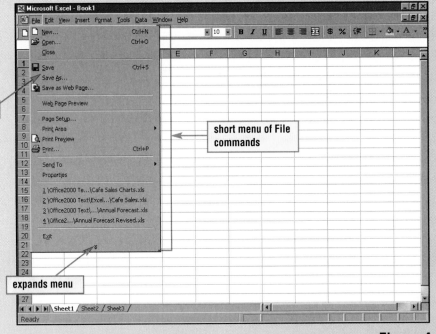

short menu of File commands

expands menu

Figure 4

When a menu is first opened, it displays a short version of commands. The short menu displays basic commands when the application is first used. As you use the application, those commands you use frequently are listed on the short menu and others are hidden. Because the short menu is personalized automatically to the user's needs, different commands may be listed on your File menu than appear in Figure 4 above.

An expanded version will display automatically after the menu is open for a few seconds (see Figure 5). If you do not want to wait for the expanded version to appear, you can click ✻ at the bottom of the menu and the menu list will expand to display all commands.

You can double-click the menu name to show the expanded menu immediately.

Your screen should be similar to Figure 5.

Figure 5

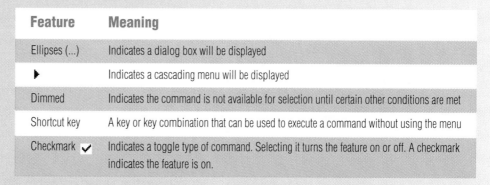

command on hidden menu

expanded menu of File commands

The commands that are in the hidden menu appear on a light gray background. Once one menu is expanded, others are expanded automatically until you choose a command or perform another action.

2
- Point to each menu in the menu bar to see the expanded menu for each.

- Point to the File menu again.

Many commands have images next to them so you can quickly associate the command with the image. The same image appears on the toolbar button for that feature.

Menus may include the following features (not all menus include all features):

Feature	Meaning
Ellipses (...)	Indicates a dialog box will be displayed
▶	Indicates a cascading menu will be displayed
Dimmed	Indicates the command is not available for selection until certain other conditions are met
Shortcut key	A key or key combination that can be used to execute a command without using the menu
Checkmark ✓	Indicates a toggle type of command. Selecting it turns the feature on or off. A checkmark indicates the feature is on.

Once a menu is open, you can *select* a command from the menu by pointing to it. A colored highlight bar, called the **selection cursor**, appears over the selected command. If the selected command line displays a right-facing arrow, a submenu of commands automatically appears when the command is selected. This is commonly called a **cascading menu**.

3 ━━■ Point to the Send To command to display the cascading menu.

Your screen should be similar to Figure 6.

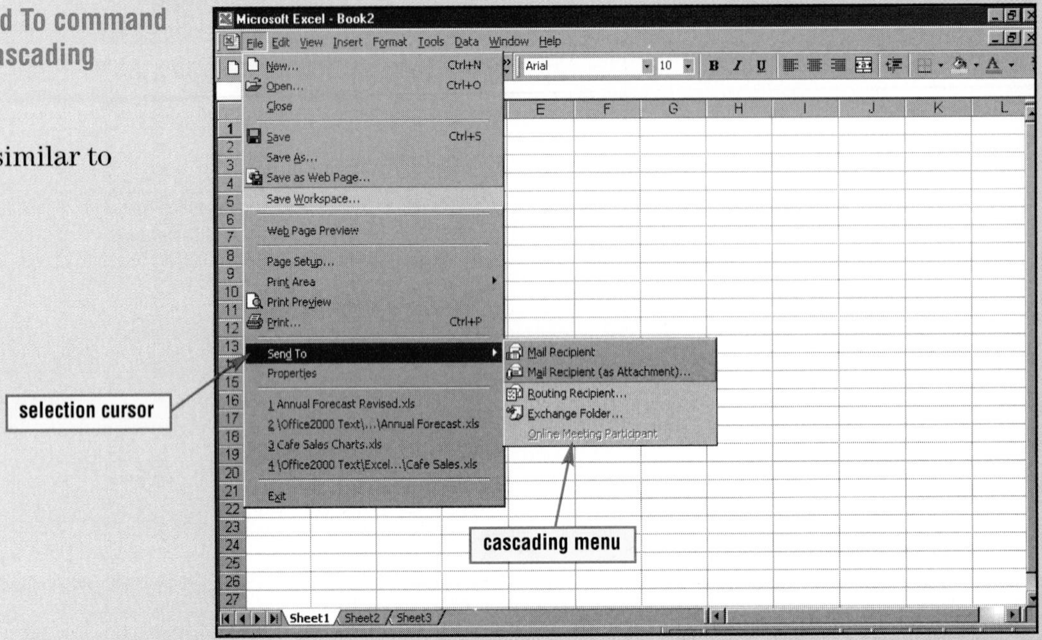

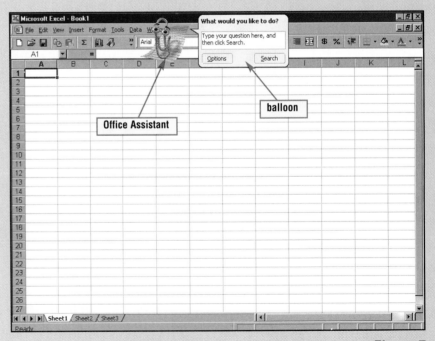

Figure 6

You can also type the underlined command letter to choose a command. If the command is already selected, you can press ←Enter to choose it.

Then to *choose* a command, you click on it. When the command is chosen, the associated action is performed. You will use a command in the Help menu to access the Microsoft Office Assistant and Help feature.

Note: If your Office Assistant feature is already on, as shown in Figure 7, skip step 4.

4 ━■ Point to Help.

■ Choose Show the Office Assistant.

If the Assistant does not appear, your school has disabled this feature. If this is the case, choose Help/Microsoft Excel Help and skip to the section Using Help.

Your screen should be similar to Figure 7.

Figure 7

The command to display the Assistant has been executed, and the Office Assistant character is displayed. Because there are a variety of Office Assistant characters, your screen may display a different character than shown here.

Using the Office Assistant

When the Office Assistant is on, it automatically suggests help topics as you work. It anticipates what you are going to do and then makes suggestions on how to perform the task. In addition, you can activate the Assistant at any time to get help on features in the Office application you are using. When active, the Office Assistant balloon appears and displays a prompt and a text box in which you can type the topic you want help on.

1 ■ If the balloon is not displayed as in Figure 7 above, click the Office Assistant character to activate it.

You will ask the Office Assistant to provide information on the different ways you can get help while using the program.

2 ■ Type **How do I get help?**

■ Click [Search].

Your screen should be similar to Figure 8.

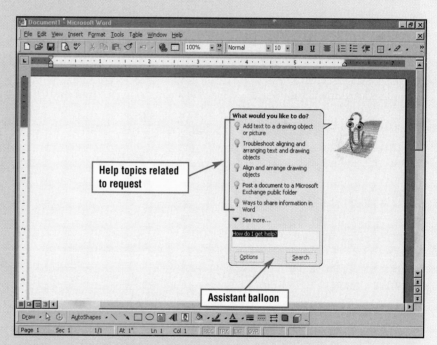

Figure 8

The balloon displays a list of related topics from which you can select.

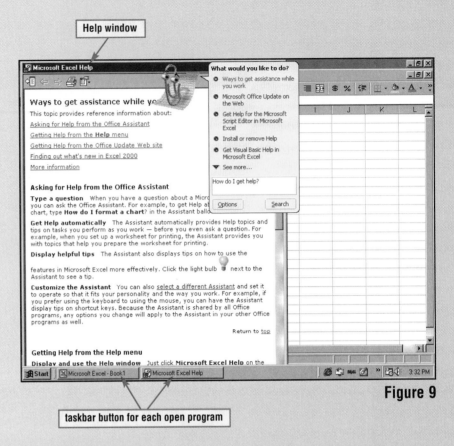

Figure 9

3 ▪ Click See more....

▪ Click Ways to get assistance while you work.

Your screen should be similar to Figure 9.

The Help program has been opened and displays the selected topic. Because Help is a separate program, it appears in its own window. The taskbar displays a button for both open windows. Now that Help is open, you no longer need to see the Assistant.

> You can also press [F1] to open Help if the Office Assistant is not on.

4 ▪ Click [Options].

▪ Select Use the Office Assistant to clear the checkmark.

▪ Click [OK].

▪ Click [Microsoft Excel Help] in the taskbar to switch back to the Help window.

> **Additional Information**
>
> The [Options] button is used to change the Office Assistant settings so it provides different levels of help, or to select a different Assistant character.

Using Help

In the Help window, the toolbar buttons help you use different Help features and navigate within Help. The ◁▤ Show button displays the Help Tabs frame.

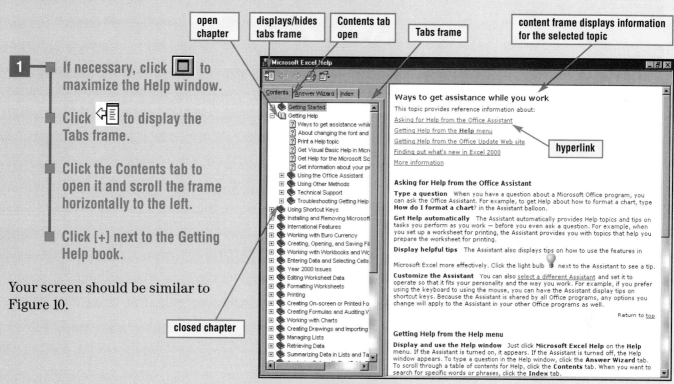

Figure 10

1 ■ If necessary, click ▢ to maximize the Help window.

■ Click ◁📄 to display the Tabs frame.

■ Click the Contents tab to open it and scroll the frame horizontally to the left.

■ Click [+] next to the Getting Help book.

Your screen should be similar to Figure 10.

The Help window is divided into two vertical frames. **Frames** divide a window into separate, scrollable areas that can display different information. The left frame in the Help window is the Tabs frame. The three folder-like tabs—Contents, Index, and Search—are used to access the three different means of getting Help information. The open tab appears in front of the other tabs and displays the available options for the feature. The right frame is the content frame. It displays the content for the located information.

The Contents tab displays a table of contents listing of topics in Help. Clicking on an item preceded with a 📖 opens a "chapter," which expands to display additional chapters or specific Help topics. Chapters are preceded with a 📖 icon and topics with a ❓ icon.

The content frame displays the selected Help topic. It contains more information than can be displayed at one time.

2 ■ Using the scroll bar, scroll the right frame to the bottom of the Help topic.

■ Scroll back to the top of the Help topic.

USING A HYPERLINK

The mouse pointer appears as 🖑 when pointing to a hyperlink.

Another way to move in Help is to click a hyperlink. A **hyperlink** is a connection to a location in the current document, another document, or the World Wide Web. It commonly appears as colored or underlined text. Clicking the hyperlink moves to the location associated with the hyperlink.

1 ■ **Click the** Asking for Help from the Office Assistant **hyperlink.**

Your screen should be similar to Figure 11.

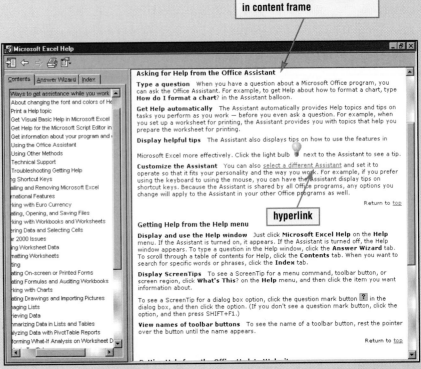

Figure 11

Help quickly jumps to the selected topic and displays the topic heading at the top of the frame.

2 ■ **Read the information displayed on this topic.**

■ **Click the** select a different Assistant **hyperlink.**

Your screen should be similar to Figure 12.

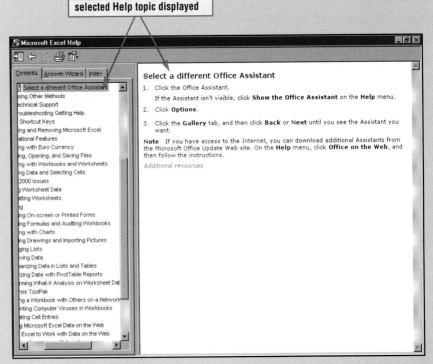

Figure 12

The Help topic about selecting a different Assistant is displayed. Notice the Contents list now highlights this topic, indicating it is the currently selected topic. Other hyperlinks may display a definition of a term.

3 ▬ **Click** the Internet **hyperlink.**

Your screen should be similar to Figure 13.

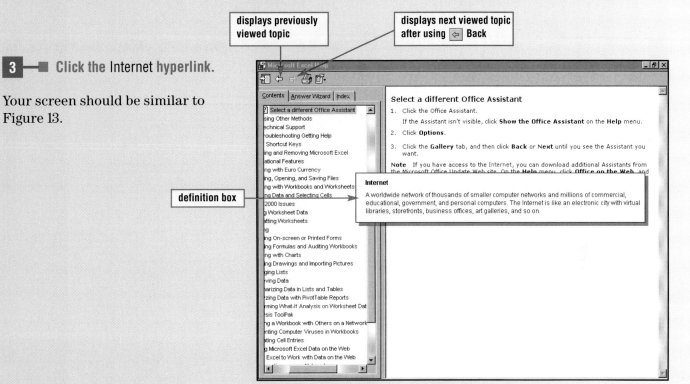

Figure 13

A box containing a definition of the Internet is displayed.

4 ▬ **Click on the definition box to clear it.**

To quickly return to the previous topic,

5 ▬ **Click** ⇦ **Back.**

The previous topic is displayed again.

The ⇨ Forward button is available after using ⇦ Back and can be used to move to the next viewed topic.

USING THE INDEX TAB

To search for Help information by entering a word or phrase for a topic, you can use the Index tab.

1 ■ Open the Index tab.

Your screen should be similar to Figure 14.

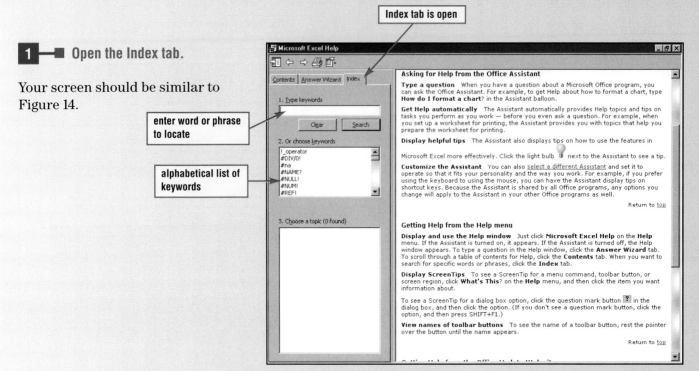

Figure 14

The Index tab consists of a text box where you can type a word or phrase that best describes the topic you want to locate. Below it is a list box displaying a complete list of Help keywords in alphabetical order. You want to find information about using the Index tab.

2 ■ Type **index** in the text box.

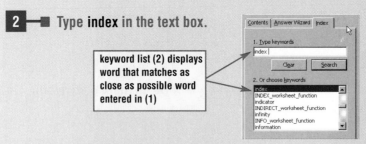

The keyword list jumps to the word "index." To locate all Help topics containing this word,

3 ■ Click [Search] .

Your screen should be similar to Figure 15.

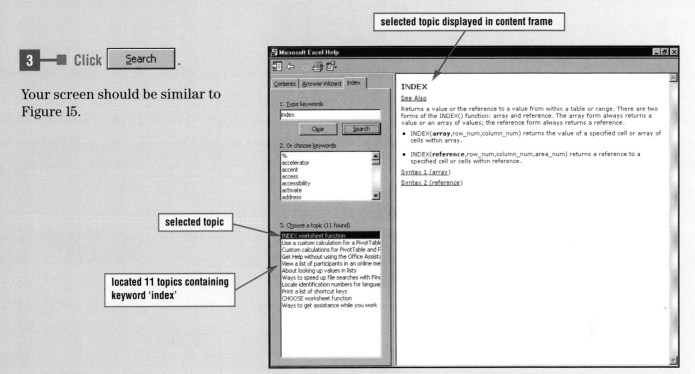

Figure 15

The topic list displayed the 11 located Help topics containing this word and displays the information on the first topic in the content frame. However, many of the located topics are not about the Help Index feature. To narrow the search more, you can add another word to the keyword text box.

4 ■ Type **help** in the keyword text box following the word index.

■ Click [Search] .

Your screen should be similar to Figure 16.

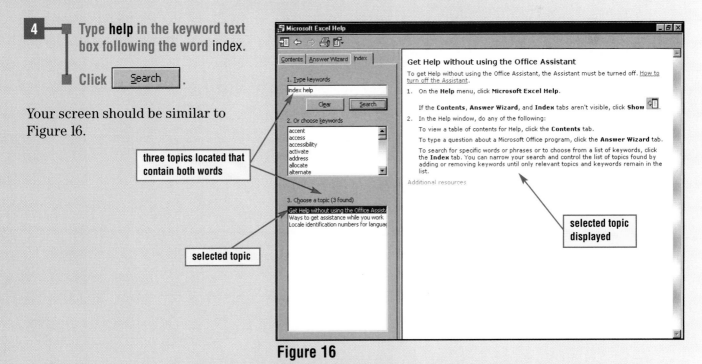

Figure 16

Now only three topics were located that contain both keywords. The first topic Get Help without using the Office Assistant is selected and displayed in the content frame.

USING THE ANSWER WIZARD

Another way to locate Help topics is to use the Answer Wizard tab. This feature works just like the Office Assistant to locate topics. You will use this method to locate Help information on toolbars.

1 Open the <u>A</u>nswer Wizard tab.

Type **How do toolbars work?** in the text box.

Click <u>S</u>earch .

Additional Information

The search term does not need to be worded as a question. It can also be a word or phrase.

Your screen should be similar to Figure 17.

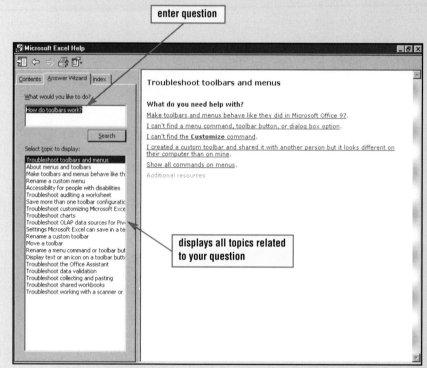

Figure 17

The topic list box displays all topics that the Answer Wizard considers may be related to the question you entered.

2 ■ Select About menus and toolbars from the topic list.

Your screen should be similar to Figure 18.

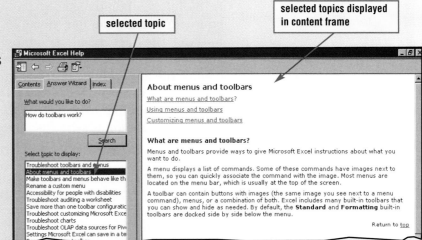

selected topic

selected topics displayed in content frame

Figure 18

3 ■ Click 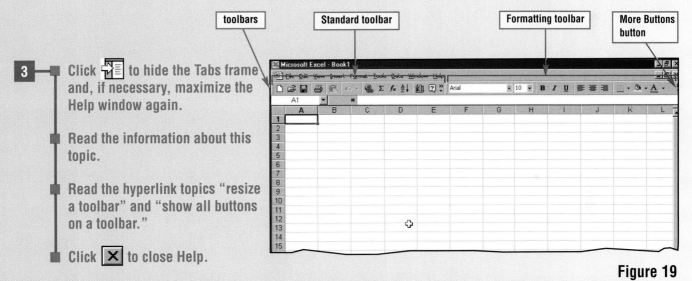 to hide the Tabs frame and, if necessary, maximize the Help window again.

■ Read the information about this topic.

■ Read the hyperlink topics "resize a toolbar" and "show all buttons on a toolbar."

■ Click ☒ to close Help.

Your screen should be similar to Figure 19.

toolbars   Standard toolbar   Formatting toolbar   More Buttons button

Figure 19

The Help window is closed, and the Excel window is displayed again.

Using Toolbars

While using Office 2000, you will see that many toolbars open automatically as different tasks are performed. Toolbars initially display the basic buttons. Like menus they are personalized automatically, displaying those buttons you use frequently and hiding others. The More Buttons ⸾ button located at the end of a toolbar displays a drop-down button list of those buttons that are not displayed. When you use a button from this list, it then is moved to the toolbar, and a button that has not been used recently is moved to the More Buttons list.

Initially, Excel displays two toolbars, Standard and Formatting, on one row below the menu bar (See Figure 19). The Standard toolbar contains buttons that are used to complete the most frequently used menu commands. The Formatting toolbar contains buttons that are used to change the appearance or format of the document. However, your screen may display different toolbars in different locations. If you right-click on a toolbar, the toolbar shortcut menu is displayed. Using this menu, you can specify which toolbars are displayed. To see which toolbars are open,

1—■ **Right-click on any toolbar.**

> The menu equivalent is **V**iew/**T**oolbars.

Your screen should be similar to Figure 20.

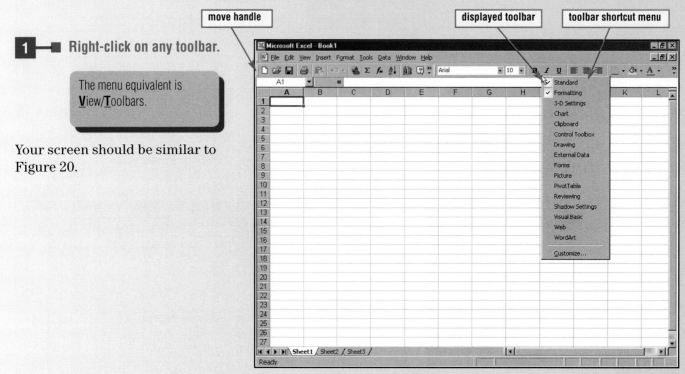

Figure 20

The toolbar shortcut menu displays a list of toolbar names. Those that are currently displayed are checked. Clicking on a toolbar from the list will display it onscreen. Clicking on a checked toolbar will hide the toolbar.

2—■ **If necessary, clear the checkmark from all toolbars other than the Standard and Formatting toolbars.**

There should now only be two open toolbars. When a toolbar is opened, it may appear docked or floating. A **docked** toolbar is fixed to an edge of the window and displays the move handle ▐ . Dragging this bar up or down allows you to move the toolbar. If multiple toolbars share the same row, dragging the bar left or right adjusts the size of the toolbar. If docked, a toolbar can occupy a row by itself, or several can be on a row together. A **floating** toolbar appears in a separate window that can be moved by dragging the title bar.

3 Drag the move handle of the Standard toolbar into the workspace.

> The mouse pointer appears as ✛ when you point to the ⫾ of any toolbar.

Your screen should be similar to Figure 21.

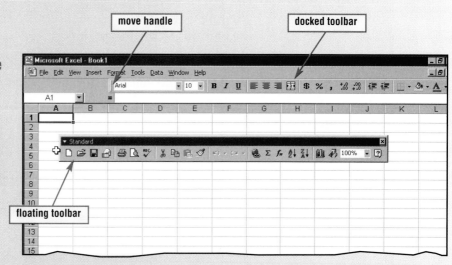

Figure 21

The Standard toolbar is now floating and can be moved to any location in the window by dragging the toolbar title bar. If you move it to the edge of the window, it will attach to that location and become a docked toolbar. A floating toolbar can also be sized by dragging the edge of the toolbar.

4 Move the floating toolbar to the left end of the row below the menu bar.

If necessary, move the Formatting toolbar to the right end of the same row as the Standard toolbar.

Your screen should be similar to Figure 22.

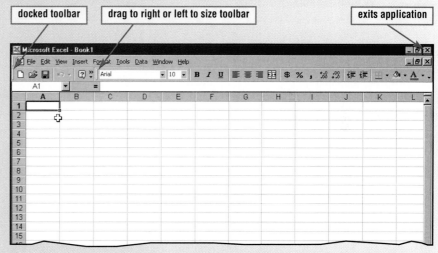

Figure 22

Additional Information

Double-clicking a toolbar when multiple toolbars share the same row minimizes or maximizes the toolbar size.

The two toolbars now occupy a single row. The size of each toolbar can be adjusted to show more or fewer buttons by dragging the move handle.

5 Drag the ⫾ of the Formatting toolbar to the right or left as needed until each bar occupies approximately half the row space.

To quickly identify the toolbar buttons, you can display the button name by pointing to the button.

6 ■ Point to any button on the Standard toolbar to see the ScreenTip displaying the button name.

Exiting an Office Application

The Exit command on the File menu can be used to quit most Windows programs. In addition, you can click the ☒ Close button in the application window title bar.

1 ■ Click ☒ Close.

The application window is closed, and the desktop is visible again.

Key Terms

cascading menu xxviii	ScreenTip xxiv
desktop xxii	scroll arrows xxv
docked xxxviii	scroll bar xxv
floating xxxviii	scroll box xxv
frame xxxi	selection cursor xxvii
hyperlink xxxi	shortcut menu xxvi
icon xxii	Start button xxii
menu xxvi	status bar xxv
menu bar xxv	taskbar xxii
mouse xxii	toolbar xxv
mouse pointer xxii	workspace xxv

Command Summary

Command	Shortcut Keys	Button	Action
Start/Programs			Opens program menu
File/Exit	Alt + F4	☒	Exits Excel program
View/Toolbars			Hides or displays toolbars
Help/Microsoft Excel Help	F1		Opens Help window
Help/Show the Office Assistant			Displays Help's Office Assistant

Overview of Excel 2000

What Is an Electronic Spreadsheet?

The electronic spreadsheet, or worksheet, is an automated version of the accountant's ledger. Like the accountant's ledger, it consists of rows and columns of numerical data. Unlike the accountant's ledger, which is created on paper using a pencil, an eraser, and a calculator, the electronic spreadsheet is created using a computer system and an electronic spreadsheet application software program.

In contrast to a word processor, which manipulates text, an electronic spreadsheet manipulates numerical data. The first electronic spreadsheet software program, VisiCalc, was offered on the market in 1979. Since then the electronic spreadsheet program has evolved into a powerful business tool that has revolutionized the business world.

The electronic spreadsheet eliminates the paper, pencil, and eraser. With a few keystrokes the user can quickly change, correct, and update the data. Even more impressive is the spreadsheet's ability to perform calculations from very simple sums to the most complex financial and mathematical formulas. The calculator is replaced by the electronic spreadsheet. Analysis of data in the spreadsheet has become a routine business procedure. Once requiring hours of labor and/or costly accountants' fees, data analysis is now available almost instantly using electronic spreadsheets.

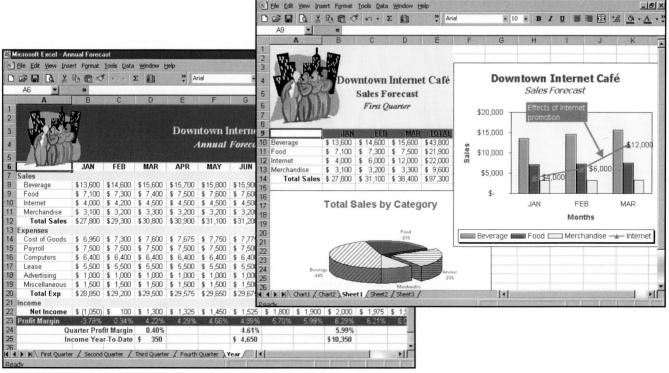

Nearly any job that uses rows and columns of numbers can be performed using an electronic spreadsheet. Typical uses of electronic spreadsheets are for budgets and financial planning in both business and personal situations.

Excel 2000 helps you create well-designed spreadsheets that produce accurate results. The application not only makes it faster to create the spreadsheet, but produces a professional-appearing result. The advantages are in the ability of the spreadsheet program to quickly edit and format data, perform calculations, create charts, and print the spreadsheet.

The data entered in an electronic spreadsheet can be edited and revised using the program commands. Numeric or text data is entered into the worksheet in a location called a cell. These entries can then be erased, moved, copied, or edited. Formulas can be entered that perform calculations using data contained in specified cells. The results of the calculations are displayed in the cell containing the formula.

The design and appearance of the spreadsheet can be enhanced in many ways. There are several commands that control the format or display of a numeric entry in a cell. For instance, numeric entries can be displayed with dollar signs or with a set number of decimal places. Text or label entries in a cell can be displayed centered or left- or right-aligned to improve the spreadsheet's appearance. You can further enhance the appearance of the spreadsheet by changing the type style and size and by adding special effects such as bold, italic, borders, boxes, drop shadows, and shading around selected cells. Columns and rows can be inserted and deleted. The cell width can be changed to accommodate entries of varying lengths.

You can play with the values in the worksheet to see the effect of changing specific values on the worksheet. This is called what-if or sensitivity analysis. Questions that once were too expensive to ask or took too long to answer can now be answered almost instantly and with little cost. Planning that was once partially based on instinct has been replaced to a great extent with facts. However, any financial planning resulting from the data in a worksheet is only as accurate as that data and the logic behind the calculations.

Excel 2000 also has the ability to produce a visual display of the data in the form of graphs or charts. As the values in the worksheet change, a graph referencing those values automatically reflects the new values. These graphs are a tool for visualizing the effects of changing values in a worksheet. You can also include a graph with the spreadsheet data. This way you can display and print it with the data it represents. You can also enhance the appearance of a graph by using different type styles and sizes, adding three-dimensional effects, and including text and objects such as lines and arrows.

Another feature is the ability to open and use multiple spreadsheet files at the same time. Additionally, you can create multiple spreadsheets within a file, called 3-D spreadsheets. Even more important is the ability to link spreadsheets so that when data in one file changes, it automatically updates the linked data in another file.

Case Study for Excel 2000 Tutorials

The Downtown Internet Café is a new concept in coffeehouses, combining the delicious aromas of a genuine coffeehouse with the fun of using the Internet. You are the new manager for the coffeehouse and are working with the owner, Evan, to develop a financial plan for the next year.

Before You Begin

To the Student

The following assumptions have been made:

■ Microsoft Excel 2000 has been properly installed on your computer system.

■ The data disk contains the data files needed to complete the series of Excel 2000 tutorials and practice exercises. These files are supplied by your instructor.

■ You are already familiar with how to use Windows and a mouse.

To the Instructor

By default, Office 2000 installs the most commonly used components and leaves others, such as the Solver and Database Query, to be installed when first accessed. It is assumed that these additional features have been installed prior to students using the tutorials.

Please be aware that the following settings are assumed to be in effect for the Excel 2000 program. These assumptions are necessary so that the screens and directions in the manual are accurate.

■ The Standard and Formatting toolbars share one row. The ScreenTips feature is active. (Use Tools/Customize/Options.)

■ The Office Assistant feature is not on (Right click on the Assistant, Select **O**ptions and clear the Use the Office Assistant option.)

■ The Normal view is on. Zoom is 100 percent. (Use View/Normal; View/Zoom/100%.)

■ All default settings for a new workbook are in effect including a default font size of 10 pt.

In addition, all figures in the tutorials reflect the use of a standard VGA display monitor set at 800 by 600. If another monitor setting is used, there may be more or fewer rows and columns displayed in the window than in the figures. The 800 by 600 setting displays rows 1 through 27 and columns A through L. This setting can be changed using Windows setup.

Microsoft Office Shortcut Bar

The Microsoft Office Shortcut Bar (shown below) may be displayed automatically on the Windows desktop. Commonly it appears in the right side of the desktop; however, it may appear in other locations, depending upon your setup. The Shortcut Bar on your screen may display different buttons. This is because the Shortcut Bar can be customized to display other toolbar buttons.

The Office Shortcut Bar makes it easy to open existing documents or to create new documents using one of the Microsoft Office applications. It can also be used to send e-mail, add a task to a to-do list, schedule appointments using Schedule[+], or add Contacts or Notes.

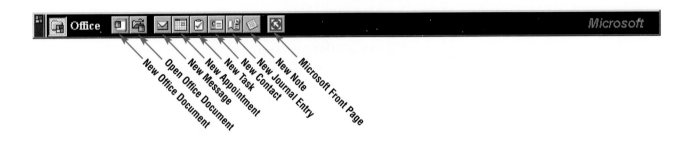

Instructional Conventions

Hands-on instructions you are to perform appear as a sequence of numbered blue steps. Within each step, a series of pink bullets identifies the specific actions that must be performed. Step numbering begins over within each main topic heading throughout the tutorial.

Command sequences you are to issue appear following the word "Choose." Each menu command selection is separated by a /. If the menu command can be selected by typing a letter of the command, the letter will appear underlined and bold. Items that need to be highlighted will follow the word "Select." You can select items with the mouse or directional keys.

EXAMPLE

1 ■ Choose **F**ile/**O**pen

■ **Select** Forecast.

Commands that can be initiated using a button and the mouse appear following the word "Click." The icon (and the icon name if the icon does not include text) is displayed following Click. The menu equivalent and keyboard shortcut appear in a margin note when the action is first introduced.

EXAMPLE

The menu equivalent is **F**ile/**O**pen and the keyboard shortcut is [Ctrl] + O.

1 — Click  Open

Black text identifies items you need to select or move to. Information you are asked to type appears in black and bold.

EXAMPLE

1 — Move to B3.

Type **Sales Forecast**.

Creating and Editing a Worksheet

Competencies

After completing this tutorial, you will know how to:

1. Enter, edit, and clear cell entries.
2. Save, close, and open workbooks.
3. Specify ranges.
4. Copy and move cell entries.
5. Enter formulas and functions.
6. Adjust column widths.
7. Change cell alignment.
8. Format cells.
9. Insert rows.
10. Insert and size a ClipArt graphic.
11. Enter and format a date.
12. Preview and print a worksheet.

Case Study

You are excited about your new position as manager and financial planner for a local coffeehouse. Evan, the owner, has hired you as part of a larger effort to increase business at the former Downtown Café. Evan began this effort by completely renovating his coffeehouse, installing Internet

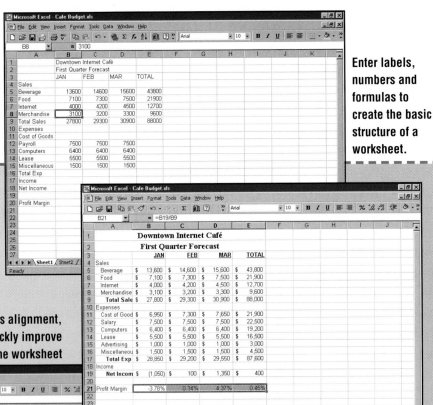

Enter labels, numbers and formulas to create the basic structure of a worksheet.

Basic formatting, such as alignment, indents, and numeric styles quickly improve the appearance of the worksheet

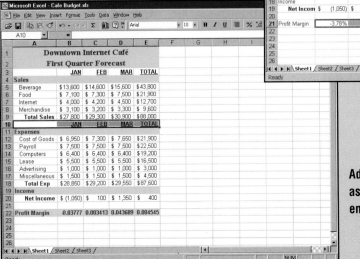

Adding color text and background fill as well as clipart (shown in final printout) further enhances the worksheet appearance.

hookups and outlets for laptops, and changing its name to the Downtown Internet Café. You and Evan expect to increase sales by attracting Internet-savvy café-goers, who, you hope, will use the Downtown Internet Café as a place to meet, study, or just relax.

Evan wants to create a forecast estimating sales and expenses for the first quarter. As part of a good business plan, you and Evan need a realistic set of financial estimates and goals.

In this tutorial, you will help with the first quarter forecast by using Microsoft Excel 2000, a spreadsheet application that can store, manipulate, and display numeric data. You will learn to enter numbers, perform calculations, copy data, label rows and columns as you create the basic structure of a worksheet for the Downtown Internet Café. You will then learn how to enhance the worksheet using formatting features and by inserting a ClipArt graphic as shown here.

Downtown Internet Café
First Quarter Forecast

	JAN	FEB	MAR	TOTAL
Sales				
Beverage	$13,600	$14,600	$15,600	$43,800
Food	$ 7,100	$ 7,300	$ 7,400	$21,800
Internet	$ 4,000	$ 4,200	$ 4,500	$12,700
Merchandise	$ 3,100	$ 3,200	$ 3,300	$ 9,600
Total Sales	$27,800	$29,300	$30,800	$87,900
	JAN	FEB	MAR	TOTAL
Expenses				
Cost of Goods	$ 6,950	$ 7,300	$ 7,600	$21,850
Salary	$ 7,500	$ 7,500	$ 7,500	$22,500
Computers	$ 6,400	$ 6,400	$ 6,400	$19,200
Lease	$ 5,500	$ 5,500	$ 5,500	$16,500
Advertising	$ 1,000	$ 1,000	$ 1,000	$ 3,000
Miscellaneous	$ 1,500	$ 1,500	$ 1,500	$ 4,500
Total Exp	$28,850	$29,200	$29,500	$87,550
Income				
Net Income	$ (1,050)	$ 100	$ 1,300	$ 350
Profit Margin	-3.78%	0.34%	4.22%	0.40%

S. Name
February 7, 2001

Concept Overview

The following concepts will be introduced in this tutorial:

1   **Worksheet Development** Worksheet development consists of four stages: planning, entering and editing, testing, and formatting.

2   **Types of Entries** The information or data you enter in a cell can be text, numbers, or formulas.

3   **Column Width** The size or width of a column controls how much information can be displayed in a cell.

4   **Range** A selection consisting of two or more cells on a worksheet is a range.

5   **Formulas** A formula is an entry that performs a calculation.

6   **Relative Reference** A relative reference is a cell or range reference in a formula whose location is interpreted by Excel in relation to the position of the cell that contains the formula.

7   **Functions** Functions are prewritten formulas that perform certain types of calculations automatically.

8   **Automatic Recalculation** Excel automatically recalculates formulas whenever a change occurs in a referenced cell.

9   **Alignment** Alignment settings allow you to change the horizontal and vertical placement and the orientation of an entry in a cell.

10   **Fonts** Fonts consist of typefaces, point sizes, and styles that can be applied to characters to improve their appearance.

11   **Character Effects** Different character effects can be applied to selections to add emphasis or interest to a document.

12   **Number Formats** Number formats affect how numbers look onscreen and when printed.

13   **Graphics** A graphic is a nontext element or object, such as a drawing or picture, that can be added to a document.

Exploring the Excel Window

As part of the renovation of the Downtown Internet Café, new computers and the most current versions of software programs were installed, including the latest version of the Microsoft Office suite of applications, Office 2000. You will use the spreadsheet application Excel 2000 included in the Office suite to create the first quarter forecast for the Café.

1 ■ Start Excel 2000.

■ If necessary, maximize the Excel application window.

After a few moments, the Excel application window is displayed. Your screen should be similar to Figure 1–1.

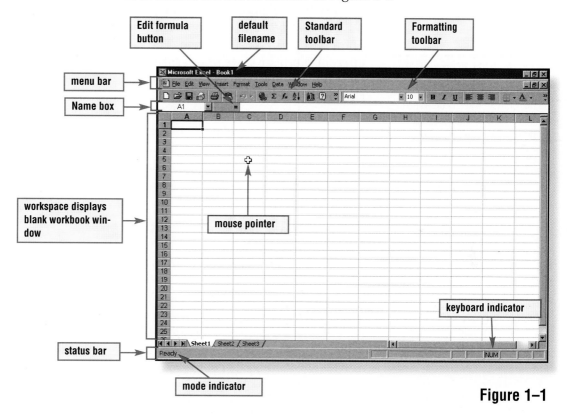

Figure 1–1

The Excel window title bar displays the program name, Microsoft Excel, followed by the file name Book1, the default name of the file displayed in the workbook window. The menu bar below the title bar displays the Excel program menu. It consists of nine menus that provide access to the commands and features you will use to create and modify a worksheet.

The toolbars, normally located below the menu bar, contain buttons that are mouse shortcuts for many of the menu items. The **Standard toolbar** contains buttons that are used to complete the most frequently used menu commands. The **Formatting toolbar** contains buttons that are used to change the appearance or format of the document. Excel includes 23 different toolbars. Many of the toolbars appear automatically as you use different features. Your screen may display other toolbars if they were on when the program was last exited.

Below the toolbars is the **formula bar**. The formula bar displays entries as they are made and edited in the workbook window. The **Name box**, located at the left end of the formula bar, provides information about the selected item. The Edit Formula button is used to create or edit a formula.

The **workspace** currently displays a blank workbook window, which is maximized and occupies the entire space. A **workbook** is an Excel file that stores the information you enter using the program. Excel calls a window that displays a workbook file a **workbook window**. You can have multiple workbook files open at once, each displayed in their own workbook window in the workspace. You will learn about the different parts of the workbook window shortly.

The mouse pointer probably appears as a ↖ or ✚ on your screen. The mouse pointer changes shape depending upon the task you are performing or where the pointer is located on the window.

The status bar at the bottom of the Excel window displays information about various Excel settings. The left side of the status bar displays the current mode or state of operation of the program (Ready). When Ready is displayed, you can move around the workbook, enter data, use the function keys, or choose a command. As you use the program, the status bar displays the current mode. The modes will be discussed as they appear throughout the tutorials. The right end of the status bar displays eight boxes that display additional information as features are used.

Finally, your screen may display the Office Assistant. This feature provides quick access to online Help.

Exploring the Workbook Window

The workbook window displays a new blank workbook file containing three blank sheets. A sheet is used to display different types of information, such as financial data or charts. Whenever you open a new workbook, it displays a worksheet.

A **worksheet**, also commonly referred to as a **spreadsheet**, is a rectangular grid of **rows** and **columns** used to enter data. It is always part of a workbook and is the primary type of sheet you will use in Excel. The worksheet is much larger than the part you are viewing in the window. The worksheet actually extends 256 columns to the right and 65,536 rows down.

Additional Information

If your status bar displays NUM, this is a keyboard indicator that tells you the NumLock key is on. When on, using the numeric keypad enters numbers. When off, it moves the cell selector. Pressing [Num Lock] on your keyboard toggles between these settings.

Additional Information

The text assumes the Office Assistant is not activated. See Introducing Common Office 2000 Features to learn about this feature and how to turn it off.

The default workbook opens with three worksheets. The number of sheets in a workbook is limited only by the available memory on your computer.

Workbook file

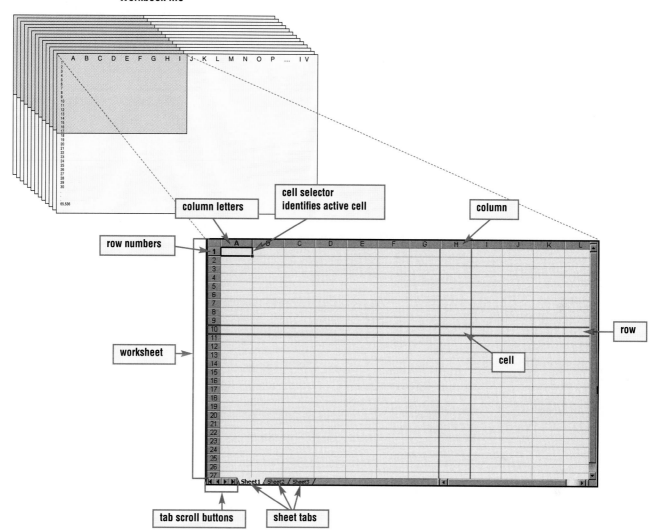

column letters

cell selector
identifies active cell

column

row numbers

row

worksheet

cell

tab scroll buttons

sheet tabs

The **row numbers** along the left side and the **column letters** across the top of the workbook window identify each worksheet row and column. The intersection of a row and column creates a **cell**. Notice the heavy border, called the **cell selector**, surrounding the cell located at the intersection of column A and row 1. The cell selector identifies the **active cell**, which is the cell your next entry or procedure affects. Additionally, the Name box in the formula bar displays the **reference**, consisting of the column letter and row number of the active cell. The reference of the active cell is A1.

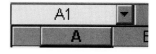

Each sheet in a workbook is named. The default names are Sheet1, Sheet2, and so on, displayed on **sheet tabs** at the bottom of the workbook window. The name of the **active sheet**, which is the sheet you can work in, appears bold. The currently displayed worksheet in the workspace, Sheet1, is the active sheet.

1━■ **Click the Sheet 2 tab.**

Your screen should be similar to
Figure 1–2.

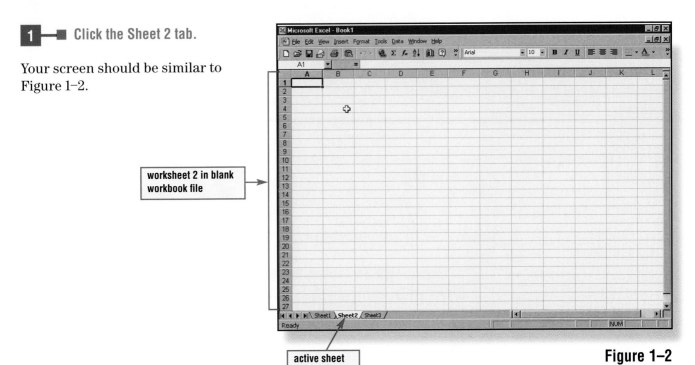

worksheet 2 in blank
workbook file

active sheet

Figure 1–2

An identical blank worksheet is displayed in the window. The Sheet2 tab
letters are bold, the background is highlighted, and it appears in front of
the other sheet tabs to show it is the active sheet.

2━■ **Click the Sheet 1 tab to make it the active sheet again.**

The sheet tab area also contains **tab scroll buttons**, which are used to scroll
tabs right or left when there are more worksheet tabs than there is available
space. You will learn about these features throughout the tutorials.

Moving around the Worksheet

You can use the directional keys in
the numeric keypad (with NumLock
off) or, if you have an extended keyboard, you can use the separate directional keypad area.

Either the mouse or the keyboard can be used to move the cell selector
from one cell to another in the worksheet. To move using a mouse, simply
point to the cell you want to move to and click the mouse button.
Depending upon what you are doing, using the mouse to move may not be
as convenient as using the keyboard, in which case the directional keys can
be used. To use the mouse, then the keyboard to move the cell selector,

1 ■— ■ Click cell B3.

■ Press → (3 times).

■ Press ↓ (4 times).

Your screen should be similar to
Figure 1–3.

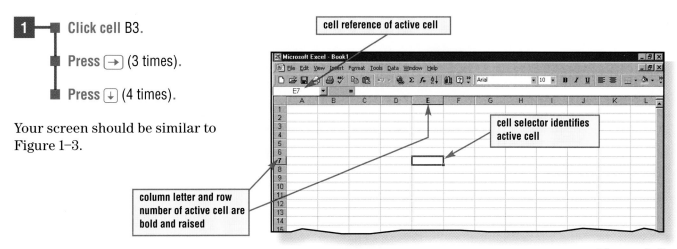

Figure 1–3

The cell selector is now in cell E7, making this cell the active cell. The
Name box displays the cell reference. In addition, the row number and column letter appear bold and raised to further identify the location of the
active cell. To return quickly to the upper-left corner, cell A1, of the worksheet,

2 ■— ■ Press Ctrl + Home.

As you have learned, the worksheet is much larger than the part you are
viewing in the window. To see an area of the worksheet that is not currently in view, you need to scroll the window. Either the keyboard or the
mouse can be used to quickly scroll a worksheet Again, both methods are
useful depending upon what you are doing. The key and mouse procedures shown in the table that follows can be used to move around the
worksheet. In addition, if you hold down the arrow keys, the Alt + Page Up
or Alt + Page Down keys, or the Page Up or Page Down keys, you can quickly
scroll through the worksheet. As you scroll the worksheet using the keyboard, the cell selector moves to the new location. When you use the
mouse and the scroll bar, however, the cell selector does not move until
you click on a cell that is visible in the window.

Keys	Action
Arrow keys ← ↑ → ↓	Moves cell selector one cell in direction of arrow
Page Down	Moves cell selector down one full window
Page Up	Moves cell selector up one full window
Alt + Page Down	Moves cell selector right one full window
Alt + Page Up	Moves cell selector left one full window
Ctrl + Home	Moves cell selector to upper left corner cell of worksheet
Home	Moves cell selector to beginning of row
End →	Moves cell selector to last-used cell in row
End ↓	Moves cell selector to last-used cell in column

Mouse	Action
Click cell	Moves cell selector to selected cell
Click scroll arrow	Scrolls worksheet one row/column in direction of arrow
Click above/below scroll box	Scrolls worksheet one full window up/down
Click right/left of scroll box	Scrolls worksheet one full window right/left
Drag scroll box	Scrolls worksheet multiple windows up/down or right/left

Additional Information

The position of the scroll box indicates the relative location of the area you are viewing within the worksheet and the size indicates the proportional amount of the used area.

To see the rows immediately below row 27 and the columns to the right of column L,

3 ■ Press Page Down.

   ■ Press Alt + Page Down.

Your screen should be similar to Figure 1–4.

Your screen may display more or fewer rows and columns depending on your screen and system settings.

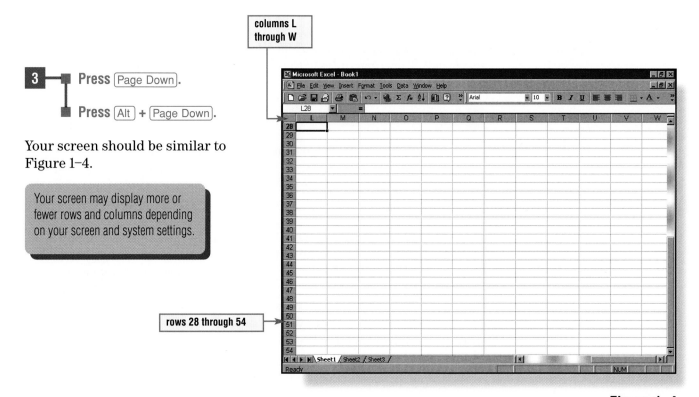

columns L through W

rows 28 through 54

Figure 1–4

The worksheet scrolled one full window upward and left and the window displays rows 28 through 54 and columns L through W of the worksheet.

4 ■ Scroll the worksheet with the mouse using the scroll bar.

   ■ Practice moving the cell selector around the worksheet using each of the keys presented in the table above.

   ■ Move to A1.

Additional Information

When you use the scroll bar to scroll the worksheet, the cell selector does not move. When you drag the scroll box, a ScreenTip appears showing the column or row location that will appear when you stop scrolling.

Row: 1

You can use the mouse or the keyboard with most of the exercises in these tutorials. As you use both the mouse and the keyboard, you will find that it is more efficient to use one or the other in specific situations.

Planning the Worksheet

Now that you are familiar with the parts of the worksheet, you are ready to create the worksheet showing the forecast for the first three months of operation for the Downtown Internet Café. As you create a worksheet, the development progresses through several stages.

Concept ① Worksheet Development

Worksheet development consists of four stages: planning, entering and editing, testing, and formatting. The objective is to create a well-designed worksheet that produces accurate results and is clearly understood, adaptable, and efficient. You will find that you will generally follow these steps in order for your first draft of a worksheet. However, you will probably retrace steps such as editing and formatting as the worksheet develops.

1. Plan
Your first step is to specify the purpose of the worksheet and how it should be organized. This means clearly identifying the data that will be input, the calculations that are needed to achieve the results, and the output that is desired. As part of the planning step, it is helpful to sketch out a design of the worksheet to organize the worksheet's structure. The design should include the worksheet title and row and column headings that identify the input and output. Additionally, sample data can be used to help determine the formulas needed to produce the output.

2. Enter and edit
After planning the worksheet, your next step is to create the structure of the worksheet using Excel by entering the worksheet labels, data, and formulas. As you create the worksheet, you are bound to make errors that need to be corrected or edited or you will need to revise the content of what you have entered to make it clearer, or to add or delete information.

3. Test
Once your worksheet structure is complete, you are ready to test the worksheet for errors. Several sets of real or sample data are used as the input, and the resulting output is verified. The input data should include a full range of possible values for each data item to ensure the worksheet can function successfully under all possible conditions.

4. Format
Enhancing the appearance of the worksheet to make it more readable or attractive is called formatting. This step is usually performed when the worksheet is near completion. It includes many features such as boldfaced text, italics, and color.

As the complexity of the worksheet increases, the importance of following the design process increases. Even for simple worksheets like the one you will create in this tutorial, the design process is important.

During the planning phase, you have spoken with the café manager regarding the purpose of the worksheet and the content in general. The primary purpose is to develop a forecast for sales and expense for the next year. Evan first wants you to develop a worksheet for the first quarter forecast and to then extend it by quarters for the year. After reviewing past budgets and consulting with Evan, you have designed the basic layout for the first quarter forecast for the café as shown below.

Downtown Internet Café
First Quarter Forecast

Sales:

Beverage	January	February	March	Total
	$ 13,600	$ 14,600	$15,600	# 43,800 (sum of beverage sales)
Food	XX, XXX			
Total Sales	$ XX,XXX (sum of monthly sales)	$ XX,XXX	$XX,XXX	$XXX,XXX (sum of total sales)

Expenses:

Cost of Goods	$(.25 * beverage sales + 50 * food sales)			$(sum of cost of goods)
Salary				
Total Expenses	$XX,XXX (sum of monthly expenses)	$XX,XXX	$XX,XXX	$XXX,XXX (sum of total expenses)

Income
Net Income $(Total Sales − Total Expenses)
Profit Margin $(Total Expenses ÷ Total Sales)

Entering Data

As you can see, the budget contains both descriptive text entries and numeric data. These are the two types of entries you can make in a worksheet.

Concept ② Types of Entries

The information or data you enter in a cell can be text, numbers, or formulas. **Text** entries can contain any combination of letters, numbers, spaces, and any other special characters. **Number** entries can include only the digits 0 to 9 and any of the special characters, + − ( ) , . / $ % E e. Number entries are used in calculations. An entry that begins with an equal sign (=) is a **formula**. Formula entries perform calculations using numbers or data contained in other cells. The resulting value is a **variable** value because it can change if the data it depends on changes. In contrast, a number entry is a **constant** value. It does not begin with an equal sign and does not change unless you change it directly by typing in another entry.

First you will enter the worksheet **headings**. Row and column headings are entries that are used to create the structure of the worksheet and describe other worksheet entries. Generally, headings are text entries. The column headings in this worksheet consist of the three months (January through March) and a total (sum of entries over three months) located in columns B through E. To enter data in a worksheet, you must first select the cell where you want the entry displayed. The column heading for January will be entered in cell B2.

1 ■ Move to B2.

■ Type **J**

Your screen should be similar to Figure 1–5.

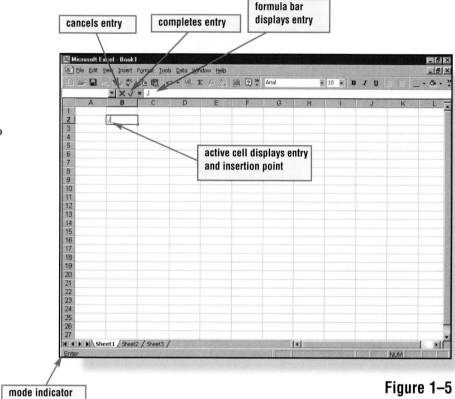

Figure 1–5

Several changes have occurred in the window. As you type, the entry is displayed both in the active cell and in the formula bar. An insertion point appears in the active cell and marks your location in the entry. Two new buttons, ☒ and ☑, appear in the formula bar. They can be used by the mouse to complete your entry or cancel it.

Notice also that the mode displayed in the status bar has changed from Ready to Enter. This notifies you that the current mode of operation in the worksheet is entering data. To continue entering the heading,

If you made an error while typing the entry, use (Backspace) to erase the characters back to the error. Then retype the entry correctly.

2 ■ Type **anuary**

Although the entry is displayed in both the active cell and the formula bar, you need to press the (←Enter) key or click ☑ to complete your entry. If you press (Esc) or click ☒, the entry is cleared and nothing appears in the cell. Since your hands are already on the keyboard, it is quicker to press (←Enter) than it is to use the mouse to click ☑.

3 ━■ Press ←Enter.

Your screen should be similar to Figure 1–6.

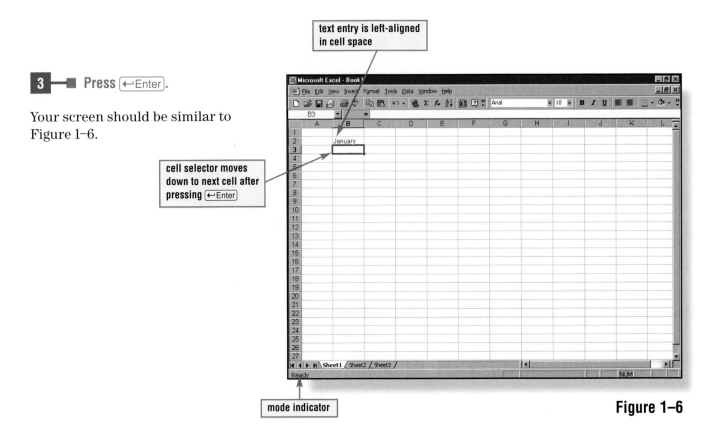

text entry is left-aligned in cell space

cell selector moves down to next cell after pressing ←Enter

mode indicator

Figure 1–6

Pressing ⇧Shift + ←Enter to complete an entry moves the cell selector up a cell, and Ctrl + ←Enter completes the entry without moving the cell selector.

The entry January is displayed in cell B2, and the mode has returned to Ready. In addition, the cell selector has moved to cell B3. Whenever you use the ←Enter key to complete an entry, the cell selector moves down one cell.

Notice that the entry is positioned to the left side of the cell space. The positioning of cell entries in the cell space is called alignment. By default, text entries are displayed left-aligned. You will learn more about this feature later in the tutorial.

Clearing an Entry

After looking at the entry, you decide you want the column headings to be in row 3 rather than in row 2. This will leave more space above the column headings for a worksheet title.

The Delete key can be used to clear the contents from a cell. To remove the entry from cell B2 and enter it in cell B3,

The menu equivalent is Edit/Clear/Contents. Clear Contents is also an option on the shortcut menu.

1 ━■ Move to B2.

■ Press Delete.

■ Move to B3.

■ Type **January**

■ Click .

The cell selector remains in the active cell when you use 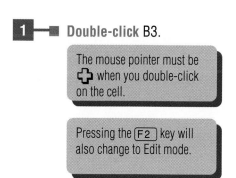 to complete an entry. In Figure 1–7, because the cell selector is positioned on a cell containing an entry, the contents of the cell are displayed in the formula bar.

Editing an Entry

- -

You would like to change the heading from January to JAN. An entry in a cell can be entirely changed in the Ready mode or partially changed or edited in the Edit mode. To use the Ready mode, you move the cell selector to the cell you want to change and retype the entry the way you want it to appear. As soon as a new character is entered, the existing entry is cleared.

Generally, however, if you need to change only part of an entry, it is quicker to use the Edit mode. To change to Edit mode, double-click on the cell whose contents you want to edit.

1 ▪ **Double-click** B3.

> The mouse pointer must be ✚ when you double-click on the cell.

> Pressing the F2 key will also change to Edit mode.

Your screen should be similar to Figure 1–7.

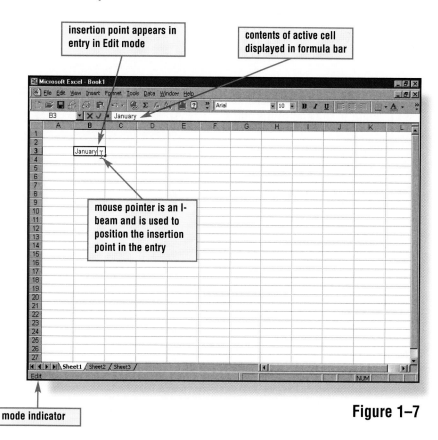

Figure 1–7

The status bar shows that the new mode of operation is Edit. The insertion point appears in the entry, and the mouse pointer changes to an I-beam when positioned on the cell. The mouse pointer can now be used to move the insertion point in the entry by positioning the I-beam and clicking.

In addition, in the Edit mode, the following keys can be used to move the insertion point:

Key	Action
Home	Moves insertion point to beginning of entry
End	Moves insertion point to end of entry
→	Moves insertion point one character right
←	Moves insertion point one character left

Additional Information

You can also use Ctrl + Delete to delete everything to the right of the insertion point.

Once the insertion point is appropriately positioned, you can edit the entry by removing the incorrect characters and typing the correct characters. The Delete key erases characters at the insertion point, and the Backspace key erases characters to the left of the insertion point. To change this entry to JAN,

2 ■ If necessary, **move** the insertion point to the end of the entry.

■ Press Backspace (4 times).

■ Press Home.

■ Press Caps Lock.

■ Press →.

■ Press Insert.

■ Type **A**

Your screen should be similar to Figure 1–8.

capital letters produced automatically when caps lock key is on

insertion point changes to a highlight when overwrite is on

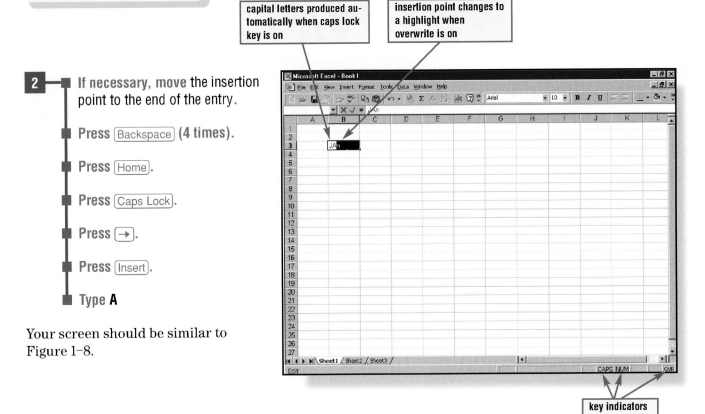

key indicators

Figure 1–8

The four characters at the end of the entry were deleted using Backspace. Turning on the Caps Lock feature produced an uppercase letter A without having to hold down ⇧Shift. Finally, by pressing Insert the program switched from inserting text to overwriting text as you typed. The insertion point changes to a highlight to show the character will be replaced. The status bar displays CAPS and OVR to let you know these features are on.

Overwrite is automatically turned off when you leave Edit mode or if you press [Insert] again.

3 ■ Type **N**

■ Press [←Enter].

The new heading JAN is entered into cell B3, replacing January. As you can see, editing will be particularly useful with long or complicated entries.

Next you will enter the remaining three headings in row three. You can also complete an entry by moving to any other worksheet cell. To try this,

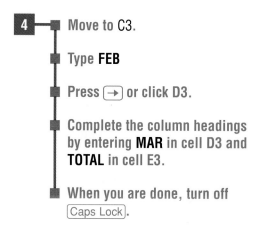

4 ■ Move to **C3**.

■ Type **FEB**

■ Press [→] or click **D3**.

■ Complete the column headings by entering **MAR** in cell D3 and **TOTAL** in cell E3.

■ When you are done, turn off [Caps Lock].

Your screen should be similar to Figure 1–9.

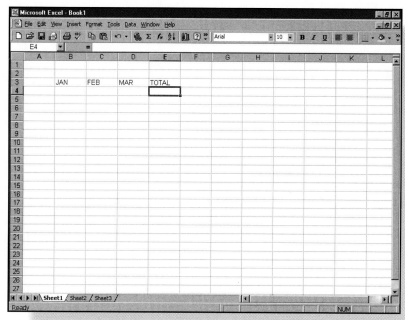

Figure 1–9

Using AutoCorrect

Above the column headings, in rows 1 and 2, you want to enter a title for the worksheet. While entering the title, you will intentionally misspell the words First and Quarter to demonstrate how the AutoCorrect feature of Office works. The **AutoCorrect** feature automatically corrects common typing errors as they are made. Office 2000 contains a list of words that are commonly spelled incorrectly or typed incorrectly. When you misspell one of the words in the list, Excel will automatically correct the spelling for you. For example, it will automatically capitalize the days of the week. If you commonly spell a word wrong that is not in the AutoCorrect list, you can manually add it to the list. This word is added to the list on the computer you are using and will be available to anyone who uses the machine after you.

1 ■ Move to B1.

■ Type **Downtown Internet Cafe**

■ Press ⏎Enter.

■ Type **Firts Quater Forecast**

■ Press ⏎Enter.

Your screen should be similar to Figure 1–10.

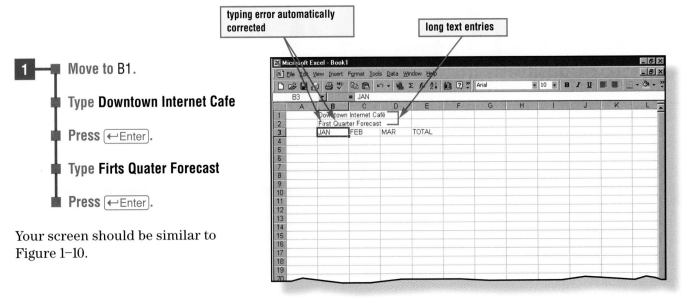

Figure 1–10

The AutoCorrect feature automatically changed the spelling of cafe to include the accent mark and corrected the two typing errors. When a text entry is longer than the cell's column width, Excel will display as much of the entry as it can. If the cell to the right is empty, the whole entry will be displayed. If the cell to the right contains an entry, the overlapping part of the entry is not displayed.

Next the row headings need to be entered into column A of the worksheet. The row headings and what they represent are shown below:

Heading	Represents
Sales	
Beverage	Income from sale of drinks (espresso, gourmet coffee, cold drinks)
Food	Income from sales of sandwiches and salads
Internet	Income from Internet connection time charges
Merchandise	Income from sale of Café T-shirts, mugs, and so forth
Total Sales	Sum of all sales
Expenses	
Cost of Goods	Cost of beverage and food items sold
Salary	Personnel expenses
Computers	Monthly payment for computer hardware
Lease	Monthly lease expense
Miscellaneous	Monthly expenses for T1 line, phone, electricity, water, trash removal, etc.
Income	
Net Income	Total sales minus total expenses
Profit Margin	Net income divided by total sales

2 ■ Complete the row headings for the Sales portion of the worksheet by entering the following headings in the indicated cells:

Cell	Heading
A4	**Sales**
A5	**Beverage**
A6	**Food**
A7	**Internet**
A8	**Merchandise**
A9	**Total Sales**

Remember to press ⏎Enter or an arrow key to complete the last entry.

Your screen should be similar to Figure 1–11.

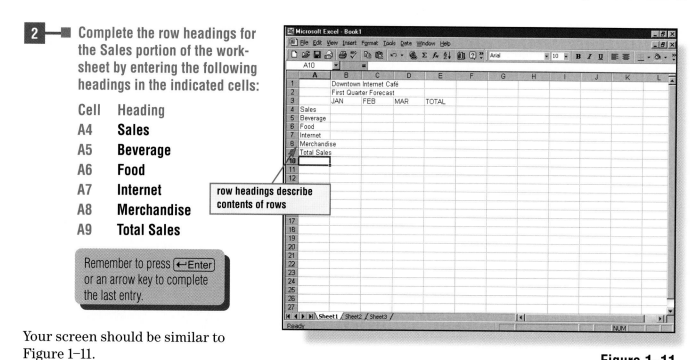

Figure 1–11

Entering Numbers

Next you will enter the expected beverage sales numbers for January through March into cells B5 through D5. As you learned earlier, number entries can include the digits 0 to 9 and any of these special characters: + − ( ) , . / $ % E e. When entering numbers, it is not necessary to type the comma to separate thousands or the currency ($) symbol. You will learn about adding these symbols later.

To enter the expected beverage sales for January,

1 ■ Move to B5.

■ Type **13600**

■ Press ⏎Enter.

You can use the number keys above the alphabetic keys or the numeric keypad area to enter numbers. If you use the numeric keypad, the Num Lock key must be on.

Your screen should be similar to Figure 1–12.

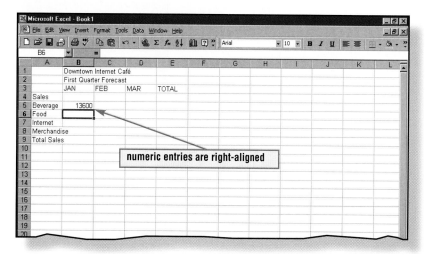

Figure 1–12

Unlike text entries, Excel displays number entries right-aligned in the cell space by default.

2 In the same manner, enter the January sales numbers for the remaining items using the values shown below.

Cell	Number
B6	7100
B7	3600
B8	3100

Your screen should be similar to Figure 1–13.

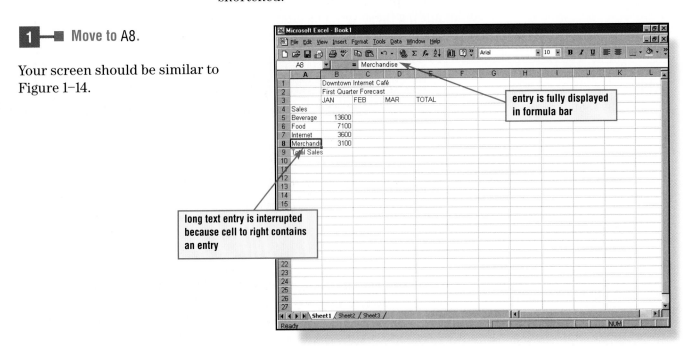

Figure 1–13

Adjusting Column Widths

After entering the numbers for January in column B, any long headings in column A were cut off or interrupted. Notice that the entry in cell A8 is no longer completely displayed. It is a long text entry and because the cell to the right (B8) now contains an entry, the overlapping part of the entry is shortened.

1 Move to A8.

Your screen should be similar to Figure 1–14.

entry is fully displayed in formula bar

long text entry is interrupted because cell to right contains an entry

Figure 1–14

You can now see the entire entry is fully visible in the formula bar and that only the display of the entry in the cell has been shortened. To allow the long text entries in column A to be fully displayed, you can increase the column's width.

Concept 3 Column Width

The size or width of a column controls how much information can be displayed in a cell. A text entry that is larger than the column width will be fully displayed only if the cells to the right are blank. If the cells to the right contain data, the text is interrupted. On the other hand, when numbers are entered in a cell, the column width is automatically increased to fully display the entry.

The default column width setting in Excel is 8.43. The number represents the average number of digits that can be displayed in a cell using the standard font. The column width can be any number from 1 to 255.

When the worksheet is printed, it appears as it does currently on the screen. Therefore, you want to increase the column width to display the largest entry. Likewise, you can decrease the column width when the entries in a column are short.

Additional Information

You can also adjust the size of any row by dragging the row divider line or by using F**o**rmat/**R**ow/H**e**ight.

The menu equivalent is F**o**rmat/**C**olumn/**W**idth.

The column width can be quickly adjusted by dragging the boundary line located to the right of the column letter. Dragging it to the left decreases the column width, while dragging it to the right increases the width. As you drag, a temporary column reference line shows where the new column will appear and a ScreenTip displays the width of the column.

2 ■ **Point to the boundary line to the right of the column letter A and drag the mouse pointer to the right.**

> The mouse pointer changes to ↔ when you can size a column.

■ **When the ScreenTip displays 15.00, release the mouse button.**

Your screen should be similar to Figure 1–15.

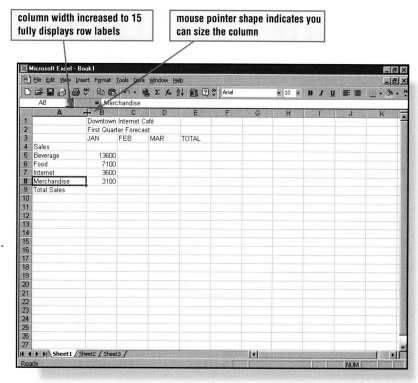

column width increased to 15 fully displays row labels

mouse pointer shape indicates you can size the column

Figure 1–15

Now, however, the column width is wider than you need. Another way to change the column width is to automatically adjust the width to fit the column contents.

3 ▪— **Double-click the A column boundary line.**

> The menu equivalent is Format/Column/AutoFit Selection.

Your screen should be similar to Figure 1–16.

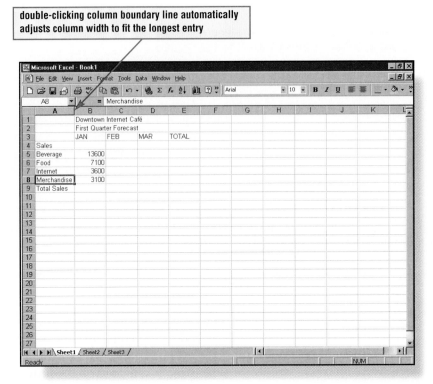

double-clicking column boundary line automatically adjusts column width to fit the longest entry

Figure 1–16

The column width is sized to just slightly larger than the longest cell contents.

Saving and Closing a Workbook

The rest of the row headings, sales values, and several of the expense numbers for the month of January have already been entered and saved on your data disk in a file called Café Forecast. Before opening this workbook file, you will save and close the current workbook.

While you work on a document, your changes are stored in memory. Not until you save the document as a file on a disk are you safe from losing your work due to a power failure or other mishap. When you save a file, you need to specify the location where you want the file stored and a file name. The Save and Save As commands on the File menu can be used to save a file. The Save command saves a document using the same path and file name by replacing the contents of the existing disk file with the changes you have made. The Save As command allows you to select the path and provide a different file name. This command lets you save both an original version of a document and a revised document as two separate files. When a workbook is saved for the first time, either command can be used.

Additional Information

As a backup against the accidental loss of work due to power failure or other mishap, you may want to install the AutoSave add-in feature. This feature automatically saves your work at the set time intervals you specify.

1 Place your data disk in drive A (or the appropriate drive for your system).

■ Click 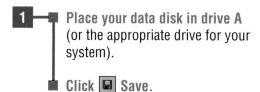 Save.

> The menu equivalent is **F**ile/**S**ave and the keyboard shortcut is Ctrl + S.

Your screen should be similar to Figure 1–17.

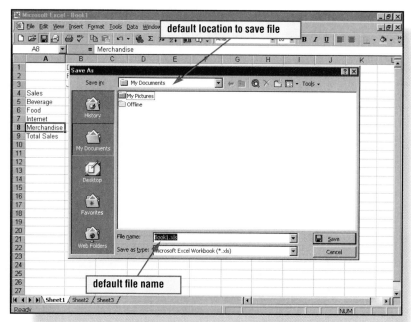

Figure 1–17

Additional Information

Windows documents can have up to 256 characters in the file name. Names can contain letters or numbers. Special symbols cannot be used with the exception of the _, -, '.

The Save As dialog box is displayed in which you specify the location to save the file and the file name. The Save In list box displays the default location where files are stored. The list box displays the names of any Excel files stored in that location. The File Name list box displays the default workbook file name, Book1. Notice the default name is highlighted, indicating it is selected and will be replaced as you type the new name. First you will change the file name to Forecast.

2 Type **Forecast**.

Your screen should be similar to Figure 1–18.

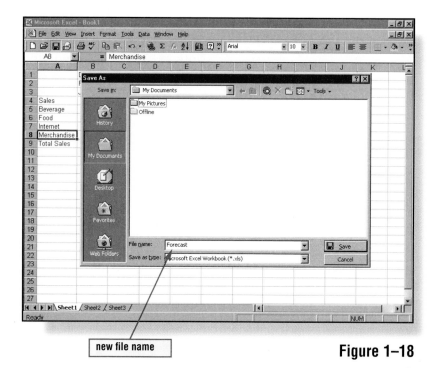

Figure 1–18

The default file name is replaced with new file name. Next you need to change the location to the drive containing your data disk.

3 ■ Open the Save In list box.

■ Select 3½ Floppy (A:) (or the appropriate drive for your system) from the Save In drop-down list.

> If an error message is displayed, check that your disk is properly inserted in the drive and click ☐ Retry.

Your screen should be similar to Figure 1–19.

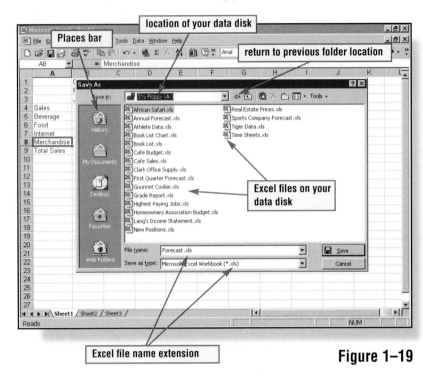

Figure 1–19

> Your file list may display more file names than shown here.

Now the name list box displays the names of all Excel files on your data disk. You can also select the location to save from the Places bar along the left side of the dialog box. The icons bring up a list of recently accessed files and folders, the contents of the My Documents and Favorites folder, the Windows desktop, and the remote WebFolders list. Selecting a folder from one of these lists changes to that location. You can also click the ⇦ button in the toolbar to return to folders that were previously opened during the current session.

Notice that Excel added the xls file extension to the file name. This is the default extension for Excel workbook documents.

4 ■ Click  .

Your screen should be similar to Figure 1–20.

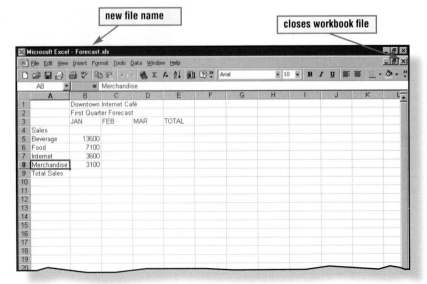

Figure 1–20

The new file name is displayed in the worksheet window title bar. The worksheet data that was on your screen and in the computer's memory is now saved on your data disk in a new file called Forecast. You are now ready to close the workbook file.

The menu equivalent is **F**ile/**C**lose.

5 ▬ Click ☒ **Close Window (in the menu bar).**

Because you did not make any changes to the document since saving it, the document window is closed immediately and the Excel window displays an empty workspace. If you had made additional changes, Excel would ask if you wanted to save the file before closing it. This prevents the accidental closing of a file that has not been saved first.

Note: If you are running short on lab time, this is an appropriate place to end your session.

Opening a Workbook File

You are now ready to open the workbook file named Café Budget.

1 ▬ Click ☞ **Open.**

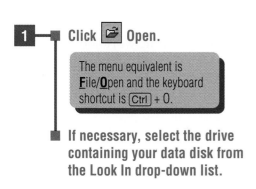

The menu equivalent is **F**ile/**O**pen and the keyboard shortcut is [Ctrl] + O.

If necessary, select the drive containing your data disk from the Look In drop-down list.

Your screen should be similar to Figure 1–21.

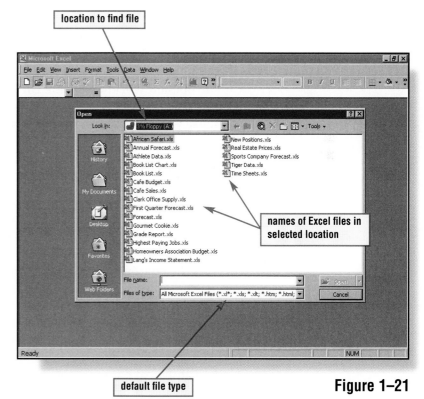

location to find file

names of Excel files in selected location

default file type

Figure 1–21

If your screen does not display file extensions, your Windows program has this option deactivated.

From the Open dialog box, you specify the name and location of the file to open. The file list area displays the names of all Microsoft Excel files on your data disk. Only Excel files are displayed; this is the default setting in the Files of Type text box. The file you want to open is Café Budget.

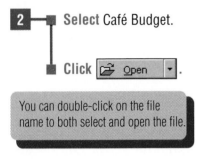

2 — ■ Select Café Budget.

■ Click 🖼 Open ▾ .

> You can double-click on the file name to both select and open the file.

Your screen should be similar to Figure 1–22.

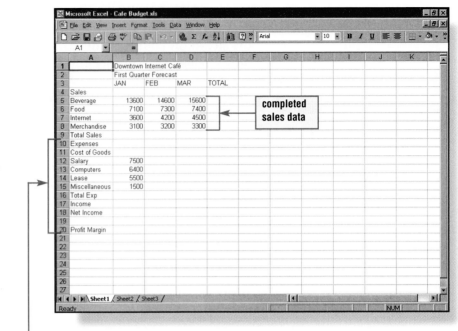

completed sales data

new row labels and expense values

Figure 1–22

The new workbook file is loaded and displayed in the workbook window. The opened workbook, Café Budget, contains the additional sales values for February and March, the expense row headings, and several of the expense values for the month of January.

Copying Data

Next you want to enter the estimated expenses for salary, computers, lease, and miscellaneous for February and March. They are the same as the January expense numbers. Because these values are the same, instead of entering the same number repeatedly into each cell you can quickly copy the contents of one cell to another.

The contents of worksheet cells can be duplicated (copied) to other locations in the worksheet using the Copy and Paste commands on the Edit menu or their toolbar shortcuts. First you use the Copy command to copy the cell contents to the Clipboard. Then you move to the new location where you want the contents copied and use the Paste command to insert the Clipboard contents into the selected cells. Be careful when pasting to the new location because any existing entries are replaced.

To use the Copy command, you first must select the cell or cells containing the data to be copied. This is called the **copy area** or **source**.

First you will copy the value in cell B12 into cells C12 and D12.

Additional Information

Office 2000 contains an Office clipboard in addition to the Windows clipboard. Only one item can be stored in the Windows clipboard while up to 12 items can be stored in the Office 2000 clipboard. The Office 2000 clipboard allows you to copy multiple items from various Office documents and paste all or part of the collection of copied items into another Office document.

1 ■ Move to B12.

■ Click 📋 Copy.

> The menu equivalent is **E**dit/**C**opy and the shortcut key is [Ctrl] + C. Copy is also available on the shortcut menu.

Your screen should be similar to Figure 1–23.

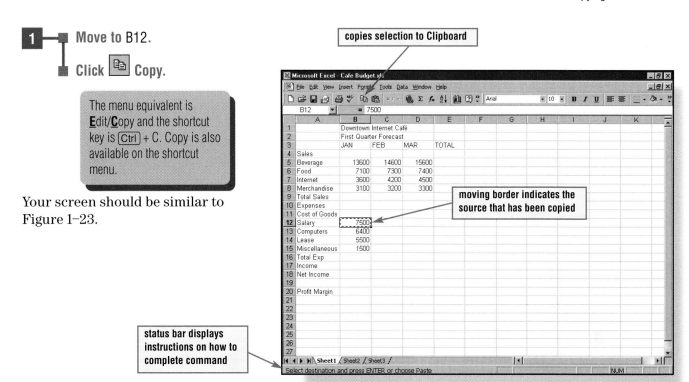

Figure 1–23

Additional Information

While the moving border is still displayed, you can also simply press [↵Enter] to paste. However, using this method clears the contents of the Clipboard immediately so it can only be used once.

A moving border identifies the source and indicates that the contents have been copied to the Clipboard. The instructions displayed in the status bar tell you to select a **destination**, also called the **paste area**, where you want the contents copied. To specify cell C12 as the destination,

2 ■ Move to C12.

■ Click 📋 Paste.

> The menu equivalent is **E**dit/**P**aste and the shortcut key is [Ctrl] + V. Paste is also available on the shortcut menu.

Your screen should be similar to Figure 1–24.

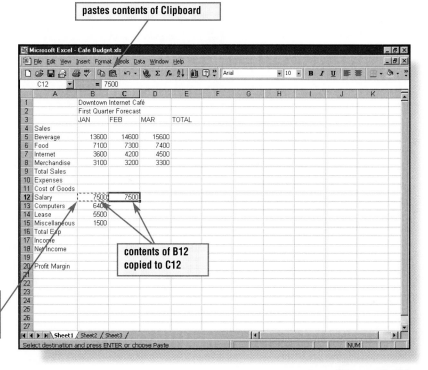

Figure 1–24

The moving border is still displayed indicating the Clipboard still contains the copied entry. Now you can complete the data for the Salary row by pasting the value again from the Clipboard into cell D12.

3 ▪ Move to D12.

   ▪ Click  Paste.

Selecting a Range

Now you need to copy the Computers value in cell B13 to February and March. You could copy and paste the contents individually into each cell. It is much faster, however, to select a paste area that consists of multiple cells, called a range, and paste the contents to all cells in the selection at once.

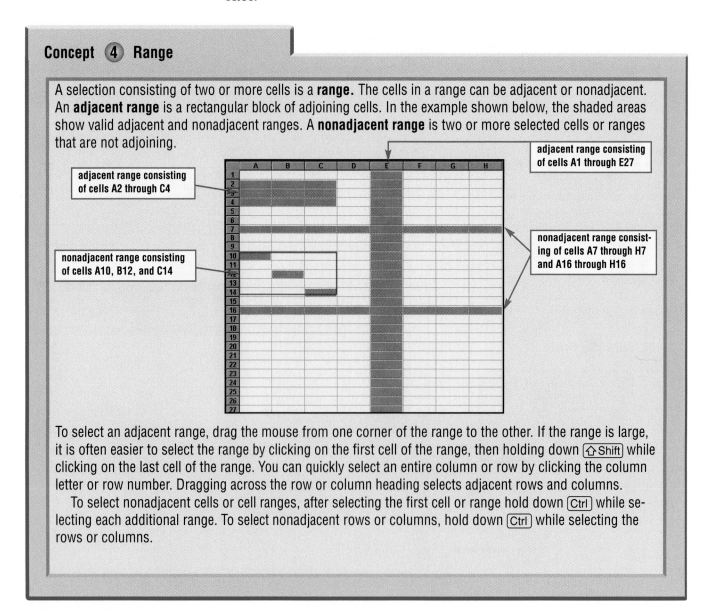

Concept ④ Range

A selection consisting of two or more cells is a **range.** The cells in a range can be adjacent or nonadjacent. An **adjacent range** is a rectangular block of adjoining cells. In the example shown below, the shaded areas show valid adjacent and nonadjacent ranges. A **nonadjacent range** is two or more selected cells or ranges that are not adjoining.

adjacent range consisting of cells A2 through C4

nonadjacent range consisting of cells A10, B12, and C14

adjacent range consisting of cells A1 through E27

nonadjacent range consisting of cells A7 through H7 and A16 through H16

To select an adjacent range, drag the mouse from one corner of the range to the other. If the range is large, it is often easier to select the range by clicking on the first cell of the range, then holding down (⇧Shift) while clicking on the last cell of the range. You can quickly select an entire column or row by clicking the column letter or row number. Dragging across the row or column heading selects adjacent rows and columns.

To select nonadjacent cells or cell ranges, after selecting the first cell or range hold down (Ctrl) while selecting each additional range. To select nonadjacent rows or columns, hold down (Ctrl) while selecting the rows or columns.

To complete the data for the Computer row, you want to copy the value in cell B13 to the Clipboard and then copy the Clipboard contents to the range of cells C13 through D13.

1 — Move to B13

Click 📋 Copy

Drag to select cells C13 to D13.

> You can also hold down
> ⇧ Shift and use the directional keys to select a range.

Click 📋 Paste.

> The paste area does not have to be adjacent to the copy area.

Your screen should be similar to Figure 1–25.

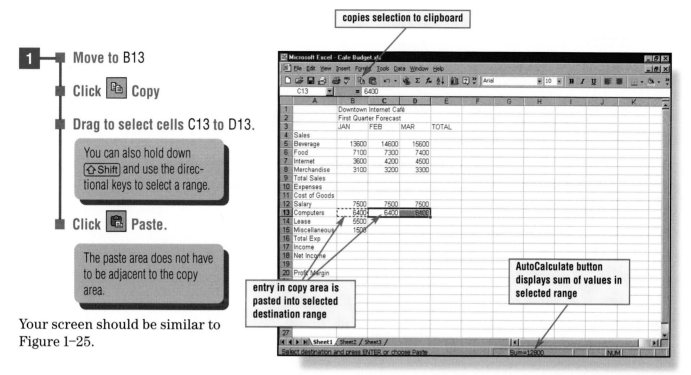

Figure 1–25

The destination range is highlighted and identified by a dark border surrounding the selected cells. The entry copied from cell B13 was pasted into the selected destination range. Also notice the AutoCalculate button in the status bar is now active. This button displays the sum of values in a selected range of cells. It can also display the average, count, minimum, or maximum values in a range by selecting the appropriate option from the button's shortcut menu.

Copying Using the Fill Handle

Next you will copy the January Lease expenses to cells C14 through D14 and Miscellaneous expenses to cells C15 through D15. You can copy both values at the same time across the row by first specifying a range as the source area.

1 — Drag to select cells B14 through B15.

Another way to copy is to drag the **fill handle,** the black box in the lower-right corner of the selection.

2 ■ **Point to the fill handle and when the mouse pointer is a ➕, drag the mouse to extend the selection to cells C14 through D15.**

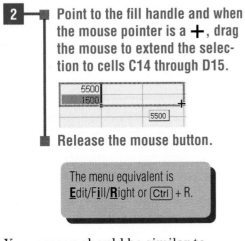

■ **Release the mouse button.**

The menu equivalent is
Edit/**Fi**ll/**R**ight or Ctrl + R.

Your screen should be similar to
Figure 1–26.

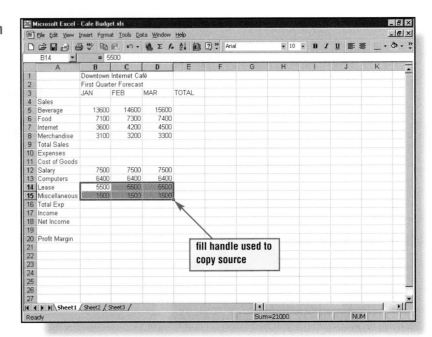

fill handle used to copy source

Figure 1–26

The range of cells to the right of the source is filled with the same value as in the active cell. The Fill command does not copy the source to the Clipboard; therefore, you cannot paste the source multiple times.

Review of Copying Methods

To review, you have learned two methods to copy an entry:

1. Use the Copy and Paste commands: **E**dit/**C**opy (Ctrl +C) or 🗐 and **E**dit/**P**aste (Ctrl + V) or 📋 .

2. Use the **E**dit/**Fi**ll command: **R**ight, **L**eft, **U**p, or **D**own or drag the fill handle.

When you use the Copy command, the contents are copied to the Clipboard and can be copied to any location in the worksheet, another workbook, or another application. When you use **E**dit/**Fi**ll or drag the fill handle, the destination must be in the same row or column as the source, and the source is not copied to the Clipboard.

Entering Formulas

The remaining entries that need to be made in the worksheet are formula entries.

Concept ⑤ Formulas

A **formula** is an entry that performs a calculation. The result of the calculation is displayed in the cell containing the formula. A formula always begins with an equal sign (=), which defines it as a numeric entry. Formulas use the following arithmetic operators to specify the type of numeric operation to perform:

Symbol	Operation
+	addition
−	subtraction
/	division
*	multiplication
^	exponentiation

In a formula that contains more than one operator, Excel performs the calculation in the following **order of precedence:**

Exponentiation

Multiplication and division

Addition and subtraction.

This order can be overridden by enclosing the operation you want performed first in parentheses. Excel evaluates operations in parentheses working from the innermost set of parentheses out. For example, in the formula =5*4−3, Excel first multiplies 5 times 4 to get 20, and then subtracts 3 for a total of 17. If you enter the formula as =5*(4−3), Excel first subtracts 3 from 4 because the operation is enclosed in parentheses. Then Excel multiplies the result, 1, by 5, for a final result of 5. If two or more operators have the same order of precedence, calculations are performed in order from left to right.

The values on which a numeric formula performs a calculation are called **operands**. Numbers or cell references can be operands in a formula. Usually cell references are used, and when the numeric entries in the referenced cell(s) change, the result of the formula is automatically recalculated. You can also use single-word row and column headings in place of cell references and formulas.

The first formula you will enter will calculate the total Beverage sales for January through March by summing the numbers in cells B5 through D5. You will use cell references in the formula as the operands and the + arithmetic operator to specify addition. A formula is entered in the cell where you want the calculated value to be displayed.

1 ■ Move to E5.

■ Type =

■ Type b5+c5+d5

> Cell references can by typed in either uppercase or lower-case letters. Spaces between parts of the formulas are optional.

■ Press ⏎Enter.

> If you enter a formula incorrectly, Excel displays an error in the cell or message box proposing a correction.

■ Move to E5.

Your screen should be similar to Figure 1–27.

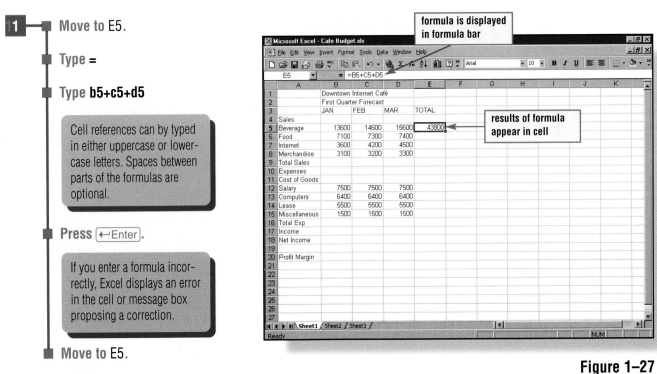

Figure 1–27

The number 43800 is displayed in cell E5 and the formula that calculates this value is displayed in the formula bar.

Copying Formulas

The formulas to calculate the total sales for rows 5 through 8 can be entered next. Just like text and numeric entries, you can copy formulas from one cell to another.

1 ■ Copy the formula in cell E5 to cells E6 through E8 using any of the copying methods.

■ Move to E6.

Your screen should be similar to Figure 1–28.

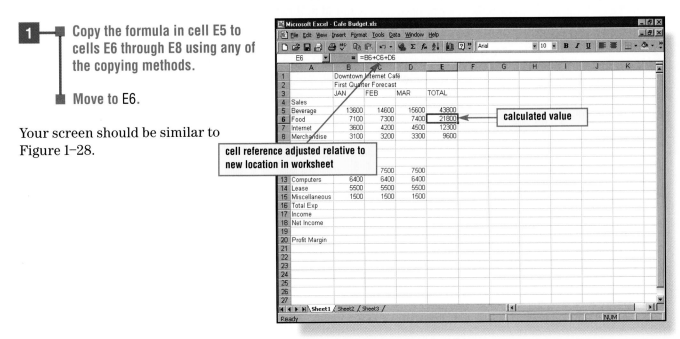

Figure 1–28

The number 21800 is displayed in the cell. The formula displayed in the formula bar is =B6+C6+D6. The formula to calculate the Food total sales is not an exact duplicate of the formula used to calculate the Beverage total sales (=B5+C5+D5). Instead the cells referenced in the formula have been changed to reflect the new location of the formula in row 6. This is because the references in the formula are relative references.

Concept ⑥ Relative Reference

A **relative reference** is a cell or range reference in a formula whose location is interpreted by Excel in relation to the position of the cell that contains the formula. For example, in the formula to calculate total beverage sales in cell E5, the cell reference to B5 tells Excel to use the contents of the cell three cells to the left of the cell containing the formula. When a formula is copied, the referenced cells in the formula automatically adjust to reflect the new worksheet location. The relative relationship between the referenced cell and the new location is maintained. Because relative references automatically adjust for the new location, the relative references in a copied formula refer to different cells from the references in the original formula. The relationship between cells in both the copied and pasted formula is the same although the cell references are different.

	B	C	D	E
5	13600	14600	15600	=B5+C5+D5
6	7100	7300	7400	=B6+C6+D6
7	3600	4200	4500	=B7+C7+D7
8	3100	3200	3300	=B8+C8+D8

2 ■ Move to E7 and E8.

The formulas in these cells have also changed to reflect the new row location and to appropriately calculate the total based on the sales.

Entering Functions

Next you will calculate the monthly total sales. The formula to calculate the total sales for January needs to be entered in cell B9 and copied across the row. You could use a formula similar to the formula used to calculate the category sales in column E. The formula would be =B5+B6+B7+B8. However, it is faster and more accurate to use a function.

Concept Functions

Functions are prewritten formulas that perform certain types of calculations automatically. The **syntax** or rules of structure for entering all functions is:

Function name (argument1, argument2,...)

The function name identifies the type of calculation to be performed. Most functions require that you enter one or more arguments following the function name. An **argument** is the data the function uses to perform the calculation. The type of data the function requires depends upon the type of calculation being performed. Most commonly, the argument consists of numbers or references to cells that contain numbers. The argument is enclosed in parentheses, and multiple arguments are separated by commas. If a function starts the formula, enter an equal sign before the function name (=SUM(D5:F5)/25).

Excel includes several hundred functions* divided into 9 categories. Some common functions and the results they calculate are shown below.

Category	Function	Calculates
Financial	PMT	Calculates the payment for a loan based on constant payments and a constant interest rate
	PV	Returns the present value of an investment; the total amount that a series of future payments is worth now
Time & Date	TODAY	Returns the serial number that represents today's date
	DATE	Returns the serial number of a particular date
	NOW	Returns the serial number of the current date and time
Math & Trig	SUM	Adds all the numbers in a range of cells
	ABS	Returns the absolute value of a number, a number without its sign
Statistical	AVERAGE	Returns the average (arithmetic mean) of its arguments
	MAX	Returns the largest value in a set of values; ignores logical values and text
Lookup & Reference	COLUMNS	Returns the number of columns in an array or reference
	CHOOSE	Chooses a value or action to perform from a list of values, based on an index number
Database	DSUM	Adds the numbers in the field (column) or records in the database that match the conditions you specify
	DAVERAGE	Averages the values in a column in a list or database that match conditions you specify
Text	DOLLAR	Converts a number to text, using currency format
	UPPER	Converts text to uppercase
Logical	IF	Returns one value if a condition you specify evaluates to True and another value if it evaluates to False
	AND	Returns True if all its arguments are True; returns False if any arguments are False
Information	ISLOGICAL	Returns True if value is a logical value, either True or False
	ISREF	Returns True if value is a reference

*Use Help for detailed explanations of every function.

You will use the SUM function to calculate the total sales for January. Because the SUM function is the most commonly used function, it has its own toolbar button.

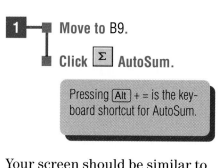

1 Move to B9.

Click Σ AutoSum.

> Pressing [Alt] + = is the keyboard shortcut for AutoSum.

Your screen should be similar to Figure 1–29.

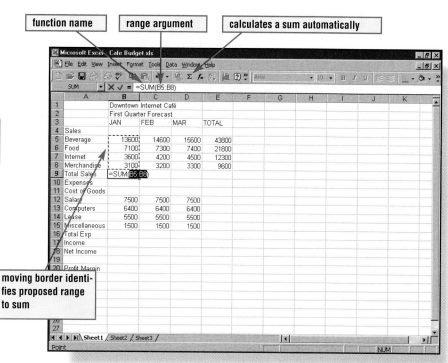

Figure 1–29

Additional Information

The AutoSum button can also calculate a grand total if your worksheet contains subtotals. Select a cell below or to the right of a cell that contains a subtotal and then click Σ AutoSum.

Excel automatically proposes a range based upon the data above or to the left of the active cell. The name of the function followed by the range argument enclosed in parentheses is displayed in the formula bar. Excel displays a range reference as the topmost cell and bottommost cell in the range separated by a colon (B5:B8). To accept the proposed range and enter the function,

2 Click ✓ Enter.

> If you used the [←Enter] key, move to B9.

Your screen should be similar to Figure 1–30.

Figure 1–30

The result, 27400, calculated by the SUM function is displayed in cell B9.

Next you need to calculate the total sales for February and March and the Total column.

3 ■ **Copy the function from cell B9 to cells C9 through E9.**

■ **Move to C9.**

The result calculated by the function, 29300, is displayed in cell C9 and the copied function is displayed in the formula bar. The range reference in the function adjusted relative to its new cell location because it is a relative reference.

Testing the Worksheet

Now that you have created the worksheet structure and entered some sample data for the forecasted sales for the first quarter, you want to test the formulas to verify they are operating correctly. A simple way to do this is to use a calculator to verify that the correct result is displayed. You can then further test the worksheet by changing values and verifying that all cells containing formulas that reference the value are appropriately recalculated.

After considering the sales estimates for the three months, you decide that the estimated Internet sales for January are too low and you want to increase this number from 3600 to 4000.

1 ■ **Change the entry in cell B7 to 4000.**

Your screen should be similar to Figure 1–31.

increasing sales value by 400 increases total sales in B9, E7 and E9 by 400

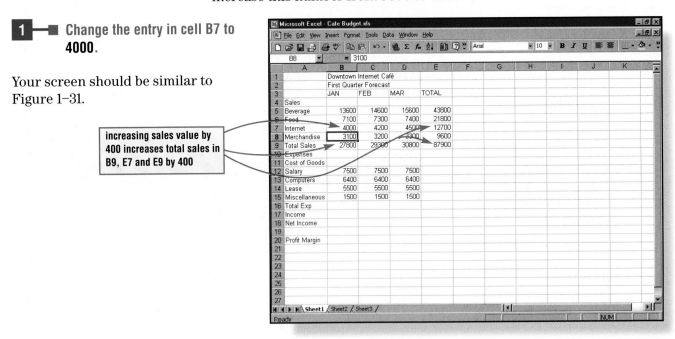

Figure 1–31

The Internet total in cell E7 has been automatically recalculated. The number displayed is now 12700. Likewise, the January total in cell B9 and the grand total in cell E9 have increased by 400 to reflect the change in cell B7.

Concept 8 Automatic Recalculation

The **automatic recalculation** of a formula whenever a number in a referenced cell in the formula changes is one of the most powerful features of electronic worksheets. Only those formulas directly affected by a change in the data are recalculated. This is called **minimal recalculation**. Without this feature, in large worksheets it could take several minutes to recalculate all formulas each time a number is changed in the worksheet. The minimal recalculation feature decreases the recalculation time by recalculating only dependent formulas.

The formulas in the worksheet are correctly calculating the desired result. The Sales portion of the worksheet is now complete.

Using Pointing to Enter a Formula

Next you will enter the formula to calculate the cost of goods sold. These numbers are estimated by using a formula to calculate the number as a percent of sales. As a general rule, the Café calculates beverage expenses at 25 percent of beverage sales and food expenses at 50 percent of food sales.

Rather than typing in the cell references for the formula, you will enter them by selecting the worksheet cells. In addition, to make the process of entering and copying entries even easier, you can enter data into the first cell of a range and have it copied to all other cells in the range at the same time by using [Ctrl] + [←Enter] to complete the entry. You will use this feature to enter the formulas to calculate the beverage expenses for January through March. This formula needs to first calculate the beverage cost of goods at 25 percent and add it to the food cost of goods calculated at 50 percent.

Additional Information

The cells can be adjacent or non-adjacent.

1
- Select B11 through D11.
- Type =
- Click cell B5.

Even when a range is selected, you can still point to specify cells in the formula. You can also use the direction keys to move to the cell.

Your screen should be similar to Figure 1–32.

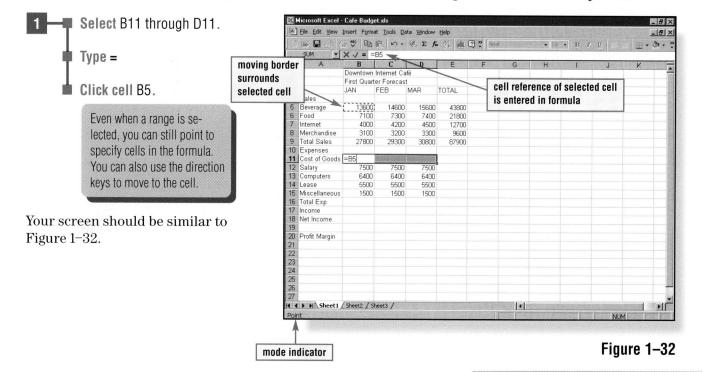

Figure 1–32

Notice that the status bar displays the current mode as Point. This tells you the program is allowing you to select cells by highlighting them. The cell reference, B5, is entered following the = sign. To continue the formula and enter the percentage value to multiply by,

2 Type ***25%**

Next you need to add the food percentage to the formula,

3 Type **+**

Click on B6.

Type ***50%**

Press Ctrl + ↵Enter.

Your screen should be similar to Figure 1–33.

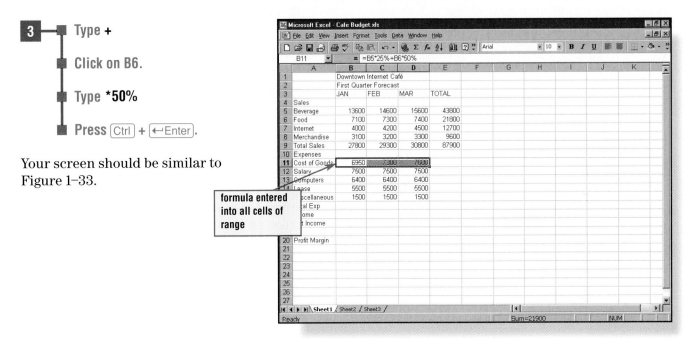

formula entered into all cells of range

Figure 1–33

The formula to calculate the January cost of goods expense was entered in cell B11 and copied to all cells of the selected range. You can now calculate the total expenses in row 11 and column E. To do this quickly, you will preselect the range and use the AutoCalculate button.

4 Select B16 through D16.

Click Σ .

In a similar manner, enter sum functions to calculate the expenses in column E.

The next formula to be entered will calculate the net income. Net income is calculated by subtracting total expenses from total sales.

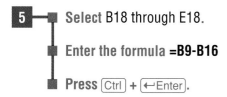

5 ■ Select B18 through E18.

■ Enter the formula **=B9-B16**

■ Press Ctrl + ←Enter.

Your screen should be similar to Figure 1-34.

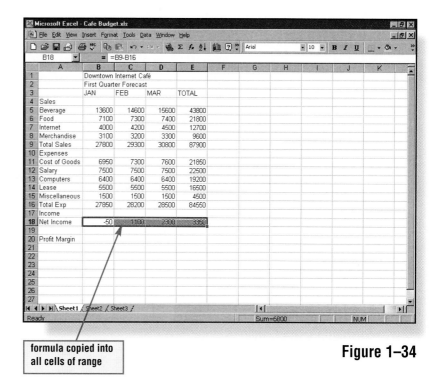

formula copied into all cells of range

Figure 1-34

The formula is quickly entered into all cells of the range. The final formula you need to enter is to calculate the profit margin.

6 ■ Select B20 through E20.

■ Enter the formula **=B18/B9**

■ Press Ctrl + ←Enter.

Your screen should be similar to Figure 1-35.

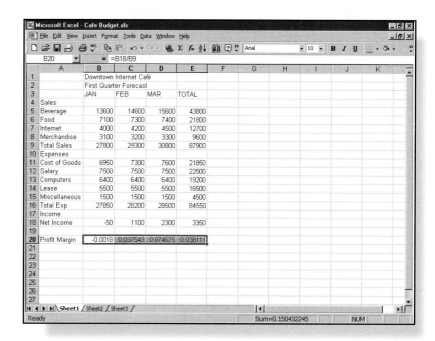

Figure 1-35

The profit margins are calculated and displayed in cells B20 through E20.

Inserting Rows

To delete a row or column, move to it and choose **E**dit/**D**elete/Entire **R**ow or Entire **C**olumn.

Finally, you realize you forgot to include a row for the Advertising expenses. To add this data, you will insert a blank row below the Lease row. To indicate where you want to insert a single blank row, move the cell pointer to the row immediately below the row where you want the new row inserted. If you want to insert multiple rows, select a range of rows and Excel inserts the same number of rows you selected in the range.

1 ■ Move to A15.

■ Choose **I**nsert/**R**ows.

The Insert and Delete commands are also available on the shortcut menu.

■ Enter the label **Advertising** in cell A15 and the value **1000** in cells B15 through D15.

■ Copy the function from cell E14 to E15 to calculate the Total Advertising expense.

Your screen should be similar to Figure 1–36.

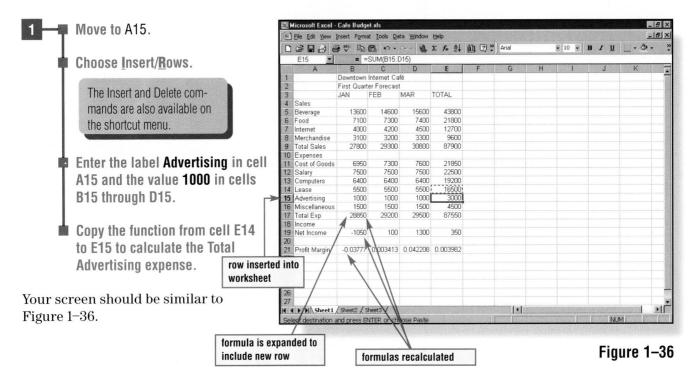

row inserted into worksheet

formula is expanded to include new row

formulas recalculated

Figure 1–36

The range in the formula to calculate monthly total expenses in row 17 has been revised to include the data in the inserted row. Additionally the net income in row 19 and profit margin in row 21 have been recalculated to reflect the change in data.

Additional Information

In a similar manner, you can insert blank columns by moving the cell pointer to the right of the column where you want to insert the new column and use **I**nsert/**C**olumn.

Formatting the Worksheet

Now that many of the worksheet values are entered, you want to improve the appearance of the worksheet by changing the format of the headings. **Format** controls how information is displayed in a cell and includes such features as font (different type styles and sizes), color, patterns, borders, and number formats such as commas and dollar signs. Applying different formats greatly improves both the appearance and readability of the data in a worksheet.

Changing Cell Alignment

You decide the column headings would look better if they were right-aligned in their cell spaces. Then they would appear over the numbers in the column. Alignment is a basic format setting that is used in most worksheets.

Concept 9 **Alignment**

Alignment settings allow you to change the horizontal and vertical placement and the orientation of an entry in a cell. Horizontal placement allows you to left-, center-, or right-align text and number entries in the cell space. Entries can also be indented within the cell space, centered across a selection, or justified. You can also fill a cell horizontally with a repeated entry. Vertical placement allows you to specify whether the cell contents are displayed at the top, centered, or at the bottom of the vertical cell space or justified vertically. Orientation changes the angle of text in a cell by varying the degrees of rotation. Examples of the basic alignment settings are shown below.

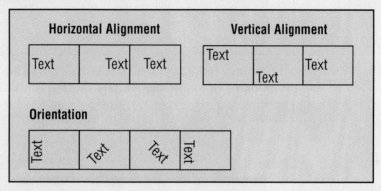

The default horizontal alignment is left for a text entry and right for a number entry. Vertical alignment is bottom for both types of entries.

First you will change the column heading in cell B3 to right-aligned using the Format menu.

1 ■ Move to B3.

■ Choose Format/Cells.

The shortcut key is Ctrl + 1.
Format Cells is also an option
on the shortcut menu.

■ Open the Alignment tab.

Your screen should be similar to
Figure 1–37.

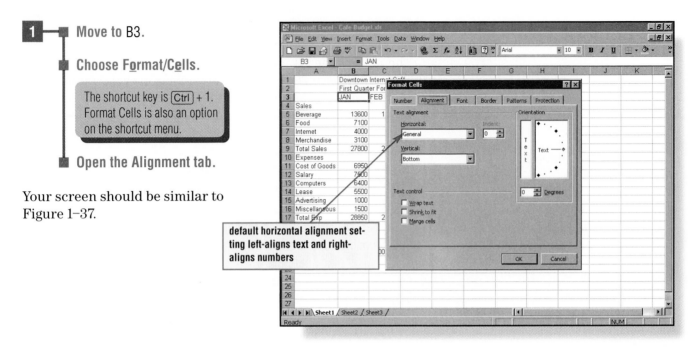

Figure 1–37

The Alignment tab shows the default horizontal alignment setting is
General. This setting left-aligns text entries and right-aligns number entries. You want to change the horizontal alignment of the entry to right-
aligned.

2 ■ Open the Horizontal drop-down
list box.

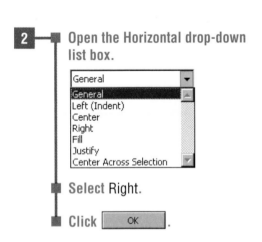

■ Select Right.

■ Click ☐ OK ☐.

Your screen should be similar to
Figure 1–38.

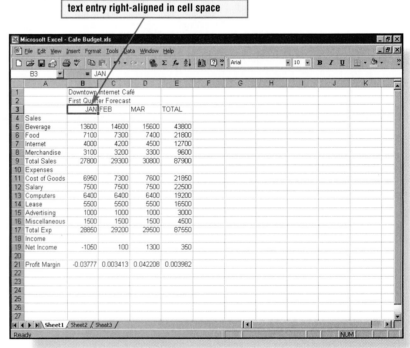

Figure 1–38

A quicker way to change the alignment is to use the Formatting toolbar shortcuts shown below:

Shortcut	Action
	Align Left
	Center
	Align Right

You can quickly align a range of cells by selecting the range and then using the command or button. A quick way to select a range of filled cells is to hold down ⇧Shift and double-click on the edge of the active cell in the direction in which you want the range expanded. For example, to select the range to the right of the active cell, you would double-click the right border. To right-align the remaining column entries,

> If you do not hold down ⇧Shift while double-clicking on a border, the cell selector moves to the last-used cell in the direction indicated.

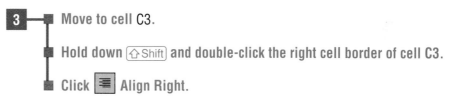

3 — Move to cell C3.

Hold down ⇧Shift and double-click the right cell border of cell C3.

Click Align Right.

> The menu equivalent is **F**ormat/C**e**lls/Alignment/**H**orizontal/Right.

The entries in the selected range are right-aligned in their cell spaces.

Indenting Entries

Next you would like to indent the row headings in cells A5 through A8 and A11 through A16 from the left edge of the cell. You want to indent the headings in both ranges at the same time. To select a nonadjacent range, you select the first cell or range of cells and then hold down Ctrl and select the other cells. To select the cells and indent them,

1 ■ Select A5 through A8.

■ Hold down Ctrl.

■ Select A11 through A16.

■ Release the Ctrl key.

■ Click 🔄 Increase Indent.

> The menu equivalent is
> Format/Cells/Alignment/
> Horizontal/Left(Indent)/1.

Your screen should be similar to
Figure 1–39.

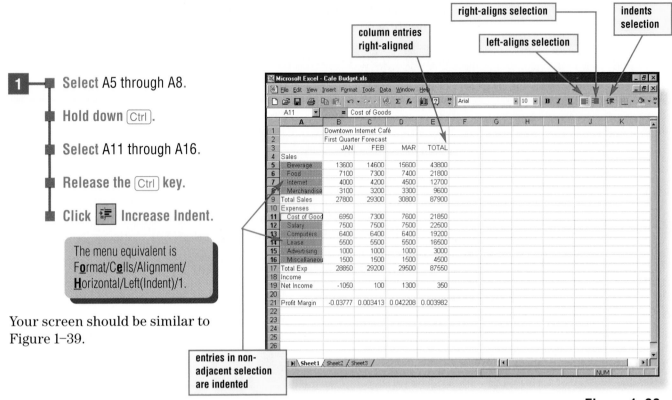

Figure 1–39

Each entry in the selected range is indented two spaces from the left edge
of the cell. You would also like to indent the Total Sales, Total Exp, and Net
Income headings four spaces.

2 ■ Select A9, A17, and A19.

■ Click 🔄 Increase Indent
(2 times).

Your screen should be similar to
Figure 1–40.

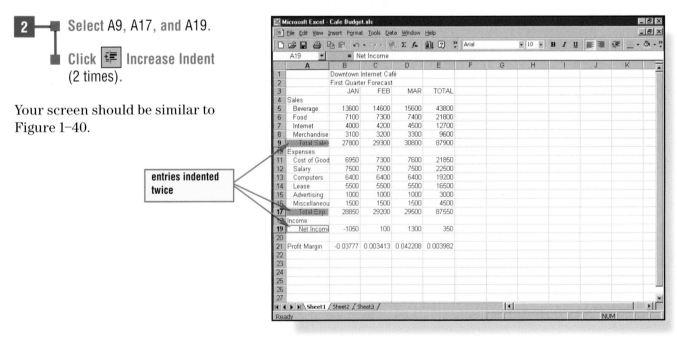

Figure 1–40

Additional Information

If you move cells containing formulas, the formulas are not adjusted relative to their new worksheet location.

As you drag, an outline of the cell appears and the mouse pointer displays the cell reference to show its new location in the worksheet.

Moving Cell Contents

Next you want to center the worksheet titles across columns A through E so they are centered over the worksheet data. Before you can do this, however, you need to first move the two titles into the leftmost cell of the range. You could cut and paste the contents, or you can drag the cell border to move the cell contents. This is similar to copying by dragging. Dragging is quickest and most useful when the distance between cells is short and they are visible within the window, whereas Cut and Paste is best for long-distance moves.

1
- **Select cells** B1 and B2.
- **Point to the border of the range selection and when the mouse pointer shape is , drag the mouse pointer to cell A1:A2 and release the mouse button.**

Your screen should be similar to Figure 1–41.

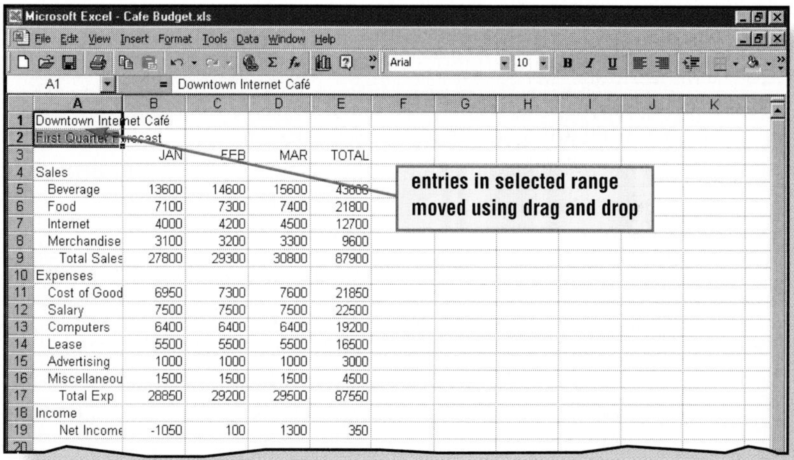

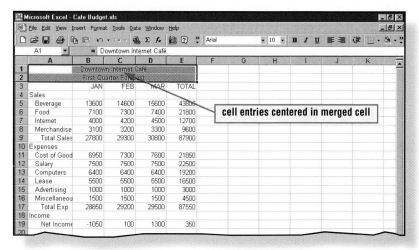

Figure 1–41

The cell contents are copied into cells A1 and A2 and cleared from the original cells.

Centering across a Selection

Now you are ready to center the worksheet title across cells A1 through E2.

1
- **Select** A1 through E2.
- **Choose Format/Cells**
- **From the Horizontal drop-down list, select** Center Across Selection.
- **Click** OK.

Your screen should be similar to Figure 1–42.

Figure 1–42

Excel has centered the contents of the leftmost cells of the range within the selected range.

Additional Information

The Font settings are common to all Office 2000 programs.

Changing Fonts and Font Styles

Finally, you want to improve the worksheet appearance by enhancing the appearance of the title. One way to do this is to change the font and font size used in the title.

Concept Fonts

A **font**, also commonly referred to as a **typeface**, is a set of characters with a specific design. The designs have names such as Times New Roman and Courier. Using fonts as a design element can add interest to your document and give readers visual cues to help them find information quickly.

There are two basic types of fonts, serif and sans serif. **Serif** fonts have a flair at the base of each letter that visually leads the reader to the next letter. Two common serif fonts are Roman and Times New Roman. Serif fonts generally are used in paragraphs. **Sans serif** fonts do not have a flair at the base of each letter. Arial and Helvetica are two common sans serif fonts. Because sans serif fonts have a clean look, they are often used for headings in documents. It is good practice to use only two types of fonts in a document, one for text and one for headings. Too many styles can make your document look cluttered and unprofessional.

Each font has one or more sizes. Size is the height and width of the character and is commonly measured in points, abbreviated pt. One point equals about 1/72 inch, and text in most documents is 10 pt. or 12 pt.

Here are several examples of the same text in various fonts and sizes.

Typeface	Font Size (12 pt./18 pt.)
Arial	This is 12 pt. This is 18 pt.
Courier New	This is 12 pt. This is 18 pt.
Times New Roman	This is 12 pt. This is 18 pt.

The fonts on your computer system will be either printer or TrueType fonts. TrueType fonts appear onscreen as they will appear when printed. They are installed when Windows is installed. Printer fonts are supported by your printer and are displayed as close as possible to how they will appear onscreen, but may not match exactly when printed.

1 Select A1 and A2.

Open the [Arial] Font drop-down list box.

The menu equivalent is F**o**rmat/C**e**lls/**F**ont.

Your screen should be similar to Figure 1–43.

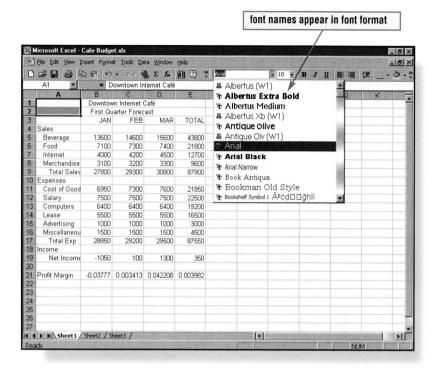

font names appear in font format

Figure 1–43

The Font drop-down menu displays examples of the available fonts in alphabetical order. The default worksheet font, Arial, is highlighted.

2 Select Times New Roman.

Your screen should be similar to Figure 1–44.

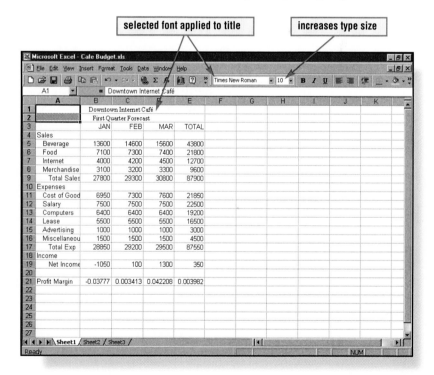

selected font applied to title   increases type size

Figure 1–44

The title appears in the selected typeface and the Font button displays the name of the font in the active cell.

Next you will increase the font size to 14.

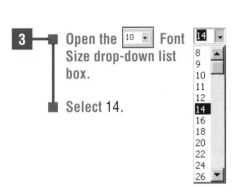

> **3** Open the `10` Font Size drop-down list box.
>
> ■ Select `14`.

Your screen should be similar to Figure 1–45.

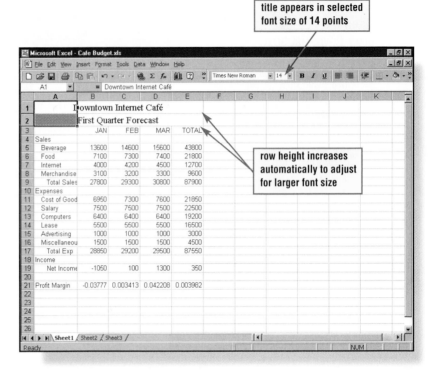

Figure 1–45

Notice that the height of the row has increased to accommodate the larger font size of the heading.

Changing Character Effects

In addition to changing font and font size, you can apply different character effects to enhance the appearance of text.

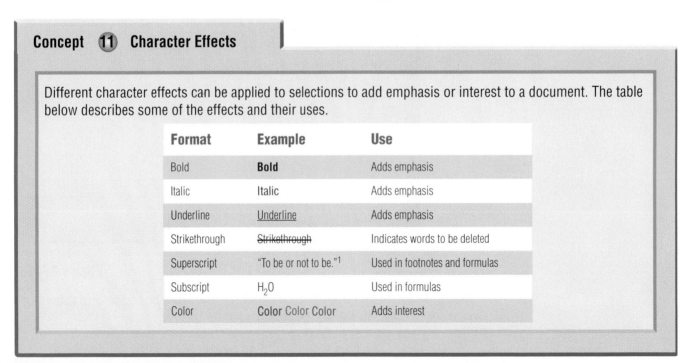

Concept 11 Character Effects

Different character effects can be applied to selections to add emphasis or interest to a document. The table below describes some of the effects and their uses.

Format	Example	Use
Bold	**Bold**	Adds emphasis
Italic	*Italic*	Adds emphasis
Underline	<u>Underline</u>	Adds emphasis
Strikethrough	~~Strikethrough~~	Indicates words to be deleted
Superscript	"To be or not to be."[1]	Used in footnotes and formulas
Subscript	H_2O	Used in formulas
Color	**Color** Color Color	Adds interest

You want to add bold, italic, and underlines to several worksheet entries. First you will bold the two title lines.

Your screen should be similar to Figure 1–46.

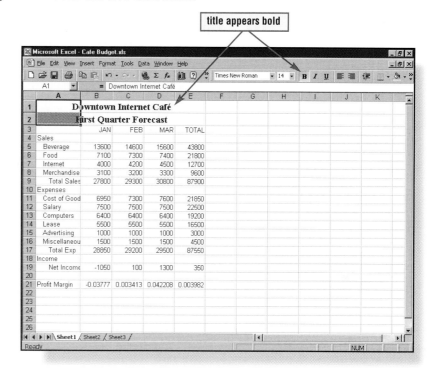

Figure 1–46

Next you would like to bold, underline, and italicize some of the other entries in the worksheet.

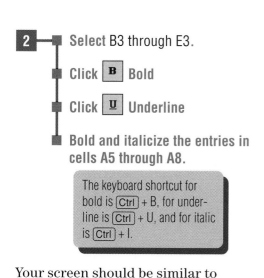

> The keyboard shortcut for bold is Ctrl + B, for underline is Ctrl + U, and for italic is Ctrl + I.

Your screen should be similar to Figure 1–47.

Figure 1–47

Using Undo

Sometimes formatting changes you make do not have the expected result. In this case, you feel that the sales category names would look better without the formatting. To quickly undo the last two actions you performed,

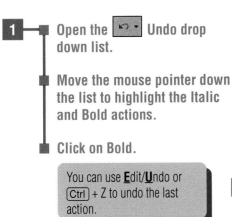

1 ▪ Open the 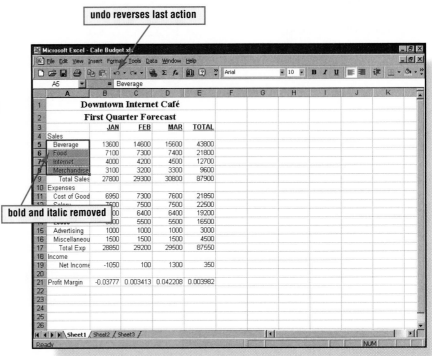 Undo drop down list.

▪ Move the mouse pointer down the list to highlight the Italic and Bold actions.

▪ Click on Bold.

> You can use **E**dit/**U**ndo or [Ctrl] + Z to undo the last action.

Your screen should be similar to Figure 1–48.

Figure 1–48

> **Additional Information**
>
> If you change your mind, use Edit/Redo (⌐▾ or [Ctrl] + y). Repeatedly using the Undo or Redo buttons performs the actions in the list one by one.

The two actions you selected are undone. Undo reverses the selected actions regardless of the current cell pointer location.

Using Format Painter

You do think, however, that the Total Sales, Total Exp, and Net Income labels would look good in bold.

1 ▪ Apply bold to cell A9.

You could repeat the same sequence for cell A17, but a quicker method is to copy the format from one cell to another using ▧ Format Painter on the Standard toolbar. To copy the format of the active cell to the other cells and turn off the feature when you are done,

2 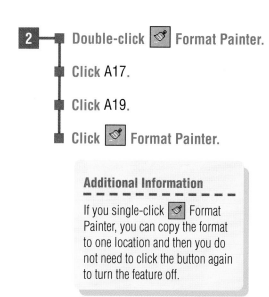 Double-click Format Painter.

Click A17.

Click A19.

Click Format Painter.

Additional Information

If you single-click Format Painter, you can copy the format to one location and then you do not need to click the button again to turn the feature off.

Your screen should be similar to Figure 1–49.

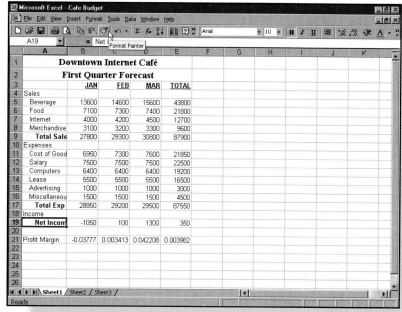

Figure 1–49

The formatting was quickly added to each cell as it was selected and the feature is off.

Formatting Numbers

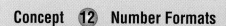

You also want to improve the appearance of the numbers in the worksheet by changing their format.

Concept ⑫ Number Formats

Number formats affect how numbers look onscreen and when printed. They do not affect the way Excel stores or uses the values in calculations. The default number format setting in a worksheet is General. In most cases when you enter numbers, the numbers appear just as you enter them, unformatted. Unformatted numbers are displayed without a thousands separator such as a comma, with negative values preceded by a – (minus sign), and with as many decimal place settings as cell space allows.

In some cases, formats are applied to number entries depending on the symbols you used when entering the data. The table below shows samples of how Excel automatically formats a number based on how it appears when you enter it.

Entry	Format
10,000	Comma
$102.20	Currency with two decimal places
90%	Percent with zero decimal places
10/30/98	Date
9:10	Time

First you will change the number format of cells B5 through E8 to display dollar signs, commas, and decimal places.

1 ■ Select cells B5 through E9.

■ Choose Format/Cells.

■ If necessary, open the Number tab.

■ From the Category list box, select Currency.

Your screen should be similar to Figure 1–50.

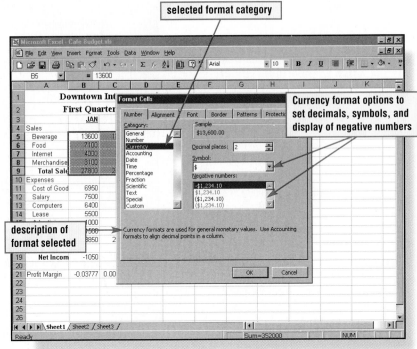

Figure 1–50

The Currency category includes options that allow you to specify the number of decimal places, how negative numbers will appear, and whether a currency symbol such as a dollar sign will be displayed.

2 ■ Click [OK] to use the default Currency format settings.

Your screen should be similar to Figure 1–51.

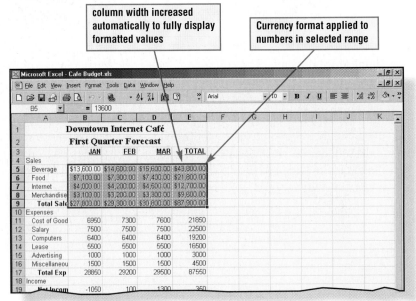

Figure 1–51

The number entries in the selected range appear with a currency symbol, comma, and two decimal places. The column widths increased automatically to fully display the formatted values.

A second format category that displays numbers as currency is Accounting. To see how this format looks,

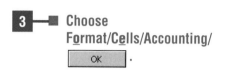

3 ━ Choose Format/Cells/Accounting/ OK .

Your screen should be similar to Figure 1–52.

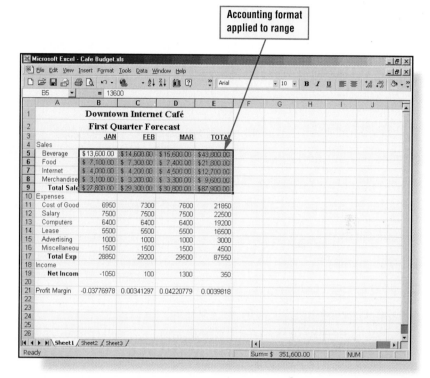

Figure 1–52

The numbers now appear in Accounting format. The primary difference between the Accounting and the Currency formats is that the Accounting format aligns numbers at the decimal place and places the dollar sign in a column at the left edge of the cell space. In addition, it does not allow you to select different ways of displaying negative numbers but displays them in black in parentheses. You decide the Accounting format will make it easier to read the numbers in a column.

As you look at the numbers, you decide it is not necessary to display the decimal places since most of the values are whole numbers. To do this,

The 🔢 button increases the number of decimal places.

4 ━ Click 🔢 Decrease decimal (2 times).

You want to quickly apply the same formats to the expense range of cells.

5 ■ Click 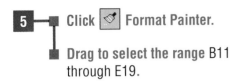 Format Painter.

■ Drag to select the range B11 through E19.

Your screen should be similar to Figure 1–53.

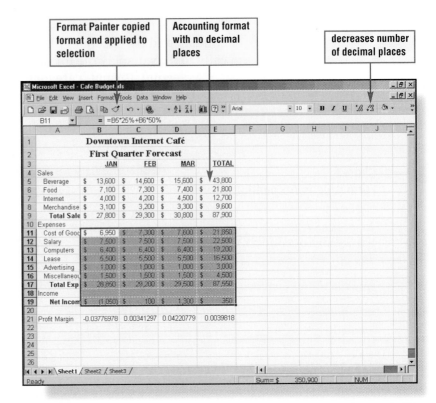

Figure 1–53

You would also like the Profit Margin to be displayed as a percentage with two decimal places.

6 ■ Select B21 through E21.

■ Choose F**o**rmat/C**e**lls Percentage/ OK .

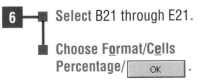

Your screen should be similar to Figure 1–54.

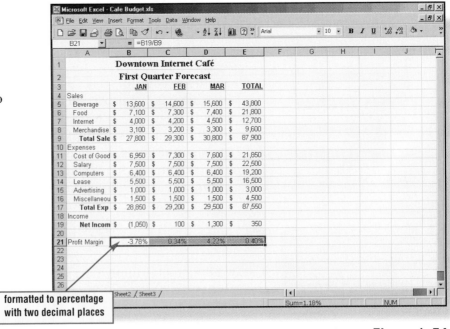

Figure 1–54

Now that the numbers are displayed as a percentage and the number of decimal places has been decreased, the column widths are larger than they need to be. Because Excel does not automatically reduce column widths, you need to make this change yourself. You will use the AutoFit feature to adjust the column widths for all cells in columns A through E.

7 Click the A column letter and drag to the right to expand the selection to include column E.

Double-click any column border line in the selection to AutoFit the selection.

Additional Information

You could also press Ctrl + A or click the button at the intersection of the row numbers and column letters to select the entire worksheet and then double-click on any border line to adjust the column widths of all columns containing entries.

Your screen should be similar to Figure 1–55.

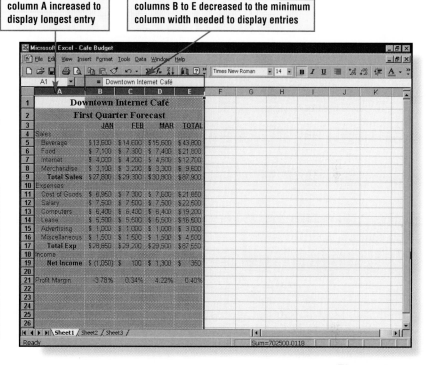

column A increased to display longest entry

columns B to E decreased to the minimum column width needed to display entries

Figure 1–55

The width of columns B through E automatically decreased to the minimum column width needed to fully display the entries. The width of column A increased to accommodate the longest entry.

Adding Color

The last formatting change you would like to make to the worksheet is to add color to the text and to the background of selected cells. First you will change the color of the text.

1 ■ Select A1 through A2.

■ Open the [A ▾] Font Color palette.

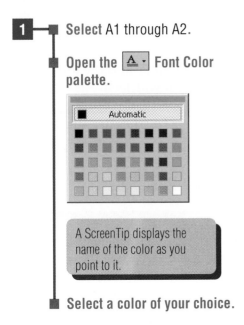

■ Select a color of your choice.

A ScreenTip displays the name of the color as you point to it.

Your screen should be similar to Figure 1–56.

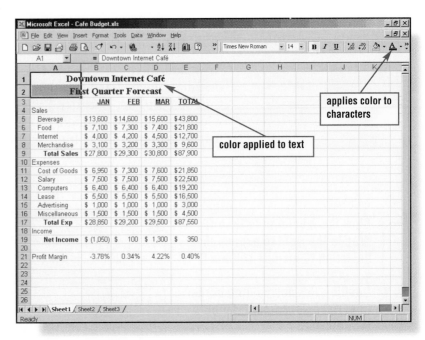

Figure 1–56

This text will use the cell fill color of yellow and the title text of blue.

The selected color appears in the button and can be applied again simply by clicking the button. Next you will change the cell background color, also called the fill color.

2 ■ Select A1 through E2.

■ Open the [🖌 ▾] Fill Color palette.

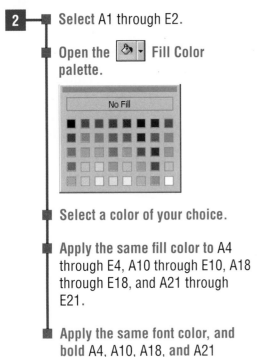

■ Select a color of your choice.

■ Apply the same fill color to A4 through E4, A10 through E10, A18 through E18, and A21 through E21.

■ Apply the same font color, and bold A4, A10, A18, and A21 through E21.

Your screen should be similar to Figure 1–57.

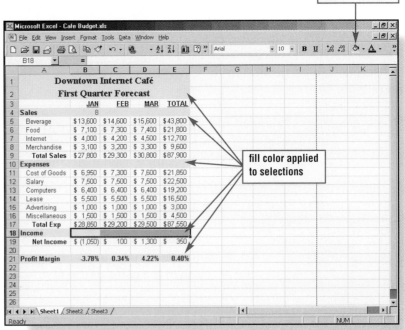

Figure 1–57

Inserting Copied Cells

Although the formatting you added to the titles makes the worksheet easier to read, you decide you need to display month headings above the expense columns. To do this quickly, you can insert copied data between existing data. To indicate where to place the copied text, you move the cell pointer to the upper-left cell of the area where you want the selection inserted and specify the direction you want to shift the surrounding cells.

1 ■ Copy the contents of cells A3 through E3.

■ Move to A10.

■ Choose Insert/Copied Cells.

■ If necessary, select Shift cells down from the Insert Paste dialog box.

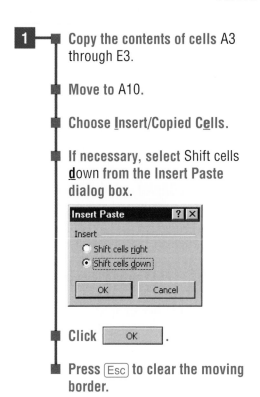

■ Click [OK].

■ Press [Esc] to clear the moving border.

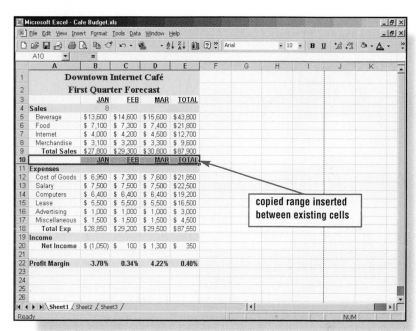

Figure 1–58

Your screen should be similar to Figure 1–58.

Additional Information

You can also insert moved text between existing cells by cutting the selection and choosing Cut Cells from the Insert menu.

The copied data is inserted into the existing row (10) and all entries below are moved down one row. The formats applied to the selection you copied are also copied.

Inserting and Sizing Graphics

Finally you want to add a graphic to add interest. A ClipArt image is one of several different graphic objects that can be added to an Excel document.

Concept ⑬ Graphics

A **graphic** is a nontext element or object, such as a drawing or picture, that can be added to a document. An **object** is an item that can be sized, moved, and manipulated. A graphic can be a simple drawing object consisting of shapes such as lines and boxes that can be created using features on the Drawing toolbar. A **drawing object** is part of your Excel document. A **picture** is an illustration such as a scanned photograph. It is a graphic created from another program. Pictures are inserted as embedded objects. An **embedded object** becomes part of the Excel document and can be opened and edited using the source program, the program in which it was created.

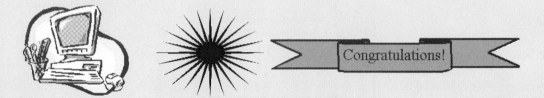

Picture files can be obtained from a variety of sources. Many simple drawings called **ClipArt** are available in the Clip Gallery that comes with Office 2000. You can also create graphic files using a scanner to convert any printed document, including photographs, to an electronic format. Most images that are scanned and inserted into documents are stored as Windows bitmap files (.bmp). All types of graphics, including ClipArt, photographs, and other types of images can be found on the Internet. These files are commonly stored as .jpg or .pcx files. Keep in mind that any images you locate on the Internet may be copyrighted and should be used only with permission. You can also purchase CDs containing graphics for your use.

A graphic object can be manipulated in many ways. You can change its size, add borders or shading, or move it to another location on the page, including in the margins or on top of or below other objects. It cannot, however, be placed behind the worksheet data.

You want to insert a ClipArt graphic to the right of the data in the worksheet.

1 ■ Move to F3.

■ Choose **I**nsert/**P**icture/**C**lipArt

Your screen should be similar to
Figure 1–59.

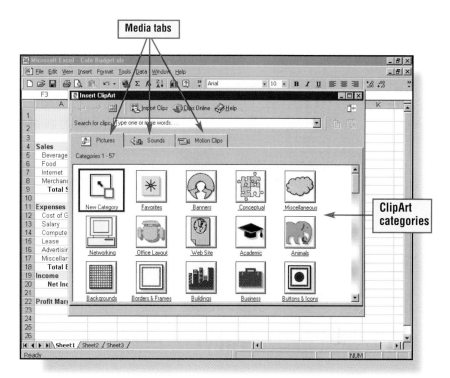

Figure 1–59

Your ClipArt categories may be different from Figure 1–59.

The Insert ClipArt dialog box Media tabs organize the different media by
type. The Pictures tab contains clip art, photographs, scanned images,
drawings, and other graphics. Sound effects and music files are in the
Sounds tab, and videos and animation files are in the Motion Clips tab.
The clip art you want is in the People category in the Pictures tab.

2 ■ If necessary, open the
Pictures tab.

■ Click [icon].

This picture can also be
found in the People at Work
category.

Your screen should be similar to
Figure 1–60.

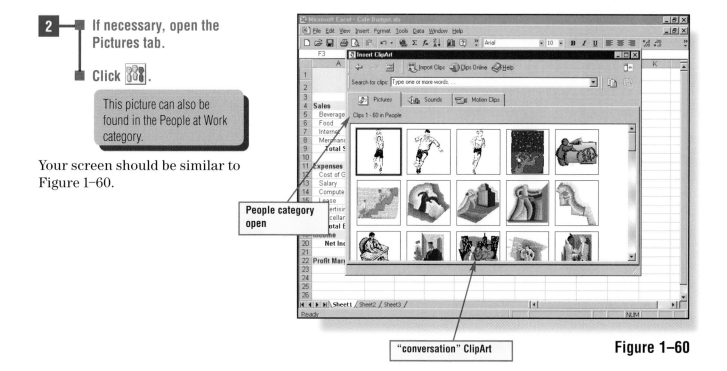

Figure 1–60

Icons of the ClipArt images available in the People category are displayed. Pointing to an image displays the image name in a ScreenTip. You want to insert the ClipArt named "conversation."

3 ▪ Click 🖼 conversation.

▪ From the Common Task pop-up menu click 🔲 Insert Clip.

▪ Click ✖ to close the dialog box.

> If this graphic is not available in the Clip Gallery, choose Insert/Picture and select Conversation.wmf from your data disk.

Your screen should be similar to Figure 1–61.

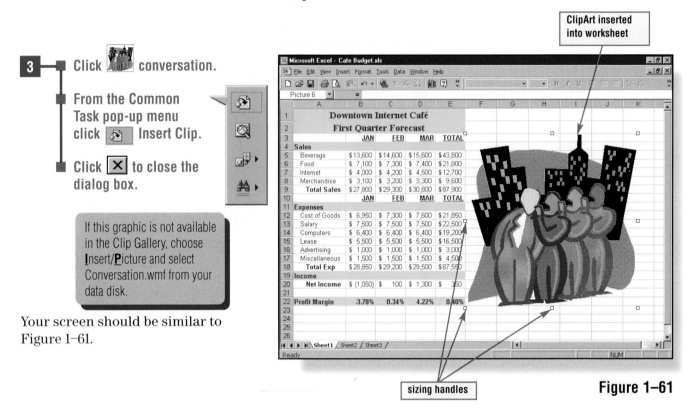

Figure 1–61

> The Picture toolbar may automatically display when a graphic object is selected.

The ClipArt image is inserted in the document at the current cell. Frequently, when a graphic is inserted, its size will need to be adjusted. In this case you want to reduce its size. The picture is surrounded by eight boxes, called **sizing handles**, indicating it is a selected object and can now be sized and moved anywhere in the document. The handles are used to size the object, much as you would size a window. A graphic object is moved by dragging it to the new location.

You want to reduce the graphic size to cells F4 through J22, approximately.

4 Point to the lower-right corner handle.

> The mouse pointer changes to ⤡, just as it does when resizing a window.

Drag the mouse to reduce the size of the graphic to cover cells F4 through J22.

> Dragging a corner handle maintains the original proportions of the picture.

Move to A1.

Your screen should be similar to Figure 1–62.

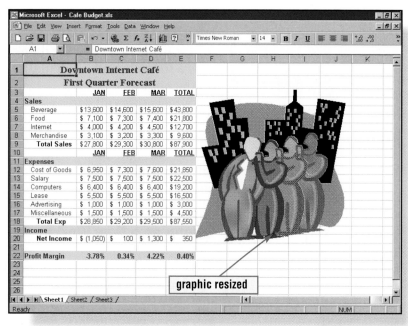

Figure 1–62

The three-month forecast is now complete.

Entering a Date

Now that the worksheet is complete, you want to include your name and the date in the worksheet as documentation.

1 Enter your first initial and last name in cell A24.

Enter the current date in cell A25 in the format mm/dd/yyyy (for example, 10/10/2001).

Move to A25.

Your screen should be similar to Figure 1–63.

> Your date may be formatted differently, depending on the last-used date format on your system.

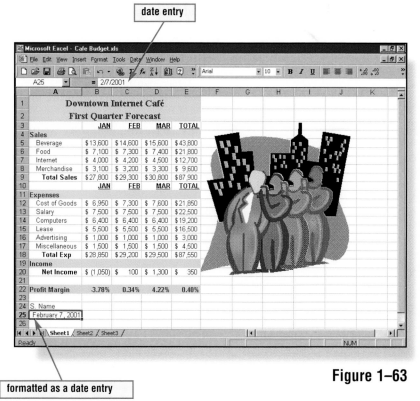

Figure 1–63

EXCEL 2000

Use F**o**rmat/C**e**lls/Number/Date to change the date format.

Excel automatically recognized your entry as a date and formatted the entry appropriately. The entry is displayed in the formula bar as you enter it. If you had preceded the date entry with =, Excel would have interpreted it as a formula and a calculation of division would have been performed on the numbers.

Excel stores all dates as serial numbers with each day numbered from the beginning of the century; the date serial number 1 corresponds to the date January 1, 1900, and the integer 65380 is December 31, 2078. The integers are assigned consecutively beginning with 1 and ending with 65,380. They are called **date numbers**. Conversion of the date to a serial number allows dates to be used in calculations.

Saving as a New Workbook

Now you are ready to save the changes you have made to the workbook file to your data disk.

1 ■ Choose **F**ile/Save **A**s

■ Edit the file name to **Café Forecast**.

■ If the Save In location is not correct, select the appropriate location from the drop-down list.

■ Click  .

Previewing and Printing a Workbook

If you have printer capability, you can print a paper copy, also called a printout or hard copy, of the worksheet.

1 ■ If necessary, turn the printer on and check to see that it is online.

Before printing, you may want to preview how the worksheet will appear on the printed page. To do this,

2 ── Click 📖 Print Preview.

> The menu equivalent is **F**ile/Print Pre**v**iew.

Your screen should be similar to Figure 1–64.

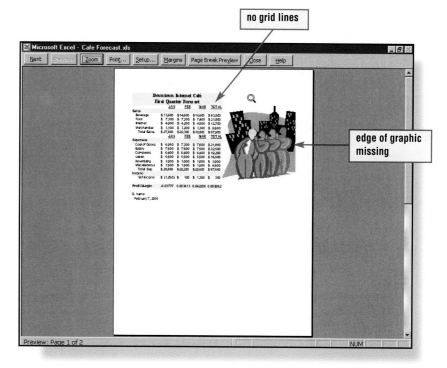

Figure 1–64

The Print Preview window displays the worksheet as it will appear on the printed page. Notice that the row and column lines are not displayed and will not print. Also notice that the right edge of the graphic is cut off because it is too large to fit on the page. You need to make the graphic smaller so that it will all print on one page.

3 ── Click Close .

Your screen should be similar to Figure 1–65.

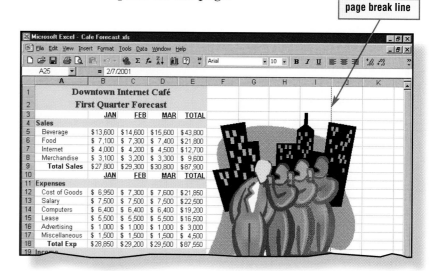

Figure 1–65

Notice the dotted line between columns I and J. This line indicates the location of the page break.

> Click on the graphic to select it.

4 ── Select the graphic and reduce it in size to just fit within the page break.

── Preview the worksheet again.

You can now see that the entire graphic is displayed and will print on the page. While previewing, you can change from full-page view to a magnified view by clicking on the preview page when the mouse pointer appears as a .

5 Click the worksheet title.

> The area you click on is the area that will display in the Preview window.

Your screen should be similar to Figure 1–66.

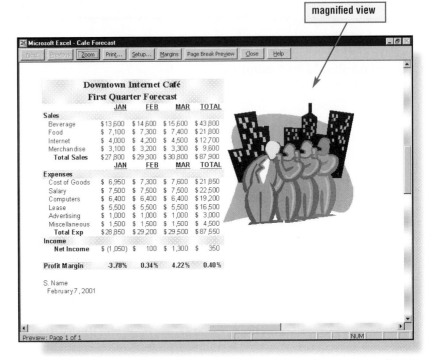

Figure 1–66

The worksheet is displayed in the actual size it will appear when printed.

6 Click on the worksheet again to return to full-page view.

Click Print... .

Your screen should be similar to Figure 1–67.

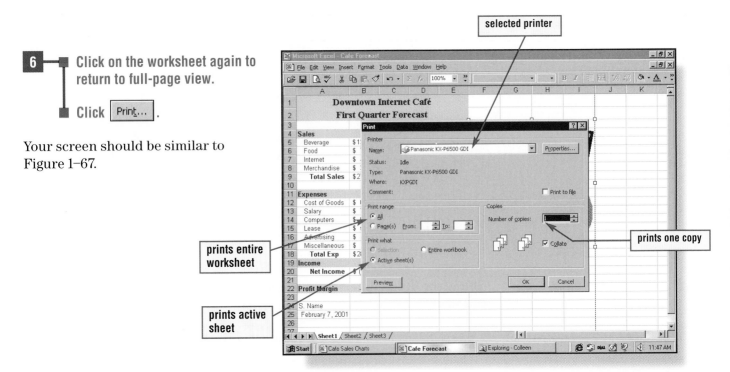

Figure 1–67

From the Print dialog box, you need to specify the printer you will use and the document settings. The printer that is currently selected is displayed in the Name drop-down list box in the Printer section of the dialog box.

7 If you need to change the selected printer to another printer, open the Na**m**e drop-down list box and select the appropriate printer (your instructor will tell you which printer to select).

The Print Range area of the Print dialog box lets you specify how much of the document you want printed. The All setting prints the entire document and Pages prints only the pages you specify. The Print what options are used to restrict the printing to a selection, the active sheet, or the entire workbook. The default settings of All and Active sheet are correct. In the Copies section, the default setting of one copy of the document is acceptable. To begin printing using the settings in the Print dialog box,

> The menu equivalent is **F**ile/**P**rint and the keyboard shortcut is Ctrl + P. You can also click 🖨 to print using the default print settings.

8 Click  .

Your printer should be printing out the worksheet. Your printed output should look like the figure shown in the Case Study at the beginning of the tutorial. If you do not have a color printer, the colors appear as shades of gray.

Exiting Excel

If you want to quit or exit the Excel program at this time,

> The menu equivalent is **F**ile/E**x**it.

1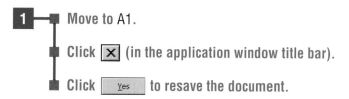

Move to A1.

Click ☒ (in the application window title bar).

Click Yes to resave the document.

Additional Information

Excel saves the file with the cell selector positioned in the same cell it was in when saved.

Concept Summary

Tutorial 1: Creating and Editing a Worksheet

Worksheet development consists of four stages; planning, entering and editing, testing, and formatting.

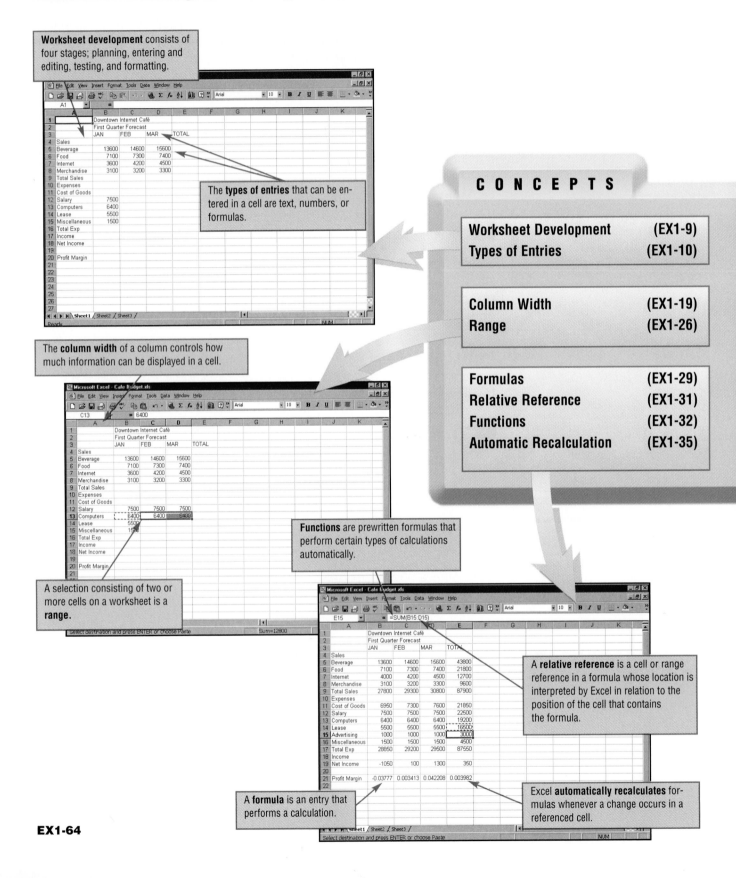

The **types of entries** that can be entered in a cell are text, numbers, or formulas.

CONCEPTS

Worksheet Development	**(EX1-9)**
Types of Entries	**(EX1-10)**
Column Width	**(EX1-19)**
Range	**(EX1-26)**
Formulas	**(EX1-29)**
Relative Reference	**(EX1-31)**
Functions	**(EX1-32)**
Automatic Recalculation	**(EX1-35)**

The **column width** of a column controls how much information can be displayed in a cell.

Functions are prewritten formulas that perform certain types of calculations automatically.

A selection consisting of two or more cells on a worksheet is a **range**.

A **relative reference** is a cell or range reference in a formula whose location is interpreted by Excel in relation to the position of the cell that contains the formula.

A **formula** is an entry that performs a calculation.

Excel **automatically recalculates** formulas whenever a change occurs in a referenced cell.

Fonts consist of typefaces, point sizes, and styles that can be applied to characters to improve their appearance.

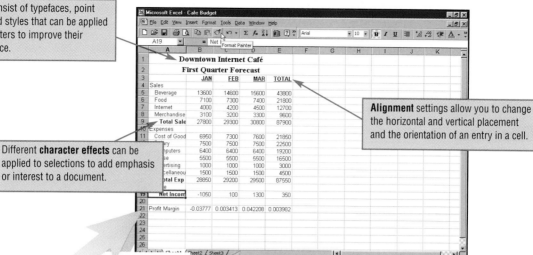

Alignment settings allow you to change the horizontal and vertical placement and the orientation of an entry in a cell.

Different **character effects** can be applied to selections to add emphasis or interest to a document.

Alignment	(EX1-39)
Fonts	(EX1-44)
Character Effects	(EX1-46)
Number Formats	(EX1-49)
Graphics	(EX1-56)

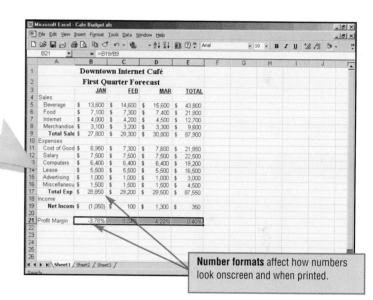

Number formats affect how numbers look onscreen and when printed.

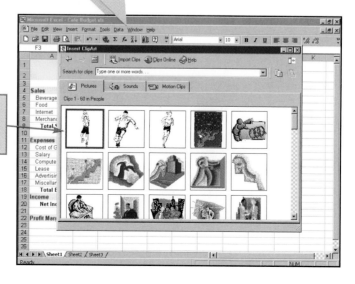

A **graphic** is a nontext element or object, such as a drawing or picture, that can be added to a document.

Tutorial Review

Key Terms

active cell   EX1-5
active sheet   EX1-5
adjacent range   EX1-26
alignment   EX1-39
argument   EX1-32
AutoCorrect   EX1-15
automatic recalculation   EX1-35
cell   EX1-5
cell selector   EX1-5
ClipArt   EX1-56
column   EX1-4
column letter   EX1-5
constant   EX1-10
copy area   EX1-24
date number   EX1-60
destination   EX1-25
drawing object   EX1-56
embedded object   EX1-56
fill handle   EX1-27
font   EX1-44
format   EX1-38
Formatting toolbar   EX1-3
formula   EX1-10, EX1-29
formula bar   EX1-4
functions   EX1-32
graphic   EX1-56
heading   EX1-11
minimal recalculation   EX1-35
Name box   EX1-4
nonadjacent range   EX1-26

number   EX1-10
number formats   EX1-49
object   EX1-56
operand   EX1-29
order of precedence   EX1-29
paste area   EX1-25
picture   EX1-56
range   EX1-26
reference   EX1-5
relative reference   EX1-31
row   EX1-4
row number   EX1-5
sans serif   EX1-44
serif   EX1-44
sheet tab   EX1-5
sizing handle   EX1-58
source   EX1-24
spreadsheet   EX1-4
Standard toolbar   EX1-3
syntax   EX1-32
tab scroll button   EX1-6
text   EX1-10
typeface   EX1-44
variable   EX1-10
workbook   EX1-4
workbook window   EX1-4
worksheet   EX1-4
workspace   EX1-4

Command Summary

Command	Shortcut Keys	Button	Action
File/Open <file name>	Ctrl + O		Opens an existing workbook file
File/Close			Closes open workbook file
File/Save <file name>	Ctrl + S		Saves current file on disk using same file name and/or location
File/Save As <file name>			Saves current file on disk using a new file name
File/Print Preview			Displays worksheet as it will appear when printed
File/Print	Ctrl + P		Prints a worksheet or an entire workbook
File/Exit			Exits Excel
Edit/Undo	Ctrl + Z		Undoes last entry, editing, or formatting change
Edit/Redo	Ctrl + Y		Restores changes after using Undo
Edit/Copy	Ctrl + C		Copies selected data to Clipboard
Edit/Paste	Ctrl + V		Pastes selections stored in Clipboard
Edit/Fill			Fills selected cells with contents of source cell
Edit/Clear/Contents	Delete		Clears cell contents
Edit/Delete/Entire Row			Deletes selected rows
Edit/Delete/Entire Column			Deletes selected columns
View/Toolbars			Displays or hides selected toolbar
Insert/Copied Cells			Inserts row and copies text from Clipboard
Insert/Rows			Inserts a blank row
Insert/Columns			Inserts a blank column
Insert/Picture/From File			Inserts picture at insertion point from disk
Format/Cells/Number/Currency			Applies Currency format to selection
Format/Cells/Number/Accounting			Applies Accounting format to selection
Format/Cells/Number/Date			Applies Date format to selection
Format/Cells/Number/Percent			Applies Percent format to selection
Format/Cells/Number/Decimal places			Increases or decreases the number of decimal places associated with a number value
Format/Cells/Alignment/Horizontal/ Left (Indent)			Left-aligns entry in cell space

Command	Shortcut Keys	Button	Action
Format/Cells/Alignment/Horizontal/Center		≡	Center-aligns entry in cell space
Format/Cells/Alignment/Horizontal/Right		≡	Right-aligns entry in cell space
Format/Cells/Alignment/Horizontal/Left (Indent)/1		≡	Left-aligns and indents cell entry one space
Format/Cells/Alignment/Horizontal/Center Across Selection			Centers cell contents across selected cells
Format/Cells/Font			Changes font and attributes of cell contents
Format/Cells/Font/Font Style/Bold	Ctrl + B	**B**	Bolds selected text
Format/Cells/Font/Font Style/Italic	Ctrl + I	*I*	Italicizes selected text
Format/Cells/Font/Underline/Single	Ctrl + U	U̲	Underlines selected text
Format/Cells/Font/Color		A ▾	Adds color to text
Format/Cells/Patterns/Color		▨ ▾	Adds color to cell background
Format/Row/Height			Changes height of selected rows
Format/Column/Width			Changes width of columns
Format/Column/Autofit Selection			Changes column width to match widest cell entry

Screen Identification

In the following worksheet, several items are identified by letters. Enter the correct term for each item in the space provided.

a. _____

b. _____

c. _____

d. _____

e. _____

f. _____

g. _____

h. _____

i. _____

j. _____

k. _____

l. _____

m. _____

n. _____

o. _____

p. _____

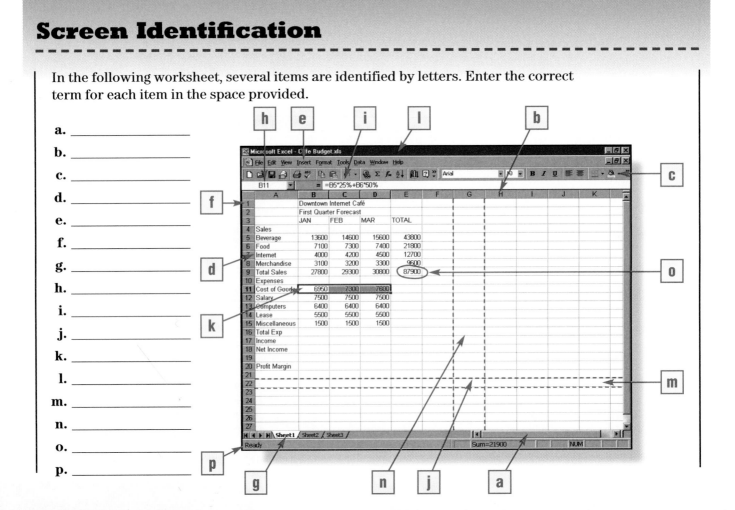

Matching

Match the lettered item on the right with the numbered item on the left.

1. source   _____   **a.** right-aligns cell entry

2. *   _____   **b.** moves cell selector to upper-left corner of worksheet

3. ▤   _____   **c.** the cell you copy from

4. Ctrl + Home   _____   **d.** two or more worksheet cells

5. .xls   _____   **e.** a cell reference

6. ▦   _____   **f.** displays current cell entry

7. =C19+A21   _____   **g.** an arithmetic operator

8. range   _____   **h.** centers text across a selection

9. D11   _____   **i.** a formula summing two cells

10. formula bar   _____   **j.** Excel workbook file name extension

Fill-In Questions

Complete the following statements by filling in the blanks with the correct terms.

1. The _____ occupies the center of the Excel window and can display multiple windows.

2. The worksheet displays a rectangular grid of _____ and _____.

3. A(n) _____ consists of two or more worksheet cells.

4. The intersection of a row and column creates a(n)_____.

5. _____ are text entries that are used to create the structure of the worksheet.

6. By default, text entries are _____ -aligned and number entries are _____ -aligned.

7. A(n) _____ consists of the column letter and row number used to identify a cell.

8. A(n) _____ is an entry that performs a calculation.

9. Without _____ recalculation, large worksheets would take several minutes to recalculate all formulas each time a number was changed.

10. _____ control how information is displayed in a cell.

Multiple Choice

Circle the correct response to the questions below.

1. The three steps in the worksheet planning phase are:
   a. specify purpose, design, use sample data
   b. outline, design, enter data
   c. specify purpose, enter data, document
   d. enter data, design and build, document

2. _____ entries can contain any combination of letters, numbers, spaces, and any other special characters.
   a. Number
   b. Variable
   c. Constant
   d. Text

3. The _____ of a column controls how much information can be displayed in a cell.
   a. size
   b. shape
   c. width
   d. alignment

4. A(n) _____ range is a rectangular block of adjoining cells.
   a. selected
   b. adjacent
   c. nonadjacent
   d. block

5. The values on which a numeric formula performs a calculation are called:
   a. operators
   b. operands
   c. accounts
   d. data

6. Whenever a formula containing _____ references is copied, the referenced cells are automatically adjusted.
   a. relative
   b. automatic
   c. fixed
   d. variable

7. A_____ is a set of characters with a specific design.
   a. font
   b. formula
   c. text entry
   d. function

8. _____can be applied to selections to add emphasis or interest to a document.

    a. Alignments

    b. Pictures

    c. Character effects

    d. Text formats

9. The currency number format can display:

    a. dollar signs

    b. commas

    c. decimal places

    d. all the above

10. A nontext element or object, such as a drawing or picture that can be added to a document, is called a(n):

    a. picture

    b. drawing

    c. graphic

    d. image

True/False

Circle the correct answer to the following questions.

1. Formulas are used to create, edit, and position graphics.	True	False
2. The default column width setting in Excel is 15.0.	True	False
3. A nonadjacent range is two or more selected cells or ranges that are adjoining.	True	False
4. A formula is an entry that performs a calculation.	True	False
5. Because relative references automatically adjust for the new location, the relative references in a copied formula refer to different cells from the references in the original formula.	True	False
6. Formulas are prewritten statements that perform certain types of calculations automatically.	True	False
7. The automatic recalculation is one of the most powerful features of electronic worksheets.	True	False
8. Font settings allow you to change the horizontal and vertical placement and the orientation of an entry in a cell.	True	False
9. Number formats affect how numbers look onscreen and when printed.	True	False
10. An embedded object becomes part of the Excel document and can be opened and edited using the source program.	True	False

Discussion Questions

1. Discuss why it is important to design a worksheet before you begin entering actual data into it.

2. What types of entries are used in worksheets? Discuss the uses of each type of entry.

3. Discuss how formulas are created. Why are they the power behind worksheets?

4. Discuss the formatting features presented in the lab. Why are they important to the look of the worksheet?

Hands-On Practice Exercises

Step by Step

Rating System ☆ Easy
☆ ☆ Moderate
☆ ☆ ☆ Difficult

1. Lisa Sutton is an employment analyst working for the state of New Jersey. One of her responsibilities is to collect and analyze data on future job opportunities in the state. Lisa has compiled a list of the jobs that are expected to offer the most new positions. Follow the directions below to complete the worksheet shown here.

   a. Open the workbook file New Positions.

   b. Begin with the title of the worksheet: Modify the label in cell B2 so that the first letter of each word is capitalized; move the label in cell B2 to A2; move the label in cell B3 to A3; center the titles in cells A2 and A3 across the columns A through D; and finally, increase the font size to 14 point.

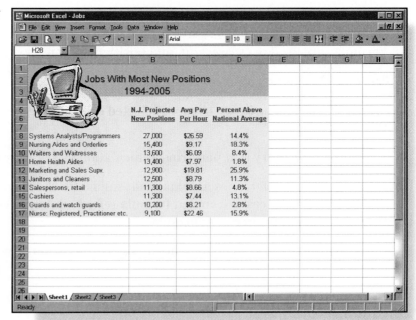

   c. Adjust the column widths so that all the data is fully displayed.

   d. Fix the spelling of Janitors in cell A13.

   e. Format the numbers in column B as number with a comma to separate thousands and 0 decimal places. Format the numbers in column C as currency with dollar signs and two decimal places. Format the numbers in column D as percent with one decimal place.

   f. Insert a new row below row 3 and a new row below row 6.

   g. Bold the titles in rows 5 and 6. Underline the titles in row 6.

   h. Center the values in columns B, C and D.

i. Add font and fill colors to the worksheet as you like.

j. Insert a ClipArt graphic of your choice from the Clip Gallery. Size and position it appropriately to fit the page.

k. Enter your name and the current date on separate rows just below the worksheet.

l. Move to cell A1. Save the workbook file as Jobs. Preview and print the worksheet.

2. Lisa Sutton, employment analyst for New Jersey, has collected data on the highest paying jobs in New Jersey and the country. Follow the directions below to complete the worksheet shown here.

a. Open the workbook file Highest Paying Jobs. Increase the column widths to fully display the data.

b. Center the titles in cells A1 and A2 over the worksheet data. Change the font of the main title line to Times New Roman 16 points. Change the font of the subtitle line to Times New Roman 14 points.

c. Insert a new row below row 2.

d. Calculate the percentage differential for Physicians and Surgeons in New Jersey to the U.S. average in cell D5. Copy the formula down the column. *Hint:* Subtract the U.S. value from the N.J. value and divide by the U.S. value.

e. Format the data in columns B and C as currency with two decimal places. Format the data in column D as a percent with two decimal places.

f. Add a column heading, Job Title, in A4. Center and bold all column headings.

g. Add formatting, such as color fill and font color of your choice, to the worksheet.

h. Insert the ClipArt image of currency (located in the Business category of the Clip Gallery or on your data disk). Move and size it to fit to the left of the title.

i. Enter your name and the current date on separate rows just below the worksheet.

j. Move to cell A1. Save the workbook file as Highest Paying Jobs Revised. Preview and print the worksheet.

3. Mark Ernster works for a national real estate company. To compare housing prices in different areas of the country, he has collected data on the average prices of existing homes in four national regional areas. Follow the directions below to complete the worksheet shown here.

a. Open the workbook file Real Estate Prices.

b. Edit the title in cell B3 so that the first letter of each word is uppercase. Center the title across columns A through G. Increase the font size to 14 and bold and apply a font color of your choice to the title.

c. Center-align and underline the column headings in row 5. Right-align cells B7 through E10. Left-align cells A7 through A10. Best-fit column A.

d. Calculate the U.S. average for 1995 in cell F7 by summing the four regional averages in the row and dividing by 4. Be careful not to include the year row headings in your calculation. Copy the formula to the other two years in cells F8 and F9.

e. Next, you would like to calculate the percent of increase from 1995 to 1996 and from 1996 to 1997. Enter the formula =(F8–F7)/F8 in cell G8. Format the formula as a percentage with two decimal places. Copy the formula to G9.

f. To calculate the 1998 projected average price, enter =B9+B9*((B9–B8)/B9) in cell B10. Copy the formula to cells C10 through F10. Copy the formula in G9 to G10.

g. Format all the prices as Accounting with zero decimal places. Increase the width of columns B through F to 10. Best-fit column G.

h. Delete row 6 and insert another blank row below the title.

i. Add fill colors to the worksheet as you like.

j. Insert the picture House.bmp from your data disk. Size and position it to fit on the left side of the title.

k. Enter your name and the current date on separate rows just below the worksheet.

l. Move to cell A1. Save and replace the workbook file Real Estate Prices. Preview and print the worksheet.

4. Will Bloomquist is a writer for his college newspaper. He has been researching an article on student athletes and has found some interesting data on student athletic participation in high school and college by men and women. Follow the directions below to complete the worksheet shown here.

a. Open the workbook Athlete Data on your data disk.

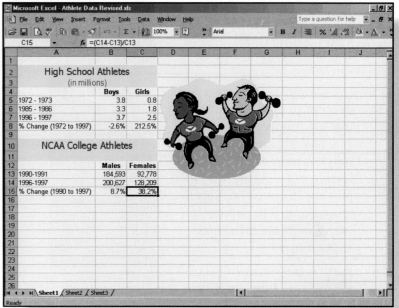

b. Center the titles in rows 2 and 3 over the worksheet data. Format the title in row 2 to Tahoma 14 points. Apply a font color and fill color of your choice to row 2. Format the subtitle in row 3 to 12 points and apply the same font and fill color as the main title.

c. Make the same changes you made to rows 2 and 3 to rows 9 and 10.

d. Bold and center the column labels in rows 4 and 11.

e. Adjust the width of column A to fully display the labels.

f. Format the data in B12 through C13 as Numbers with a thousands separator and no decimal places.

g. Calculate the % change for high school and college athletes. Format the data as a percentage with one decimal place. (*Hint:* Subtract the oldest year's data from the most recent year's and divide the result by the oldest year's value.)

h. Insert a blank row above row 9.

i. Insert the Weightlifting ClipArt graphic (located in the Sports and Leisure category of the Clip Gallery or on your data disk) to the right of the worksheet. Adjust the size and location of the picture as necessary.

j. Enter your name and the current date on separate rows below the worksheet.

k. Move to cell A1. Save and replace the workbook file as Athlete Data. Preview and print the worksheet.

5. Kent Allen works for The Mountain Lakes Homeowners Association. Using last year's final budget numbers, he is to create a projected budget for 2002. Follow the directions below to complete the worksheet shown here.

a. Open the workbook file Homeowners Association Budget. Adjust the width of column A to fully display the labels.

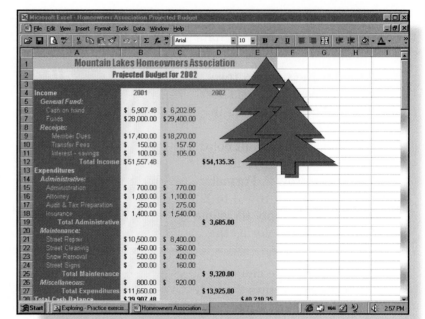

b. In column C calculate a 5 percent increase for all the income numbers for the year 2002. Calculate a 10 percent increase in administrative expenditures, a 20 percent decrease in Maintenance, and a 15 percent increase in Miscellaneous expenditures.

c. Format the data with the Accounting number format.

d. In column D calculate the totals for Total Income, Total Administrative, Total Maintenance, and Total Expenditures for 2002. In column E, calculate the Total Cash Balance by subtracting the total expenditures from the total income for 2002.

e. Indent the row label subheads and further indent the items under each subhead. Right-align the total labels.

f. Delete rows 13 and 14.

g. Change the font type, size, and color of the title lines to a format of your choice.

h. Apply character effects and color of your choice to the worksheet.

i. Insert a ClipArt image of your choice from the Clip Gallery. Position and size it to fit the page.

j. Enter your name and the current date on separate rows just below the worksheet.

k. Move to cell A1. Save and replace the workbook file as Homeowners Association Projected Budget. Preview and print the worksheet.

6. Ian Pario is a financial assistant for Clark Office Supply. He is preparing a budgeted income statement for the first quarter (January through March). Follow the directions below to complete the worksheet shown here.

a. Open the workbook file Clark Office Supply. Expand column A to fully display the labels.

b. Enter 80000 for January sales, 85000 for February sales, and 80000 for March sales.

c. Enter 1500 for each month's fixed cost.

d. Using the following information, enter formulas to calculate the other items in the budgeted income statement:

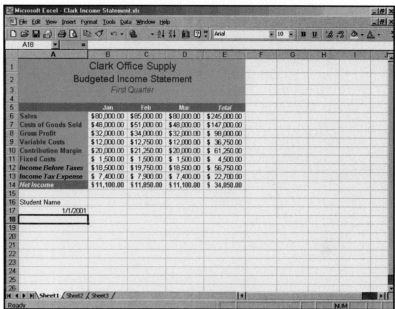

Cost of Goods Sold = 60% of Sales

Gross Profit = Sales − Cost of Goods Sold

Variable Costs = 15% of Sales

Contribution Margin = Gross Profit − Variable Costs

Income before Taxes = Contribution Margin − Fixed Costs

Income Tax Expense = 40% of Income before Taxes

Net Income = Income before Taxes − Income Tax Expense

e. Calculate the first quarter totals.

f. Use the formatting features you learned in the tutorial to enhance the worksheet.

g. Enter your name and the current date on separate rows just below the worksheet.

h. Move to cell A1. Save the workbook file as Clark Income Statement. Preview and print the worksheet.

On Your Own

7. Hank's girlfriend noticed that he gained a few extra pounds over Christmas and tactfully has suggested that he cut down on his snack foods. Hank has decided to eliminate all snacks that contain 30 percent of their calories from fat. To help him, you are to create a worksheet that lists his favorite foods, their calories per serving, and their fat grams per serving. The worksheet will use this data to calculate the percent of calories from fat for each snack.

The table below shows Hank's favorite foods and their calorie and fat content per serving. Each gram of fat contains nine calories. To calculate the percent of fat for each food, multiply the fat grams by nine and divide by the number of calories. Use the formatting features you learned in the tutorial to enhance the worksheet and to identify the snack items that have less than 30 percent calories from fat. Enter your name and the current date on separate rows just below the worksheet. Preview, save, and print the worksheet.

Food	Fat grams per serving	Calories per serving
Bagel	1	240
Cream Cheese	9	110
Hotdog	13	140
Muffin	6	200
Cookies	4.5	130
Pretzels	1	110
Chips	9	140

8. Create a personal six-month budget using a worksheet. Enter an appropriate title and use descriptive labels for your monthly expenses (food, rent, car payments, insurance, credit card payments, etc.). Enter your monthly expenses (or, if you prefer, any reasonable sample data). Use formulas to calculate total expenses for each month and to calculate the average monthly expenditures for each expense item. Enhance the worksheet using features you learned in this tutorial. Enter your name and the current date on separate rows just below the worksheet. Preview, save, and print the worksheet.

9. Lee DeLuca is the new owner and manager of a candy store called Confectionery Delights. She has four salespeople (Ann, John, Robert, and Sally) and is planning a month-long sales promotion for August. Using the four steps in the planning process, you are to plan and create a worksheet for Lee that can be used to record and analyze sales for that month.

Weekly sales data for each employee will be entered into the worksheet. Using that data, the worksheet will calculate the average and total monthly sales for each person. Additionally, it will calculate the average and total weekly sales for the store. Write a short paragraph describing how you used each of the four planning steps. With sample data in the worksheet, enter your name and the current date on separate rows just below the worksheet. Preview, save, and print the worksheet.

10. Use the library and/or the Web to locate information on employment opportunities and salary trends related to your area of study. Create a worksheet to display information relating to job titles, years of experience, and starting and top salaries for positions in your field. Calculate the median salary (the average of the starting and the top salary). Enhance the worksheet using features you learned in this tutorial. Enter your name and the current date on separate rows just below the worksheet. Preview, save, and print the worksheet.

Charting Worksheet Data

Competencies

After completing this tutorial, you will know how to:

1. Select a chart data range.
2. Change the type of chart.
3. Move the chart location.
4. Format chart elements.
5. Add chart titles and move the legend.
6. Create a combination chart.
7. Change worksheet data.
8. Add data labels, text boxes, and arrows.
9. Create, explode, and rotate a pie chart.
10. Apply patterns and color.
11. Size and align a sheet on a page.
12. Add predefined headers and footers.
13. Document, preview, and print a workbook.

Many different types of charts can be created and modified to visually represent worksheet data.

Case Study

After creating the first quarter forecast for the Downtown Internet Café, you contacted several other Internet cafes to inquire about their startup experiences. You heard many exciting success stories! Internet connections attract more customers and the typical customer stays longer at an Internet café than at a regular café. As a result, they end up spending more money.

The Chart Wizard makes it easy to create a chart from data in a worksheet.

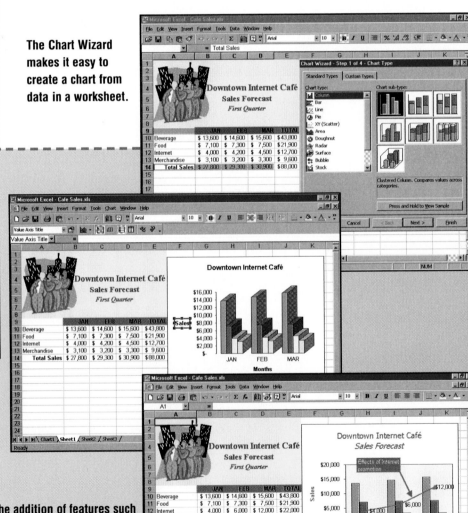

The addition of features such as data labels, text boxes, arrows, and color add emphasis to the chart.

You now believe that your initial sales estimates are too low. You too should be able to increase sales dramatically. In addition to sales of coffee and food items to customers, the Café also derives sales from charging for Internet connection time. In your discussions with other Internet café managers, you have found that Internet connection sales account for approximately 25 percent of their total sales. You would like to launch an aggressive advertising campaign to promote the new Internet aspect of the Downtown Internet Café. You believe that the campaign will lead to an increase in sales not only in Internet connection time but in food and beverage sales as well.

To convince Evan, you need an effective way to illustrate the sales growth you are forecasting. To do this, you decide to create charts of the sales projections, as charts make it easy to visually understand numeric data. Excel 2000 can create many types of charts from data in a worksheet. In this tutorial, you will learn to use Excel 2000's chart-creating and formatting features to produce several different charts of your sales estimates, as shown below.

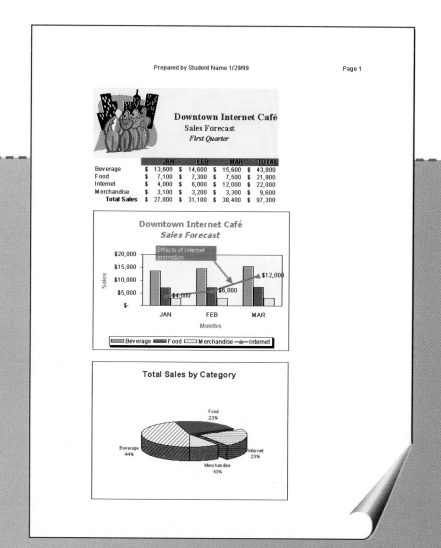

Concept Overview

The following concepts will be introduced in this tutorial:

1 **Chart Types** Different types of charts are used to represent data in different ways. The type of chart you create depends on the type of data you are charting and the emphasis you want the chart to impart.

2 **Chart Elements** Chart elements consist of a number of parts that are used to graphically display the worksheet data.

3 **Chart Objects** A chart object is a graphic object that is created using charting features included in Excel. A chart object can be inserted into a worksheet or into a special chart sheet.

4 **Groups** Because it consists of many separate objects a chart object is a group. A group is two or more objects that are treated as a single object.

5 **Data Label** Data labels provide additional information about a data marker.

6 **Text Box** A text box is a rectangular object in which you type text. Text boxes can be added to a sheet or an embedded chart.

7 **Header and Footer** Lines of text displayed below the top margin or above the bottom margin of each page are called headers and footers.

Learning about Charts

You have decided to chart the sales forecast data for the Downtown Internet Café to better see the sales trends. The sales data is in a separate workbook file named Café Sales.

1 ▬ Open the file Café Sales.

Your screen should be similar to Figure 2–1.

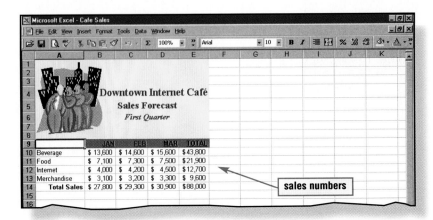

Figure 2–1

Although the worksheet shows the sales numbers for each category, it is hard to see how the different categories change over time. A visual representation of data in the form of a **chart** would convey that information in an easy-to-understand and attractive manner.

Concept (1) Chart Types

Different types of charts are used to represent data in different ways. The type of chart you create depends on the type of data you are charting and the emphasis you want the chart to impart. Excel 2000 can produce 14 standard types of graphs or charts, with many different subtypes for each standard type. In addition, Excel includes professionally designed built-in custom charts that include additional formatting and chart refinements. The basic chart types are:

Type	Description	Type	Description
	Area charts show the magnitude of change over time by emphasizing the area under the curve created by each data series.		Radar charts display a line or area chart wrapped around a central point. Each axis represents a set of data points.
	Bar charts display data as evenly spaced bars. The categories are displayed along the Y axis and the values are displayed horizontally, placing more emphasis on comparisons and less on time.		XY (scatter) charts are used to show the relationship between two ranges of numeric data.
	Column charts display data as evenly spaced bars. They are similar to bar charts, except that categories are organized horizontally and values vertically to emphasize variation over time.		Surface charts display values as what appears to be a rubber sheet stretched over a 3-D column chart. These are useful for finding the best combination between sets of data.
	Line charts display data along a line. They are used to show changes in data over time, emphasizing time and rate of change rather than the amount of change.		A bubble chart compares sets of three values. It is like a scatter chart with the third value displayed as the size of bubble markers.
	Pie charts display data as slices of a circle or pie. They show the relationship of each value in a data series to the series as a whole. Each slice of the pie represents a single value in the series.		A stock chart is a high-low-close chart. It requires three series of values in this order.
			Cylinder charts display values with a cylindrical shape.
	Doughnut charts are similar to pie charts except that they can show more than one data series.		Cone charts display values with a conical shape.
			Pyramid charts display values with a pyramid shape.

Selecting the Data to Chart

The first chart you want to create will show the total sales pattern over the three months. All charts are drawn from data contained in a worksheet. To create a new chart, you select the worksheet range containing the data you want displayed as a chart plus any row or column headings you want used in the chart. Excel then translates the selected data into a chart based upon the shape and contents of the worksheet selection.

A chart consists of a number of parts that are important to understand so that you can identify the appropriate data to select in the worksheet.

Concept (2) Chart Elements

A chart consists of a number of parts that are used to graphically display the worksheet data. The basic parts of a two-dimensional chart are shown in the figure below.

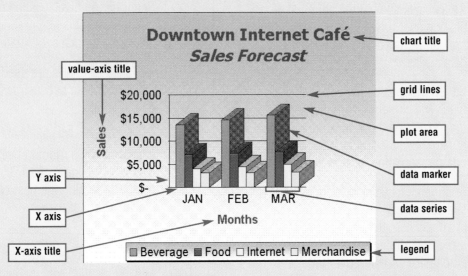

The bottom boundary line of the chart is the **X axis**. It is used to label the data being charted, such as a point in time or a category. The **category names** displayed along the X axis correspond to the headings for the worksheet data that is plotted along the X axis. The left boundary line of the chart is the **Y axis**, also called the **value axis**. This axis is a numbered scale whose numbers are determined by the data used in the chart. Typically the X-axis line is the horizontal line and the Y-axis line is the vertical line.

The selected worksheet data is visually displayed within the X- and Y-axis boundaries. This is called the **plot area**. Each group of related data, such as the numbers in a row or column of the selected area of the worksheet, is called a **data series**. Each number represented in a data series is identified by a **data marker**. A data marker can be a symbol, color, or pattern. To distinguish one data series from another, different data markers are used. In addition, chart gridlines are commonly displayed to make it easier to read the chart data. **Chart gridlines** extend from the Y-axis line across the plot area. A **legend** identifies the chart data series names and data markers that correspond to each data series.

A chart can also contain descriptive **titles** that explain the contents of the chart. The **chart title** is displayed centered above the charted data. Titles can also be used to describe the X and Y axes. The X-axis title line is called the **category-axis title**, and the Y-axis title is called the **value-axis title**.

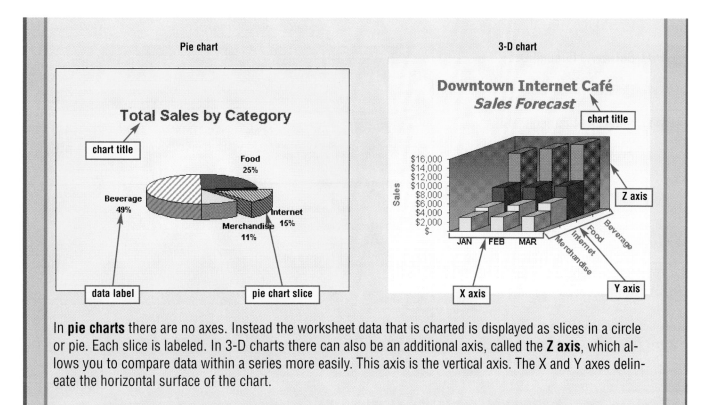

In **pie charts** there are no axes. Instead the worksheet data that is charted is displayed as slices in a circle or pie. Each slice is labeled. In 3-D charts there can also be an additional axis, called the **Z axis**, which allows you to compare data within a series more easily. This axis is the vertical axis. The X and Y axes delineate the horizontal surface of the chart.

The first chart you will create of the worksheet data will use the month labels in cells B9 through D9 to label the X axis. The numbers to be charted are in cells B14 through D14. In addition, the label Total Sales in cell A14 will be used as the chart legend, making the entire range A14 through D14.

Notice that the two ranges, B9 through D9 and A14 through D14, are not adjacent and are not the same size. When plotting nonadjacent ranges in a chart, the selections must form a rectangular shape. To do this, the blank cell A9 will be included in the selection. To specify the range and create the chart,

1 Select A9 through D9.

Hold down [Ctrl].

Select A14 through D14.

Click 📊 Chart Wizard.

> The menu equivalent is
> Insert/Chart.

Move the Chart Wizard dialog
box to right to see as much of the
worksheet as possible.

Your screen should be similar to
Figure 2–2.

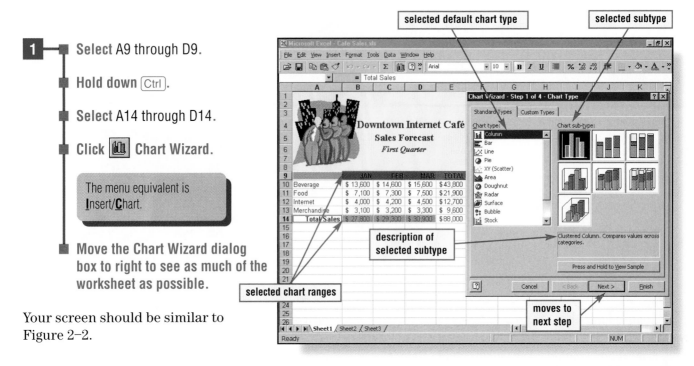

Figure 2–2

Chart Wizard is an interactive program that guides you through the
steps to create a chart. The first step is to select the chart type from the
Chart Type list box. The default chart type is a **column chart**. Each type of
chart includes many variations. The variations associated with the column
chart type are displayed as buttons in the Chart Subtype section of the dialog box. The default column subtype is a clustered column. A description
of the selected subtype is displayed in the area below the subtype buttons.
To use the default column chart type and move to the next step,

2 Click   Next >   .

Your screen should be similar to
Figure 2–3.

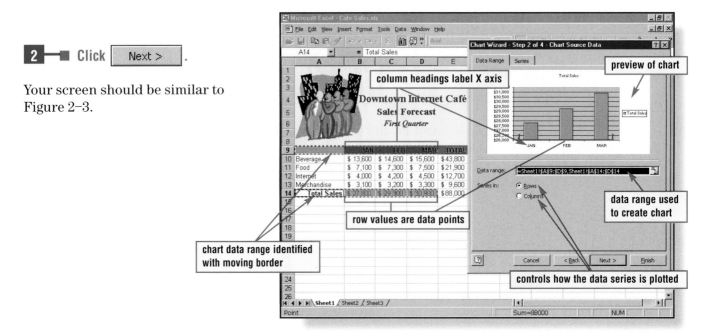

Figure 2–3

In the second Chart Wizard dialog box you specify the data range on the worksheet you want to plot. Because you selected the data range before starting the Chart Wizard, the range is correctly displayed in the Data range text box. In addition, the data range is identified with a moving border in the worksheet. The dialog box also displays a preview of the chart that will be created using the specified data and selected chart type.

The two Series In options change how Excel plots the data series from the rows or columns in the selected data range. The orientation Excel uses by default varies depending upon the type of chart selected and the number of rows and columns defined in a series. The worksheet data range that has the greater number of rows or columns appears along the X axis and the smaller number is charted as the data series. When the data series is an equal number of rows and columns, as it is in this case, the default is to plot the rows. The first row defines the X-axis category labels and the second row the plotted data. The content of the first cell in the second row is used as the legend text. To accept the default settings,

3 ▪ Click 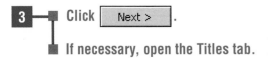.

▪ If necessary, open the Titles tab.

Your screen should be similar to Figure 2–4.

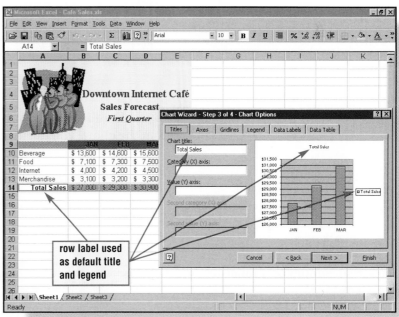

Figure 2–4

In the Step 3 dialog box, you can turn some standard options on and off and change the appearance of chart elements such as a legend and titles. To clarify the data in the chart, you will add a more descriptive chart title as well as titles along the X and Y axes. As you add the titles, the preview chart will update to display the new settings.

4 In the Chart Title text box, replace the default title with
Downtown Internet Cafe Sales

Use (Tab), not (Enter), after
typing the title text. Pressing
(Enter) is the same as clicking
Next >.

In the Category (X) Axis text box,
enter **Months**

In the Value (Y) Axis text box,
enter **Total Sales**

Your screen should be similar to
Figure 2–5.

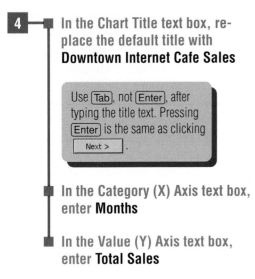
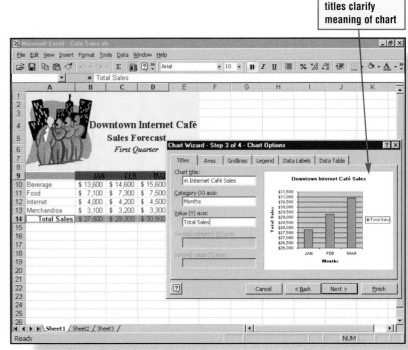

Figure 2–5

Because there is only one data range and the titles now fully explain
the data in the chart, you decide to clear the display of the legend.

5 Open the Legend tab.

Click **S**how Legend to clear the
checkmark.

Your screen should be similar to
Figure 2–6.

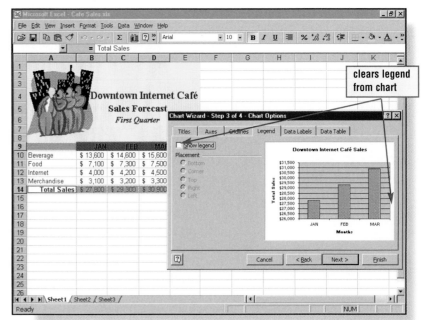

Figure 2–6

The legend is removed and the chart area resized to occupy the extra
space.

6 ■ Click Next > .

Your screen should be similar to Figure 2–7.

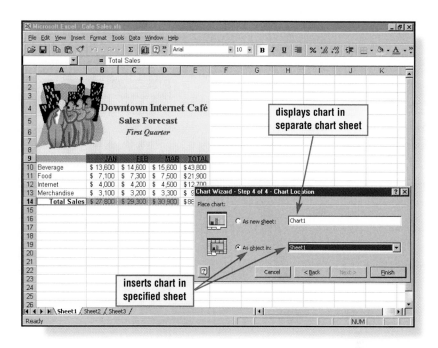

Figure 2–7

In the last step, you specify where you want the chart displayed in the worksheet. A chart can be displayed in a separate chart sheet or as an object in an existing sheet.

Concept ③ Chart Objects

A **chart object** is a graphic object that is created using charting features included in Excel. A chart object can be inserted into a worksheet or into a special chart sheet.

Charts that are inserted into a worksheet are embedded objects. An **embedded chart** becomes part of the sheet in which it is inserted and is saved as part of the worksheet when you save the workbook file. Like all graphic objects, an embedded chart object can be sized and moved in a worksheet. A worksheet can contain multiple charts. As objects are added to the worksheet, they automatically **stack** in individual layers. The stacking order is apparent when objects overlap. Stacking allows you to create different effects by overlapping objects. Because you can rearrange the stacking order, you do not have to add or create the objects in the order in which you want them to appear.

Triangle is on top of stack

Triangle is sent to the back

Square is brought to the front

A chart that is inserted into a separate chart sheet is also saved with the workbook file. Only one chart can be added to a chart sheet and it cannot be sized and moved.

You would like this chart displayed as an object in the Sales worksheet. This is the default selection. To complete the chart,

7 ■ Click [Finish] .

Your screen should be similar to Figure 2–8.

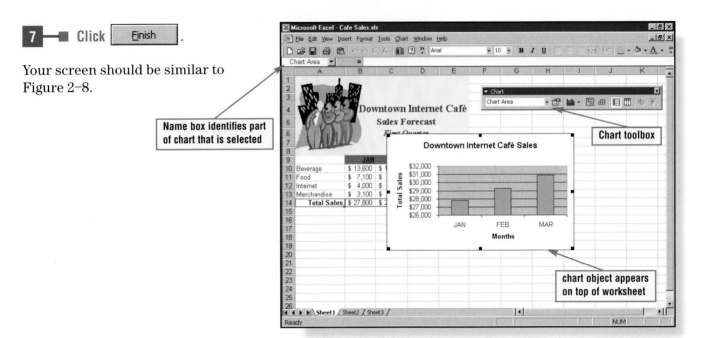

Figure 2–8

The chart with the settings you specified using the Chart Wizard is displayed on the worksheet. It covers some of the worksheet data because it is a separate chart object that can be moved and sized within the worksheet.

Notice that the name box displays Chart Area. The Name box identifies the part of the chart that is selected, in this case the entire chart and all its contents.

Also notice that the Chart toolbar is automatically displayed whenever a chart is selected. The Chart toolbar contains buttons for the most frequently used chart editing and formatting features. These buttons are identified below.

If your chart toolbar is not automatically displayed, open it by selecting it from the toolbar shortcut menu. It may also be docked already, depending on how it was last used.

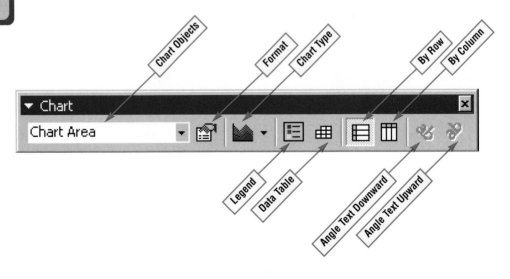

Move toolbars by dragging the title bar of the floating toolbar or move the handle ⬚ of the docked toolbar.

8 — If necessary, move the Chart toolbar to the row below the Standard and Formatting toolbars.

Moving and Sizing a Chart

You want to move the chart so that it is displayed to the right of the worksheet data. In addition, you want to increase the size of the chart. A selected chart object is moved by pointing to it and dragging it to a new location. When you move the mouse pointer into the selected chart object, it will display a chart ScreenTip to advise you of the chart element that will be affected by your action. When moving the entire chart, the ScreenTip must display Chart Area.

1 — Move the mouse pointer to different elements within the chart and note the different chart ScreenTips that appear.

■ With the chart ScreenTip displaying Chart Area, drag the chart object so that the upper-left corner is in cell F4.

The mouse pointer appears as a ✛ while dragging to move an object.

Your screen should be similar to Figure 2–9.

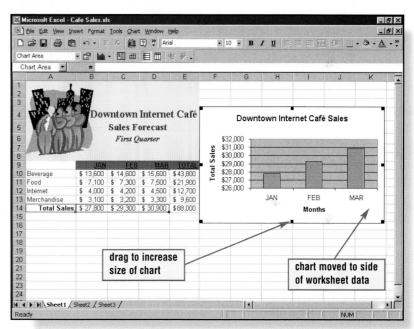

Figure 2–9

Next you will increase the size of the chart by dragging a **selection handle**. This is the same as sizing a graphic object.

2 Point to the lower-center selection handle, hold down Alt, and drag the chart box down until it is displayed over cells F4 through K20.

The mouse pointer appears as a ↕ while sizing an object.

Additional Information

If you hold down Alt while dragging to move and size a chart object, the chart automatically snaps into position or aligns with the closest worksheet cell when you release the mouse button. Release the mouse button before you release Alt.

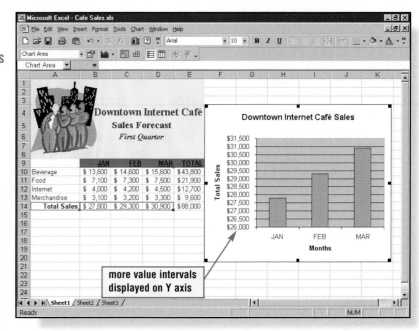

Figure 2–10

Your screen should be similar to Figure 2–10.

Your chart may show different value intervals.

As you enlarge the chart, more value intervals are displayed along the Y axis, making the data in the chart easier to read. Additionally, the fonts in the chart scale proportionally as you resize the chart. The chart includes standard formats that are applied to the selected chart subtype, such as a shaded background in the plot area and blue columns.

It is now easy to see how the worksheet data you selected is represented in the chart. Each column represents the total sales for that month in row 9. The month labels in row 3 have been used to label the X-axis category labels. The range or scale of values along the Y axis is determined from the data in the worksheet. The upper limit is the maximum value in the worksheet rounded upward to the next highest interval.

Changing the Type of Chart

The menu equivalent is **C**hart/Chart **T**ype.

Next you would like to see how the same data displayed in the column chart would look as a line chart. A **line chart** displays data as a line and is commonly used to show trends over time. This is easily done by changing the chart type using the ▦▾ Chart Type button on the Chart toolbar.

1 Open the  ▾ Chart Type drop-down list.

Click ⬚ Line Chart.

Your chart should be similar to Figure 2–11.

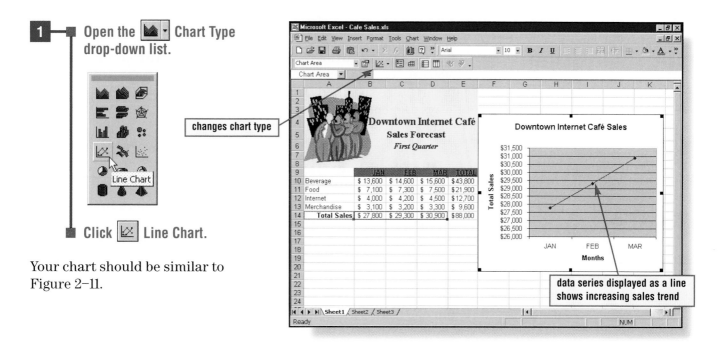

Figure 2–11

The data for the total sales for the three months is now displayed as a line. Also notice the ⬚ ▾ Chart type button displays a line chart, reflecting the last-selected chart type. The line shows the increasing sales trend from month to month. However, because the chart contains only one data series, a line chart is not very interesting or colorful. You will change it to a 3-D bar chart next.

2 Click ⬚ ▾ Chart Type.

Click ⬚ 3-D Bar Chart.

Your chart should be similar to Figure 2–12.

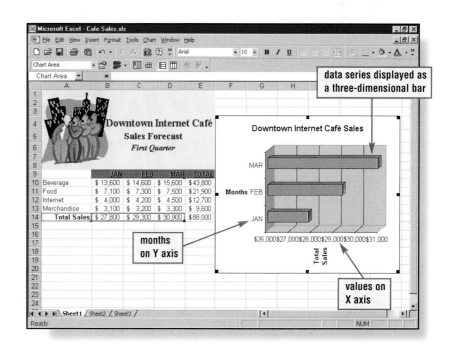

Figure 2–12

The 3-D bar chart reverses the X and Y axes and displays the data series as a three-dimensional bar. This chart makes it easy to compare the total sales values for the three months and is a lot more colorful.

As you can see, it is very easy to change the chart type and format once the data series are specified. The same data can be displayed in many different ways. Depending upon the emphasis you want the chart to make, a different chart style can be selected.

Moving the Chart Location

After modifying this chart, you decide that you are more interested in comparing the sales categories for each month rather than total sales. You could delete the chart simply by pressing Delete while it is selected; however, you decide just to move it to another location in the workbook for now.

When a chart is selected, the Data menu changes to the Chart menu. In addition, many of the commands under the other menus have changed to commands that apply to charts only. The Chart menu contains commands that can be used to modify the chart.

> **Chart**
>
> Chart Type...
> Source Data...
> Chart Options...
> Location...
>
> Add Data...
> Add Trendline...
>
> 3-D View...

1 ━■ Choose Chart/Location

Your screen should be similar to Figure 2–13.

moves selected chart to specified location in workbook

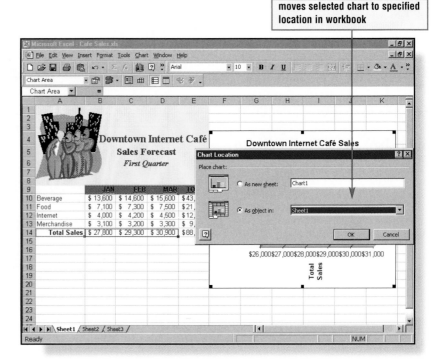

Figure 2–13

2 Choose the As new <u>s</u>heet option.

Click [OK].

Your chart should be similar to Figure 2–14.

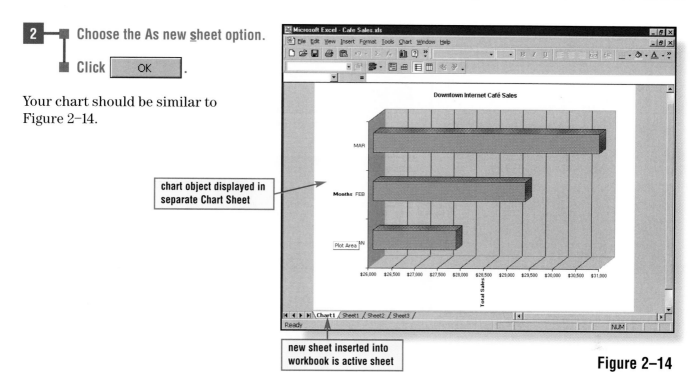

chart object displayed in
separate Chart Sheet

new sheet inserted into
workbook is active sheet

Figure 2–14

The bar chart is now an object displayed in a separate chart sheet. Generally, you display a chart in a chart sheet when you want the chart displayed separately from the associated worksheet data. The chart is still automatically linked to the worksheet data from which it was created.

The new chart sheet named Chart1 was inserted to the left of the worksheet, Sheet1. The Chart sheet is the active sheet, or the sheet you are currently viewing and working in. To display Sheet1 containing the worksheet data,

> You can also press [Ctrl] + [Pg Up] to move to the next sheet and [Ctrl] + [Pg Dn] to move to the previous sheet.

3 Click the Sheet1 tab.

Creating a Chart with Multiple Data Series

Now you are ready to continue your analysis of sales trends. You want to create a second chart to display the sales data for each category for the three months. You could create a separate chart for each category and then compare the charts; however, to make the comparisons between the categories easier, you will display all the categories on a single chart.

The data for the three months for the four categories is in cells B10 through D13. The month headings (X-axis data series) are in cells B9 through D9, and the legend text is in the range A10 through A13. To specify the chart data series,

1 ■ Select A9 through D13.

■ Click 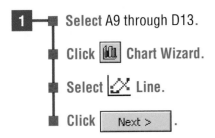 Chart Wizard.

■ Select Line.

■ Click Next >.

Your screen should be similar to Figure 2–15.

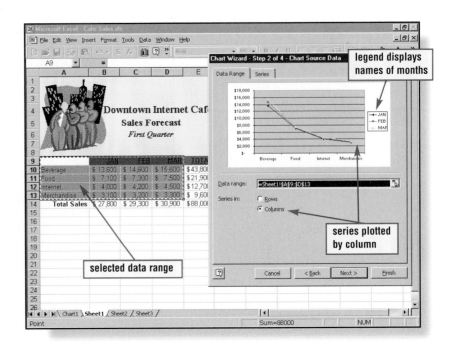

Figure 2–15

When plotting the data for this chart, Excel selected Columns as the data series orientation because there are fewer columns than rows in the data range. This time, however, you want to change the data series to Rows so that the months are along the X axis.

> If you want to change the series orientation of an existing chart, you can use ☰ By Row or ☷ By Column in the Chart toolbar.

2 ■ Select Rows.

Your screen should be similar to Figure 2–16.

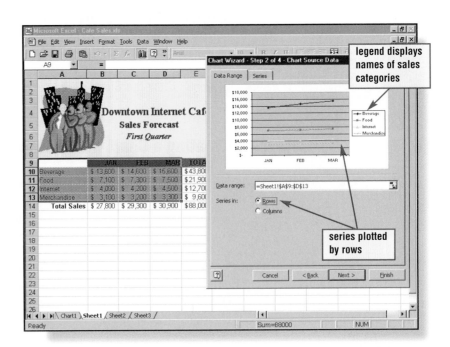

Figure 2–16

The sample chart is redrawn with the new orientation. The line chart now compares the sales by month rather than by category. The Legend displays the names of the sales categories.

3 ■ Click [Next >] .

■ Open the Titles tab.

■ Enter the following titles:

Title	Entry
Chart title	**Downtown Internet Café Sales Forecast**
Category (X) axis	**Months**
Value (Y) axis	**Sales**

Because you want this chart embedded in the worksheet, you can skip the next step, which accepts the default, and finish the chart.

4 ■ Click [Finish] .

■ Move and size the chart until it covers cells F2 through K19.

Your screen should be similar to Figure 2–17.

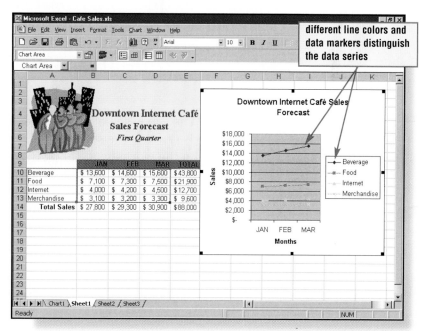

Figure 2–17

A different line color and data marker identify each data series and are reflected in the legend. The line chart shows that sales in all categories are increasing, with the sharpest increase occurring in beverage sales.

Applying a Custom Chart Type

Although the line chart shows the sales trends for the three months for the sales categories, again it does not look very interesting. You decide to look at several other chart types to see if you can improve the appearance.

First you would like to see the data represented as an area chart. An **area chart** represents data the same as a line chart, but in addition, it shades the area below each line to emphasize the degree of change.

1 Click [icon] ▾ to open the Chart type drop-down list.

Click [icon] Area Chart.

Your chart should be similar to Figure 2–18.

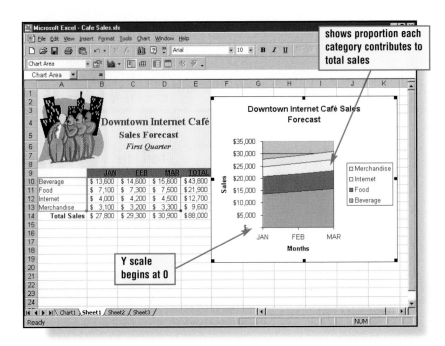

Figure 2–18

The Y-axis scale has changed to reflect the new range of data. The new Y-axis range is the sum of the five categories, or the same as the total number in the worksheet. Using this chart type, you can see the magnitude of change each category contributes to the total sales in each month.

Because this is not the emphasis you want to show, you decide to continue looking at other types of charts. Because not all chart types are available from the Chart Type drop-down list, you will use the Chart Type menu option in the Chart menu instead.

2 Choose **C**hart/Chart **T**ype.

Your screen should be similar to Figure 2–19.

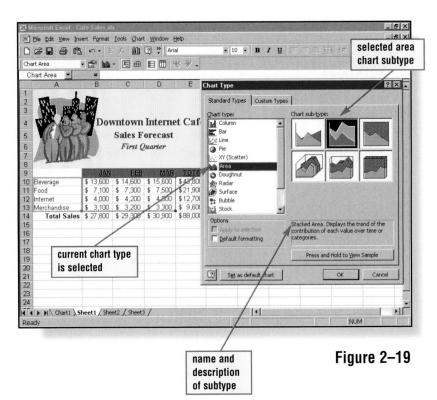

Figure 2–19

The Chart Type dialog box contains the same options as the Chart Wizard - Step 1 dialog box. The current chart type, Area, is the selected option. You want to see how this data will look as a stacked-column chart.

3
- Select 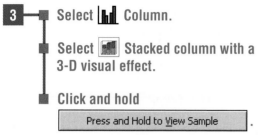 Column.
- Select ▦ Stacked column with a 3-D visual effect.
- Click and hold
  > Press and Hold to View Sample

Your screen should be similar to Figure 2–20.

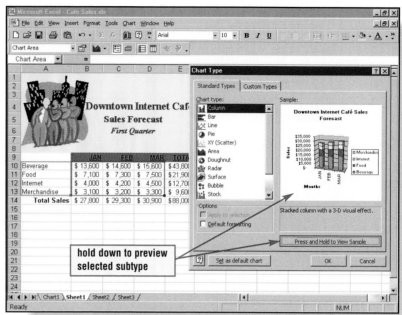

Figure 2–20

The sample chart is redrawn showing the data as a **stacked-column chart**. This type of chart also shows the proportion of each sales category to the total sales. To see what other types of charts are available,

4
- Open the Custom Types tab.
- Click  Area Blocks.

Your screen should be similar to Figure 2–21.

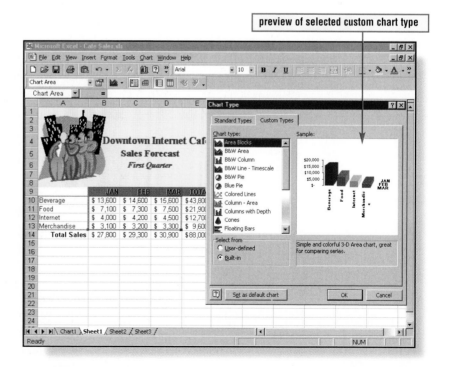

Figure 2–21

The sample area shows how the data you selected for the chart will appear in this style. Custom charts are based upon standard types that are enhanced with additional display settings and custom formatting. Although this is interesting, you feel the data is difficult to read.

5 Select several other custom chart types to see how the data appears in the Sample area.

Select Columns with Depth.

Your screen should be similar to Figure 2–22.

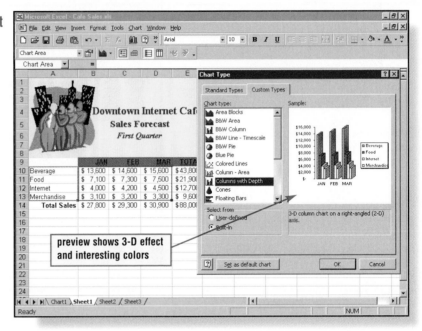

Figure 2–22

This chart shows the sales for each category for each month with more interesting colors and three-dimensional depth.

6 Click  OK .

Your screen should be similar to Figure 2–23.

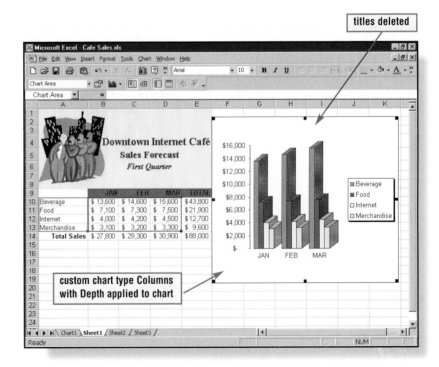

Figure 2–23

Adding Chart Titles

Unfortunately, when applying a custom chart type, the chart titles are deleted and you need to add them again.

1 Choose <u>C</u>hart/Chart <u>O</u>ptions.

In the Titles tab, enter the following titles:

Title	Entry
Chart title	Downtown Internet Café
Category (X) axis	Months
Value (Z) axis	Sales

Your screen should be similar to Figure 2–24.

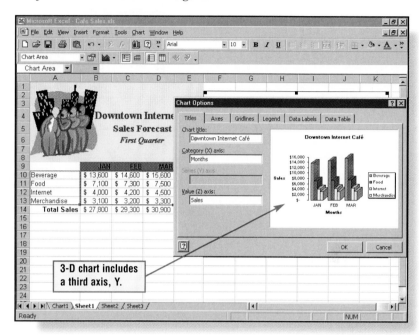

Figure 2–24

Notice that this time instead of entering the Value axis data in the Y axis, you entered it in the Z axis. This is because the Y axis is used as a Series axis on a three-dimensional chart. This three-dimensional chart only has one series of data so the Y axis is not used.

Moving the Legend

While looking at the preview chart, you decide to move the legend below the X axis.

1 Open the Legend tab.

Select Botto<u>m</u>.

Click [OK] .

Your screen should be similar to Figure 2–25.

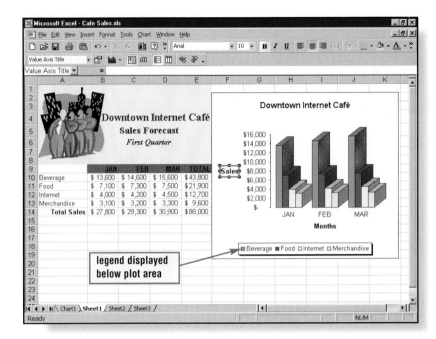

Figure 2–25

The legend is centered below the plot area of the chart and resized to fit the space.

Formatting Chart Elements

Next you want to improve the appearance of the chart by applying formatting to the different chart parts. All the different parts of a chart are separate objects. Because a chart consists of many separate objects, it is a group.

Concept ④ Groups

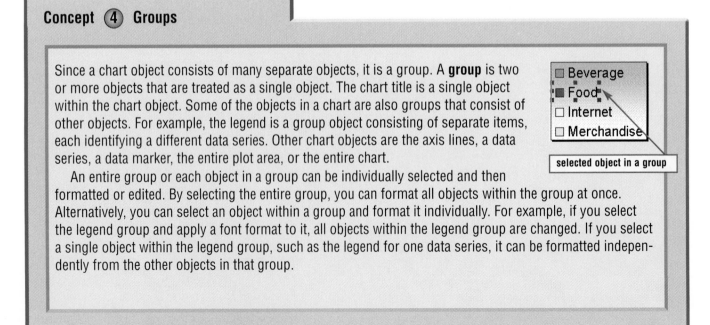

Since a chart object consists of many separate objects, it is a group. A **group** is two or more objects that are treated as a single object. The chart title is a single object within the chart object. Some of the objects in a chart are also groups that consist of other objects. For example, the legend is a group object consisting of separate items, each identifying a different data series. Other chart objects are the axis lines, a data series, a data marker, the entire plot area, or the entire chart.

An entire group or each object in a group can be individually selected and then formatted or edited. By selecting the entire group, you can format all objects within the group at once. Alternatively, you can select an object within a group and format it individually. For example, if you select the legend group and apply a font format to it, all objects within the legend group are changed. If you select a single object within the legend group, such as the legend for one data series, it can be formatted independently from the other objects in that group.

The first formatting change you want to make is to improve the appearance of the chart title.

1 ▬ **Click on the chart title to select it.**

Your screen should be similar to Figure 2–26.

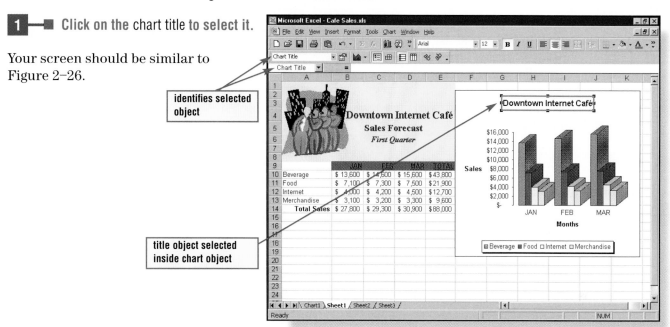

identifies selected object

title object selected inside chart object

Figure 2–26

The title is surrounded by a dotted border and selection handles, indicating that it is the selected object and will be affected by any changes you make. In addition, the Name box and Chart Objects button display Chart Title as the selected chart object.

As different objects in the chart are selected, the commands on the Format menu change to commands that can be used on the selected object. In addition, the 🗐 Format Object button to the right of the Chart Object button can be used to format the selected object.

2 ▬ **Click 🗐 Format Chart Title.**

> The menu equivalent is Format/**S**elected Chart Title and the shortcut is Ctrl+1.

▬ **Open the Font tab.**

Your screen should be similar to Figure 2–27.

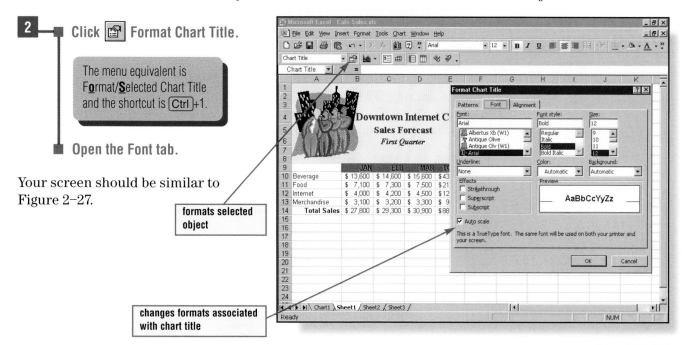

formats selected object

changes formats associated with chart title

Figure 2–27

The Format Chart Title dialog box is used to change the patterns, font, and placement of the title.

3 ■ Select Tahoma from the Font list.

■ Select 14 from the Size list.

■ Select Violet (3rd row, 6th column) from the Color list.

■ Click **OK** .

Your screen should be similar to Figure 2–28.

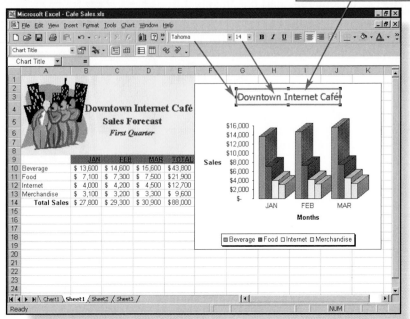

chart title formatted to new font, size, and color

Figure 2–28

Next you want to change color of axis titles. A quicker way to make many formatting changes is to use the Formatting toolbar buttons.

4 ■ Click the category-axis title Months.

■ Open the **A** ▾ Font Color palette and change the color to violet.

■ Change the color of the Sales title to violet in the same manner.

■ Click outside the Sales title to clear the selection.

Additional Information

You can also use ▨ Angle Text Downward or ▨ Angle Text Upward to quickly change the angle of a label to 45 degrees.

You also want to change the orientation of the Sales title along the axis so it is parallel with the axis line. To do this, you will rotate the label 90 degrees. You can quickly select a chart object and open the related Format dialog box by double-clicking the object.

5 ▪ Double-click the Sales title to open the Format dialog box.

▪ Open the Alignment tab.

▪ Drag the Orientation indicator arrow upward to rotate the text 90 degrees.

Your screen should be similar to Figure 2–29.

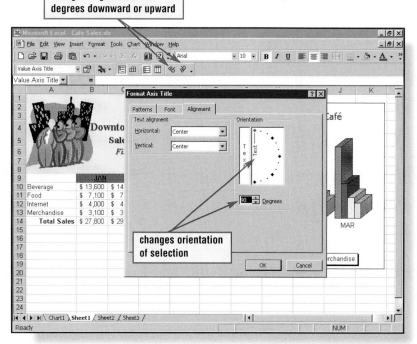

Figure 2–29

You could also enter a positive number in the degree box to rotate the selection from lower left to upper right or a negative number to rotate text in the opposite direction. Alternatively, you can use the degree scroll buttons to increase and decrease the degrees.

6 ▪ Click .

The Sales label is now displayed parallel with the Y-axis line.

Finally, you want to add a second line to the chart title. You can select individual sections of text and apply formatting to them just as you would format any other text entry.

7 ▪ Select the chart title.

▪ Click at the end of the title to place the insertion point.

▪ Press Enter.

▪ Type **Sales Forecast**.

▪ Select (highlight) the words Sales Forecast.

▪ Click *I* Italic.

▪ Click in the title to clear the selection.

Your screen should be similar to Figure 2–30.

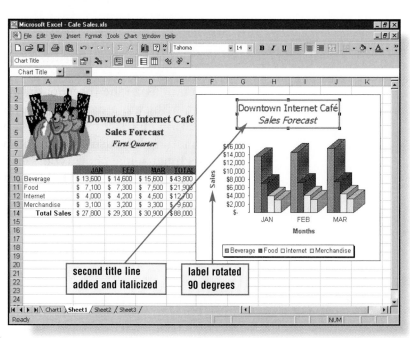

Figure 2–30

Copying a Chart

Now you want to create another chart that will emphasize the sales trend for the Internet connection data series. This chart will use the same data series and titles as the current chart. Rather than re-create much of the same chart for the new chart, you will create a copy of the column chart and then modify it.

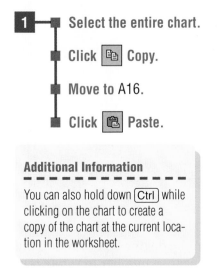

1 ■ Select the entire chart.

■ Click 📋 Copy.

■ Move to A16.

■ Click 📋 Paste.

Additional Information

You can also hold down ⌈Ctrl⌉ while clicking on the chart to create a copy of the chart at the current location in the worksheet.

Your screen should be similar to Figure 2–31.

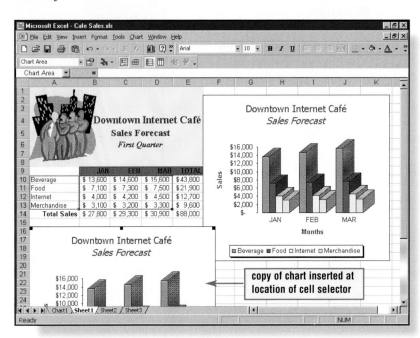

copy of chart inserted at location of cell selector

Figure 2–31

2 ■ Change the location of the copied chart to a new chart sheet (Chart2).

■ Move to Sheet1.

Creating a Combination Chart

To emphasize the Internet data, you want to display the data series as a line and all other data series as columns. This type of chart is called a **combination chart**. It uses two or more chart types to emphasize different information. Because you cannot mix a three-dimensional chart type with a one-dimensional chart type, you first need to change the chart type for the entire chart to a standard one-dimensional column chart. Then you can change the Internet data series to a line.

1 Select the chart and change the chart type to Column Chart.

■ Click on one of the yellow columns to select the Internet data series.

> Sometimes when there are many objects close together, it is easier to select the object from the Chart Objects drop-down list.

■ From the ▦ Chart Type drop-down menu, select ⬠ Line.

Your chart should be similar to Figure 2-32.

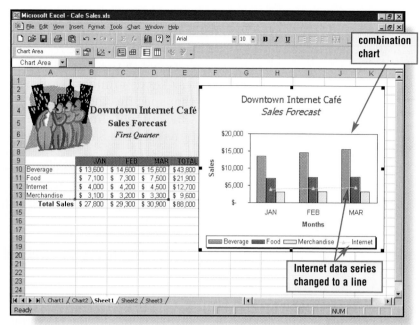

Figure 2-32

A combination chart makes it easy to see comparisons between groups of data or to show different types of data in a single chart. In this case, you can now easily pick out the Internet sales from the other sales categories.

Changing Fill Colors

As the yellow line is difficult to see on a white background, you want to change the color of the line and add a fill color to the plot area to make the line more visible.

1 Double-click on the line to select it and open the Format dialog box.

> Your ScreenTip should display Series "Internet" Point before you click.

Your screen should be similar to Figure 2-33.

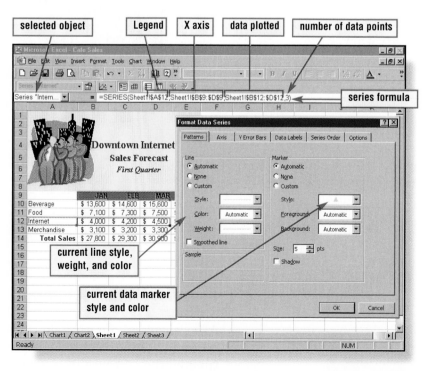

Figure 2-33

Notice that the formula bar displays a **series formula**. This formula links the chart object to the source worksheet, Sheet1. The formula contains four arguments: a reference to the cell that includes the data series name (used in the legend), references to the cells that contain the categories (X-axis numbers), references to the numbers plotted, and an integer that specifies the number of data series plotted.

The current line and data marker settings are displayed in the Patterns tab. The Sample area shows how your selections will appear.

2 ■ Open the Color palette and change the line color to sea green.

■ Open the Weight drop-down list and increase the line weight setting by one.

■ Change the Foreground and Background marker color to sea green.

■ Click OK .

Next you would like to change the plot area to ivory. You could use the Format Plot Area dialog box to change the color or the fill color button on the Formatting toolbar.

3 ■ Select the plot area.

■ Click Fill Color and select ivory.

Your screen should be similar to Figure 2–34.

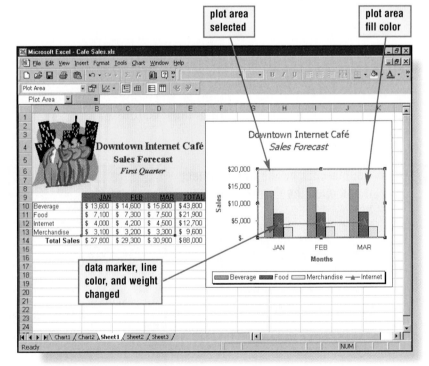

Figure 2–34

Changing Worksheet Data

After checking the worksheet and reconsidering the amounts you have budgeted for the different categories, you now feel that you have underestimated the increase in Internet sales. You are planning to heavily promote the Internet aspect of the Café and anticipate that Internet usage will increase dramatically in February and March and then level off in the following months. You want to change the worksheet to reflect this increase.

1
- Change the February Internet sales value to **6000**.

- Change the March Internet sales value to **12000**.

Your screen should be similar to Figure 2–35.

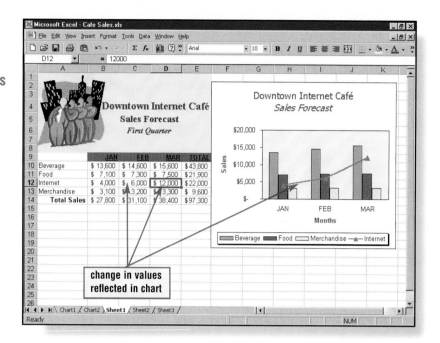

Figure 2–35

The worksheet has been recalculated and all charts that reference those worksheet cells have been redrawn to reflect the change in the data for the Internet sales. Since the chart document is linked to the source data, changes to the source data are automatically reflected in the chart.

2
- Look at the bar and column charts in the Chart1 and Chart2 sheets to see how they have changed to reflect the change in data.

- Make the Sheet1 sheet active again.

Adding Data Labels

You would also like to display data labels containing the actual numbers plotted for the Internet sales on the combination chart.

Concept ⑤   Data Label

Data labels provide additional information about a data marker. They can consist of the value of the marker, the name of the data series or category, a percent value, or a bubble size. The different types of data labels that are available depend on the type of chart and the data that is plotted.

Value data labels are helpful when the values are large and you want to know the exact value for one data series. Data labels that display a name are helpful when the size of the chart is large and it is hard to tell what value the data point is over. The percent data label is used when you want to display the percent of each series on charts that show parts to the whole. Bubble size is used on bubble charts to help the reader quickly see how the different bubbles vary in size.

---

1 ■ Double-click the Internet data series.

   ■ Open the Data Labels tab.

   ■ Select Show **v**alue.

   ■ Click [OK].

The menu equivalent is F**o**rmat/S**e**lected Data Series/Data Labels.

Your screen should be similar to Figure 2–36.

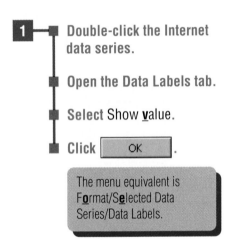

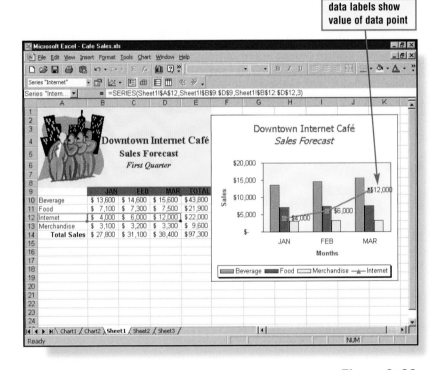

Figure 2–36

Data labels containing the actual values for Internet sales are displayed next to the data points on the line in the chart.

Adding a Text Box

- -

Because the chart reflects the Internet sales changes you made in the worksheet, you want to include a notation in the chart explaining the reason for the increase. This information can be entered in a text box.

Concept ⑥ Text Box

A **text box** is a rectangular object in which you type text. Text boxes can be added to a sheet or an embedded chart. To add one to a chart, the chart object must be selected first, otherwise the text box is added to the worksheet. A text box that is part of a chart object can be sized and moved only within the chart object. If you move the chart object, the text box moves with it. If you do not add it to the chart, it will not move as part of the chart if you move the chart to another location.

Text that is entered in a text box wraps to fit within the boundaries of the text box. This feature is called **word wrap** and eliminates the need to press [Enter] to end a line. If you change the size and shape of the text box, the text automatically rewraps on the line to adjust to the new size.

You will add a text box containing the text **Internet Promotion** to the chart to draw attention to the Internet data. A text box is created using the 🖾 Text Box button on the Drawing toolbar. To display the Drawing toolbar and create a text box,

1 — ■ Click 🖳 Drawing (on the Standard toolbar).

■ Click 🖾 Text Box.

■ Move the mouse pointer to the space above the February columns of data and drag to create a text box that is approximately 1½ inch by ½ inch.

> The mouse pointer appears as ⌶ , indicating a text box will be created as you drag the mouse.

Your screen should be similar to Figure 2–37.

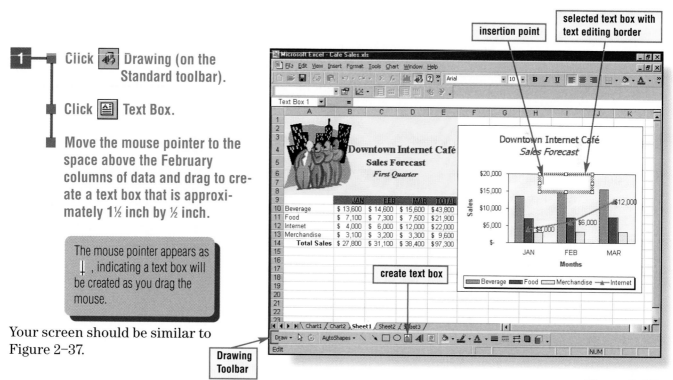

Figure 2–37

Additional Information

A dotted border around a selected object indicates that you can format the box itself. Clicking the hatched border changes it to a dotted border.

The text box is a selected object and is surrounded with a hatched border that indicates you can enter, delete, select, and format the text inside the box. It also displays an insertion point indicating that it is waiting for you to enter the text. As you type the text in the text box, do not be concerned if all the text is not visible within the text box. You will resize the box if needed to display the entire entry.

2 ■ Type **Effects of Internet promotion**

■ If necessary, adjust the size of the text box by dragging the sizing handles until it is just large enough to fully display the text on two lines.

Your screen should be similar to Figure 2–38.

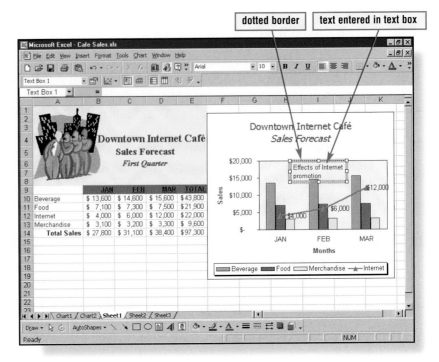

Figure 2–38

The text in the text box is difficult to read because it overlaps the plot area. To make it stand out better, you will add a fill color to the text box.

3 ■ Click the hatched text box border to turn off text editing (the insertion point disappears).

■ Open the 🖋 ▾ Fill Color drop-down menu and select a color of your choice.

> You can use the 🖋 ▾ and 🔤 ▾ buttons on either the Formatting or Drawing toolbars.

■ Select a text color of your choice from the 🔤 ▾ Font Color list.

> You can also choose Format/Text Box to format a text box.

■ Readjust the size of the text box and move it to the position displayed in Figure 2–39.

Your screen should be similar to Figure 2–39.

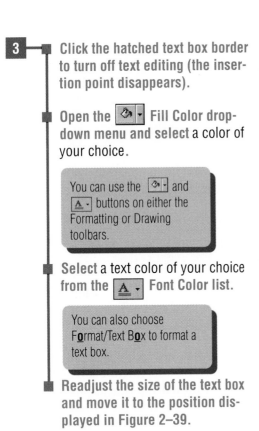

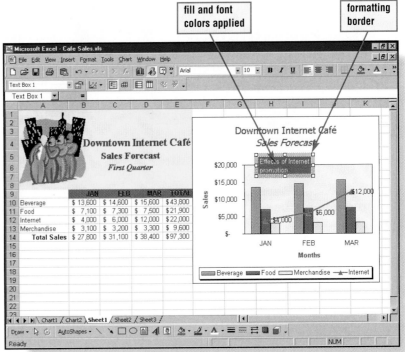

Figure 2–39

Adding Arrows

Next you want to draw an arrow from the text box to the Internet line. Like a text box, an arrow is a separate object that can be added to a worksheet or a chart.

> The mouse pointer appears as a +.

> If you hold down (Shift) while dragging, a straight horizontal line is drawn.

1 ■ Click ◥ Arrow (on the Drawing toolbar).

■ To draw the arrow, click on the right corner of the text box and drag to the Internet line. (See Figure 2–39)

A line with an arrowhead at the end is displayed. The arrow is automatically a selected object. The handles at both ends of the arrow let you adjust its size and location. You can also change the color and weight of the line to make it stand out more.

2 ■ If necessary, move and size the arrow to adjust its position as in Figure 2–40.

■ Click ✎ ▾ Line Color and select the same color for the arrow as you used for the text box.

■ Click ☰ Line Style and increase the line weight to 2¼ point.

■ Deselect the arrow.

Your screen should be similar to Figure 2–40.

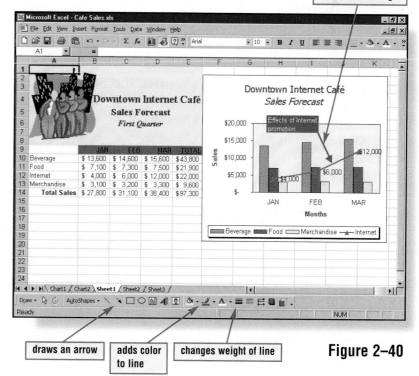

arrow with color and heavier weight

draws an arrow

adds color to line

changes weight of line

Figure 2–40

Creating a Pie Chart

The last chart you will make will use the Total worksheet data in column E. You want to see what proportion each type of sales is of all sales for the quarter. The best chart for this purpose is a pie chart. A pie chart compares parts to the whole in a manner similar to a stacked-column chart. However, each value in the range is a slice of the pie displayed as a percentage of the total.

1 ■ **Move the combination chart to top-align with cell A16 below the worksheet data.**

The use of X (category) and data series settings in a pie chart is different from their use in a column or line chart. The X series labels the slices of the pie rather than the X axis. The data series is used to create the slices in the pie. Only one data series can be specified in a pie chart.

2 ■ **Select** A10 through A13 **and** E10 through E13.

Another way to create a chart is to use the Chart Type toolbar button.

Additional Information

You can also create a chart using the default chart type (column) in a new chart sheet by selecting the data range and pressing F11.

3 ■ **If necessary, display the Chart toolbar.**

■ **Click** 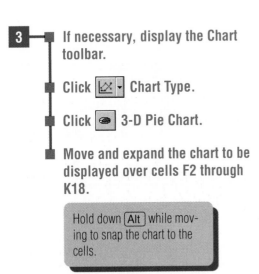 **Chart Type.**

■ **Click** 3-D Pie Chart.

■ **Move and expand the chart to be displayed over cells F2 through K18.**

Hold down Alt while moving to snap the chart to the cells.

Your screen should be similar to Figure 2–41.

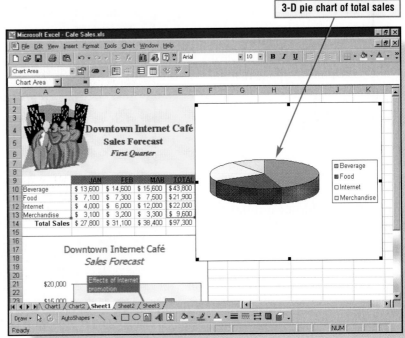

3-D pie chart of total sales

Figure 2–41

A three-dimensional pie chart is drawn in the worksheet. Each value in the data series is displayed as a slice of the pie chart. The size of the slice represents the proportion each sales category is of total sales. You need to add a chart title. In addition, you want to turn off the legend and display data labels instead to label the slices of the pie.

Formatting the Pie Chart

To clarify the meaning of the chart, you will first add a chart title. A pie chart can have only a main title because it does not contain axis lines. Then you will add labels for the slices to identify the data in the chart.

1 Choose **C**hart/Chart **O**ptions.

In the Chart Title text box of the Titles tab, enter the title **Total Sales by Category**

Open the Legend tab and clear the **S**how legend option.

> You can also click [image] Legend to turn on/off the display of the legend.

Open the Data Labels tab and select Show Label **a**nd Percent.

Click [OK].

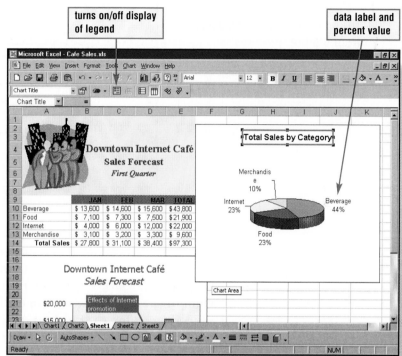

turns on/off display of legend

data label and percent value

Figure 2–42

Your chart should be similar to Figure 2–42.

The pie chart is redrawn to show the data labels and percents. The data label text box size is based on the size of the chart and the text is appropriately sized to fit in the box. Because the default size of data labels is a little too large, the entire Merchandise label does not appear on one line. To fix this, you will reduce the size of the label text. You also want to enhance the appearance of the data labels and title.

2 Select the data labels, reduce the font size until the Merchandise label is on one line, and apply formatting of your choice.

Select the title and apply formatting of your choice.

Exploding and Rotating the Pie

Next, you want to separate slightly or **explode** the Internet slice of the pie to emphasize the data.

1 ■ **Select the Internet slice.**

> To select an object within a group, select the group first and then select the object. Selection handles surround the selected object.

■ **Drag the selected slice away from the pie.**

> If all slices on the pie are selected, dragging one slice explodes all slices at the same time.

Your screen should be similar to Figure 2–43.

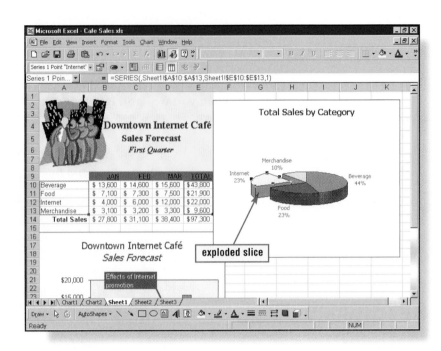

Figure 2–43

The slice is separated from the rest of the pie chart. You also want to change the position of the Internet slice so that it is toward the front of the pie. When Excel creates a pie chart, the first data point is placed to the right of the middle at the top of the chart. The rest of the data points are placed in order to the right until the circle is complete. To change the order in which the slices are displayed, you can rotate the pie chart.

2 ■ **Double-click the Internet data series.**

■ **Open the Options tab.**

■ **Change the Angle of first slice setting to 180 degrees.**

Your screen should be similar to Figure 2–44.

3 ■ **Click** OK .

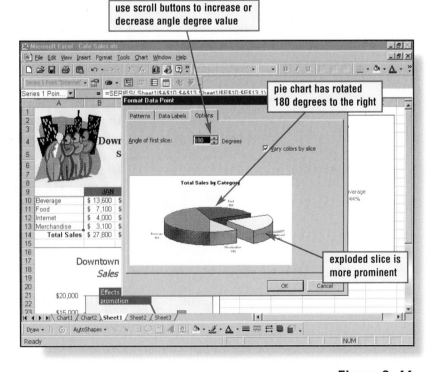

Figure 2–44

The entire pie chart has rotated 180 degrees to the right and now the Internet data slice appears toward the front of the chart.

Applying Patterns and Color

The last change you would like to make is to add patterns to the pie chart data points. As you have seen, when Excel creates a chart each data series (or data point in the case of a pie chart) is automatically displayed in a different color. Although the data series are easy to distinguish from one another onscreen, if you do not have a color printer the colors are printed as shades of gray and may be difficult to distinguish. To make the data series more distinguishable on a black-and-white printer, you can apply a different pattern to each data series object.

1 ■ **Double-click the Beverage data series slice.**

■ **Open the Pattern tab.**

Your screen should be similar to Figure 2-45.

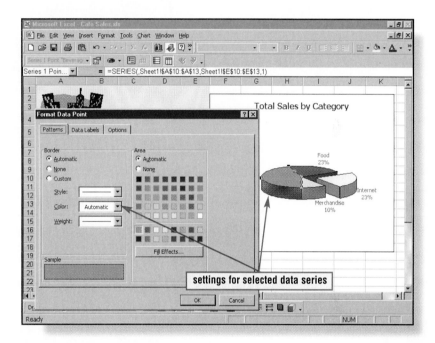

Figure 2-45

The options available in the Pattern tab vary depending upon the type of data marker that is selected. In this case, because the selected data marker is a pie slice, the options let you change the border and the background area. The current setting for the selected data marker is displayed in the sample area. This consists of a black border with a fill color of periwinkle blue. To add a pattern,

2 ■ Click [Fi̲ll Effects...] .

■ Open the Pattern tab.

Your screen should be similar to Figure 2–46.

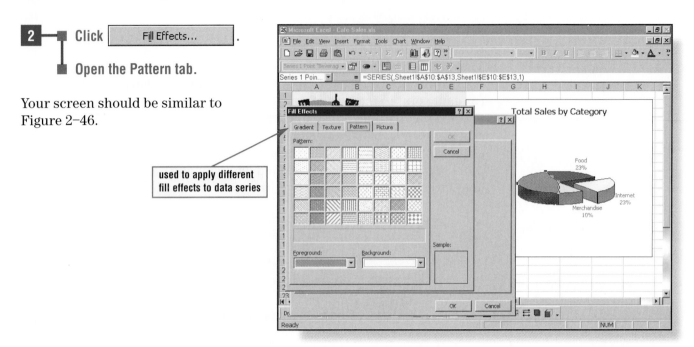

used to apply different
fill effects to data series

Figure 2–46

From the Fill Effects dialog box, you can change options for gradients, textures, patterns, and pictures used in formatting the selected object. You will add a pattern to the existing fill.

3 ■ From the Pattern palette, select a pattern of your choice.

■ Click [OK] (twice) to close both dialog boxes.

Your screen should be similar to Figure 2–47.

selected pattern is
applied to data series

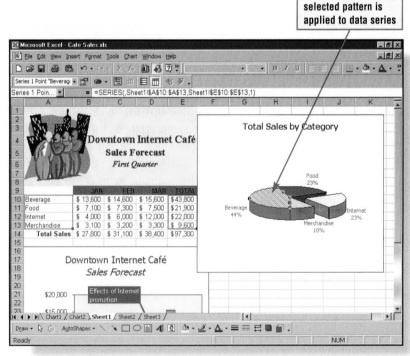

Figure 2–47

The pattern is applied to the selected data point. Next you will change the color and add pattern to the Internet data series slice.

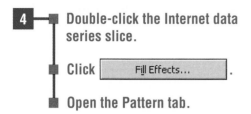

4 ■ Double-click the Internet data series slice.

■ Click [Fill Effects...].

■ Open the Pattern tab.

Your screen should be similar to Figure 2–48.

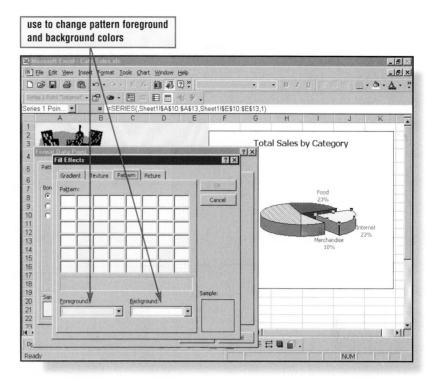

Figure 2–48

Because yellow is a light color, it is difficult to see the patterns in the Fill Effects dialog box. A pattern consists of a foreground color and a background color. The default foreground color is the same as the fill color and the background color is white. To increase the contrast, you can change the color selection of either.

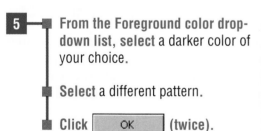

5 ■ From the Foreground color drop-down list, **select** a darker color of your choice.

■ **Select** a different pattern.

■ Click [OK] (twice).

Your chart should be similar to Figure 2–49.

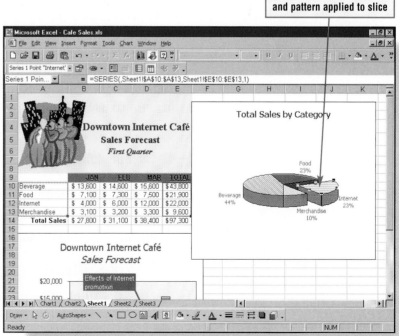

Figure 2–49

You will leave the other two data points without patterns.

6 ▪ Move the pie chart below the column chart to top-align with cell A36.

Documenting a Workbook

Now you are ready to save the changes you have made to the workbook file to your data disk. Before doing this, you want to document the workbook. Each workbook includes summary information that is associated with the file.

1 ▪ Choose **File/Properties**.

▪ Select each tab in the Properties dialog box and look at the recorded information.

▪ Open the Summary tab.

Your screen should be similar to Figure 2–50.

Figure 2–50

The Summary tab is used to specify information you want associated with the file such as a title, subject, author, keywords, and comments about the workbook file. This information helps you locate the workbook file you want to use as well as indicates the objectives and use of the workbook.

2 ▪ Enter the following information in the Summary tab.

The Author text box may be blank or may show your school or some other name. Clear the existing contents first if necessary.

Title	**Downtown Internet Café**
Subject	**Sales Forecast**
Author	**[your name]**

▪ Click **OK**.

▪ Move to cell A9 of the worksheet and save the workbook file as Café Sales Charts to your data disk.

The updated documentation has been saved with the new file.

Previewing the Workbook

It is very important before printing charts to preview how they will appear when printed. Formats that look good onscreen may not produce good printed results. Your workbook file includes two new chart sheets and a worksheet. To preview them all at once, you need to change the print setting to print the entire workbook first.

1 ▪ Choose **F**ile/**P**rint/**E**ntire workbook

▪ Click Preview .

▪ If necessary, reduce the zoom to see the full page.

Your screen should be similar to Figure 2–51.

changes settings associated with sheet you are previewing

preview of bar chart appears in shades of gray if you have a black-and-white printer

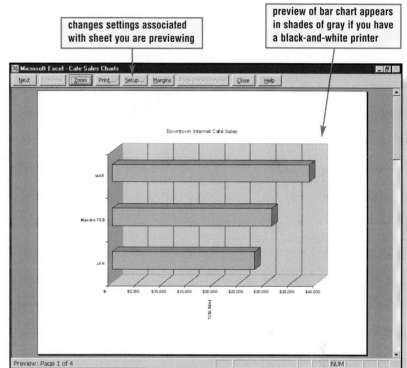

Figure 2–51

Because the bar chart is on a separate chart sheet, it is displayed on a page by itself. In addition, if you are not using a color printer, the preview displays the chart as it will appear when printed on a black-and-white printer. The colors appear as shades of gray by default. Since this chart has a dark-gray plot area fill, the bars do not stand out well. You will change the print setting associated with this chart sheet to fix this problem. The Print Preview toolbar buttons are used to access many print and page layout changes while you are previewing a document.

2 ▪ Click [Setup...] .

▪ Open the Chart tab.

Your screen should be similar to
Figure 2–52.

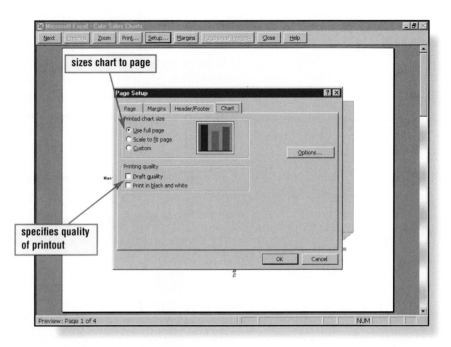

Figure 2–52

Because chart sheets print only one chart on a page, the default setting is to size the chart to fill the entire page. The Draft Quality setting sup-
presses the printing of graphics and gridlines, thereby reducing printing
time. The black-and-white option applies patterns to data series in place
of colors while leaving other areas in shades of gray. On a color printer, all
other areas are still printed in color when this option is selected.

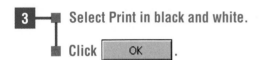

3 ▪ Select Print in black and white.

▪ Click [OK] .

Your screen should be similar to
Figure 2–53.

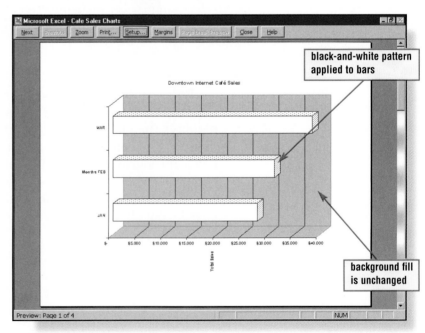

Figure 2–53

A black-and-white pattern has been applied to the bars and the background fill has not changed.

4 ━■ Click Next to see the column chart in the next Chart sheet.

This chart looks as if it will print satisfactorily using the default print settings.

5 ━■ Click Next to see the work-sheet and charts in Sheet 1.

Your screen should be similar to Figure 2–54.

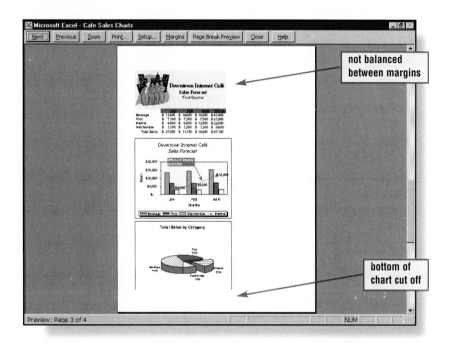

Figure 2–54

You can now see that the bottom of the pie chart exceeds the page margins and will not print on the page. You can also see that the printout will not appear balanced between the page margins. Finally, you want to include a header on each page. You will make several changes to the layout of the page to correct these problems.

Sizing the Worksheet

First you will reduce the worksheet and chart sizes so that they will fit on one page.

1 ─■ Click Setup... .

■ If necessary, open the Page tab.

Your screen should be similar to
Figure 2–55.

reduces or enlarges
to fit specific number
of pages

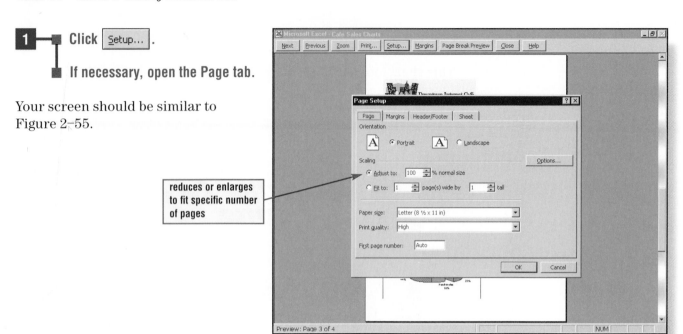

Figure 2–55

The scaling options allow you to reduce or enlarge the worksheet contents by a percentage or fit it to a specific number of pages. You want to
have the program scale the worksheet to fit on one page.

2 ─■ Select **F**it to

The default of 1 page is appropriate.

Aligning a Sheet on a Page

You would also like to center the worksheet horizontally on the page. To
make this change,

1 ━■ Open the Margins tab.

Your screen should be similar to Figure 2–56.

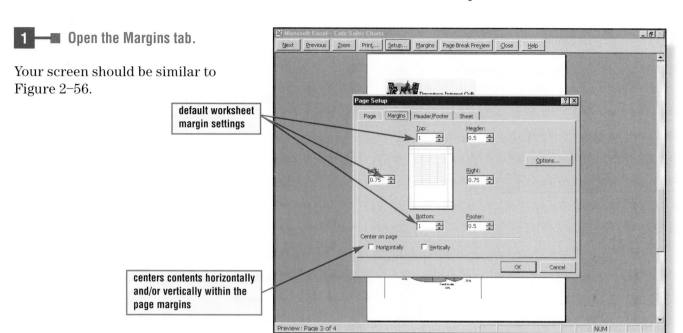

Figure 2–56

The default worksheet margin settings are displayed. They can be changed individually by adjusting the size of the settings. You want to center the worksheet data horizontally within the existing margins.

2 ━■ Select Hori<u>z</u>ontally.

Adding Predefined Headers and Footers

You would like to include your name and the date in a header.

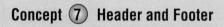

Concept ⑦ Header and Footer

A **header** is a line or several lines of text that appears at the top of each page just below the top margin. A **footer** is a line or several lines of text that appears at the bottom of each page just above the bottom margin.
   You can select from predefined header and footer text or enter your own custom text. The information contained in the predefined header and footer text is taken from the document properties associated with the worksheet and from the program and system settings. Header and footer text can be formatted like any other text. In addition, you can control the placement of the header and footer text by specifying where it should appear: left-aligned, centered, or right-aligned in the header or footer space. Information that is commonly placed in a header or footer includes the date and page number.

1 Open the Header/Footer tab.

■ Open the He**a**der drop-down list box and select the Prepared By [your name] [date], Page 3 option.

The menu equivalent is **F**ile/ Page Set**u**p/Header/Footer.

Your screen should be similar to Figure 2–57.

Additional Information

Predefined footers can be added by selecting the footer option from the **F**ooter drop-down list.

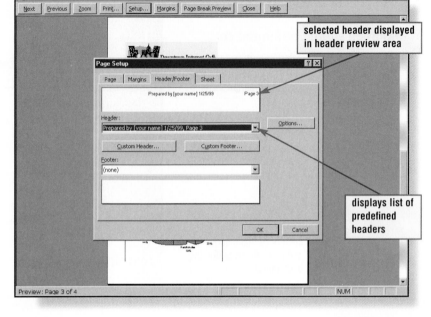

Figure 2–57

The selected header is displayed in the header area of the dialog box.

2 Click   OK   .

Your screen should be similar to Figure 2–58.

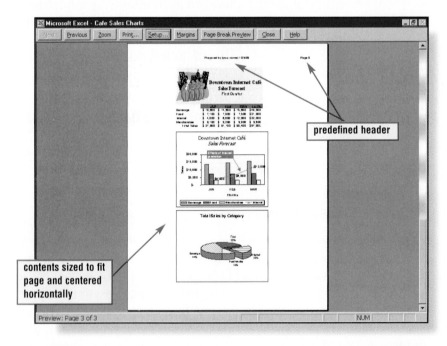

Figure 2–58

The worksheet layout settings you specified are reflected in the preview window. It now appears the way you want it to look when printed.

Click Previous to display previous sheets.

3 Add a predefined footer to the two chart sheets that displays your name, page number, and date.

Printing the Workbook

Printing a worksheet that includes charts requires a printer with graphics capability. However, the actual procedure to print is the same as printing a worksheet that does not include charts.

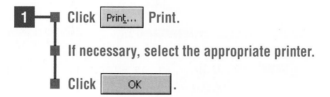

1 ■ Click Print... Print.

   ■ If necessary, select the appropriate printer.

   ■ Click OK .

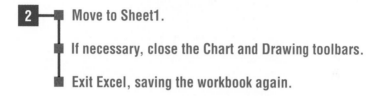

Your printer should be printing all three sheets in the workbook.

2 ■ Move to Sheet1.

   ■ If necessary, close the Chart and Drawing toolbars.

   ■ Exit Excel, saving the workbook again.

Concept Summary

Tutorial 2: Charting Worksheet Data

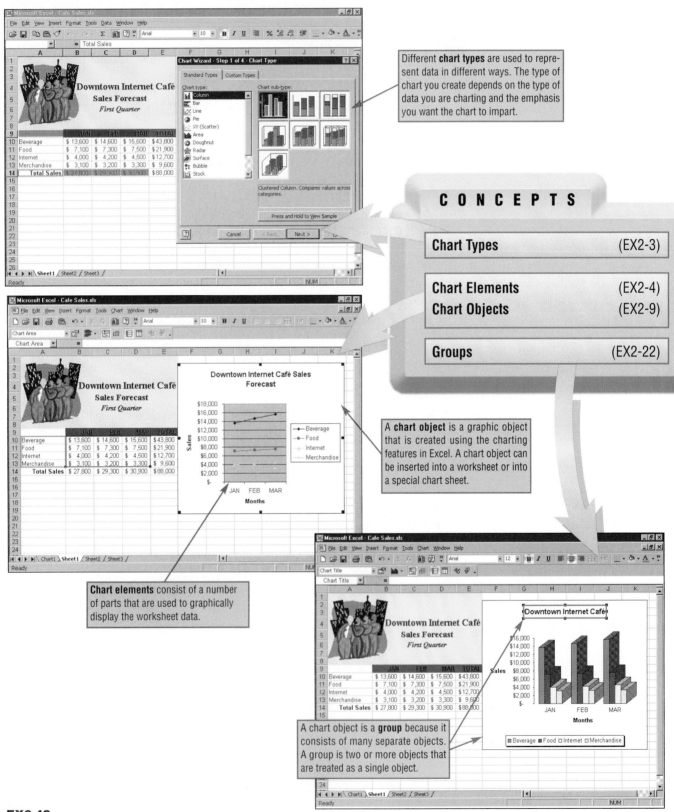

Different **chart types** are used to represent data in different ways. The type of chart you create depends on the type of data you are charting and the emphasis you want the chart to impart.

C O N C E P T S

Chart Types	(EX2-3)
Chart Elements	(EX2-4)
Chart Objects	(EX2-9)
Groups	(EX2-22)

A **chart object** is a graphic object that is created using the charting features in Excel. A chart object can be inserted into a worksheet or into a special chart sheet.

Chart elements consist of a number of parts that are used to graphically display the worksheet data.

A chart object is a **group** because it consists of many separate objects. A group is two or more objects that are treated as a single object.

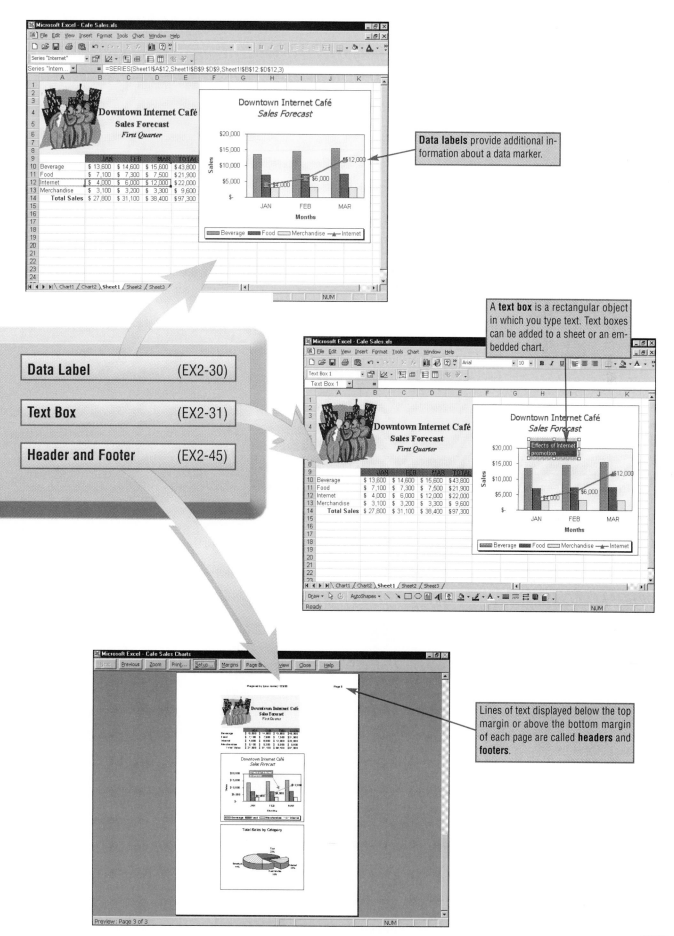

Data labels provide additional information about a data marker.

A **text box** is a rectangular object in which you type text. Text boxes can be added to a sheet or an embedded chart.

Data Label	(EX2-30)
Text Box	(EX2-31)
Header and Footer	(EX2-45)

Lines of text displayed below the top margin or above the bottom margin of each page are called **headers** and **footers**.

Tutorial Review

Key Terms

area chart   EX2-17
category-axis title   EX2-4
category name   EX2-4
chart   EX2-3
chart gridlines   EX2-4
chart object   EX2-9
chart title   EX2-4
column chart   EX2-6
combination chart   EX2-26
data label   EX2-30
data marker   EX2-4

data series   EX2-4
embedded chart   EX2-9
explode   EX2-35
footer   EX2-45
group   EX2-22
header   EX2-45
legend   EX2-4
line chart   EX2-12
pie chart   EX2-5
plot area   EX2-4
selection handle   EX2-11

series formula   EX2-28
stack   EX2-9
stacked-column chart   EX2-19
text box   EX2-31
title   EX2-4
value axis   EX2-4
value-axis title   EX2-4
word wrap   EX2-31
X axis   EX2-4
Y axis   EX2-4
Z axis   EX2-5

Command Summary

Command	Shortcut Keys	Button	Action
File/**P**rint/**E**ntire Workbook			Prints all the sheets in a workbook
File/Propert**i**es			Displays information about a file
File/Page Set**u**p/Header/Footer			Adds header and/or footer
Insert/**C**hart			Inserts chart into worksheet
F**o**rmat/S**e**lected Data Series/Data Labels	Ctrl + 1		Inserts data labels into chart
F**o**rmat/S**e**lected Legend	Ctrl + 1		Changes format of legend
F**o**rmat/S**e**lected Chart Title	Ctrl + 1		Changes format of selected chart title
F**o**rmat/S**e**lected Data Series	Ctrl + 1		Changes format of selected data series
F**o**rmat/S**e**lected Object			Changes format of embedded objects
Chart/Chart **T**ype			Changes type of chart
Chart/Chart **O**ptions			Adds options to chart
Chart/**L**ocation			Moves chart from worksheet to chart sheet

Screen Identification

1. In the following worksheet and chart, letters identify important elements. Enter the correct term for each screen element in the space provided.

a. _____   f. _____

b. _____   g. _____

c. _____   h. _____

d. _____   i. _____

e. _____

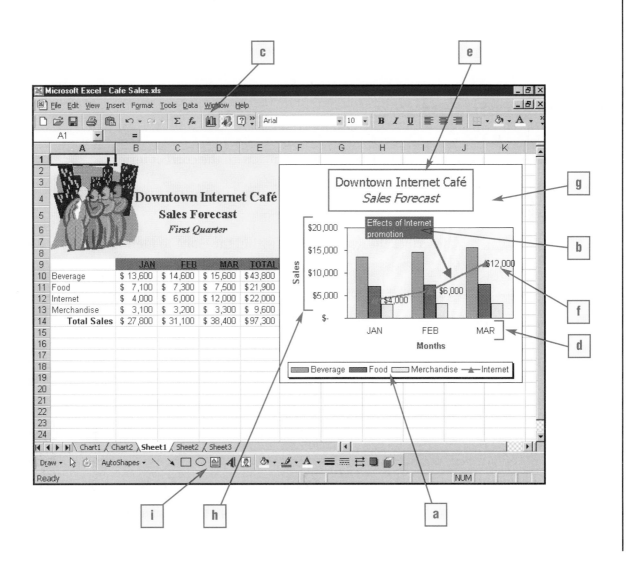

Matching

Match the lettered item on the right with the numbered item on the left.

1. chart gridlines _____ **a.** left boundary line of the chart

2. data marker _____ **b.** bottom boundary line of the chart

3. stacked-column _____ **c.** identifies each number represented in a data series

4. X axis _____ **d.** area of chart bounded by X and Y axes

5. explode _____ **e.** extend from the Y-axis line across the plot area

6. plot area _____ **f.** identifies the chart data series names and data markers

7. category-axis _____ **g.** X-axis title line

8. Y axis _____ **h.** shows proportion of each value

9. legend _____ **i.** to separate wedge slightly from other wedges of pie

10. pie chart _____ **j.** displays data as slices of a circle

Fill-In Questions

Complete the following statements by filling in the blanks with the correct terms.

1. A visual representation of data in an easy-to-understand and attractive manner is called a(n) _____.

2. A(n) _____ describes the symbols used within the chart to identify different data series.

3. The bottom boundary of a chart is the _____ and the left boundary is the _____.

4. A chart that is inserted into a worksheet is a(n) _____ object.

5. A(n) _____ chart and a(n) _____ chart both display data as a set of evenly spaced bars.

6. A(n) _____ and a(n) _____ compare parts to the whole.

7. The _____ toolbar contains buttons for the most frequently used chart editing and formatting features.

8. The _____ title is displayed centered above the charted data.

9. The black-and-white option applies _____ to data series in place of colors while leaving other areas in shades of gray.

10. When a wedge of a pie chart is separated from the other wedges, the wedge has been _____.

Multiple Choice

Circle the correct response to the questions below.

1. _____ charts are used to show changes in data over time, emphasizing time and rate of change rather than the amount of change.

   a. bar
   b. line
   c. column
   d. area

2. The _____ names displayed along the X axis correspond to the headings for the worksheet data that is plotted along the X axis.

   a. variable
   b. category
   c. value
   d. option

3. A _____ identifies the chart data series names and data markers that correspond to each data series.

   a. category
   b. value axis
   c. legend
   d. data label

4. Charts that are inserted into a worksheet are called:

   a. embedded objects
   b. attached objects
   c. inserted objects
   d. active objects

5. A(n) _____ is two or more objects that are treated as a single object.

   a. group
   b. embedded object
   c. category
   d. combined object

6. _____ can consist of the value of the marker, the name of the data series or category, a percent value, or a bubble size.

   a. legends
   b. X axis
   c. Y axis
   d. data labels

7. A(n) _____ is a rectangular object in which you type text.

    a. text box

    b. label

    c. input box

    d. embedded object

8. A _____ is a line or several lines of text that appears at the bottom of each page just above the bottom margin.

    a. footer

    b. header

    c. footing

    d. heading

9. Charts that display data as slices of a circle and show the relationship of each value in a data series to the series as a whole are called:

    a. area charts

    b. value charts

    c. pie charts

    d. bar charts

10. A chart that uses two or more chart types to emphasize different information is called a(n):

    a. area chart

    b. pie chart

    c. bar chart

    d. combination chart

True/False

Circle the correct answer to the following questions.

1.	The plot area is visually displayed within the X- and Y-axis boundaries.	True	False
2.	A bar chart displays data as a line and is commonly used to show trends over time.	True	False
3.	The Y-axis title line is called the category-axis title.	True	False
4.	An entire group or each object in a group can be individually selected and then formatted or edited.	True	False
5.	A series formula links the chart object to the source worksheet.	True	False
6.	Value data labels are helpful when the values are large and you want to know the exact value for one data series.	True	False
7.	Text that is entered in a text box wraps to fit within the boundaries of the text box.	True	False
8.	Separating slightly or exploding a slice of a pie chart emphasizes the data.	True	False

9. Patterns can be added to slices of a pie chart to make it easier to read.   True   False

10. A header is a line or several lines of text that appears at the bottom of each page just below the top margin.   True   False

Discussion Questions

1. Define each of the following terms and discuss how they are related to one another: chart type, chart element, and chart object.

2. Discuss how column and bar charts represent data. How do they differ from pie charts?

3. What type of information would best be represented by a line chart?

4. Describe how a 3-D column chart differs from a 2–D column chart.

Hands-On Practice Exercises

Step by Step

Rating System	☆ Easy
	☆ ☆ Moderate
	☆ ☆ ☆ Difficult

1. Jennifer's environmental studies paper is on the endangered Bengal tiger. She has some data saved in a worksheet on the estimated number of tigers in 1997. She has asked you to help her chart the data and make the worksheet look more attractive. The completed worksheet with charts is shown here.

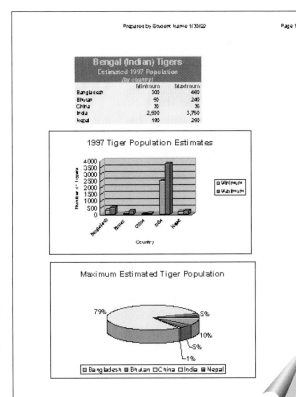

a. Open the worksheet Tiger Data on your data disk.

b. Create a clustered column with 3-D effect chart of the data in cells B6 through D11. Enter the Chart title **1997 Tiger Population Estimates**. Enter the Category (X) axis title **Country** and the Value (Z) axis **Number of Tigers**. Include the chart in the worksheet.

c. Size the chart over cells A13 through F30.

d. Rotate the Z-axis label 90 degrees. Angle the X-axis labels 45 degrees upward. Change the font size for the axis titles and legend to 10 point.

e. Create a 3-D pie chart in the worksheet showing the maximum tiger population estimates. Include the title **Maximum Estimated Tiger Population** and display percents as data labels.

f. Display the legend below the chart. Rotate the chart 90 degrees.

g. Move the pie chart below the column chart and size it appropriately.

h. Document the workbook file by adding your name as author.

i. Preview the worksheet. Add a predefined header to the worksheet that displays your name, page number, and date. Center the worksheet horizontally on the page.

j. If necessary, adjust the size and placement of the charts on the sheet so that they print on a single page. Print the worksheet.

k. Save the workbook as Tiger Charts.

2. To complete this exercise, you must have completed Exercise 3 in Tutorial 1. Mark Ernster works for a real estate company and has been collecting information on sales prices for existing homes across the country. Mark wants to graph some of the data in the worksheet for his upcoming presentation. The completed worksheet with charts is shown here.

a. Open the workbook file Real Estate Prices on your data disk.

b. Create a line chart on a separate sheet showing the housing prices for the four years for the U.S. only. Remove the legend. Title the chart appropriately. Make the line heavier and change the line and data marker color. Change the fill of the plot area to a gradient effect with two colors. Add data labels that display the values. Increase the size of the chart title and add color.

c. Create a column chart in the worksheet showing housing prices for the four regions for the four years. The X axis will display the regions and the years will be the legend. Title the chart appropriately. Move the legend to the bottom of the chart. Increase the size of the chart title and add color. Position the chart below the worksheet data and size it appropriately.

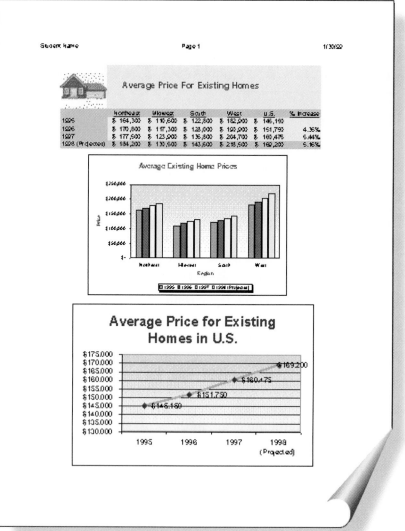

d. Change the line chart location to the worksheet and position it below the column chart. Size the chart appropriately.

e. Remove your name and date from the worksheet. Document the workbook file by adding your name as author.

f. Preview the workbook. Add a predefined header to the worksheet that displays your name, page number, and date. Center the worksheet horizontally on the page. Size the sheet to print on one page. Print the worksheet.

g. Save the workbook as Real Estate Charts.

3. Tyler Johnson works for Books Online. He has compiled a list of the 10 best-selling children's books. He would like a chart that shows management how the list price differs from the selling price of the books. The completed worksheet with charts is shown here.

a. Open the file Book List on your data disk.

b. Chart the data in columns A, C, and D by rows as a 3-D clustered bar chart.

c. Enter the Chart title Top 10 Best Selling Children's Books, the Category (X) axis as Books by Ranking and the Value (Z) axis as Price.

d. Embed the chart in the worksheet. Position the chart over cells A17 through E35.

e. Change the X-axis scale setting to 1 to label every category.

f. Add color and font refinements to the chart as you like.

g. Document the workbook file by adding your name as author.

h. Preview the worksheet. Add a predefined header to the worksheet that displays your name, page number, and date. Center the worksheet horizontally on the page. Print the worksheet.

i. Save the workbook file as Book List Chart.

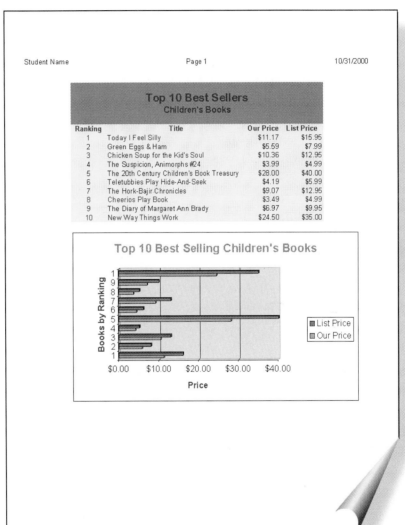

4. To complete this exercise, you must have completed Exercise 2 in Tutorial 1. Lisa Sutton is still working on her worksheets for jobs in New Jersey for her upcoming seminar. The completed chart is shown here.

a. Open the workbook file Highest Paying Jobs Revised on your data disk.

b. Create a cylindrical column chart of the data for Physicians and Surgeons, Podiatrists, Dentists, and Lawyers on a separate chart sheet.

c. Enter the chart title **Hourly Wages-N.J. vs U.S.**, the Category (X) axis title **Job Title** and the Value (Y) axis title **Hourly Wage**.

d. Add a pattern to the columns. Change the plot area fill color to ivory.

e. Increase the font size of the chart title to 16. Add color to the title. Change the axis titles to 12 point and a color of your choice.

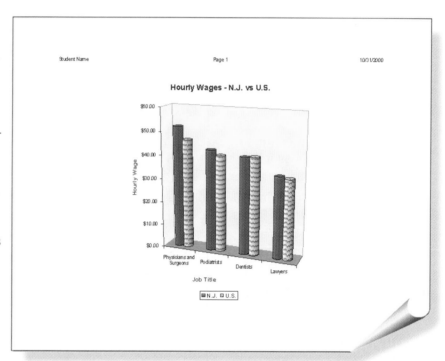

f. Position the legend at the bottom of the chart. Increase the font size of the legend to 12 pt.

g. Document the workbook file by adding your name as author.

h. Preview the chart. Add a predefined header to the chart sheet that displays your name, page number, and date. Print the chart.

i. Save the file as Highest Paying Jobs Chart.

5. To complete this exercise, you must have completed Exercise 4 in Tutorial 1. Will Bloomquist is still working on the data for his article on student athletes. The completed worksheet with charts is shown here.

a. Open the workbook Athlete Data on your data disk. Delete the picture inserted at the right of the worksheet.

b. Create an embedded line chart of the data in cells A4 through C7. Enter the chart title **High School Athletes**, the Category (X) axis title **Years** and the Value (Y) axis title **Number of Athletes**.

c. Position the chart over cells D2 through I18.

d. Edit the chart title to include the subtitle **(in millions)** on a second line. Add a color of your choice to the title.

e. Display the values for the girls next to the data points. Increase the weight of both lines.

f. Move the legend to the lower-right corner of the chart.

g. Add a text box and an arrow pointing to the girls' data line. Include the text **Steady Increase**. Format the text box and arrow as you like.

h. Add a gradient fill color to the plot area and make other chart enhancements as you like.

i. Create a 3-D pie chart on the same worksheet of the data in cells A12 through C13. Edit the chart title to **College Athletes 1990–1991**.

j. Rotate the chart so that the female slice is positioned on the right side of the chart.

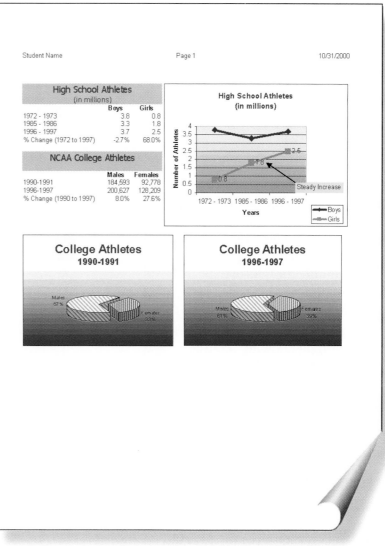

k. Remove the legend and display data labels that show the label and percent. Increase the size of the main title to 18 points and the subtitle to 14 points. Explode the female slice. Add a pattern to both slices of the pie. Add other formatting of your choice to improve the appearance of the chart.

l. Create a second 3-D pie chart on the same worksheet of the data for college athletes in 1996–1997. Format this chart to look like the chart for 1990–1991. Position the pie charts side-by-side below the worksheet. Size them appropriately.

m. Document the workbook file by adding your name as author. Remove your name and the date from the worksheet.

n. Preview the workbook. Add a predefined header to the worksheet that displays your name, page number, and date. Size the worksheet to fit on one page. Print the worksheet.

o. Save the workbook file as Student Athlete Charts.

6. Carol Hayes is the program coordinator for Fitness Lifestyles, a physical conditioning and health center. She is proposing to management that they increase their emphasis on fitness activities by expanding their exercise equipment area. To reinforce the need for this type of investment, she has found some recent data about growth in the use of exercise equipment in the last decade. She wants to create several charts of this data to emphasize the demand.

a. Create a worksheet of the following data.

	1987	1993	1997
Free Weights	24.5	31	43.2
Resistance Machines	15.3	19.4	22.5
Stationary Cycling	33.4	39.1	34.8
Treadmill	4.4	19.7	36.1
Running/Jogging	32.9	30.1	32.3

Source: American Sports Analysis study conducted by American Sports Data, Inc.

b. Add an appropriate title over the data and format the numbers to show two decimal places. Enhance the worksheet as you like to improve its appearance.

c. Create an embedded combination chart of the worksheet data showing the free weight and treadmill data as lines. Enter a chart title and appropriate X and Y axis titles. Include a text box and arrows pointing out the sharp increase in free weight and treadmill participation. Enhance the chart using features presented in the tutorial.

d. Position the chart below the worksheet. Size the chart appropriately.

e. Create a 3-D pie chart in the worksheet showing the 1997 data for the four types of equipment. Include the title **Most Used Fitness Equipment**. Remove the legend and display labels and percents as data labels. Add a pattern to two of the pie slices. Enhance the chart using features presented in the tutorial.

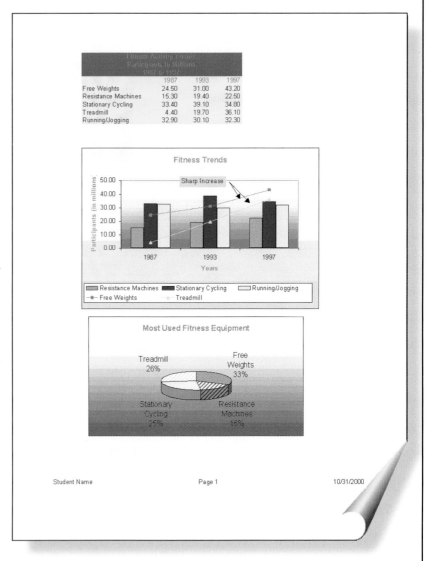

f. Move the pie chart below the combination chart and size it appropriately.

g. Document the workbook file by adding your name as author.

h. Preview the worksheet. Add a predefined footer to the worksheet that displays your name, page number, and date. Center the worksheet horizontally on the page. Print the worksheet.

i. Save the workbook file as Fitness Activity Charts.

On Your Own

7. Create a worksheet that tracks your grades. It can be a record of the test scores you received this semester, or it can be a record of your GPA each semester. Create an embedded chart that best represents your grade trends. Use the formatting techniques you have learned to change the appearance of the worksheet and the chart. Save the workbook as Grades. Include a header or footer that displays your name and the current date in the worksheet. Print the worksheet with the chart.

8. Andrew Beinbrink is learning about the stock market. Use Help to learn more about the Stock chart type. Pick four related stocks and create an embedded Stock chart of the data. Save the worksheet with the chart as Stocks. Include a header or footer that displays your name and the current date in the worksheet. Print the worksheet with the chart.

9. Kevin Tillman has started a new job with Baseball Statistics, Inc. He would like some help creating a worksheet that contains team win/loss records for the last five years. He asks you to search the Web for records. Choose a major league baseball team and locate the win/loss record for the last five years. Enter the data into a worksheet. Enhance the worksheet using the features you have learned. Create an embedded chart that displays the information over the five years. Include a header or footer that displays your name and the current date in the worksheet. Save and print the worksheet with the chart.

10. Karen Blake is thinking about purchasing a new sports utility vehicle. However, she is also concerned about the mileage per gallon ratings for the vehicles. She wants to find out the base price on several different models and the MPG rate. Use the Web or visit several local car dealerships to get this information. Create a worksheet that contains the models, base selling price, and MPG rate for each vehicle. Create an embedded combination chart of the data that shows the models along the X axis, price as the Y-axis value, and MPG rate as a secondary value Y axis. The line should represent the MPG data. Use Help for information about plotting a secondary value axis. Enhance the chart appropriately. Include a header or footer that displays your name and the current date in the worksheet. Save and print the worksheet and chart.

Managing and Analyzing a Workbook

Competencies

After completing this tutorial, you will know how to:

1. Spell-check a sheet.
2. Use Paste Function.
3. Use absolute references.
4. Apply styles.
5. Copy, move, and name sheets.
6. Use AutoFill.
7. Reference multiple sheets.
8. Zoom the worksheet.
9. Split windows and freeze panes.
10. Use what-if analysis and Goal Seek.
11. Change page orientation.
12. Add custom headers and footers.
13. Print selected sheets.

Case Study

You present your new, more optimistic, first quarter forecast for the Downtown Internet Café to Evan, who has made several formatting and design changes. He asks you to include an Average calculation and to extend the forecast for the next three quarters. He wants to hold back on your idea of an aggressive Internet sales promotion. The Café's funds are low due to

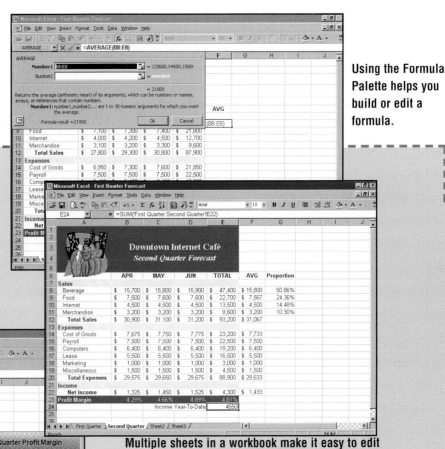

Using the Formula Palette helps you build or edit a formula.

Multiple sheets in a workbook make it easy to edit several sheets simultaneously and to perform

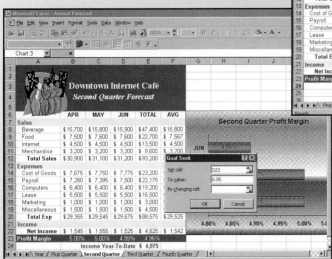

Forecasting values using what-if analysis and using charts to visually represent the change are powerful features of Excel.

the cost of the recent renovations. Evan feels that you should stick with a more conservative forecast of income derived from Internet sales. After discussing the situation, you agree that the Café will likely lose money during the first month of operations. Then the café should start to show increasing profitability. Evan stresses that the monthly profit margin should reach 5 per cent in the second quarter.

As you develop the Café's financial forecast, the worksheet grows in size and complexity. You will learn about features of Excel 2000 that help you manage a large workbook efficiently. You will also learn how you can manipulate the data in a worksheet to reach a goal using the what-if analysis capabilities of Excel. The completed annual forecast is shown here.

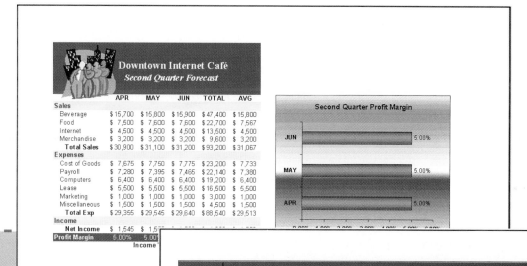

Concept Overview

The following concepts will be introduced in this tutorial:

1 **Spell Checking**   The spell checking feature locates misspelled words, duplicate words, and capitalization irregularities in the active worksheet and proposes the correct spelling.

2 **Absolute References**   An absolute reference is a cell or range reference in a formula whose location does not change when the formula is copied.

3 **Styles**   A style consists of a combination of formats that have been named and that can be quickly applied to a selection.

4 **Sheet Names**   Each sheet in a workbook can be assigned a descriptive name to identify the contents of the sheet.

5 **AutoFill**   The AutoFill feature makes entering long or complicated headings easier by logically repeating and extending the series.

6 **Sheet and 3-D References**   A formula containing sheet and 3-D references to cells in different worksheets in a workbook allows you to use data from other worksheets and to calculate new values based on this data.

7 **Split Windows**   A sheet window can be split into sections called panes to make it easier to view different parts of the sheet at the same time.

8 **Freeze Panes**   Freezing panes prevents the data in the panes from scrolling as you move to different areas in the worksheet.

9 **What-If Analysis**   What-if analysis is a technique used to evaluate the effects of changing selected factors in a worksheet.

10 **Goal Seek**   Goal Seek is a tool that is used to find the value needed in one cell to attain a result you want in another cell.

Spell Checking a Sheet

Evan, the owner of the Café, has made several changes to the first quarter forecast file. To see the file with these changes,

1 ■ Load Excel.

■ Open the worksheet file First Quarter Forecast.

Your screen should be similar to Figure 3–1.

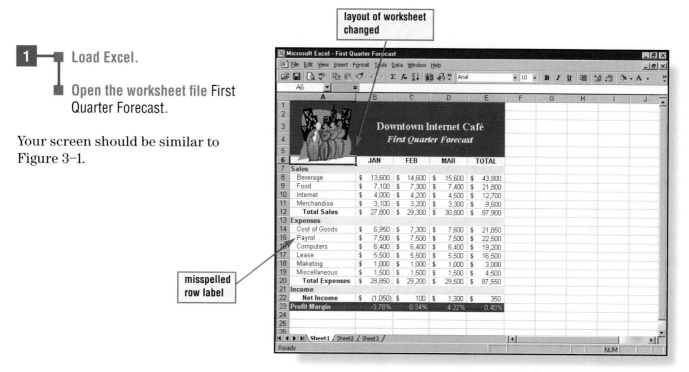

Figure 3–1

The owner changed the layout of the worksheet by moving the graphic into the title area. Additionally, several changes were made to the row labels. For example, the Salary label has been replaced with Payroll. However, the new label is misspelled. Just to make sure there are no other spelling errors, you will check the spelling of all text entries in this worksheet.

Concept ① Spell Checking

The **spell checking** feature locates misspelled words, duplicate words, and capitalization irregularities in the active worksheet and proposes the correct spelling. This feature works by comparing each word to a dictionary of words. If the word does not appear in the main dictionary or in a custom dictionary, it is identified as misspelled. The **main dictionary** is supplied with the program; a **custom dictionary** is one you can create to hold words you commonly use but that are not included in the main dictionary.

When you check spelling in Excel, the spell checking feature checks the entire active worksheet including cell values, text boxes, headers and footers, and text in embedded charts. It does not check spelling in formulas or text that results from formulas. You can also restrict the area to be checked by first selecting a range. If the formula bar is active when you check spelling, only the contents of the formula bar are checked.

Excel also includes an AutoCorrect feature that corrects typing errors automatically as you type by comparing each completed word to a list of commonly mistyped words and phrases. You can also add words and phrases you commonly mistype to the list and they will be corrected automatically as you type.

If you have Microsoft Office 2000, the spelling dictionary and listing of AutoCorrect entries is shared with the other Office applications.

Excel begins checking all worksheet entries from the active cell forward. To check the spelling in the worksheet,

2 ■ Click  Spelling.

> The menu equivalent is **T**ools/**S**pelling and the keyboard shortcut is F7 .

Your screen should be similar to Figure 3–2.

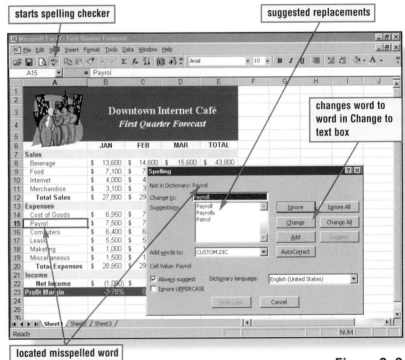

Figure 3–2

Excel 2000 immediately begins checking the worksheet for words that it cannot locate in its main dictionary. The cell selector moves to the first cell containing a misspelled word and the Spelling dialog box is displayed. The word it cannot locate in the dictionary is displayed in the first line of the dialog box. The Change to text box displays the suggested replacement. A list of other possible replacements is displayed in the Suggestions list box. If the Change to replacement is not correct, you can select from the suggestions list or type the correct word in the Change to text box.

The option buttons shown in the table below have the following effects:

Option	Effect
Ignore	Leaves selected word unchanged
Ignore All	Leaves this word and all identical words in worksheet unchanged
Change	Changes selected word to word displayed in Change to text box
Change All	Changes this word and all identical words in worksheet to word displayed in Change to text box
Add	Adds selected word to a custom dictionary so Excel will not question this word during subsequent spell checks
Suggest	Turns on the display of proposed alternatives for a misspelled word
AutoCorrect	Adds a word to the AutoCorrect list so the word will be corrected as you type

To accept the suggested replacement,

 **3** ─■ Click **Change** .

The correction is made in the worksheet, and the program continues checking the worksheet and locates another error, "Maketing."

 **4** ─■ Change this word to Marketing.

The program continues checking the worksheet. When it reaches the end of the sheet, because the cell selector was not at the beginning of the sheet when checking started, the program asks if you want to continue checking at the beginning of the sheet.

5 ─■ Click **Yes**

The program continues checking the worksheet and does not locate any other errors. A dialog box is displayed, informing you that the entire worksheet has been checked. To end spell checking,

 **6** ─■ Click **OK** .

Using Paste Function

Next you need to add a column showing the average values for the first quarter.

1 Enter the heading **AVG** in cell F6.

Move to F8.

Notice the new heading is already appropriately formatted to bold and centered. This is because Excel automatically extends formats to new cells if the format of at least three of the last five preceding columns appears that way.

You could enter a function in cell F8 to calculate the average beverage sales. However, another way is to use the Paste Function feature. This feature simplifies entering functions by prompting you to select a function from a list and then helps you enter the arguments correctly.

2 Click  Paste Function.

> The menu equivalent is Insert/Function and the keyboard shortcut is ⟨⇧ Shift⟩ + ⟨F3⟩.

Your screen should be similar to Figure 3–3.

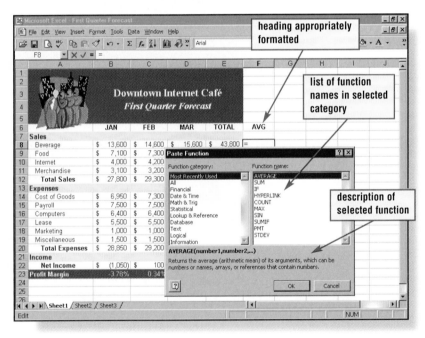

Figure 3–3

> The Most Recently Used function category initially displays 10 of the most common functions.

First you select the type of function you want to use. The Function Category list box displays the names of the function categories, and the Function Name list box displays the names of the functions in the selected category. The currently selected category is Most Recently Used. This category displays the names of the last 10 functions used.

3 ■ Select AVERAGE from the Function Name list box.

> If Average is not displayed in the list box, select it from the Statistical category.

■ Click [OK] .

Your screen should be similar to Figure 3–4.

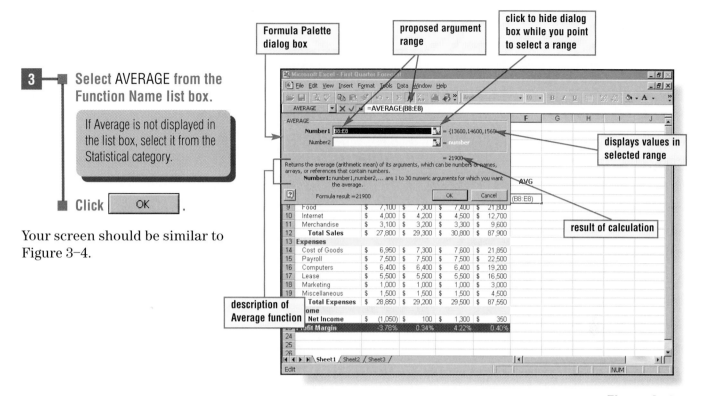

Figure 3–4

> You can also display the Formula Palette by clicking [=] Edit Formula in the Formula bar.

Additional Information

When the Formula Palette is open, the name box changes to a drop-down function list, allowing you to change the selected type of function.

Next, the Formula Palette dialog box is displayed to help you enter the arguments required for the selected function. The upper section displays the proposed argument range in the Number1 text box. Also notice the actual numbers in the selected range are displayed to the right of the textbox.

The lower section describes the Average function and what the function requires for arguments. The proposed argument range (B8:E8) is incorrect because it includes the value in the Total column, cell E8. You need to specify the correct range (B8:D8) in the Number1 text box. The numbers or the cell references containing the numbers can be entered in the text box directly, or can be entered by selecting the cell or range from the worksheet. Selecting the range is usually faster, and it avoids the accidental entry of incorrect references. To select the range B8 through D8 from the worksheet,

4 ■ Click the 📑 at the end of the Number1 text box.

■ Select B8 through D8.

Your screen should be similar to Figure 3–5.

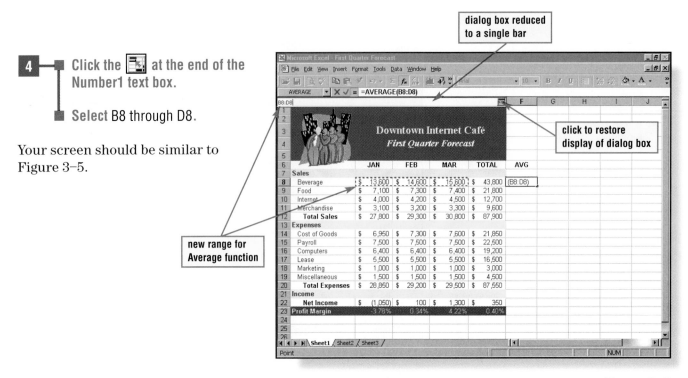

Figure 3–5

The dialog box is reduced to a single bar to allow easy access to the worksheet. The new range appears in the formula bar and the cell, as well as in the Formula Palette dialog box bar. To redisplay the dialog box and complete the function,

5 ■ Click 📑.

You can also press ⏎Enter to redisplay the dialog box.

■ Click ⬛ OK ⬛.

Your screen should be similar to Figure 3–6.

Figure 3–6

The average of the beverage sales for the quarter, 14,600, is calculated and displayed in cell F8. Notice that Excel again extended the format to the new cell, saving you the step of applying the Accounting format.

Using the Fill Handle to Delete Cell Contents

Next you need to copy the function down column F.

1 Copy the function into cells F9 through F22.

Your screen should be similar to Figure 3-7.

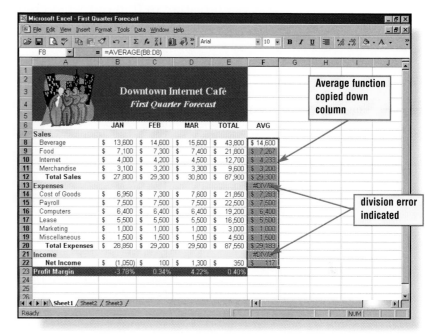

Figure 3-7

The average value has been correctly calculated for each row. Notice, however, that two cells display #DIV/0!. This indicates a division error occurred because the formula divides by zero. You will clear the formulas from these cells using the fill handle.

2 Move to cell F13.

Point to the fill handle and when the mouse pointer changes to **+**, drag upward until the cell is gray.

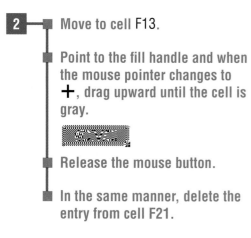

Release the mouse button.

In the same manner, delete the entry from cell F21.

Your screen should be similar to Figure 3-8.

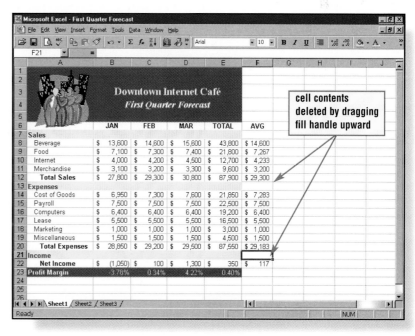

Figure 3-8

To avoid unintentionally deleting cell contents when using the fill handle, drag the fill handle out of the selected area before releasing.

Using Absolute References

While looking at the sales data in the worksheet, you decide it may be interesting to find out what contribution each sales item makes to total sales. To find out, you will enter a formula to calculate the proportion of sales by each in column G. The formula to calculate the proportion for beverage sales is Total Beverage Sales/Total Sales.

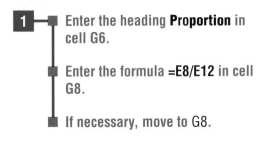

1 ■ Enter the heading **Proportion** in cell G6.

■ Enter the formula **=E8/E12** in cell G8.

■ If necessary, move to G8.

Your screen should be similar to Figure 3–9.

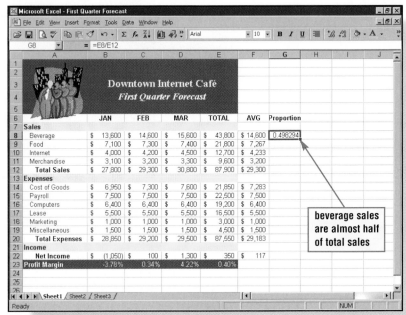

Figure 3–9

The value 0.498294 is displayed in cell G8. This shows that the beverage sales are approximately 50 percent of total sales.

Next, to calculate the proportion for Food Sales, you will copy the formula from G8 to G9. Another quick way to copy cell contents is to drag the cell border while holding down Ctrl. This method is most useful when the distance between cells is short and they are both visible in the window. It cannot be used if you are copying to a larger range than the source range.

2 ■ Point to the border of cell G8 and when the mouse pointer shape is ⌖ , hold down Ctrl and drag the mouse pointer to cell G9. Release the mouse button before releasing Ctrl.

Your screen should be similar to Figure 3–10.

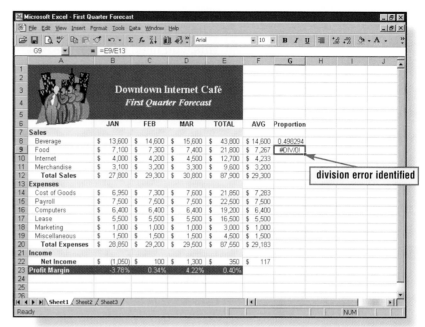

Figure 3–10

You see a #DIV/0! error is displayed in cell G9. To check the formula in that cell,

3 ■ Double-click cell G9.

Your screen should be similar to Figure 3–11.

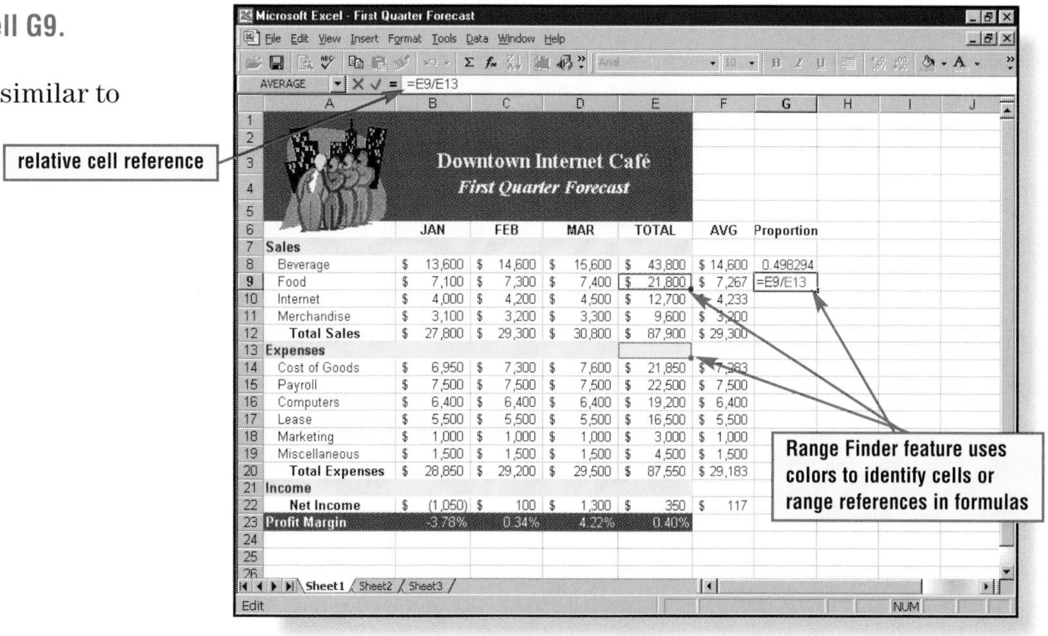

Figure 3–11

Notice that the cell references in the formula are color coded to match the borders Excel displays around the referenced worksheet cells. This is Excel's Range Finder feature. It is designed to provide visual cues to the relationships between the cells that provide values to the formulas or the cells that depend on the formulas. You can now see the error occurred because the relative reference to cell E12 adjusted correctly to the new location when the formula was copied and now references cell E13, a blank cell.

The formula in G8 needs to be entered so that the reference to the Total Sales value in cell E12 does not change when the formula is copied. To do this, you need to make the cell reference absolute.

Concept ② Absolute References

An **absolute reference** is a cell or range reference in a formula whose location does not change when the formula is copied.

To stop the relative adjustment of cell references, enter a $ (dollar sign) character before the column letter and row number. This changes the cell reference to absolute. When a formula containing an absolute cell reference is copied to another row and column location in the worksheet, the cell reference does not change. It is an exact duplicate of the cell reference in the original formula.

A cell reference can also be a **mixed reference**. In this type of reference, either the column letter or the row number is preceded with the $. This makes only the row or column absolute. When a formula containing a mixed cell reference is copied to another location in the worksheet, only the part of the cell reference that is not absolute changes relative to its new location in the worksheet.

The table below shows examples of relative and absolute references and the results when a reference in cell G8 to cell E8 is copied to cell H9.

Cell Contents of G8	Copied to Cell H9	Type of Reference
$E$8	$E$8	Absolute reference
E$8	F$8	Mixed reference (absolute row, relative column)
$E8	$E9	Mixed reference (absolute columns, relative row)
E8	F9	Relative reference

You will change the formula in cell G8 to include an absolute reference for cell E12. Then you will copy the formula to cells G9 through G11.

You can change a cell reference to absolute or mixed by typing in the dollar sign directly or by using the ABS (Absolute) key, F4. To use the ABS key, the program must be in the Edit mode and the cell reference that you want to change must be selected.

4 ■ Press (Esc) to exit from edit mode.

■ Move to G8.

■ Click on the reference to E12 in the formula bar to enter Edit mode and select the reference.

■ Press (F4).

Your screen should be similar to Figure 3-12.

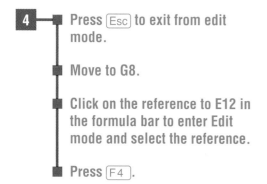

Figure 3-12

The cell reference now displays $ characters before the column letter and row number, making this cell reference absolute. If you continue to press (F4), the cell reference will cycle through all possible combinations of cell reference types. Leaving the cell reference absolute, as it is now, will stop the relative adjustment of the cell reference when you copy it again.

5 ■ Click [✓].

■ Copy the revised formula to cells G9 through G11.

■ Move to cell G9.

Your screen should be similar to Figure 3-13.

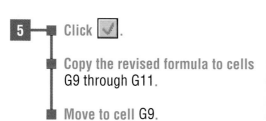

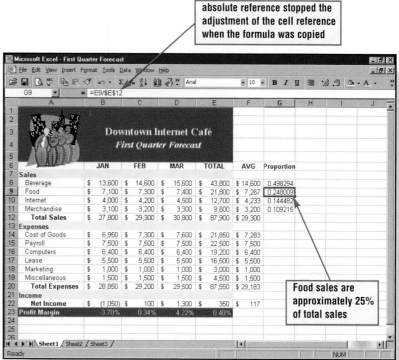

Figure 3-13

The formula has correctly adjusted the relative cell reference to Food sales in cell E9 and not adjusted the reference to E12 because it is an absolute reference.

6 ■ Move to cells G10 and G11 and confirm that the formulas were adjusted appropriately.

Applying Styles

Next you want to format the proportion values in cells G8 through G11 to display as a percent. You could apply the Percent format using the Format/Cells menu command as you did in Tutorial 1. Another way, however, is to select a predefined format style.

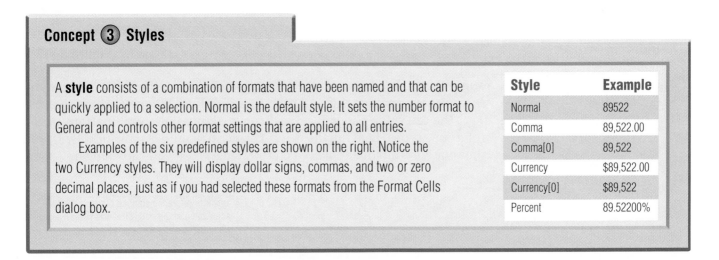

Concept ③ Styles

A **style** consists of a combination of formats that have been named and that can be quickly applied to a selection. Normal is the default style. It sets the number format to General and controls other format settings that are applied to all entries.

Examples of the six predefined styles are shown on the right. Notice the two Currency styles. They will display dollar signs, commas, and two or zero decimal places, just as if you had selected these formats from the Format Cells dialog box.

Style	Example
Normal	89522
Comma	89,522.00
Comma[0]	89,522
Currency	$89,522.00
Currency[0]	$89,522
Percent	89.52200%

1 ■ Select G8 through G11.

■ Choose Format/Style.

Your screen should be similar to Figure 3–14.

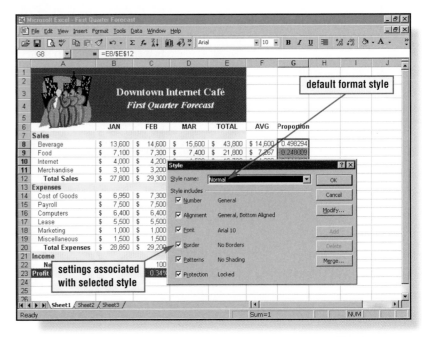

Figure 3–14

The Style dialog box displays the name of the default worksheet style, Normal, in the Style Name list box. The check boxes in the Style Includes area of the dialog box show the options that are included in this style and a description or sample. You want to use the Percent style.

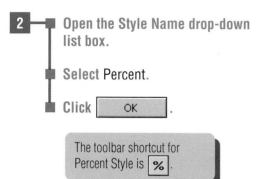

2 ● Open the Style Name drop-down list box.

● Select Percent.

● Click [OK].

The toolbar shortcut for Percent Style is [%].

Your screen should be similar to Figure 3–15.

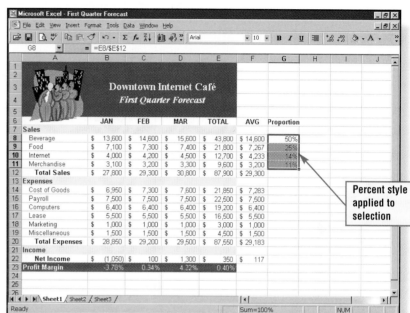

Percent style applied to selection

Figure 3–15

Additional Information

You can also quickly apply the Accounting format by selecting the Currency style or [$].

The Percent style setting automatically displays the value as a percent with no decimal places. To make the percentage more accurate, you will increase the decimal place setting to 2.

3 ● Click [.00] Increase Decimal twice.

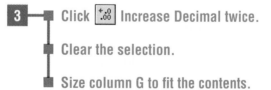

● Clear the selection.

● Size column G to fit the contents.

The calculated proportion shows the same values that a pie chart of this data would show.

Copying a Sheet

Next you want to add the second quarter forecast to the workbook. You want this data in a separate sheet in the same workbook file. To make it easier to enter the forecast for the next quarter, you will copy the contents of the first quarter forecast in Sheet1 into another sheet in the workbook. Then you will change the month headings, the title, and the number data. Although the workbook already includes two extra blank sheets, if you pasted the data into an existing sheet, the column width settings would not be copied and you would need to reset the widths. To retain column widths and to duplicate an existing sheet with all its formats, you need to create a new sheet.

To copy the active sheet into a new sheet, you hold down Ctrl while dragging the sheet tab to where you want the new sheet inserted. The mouse pointer changes to a 🏷 as you drag the mouse from one tab to another. The + indicates that the sheet is being copied. A black triangle ▼ also appears, indicating where the sheet will be inserted.

1 ■ Hold down Ctrl and click on the Sheet1 tab.

■ When the mouse pointer is a 🏷, drag the Sheet1 tab to the Sheet2 tab.

> The ▼ appears at the right side of the Sheet1 tab.

■ Release the mouse button and then release Ctrl.

Your screen should be similar to Figure 3–16.

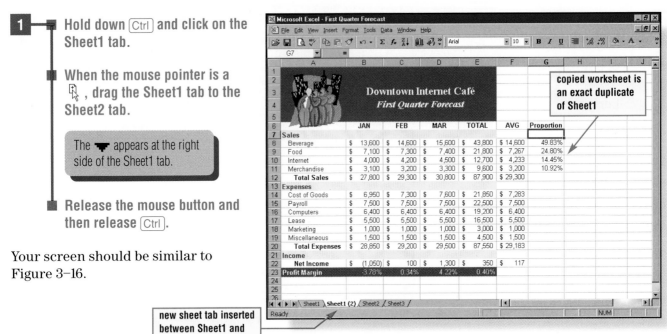

new sheet tab inserted between Sheet1 and Sheet 2

Figure 3–16

Excel 2000 names the copy of the sheet Sheet1(2) and inserts it before Sheet2. The new sheet is the active sheet and contains a duplicate of the first quarter budget in Sheet1.

Naming Sheets

As more sheets are added to a workbook, remembering what information is in each sheet becomes more difficult. To help clarify the contents of the sheets, you can rename the sheets.

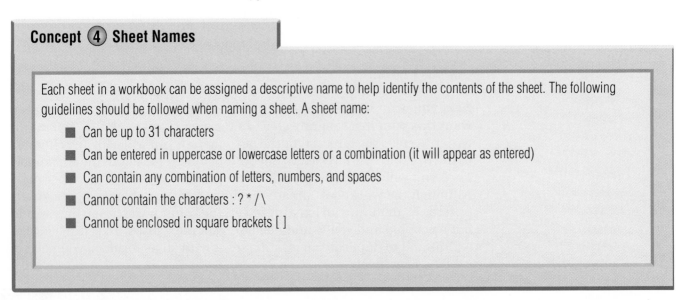

Concept ④ Sheet Names

Each sheet in a workbook can be assigned a descriptive name to help identify the contents of the sheet. The following guidelines should be followed when naming a sheet. A sheet name:

■ Can be up to 31 characters

■ Can be entered in uppercase or lowercase letters or a combination (it will appear as entered)

■ Can contain any combination of letters, numbers, and spaces

■ Cannot contain the characters : ? * / \

■ Cannot be enclosed in square brackets [ ]

Double-clicking the sheet tab activates the tab and highlights the existing sheet name. The existing name is cleared as soon as you begin to type the new name. You will change the name of Sheet1 to First Quarter and Sheet1(2) to Second Quarter.

1
- Double-click the Sheet1 tab.

- Type **First Quarter**.

- Press ←Enter.

- Change the name of the Sheet1(2) tab to **Second Quarter**.

> The menu equivalent is **F**ormat/S**h**eet/**R**ename.

Your screen should be similar to Figure 3–17.

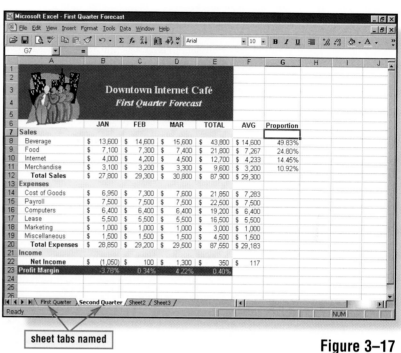

sheet tabs named

Figure 3–17

Using AutoFill

Now you can change the worksheet title and data in the second quarter sheet.

1
- Change the title in cell B4 to **Second Quarter Forecast**.

- Change the month heading in cell B6 to **APR**.

Now you need to change the remaining month headings to MAY and JUN. You will use the AutoFill feature to enter the month headings.

Concept ⑤ AutoFill

The **AutoFill** feature makes entering a series of headings easier by logically repeating and extending the series. AutoFill recognizes trends and automatically extends data and alphanumeric headings as far as you specify.

Dragging the fill handle activates the AutoFill feature if Excel recognizes the entry in the cell as an entry that can be incremented. When AutoFill extends the entries, it uses the same style as the original entry. For example, if you enter the heading for July as JUL (abbreviated with all letters uppercase), all the extended entries in the series will be abbreviated and uppercase. Dragging down or right increments in increasing order, and up or left increments in decreasing order. A linear series increases or decreases values by a constant value, and a growth series multiplies values by a constant factor.

Initial Selection	Extended series
Qtr1	Qtr2, Qtr3, Qtr4
Mon	Tue Wed Thu
Jan, Apr	Jul, Oct, Jan

A starting value of a series may contain more than one item that can be incremented, such as JAN-02, in which both the month and year can increment. If you want only one value to increment, hold down the right mouse button as you drag, and then click the appropriate command on the AutoFill shortcut menu to specify which value to increment.

The entry in cell B6, APR, is the starting value of a series of months.

2 To automatically complete the month entries, drag the fill handle to extend the range from cell B6 through cell D6.

The ScreenTip displays the entry that will appear in each cell as you drag.

Additional Information

If a series is created when you drag the fill handle that you do not want incremented, select the original values again and hold down Ctrl as you drag the fill handle. The entries will be copied, not incremented.

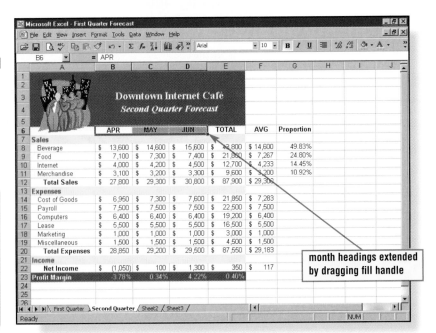

month headings extended by dragging fill handle

Your screen should be similar to Figure 3–18.

Figure 3–18

3 ■ Finally, to update the budget for April through June beverage, food, Internet, and merchandise sales, enter the new numbers as shown in the table below.

Sales	Cell	Number
Beverage	B8	15700
	C8	15800
	D8	15900
Food	B9	7500
	C9	7600
	D9	7600
Internet	B10	4500
	C10	4500
	D10	4500
Merchandise	B11	3200
	C11	3200
	D11	3200

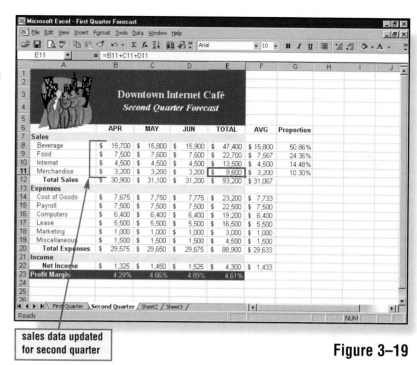

sales data updated for second quarter

Figure 3–19

Your screen should be similar to Figure 3–19.

The worksheet has been recalculated and now contains the data for the second quarter.

Referencing Multiple Sheets

You also want to display a year-to-date income total in cell E24. The formula to make this calculation will sum the total income numbers from First Quarter cell E22 and Second Quarter cell E22. To reference data in another sheet in the same workbook, you enter a formula that references cells in other worksheets.

Concept ⑥ Sheet and 3-D References

A formula that contains references to cells in other sheets of a workbook allows you to use data from multiple sheets and to calculate new values based on this data. The formula contains a **sheet reference** consisting of the name of the sheet, followed by an exclamation point and the cell or range reference. For example, the formula =Sheet2!B17 would display the entry in cell B17 of Sheet2 in the active cell of the current sheet. A formula can be created using references on multiple sheets; for example, =Sheet1!A1+Sheet2!B2. If the sheet name contains nonalphabetic characters, such as a space, the sheet name (or path) must be enclosed in single quotation marks.

The link can also be created by entering a **3-D reference** in a formula. A 3-D reference is a reference to the same cell or range on multiple sheets in the same workbook. A 3-D reference consists of the names of the beginning and ending sheets enclosed in quotes and separated by a colon. This is followed by an exclamation point and the cell or range reference. The cell or range reference is the same on each sheet in the specified sheet range. For example, the formula =SUM(Sheet1:Sheet4!H6:K6) sums the values in the range H6 through K6 of sheets 1 through 4. Any sheets stored between the starting and ending names of the reference are included. If a sheet is inserted or deleted, the range is automatically updated. 3-D references make it easy to analyze data in the same cell or range of cells on multiple worksheets.

3-D reference	Description
=SUM(Sheet1:Sheet4!H6:K6)	Sums the values in cells H6 through K6 in sheets 1, 2, 3, and 4.
=SUM(Sheet1!H6:K6)	Sums the values in cells H6 through K6 in sheet 1.
=SUM(Sheet1:Sheet4!H6)	Sums the values in cell H6 of Sheets 1, 2, 3 and 4.

Just like a formula that references cells within a sheet, a formula that references cells in multiple sheets is automatically recalculated when data in a referenced cell changes.

You will enter a 3-D reference formula in cell E24 and a descriptive text entry in cell D24.

1 ■ In cell D24 enter and right-align the entry **Income Year-To-Date**.

■ Move to E24.

■ Click Σ AutoSum.

The SUM function argument will consist of a 3-D reference to cell E22 in the First and Second Quarter sheets. Although a 3-D reference can be entered by typing it using the proper syntax, it is much easier to enter it by pointing to the cells on the sheets. To enter a 3-D reference, select the cell or range in the beginning sheet and then hold down Shift and click on the sheet tab of the last sheet in the range. This will include the indicated cell range on all sheets between and including the first and last sheet specified.

2 ■ **Click cell E22.**

■ **Hold down** (⇧Shift) **and click the First Quarter tab.**

■ **Release** (⇧Shift).

■ **Press** (←Enter).

■ **Move to E24.**

Your screen should be similar to Figure 3–20.

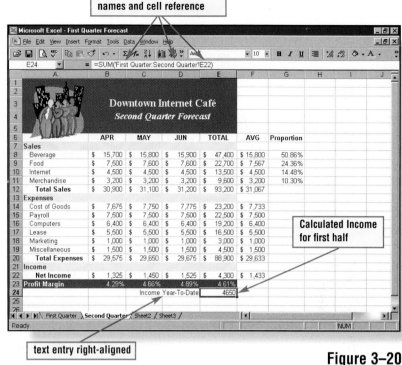

3-D reference includes sheet names and cell reference

Calculated Income for first half

text entry right-aligned

Figure 3–20

The calculated number 4650 appears in cell E24 and the function containing a 3-D reference appears in the formula bar.

You have now completed the forecast for the first half of the year.

3 ■ **Change the format of cell E24 to Accounting with zero decimal places.**

■ **Save the workbook file as First Half Forecast.**

■ **Enter your name in the workbook file documentation as the author.**

■ **Preview the entire workbook.**

■ **Add a predefined footer containing your name to both sheets.**

■ **Print both worksheets.**

■ **Close the workbook file, saving it again.**

Note: If you are running short on lab time, this is an appropriate place to end this session and begin again at a later time.

Zooming the Worksheet

You presented the completed first and second quarterly forecasts to Evan who now wants you to create worksheets for the third and fourth quarters and a combined annual forecast. Evan also wants you to show a profit margin of 5 percent at the end of the second quarter and 6 percent by the

EXCEL 2000

end of the year. You have already made several of the changes requested and saved them as a workbook file named Annual Forecast.

1 To see the revised and expanded forecast, open the workbook file Annual Forecast.

Your screen should be similar to Figure 3–21.

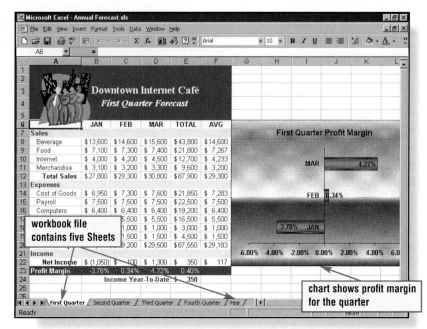

Figure 3–21

The workbook file now contains five sheets: First Quarter, Second Quarter, Third Quarter, Fourth Quarter, and Year. The Year sheet contains the forecast data for the entire 12 months. Each quarter sheet also includes a chart of the profit margin for that quarter. As you can now easily see, the profit margin by the end of the first quarter is showing a profit.

2 Click on each of the Quarter sheet tabs to view the quarterly data and profit margin chart.

Make the Year sheet active.

Your screen should be similar to Figure 3–22.

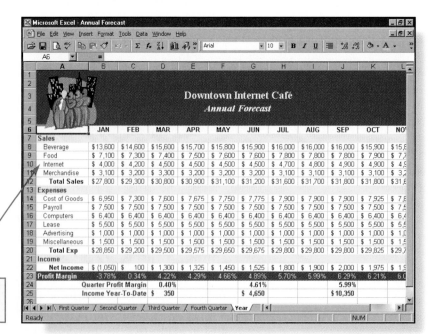

Figure 3–22

The Year sheet displays all of the quarterly data. The entire sheet, however, is not visible in the window. You can change how much information is displayed in the window to make it easier to navigate, view, and select the worksheet data by adjusting the zoom percentage. The default zoom setting is 100 percent. This setting displays data onscreen the same size that it will appear on the printed page. You can reduce or enlarge the amount of information displayed onscreen by changing the magnification from between 10 to 400 percent. You want to decrease the zoom percent to display more information in the window.

The Zoom feature is common in all Office 2000 programs.

3 ■ Open the [100% ▼] Zoom drop-down menu.

The menu equivalent is **V**iew/**Z**oom.

■ Select 75%.

The Selection option adjusts the percentage to fit the selected range in the current window size.

Your screen should be similar to Figure 3–23.

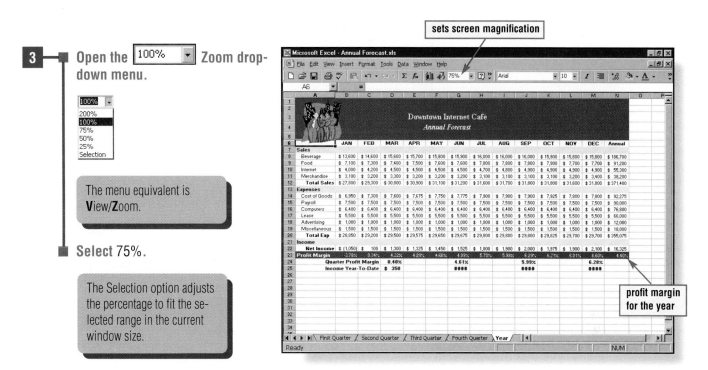

Figure 3–23

You can now see the entire worksheet and note that the total profit margin for the year is 4.4%.

4 ■ Reduce the zoom percent to 50%.

Your screen should be similar to Figure 3–24.

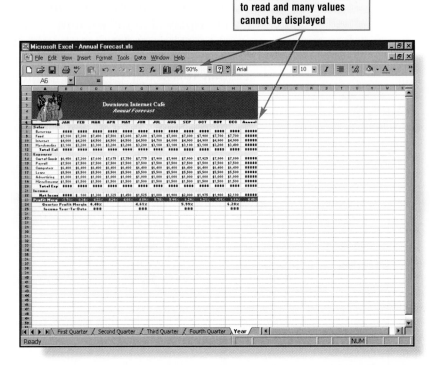

at 50% worksheet is difficult to read and many values cannot be displayed

Figure 3–24

As you reduce the percentage, more worksheet area is visible in the window. However, it gets more difficult to read and many of the values can no longer be displayed.

5 ■ Return the zoom percent back to 100%.

Moving a Sheet

Next you want to move the Annual sheet from the last position in the workbook to the first. You can quickly rearrange sheets in a workbook by dragging the sheet tab to the new location. Just as when copying a sheet, the symbol ▼ indicates where the sheet will appear.

1 Drag the Year tab to the left end of the First Quarter tab.

Your screen should be similar to Figure 3–25.

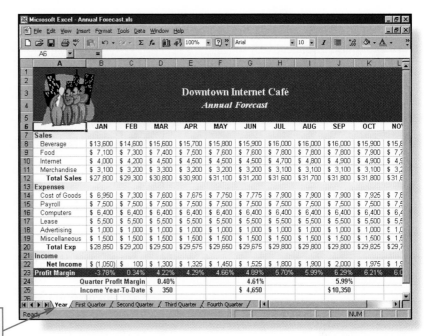

Year sheet moved to beginning of workbook file

Figure 3–25

Splitting Windows

Most of the monthly values in the Year sheet, such as cell B8, contain linking formulas that reference the appropriate cells in the appropriate quarter sheets. Others, such as the total formulas and the formula to calculate the income, do not reference cells outside the Year worksheet.

To see several of the formulas in cells that reference the quarter sheets,

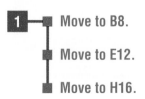

1 Move to B8.

Move to E12.

Move to H16.

Your screen should be similar to Figure 3–26.

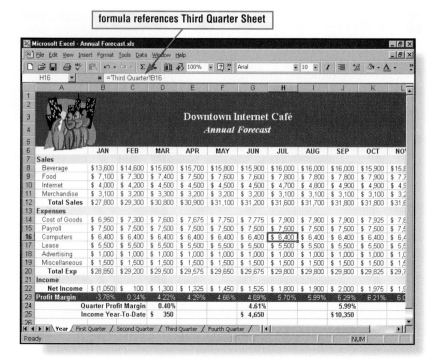

Figure 3–26

Each of these cells contained a formula that referenced a cell in the appropriate quarter sheet. To see the total formulas for the year in column N, you will move to cell N16 using the Goto feature.

2 Press F5.

Type **N16** in the Reference text box.

Click OK.

Your screen should be similar to Figure 3–27.

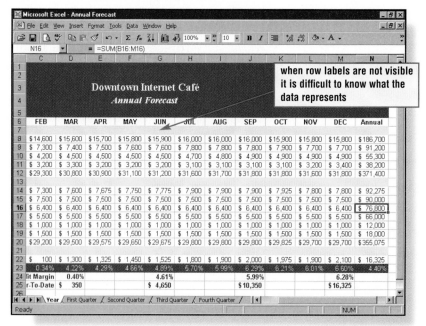

Figure 3–27

The cell pointer is now in cell N16 in the total column. The formula in this cell calculates the total of the values in row 16 and does not reference another sheet. However, it is difficult to know what the numbers represent in this row because the row headings are not visible. For example, is this number the total for the lease expenses, advertising expenses, or miscellaneous expenses? Without scrolling back to see the row headings, it is difficult to know.

Whenever you scroll a large worksheet, you will find that information you may need to view in one area scrolls out of view as you move to another area. Although you could reduce the zoom percent to view more of a worksheet in the window, you still may not be able to see the entire worksheet if it is very large. And as you saw, continuing to reduce the zoom makes the worksheet difficult to read and prevents some values from fully displaying. To view different areas of the same sheet at the same time, you can split the window into panes.

Concept ⑦ Split Windows

A sheet window can be split into sections called **panes** to make it easier to view different parts of the sheet at the same time. The panes can consist of any number of columns or rows along the top or left edge of the window. You can divide the sheet into two panes either horizontally or vertically, or into four panes if you split the window both vertically and horizontally.

Vertical Split	Horizontal Split	Four-Way Split
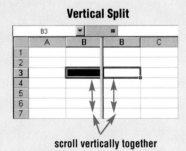	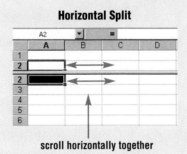	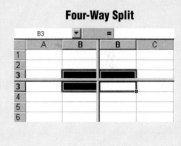
scroll vertically together	scroll horizontally together	

Each pane can be scrolled independently to display different areas of the sheet. When split vertically, the panes scroll together when you scroll vertically, but scroll independently when you scroll horizontally. Horizontal panes scroll together when you scroll horizontally, but independently when you scroll vertically.

Dragging the split box at the top of the vertical scroll bar downward creates a horizontal split, and dragging the split box at the right end of the horizontal scroll bar leftward creates a vertical split. The Window/Split command can be used to quickly create a four-way split at the active cell.

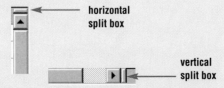

Panes are most useful for viewing a worksheet that consists of different areas or sections. Creating panes allows you to display the different sections of the worksheet in separate panes and then to quickly switch between panes to access the data in the different sections without having to repeatedly scroll to the areas.

You will split the window into two vertical panes. This will allow you to view the titles in column A at the same time as you are viewing data in column N. Pointing to the vertical split box and dragging the split bar to the left creates a vertical pane.

1 ■ Point to the vertical split box in the horizontal scroll bar.

> The mouse pointer changes to a ←‖→ to show you can drag to create a split.

■ Drag to the left and position the bar between columns D and E.

Your screen should be similar to Figure 3–28.

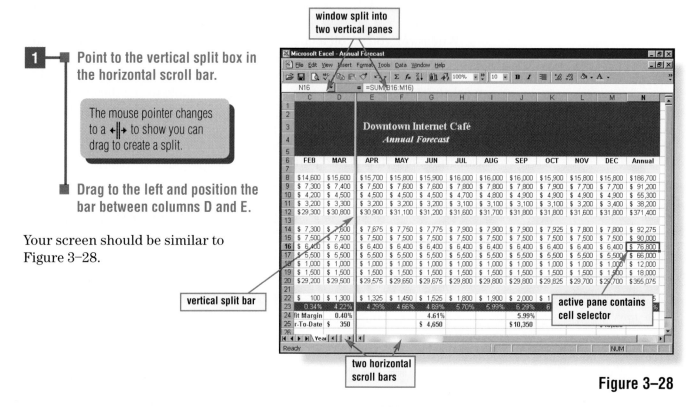

Figure 3–28

There are now two vertical panes with two separate horizontal scroll bars. The highlighted cell selector is visible in the right pane. The left pane also has a cell selector in cell N16, but it is not visible because that area of the worksheet is not displayed in the pane. When the same area of a worksheet is visible in multiple panes, the cell selector in the panes that are not active is highlighted whereas the cell selector in the **active pane** is clear. The active pane will be affected by your movement horizontally. The cell selector moves in both panes, but only the active pane scrolls.

You will scroll the left pane horizontally to display the month headings and then scroll horizontally to display the row headings.

2 ■ Click C16 in the left pane to display the active cell selector in the pane.

■ Press ← twice.

Your screen should be similar to Figure 3–29.

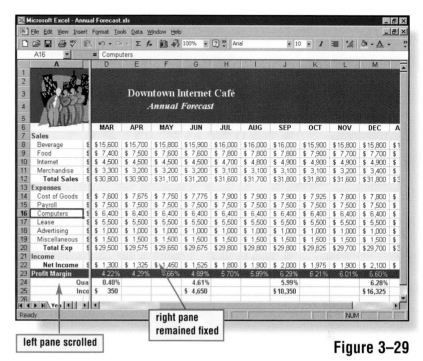

left pane scrolled

right pane remained fixed

Figure 3–29

The right pane did not scroll when you moved horizontally through the left pane to display the row headings. The cell selector in the right pane is in the same cell location as in the left pane (A16), although it is not visible.

3 ■ Drag the split bar to the right three columns.

Now you can see the data for the first quarter. To quickly compare the first quarter data to the last quarter data, you will scroll the right pane.

4 ■ Click cell E16 in the right pane.

■ Press End →.

■ Press → three times.

Your screen should be similar to Figure 3–30.

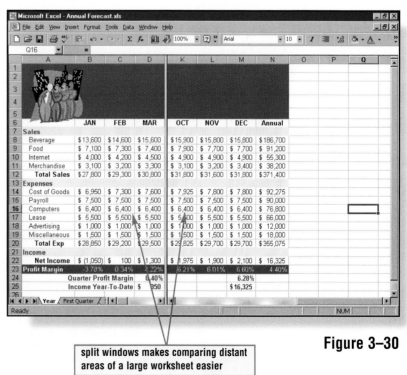

split windows makes comparing distant areas of a large worksheet easier

Figure 3–30

Now the first and last quarter data are side by side. As you can see, creating panes is helpful when you want to display and access distant areas of a worksheet quickly. After scrolling the data in the panes to display the appropriate worksheet area, you can then quickly switch between panes to make changes to the data that is visible in the pane. This saves you the time of scrolling to the area each time you want to view it or make changes to it. To clear the horizontal split from the window,

The menu equivalent is **W**indow/Remove **S**plit.

5 ■ **Double-click anywhere on the split bar.**

Freezing Panes

Another way to manage a large worksheet is to freeze panes.

Concept ⑧ Freeze Panes

Freezing panes prevents the data in the pane from scrolling as you move to different areas in a worksheet. You can freeze the information in the top and left panes of a window only. The Freeze command on the Window menu is used to freeze panes.

To create two horizontal panes with the top pane frozen, move the cell selector in the leftmost column in the window to the row below where you want the split to appear before choosing the command.

Top Pane Frozen

	A	B	C
9	**Total Sales**	$234,000	$224,000
10			
19	**Total Expenses**	$232,080	$225,880
20			
21	*INCOME*	$ 1,920	$ (1,880)
22			

To create two vertical panes with the left pane frozen, move the cell selector in the top row of the window and select the column to the right of where you want the split to appear.

Left Pane Frozen

	A	M	N
9	**Total Sales**	$670,000	$3,883,000
10			
11	*EXPENSES*		
12			
13	Advertising	$ 26,800	$ 155,320
14	Cost of Goods	$388,600	$2,252,140

To create four panes with the top and left panes frozen, click the cell below and to the right of where you want the split to appear.

Top and Left Pane Frozen

	A	E	F
3			
4		**APR**	**MAY**
11	*EXPENSES*		
12			
13	Advertising	$ 9,360	$ 8,960
14	Cost of Goods	$135,720	$129,920

This feature is most useful when your worksheet is organized using row and column headings. It allows you to keep the titles on the top and left edge of your worksheet in view as you scroll horizontally and vertically through the worksheet data.

You want to keep the month headings in row 6 and the row headings in column A visible in the window at all times while looking at the Income and Profit Margin data beginning in row 21. To do this, you will create four panes and freeze the headings in the upper and left panes. When creating frozen panes, first position the sheet in the window to display the information you want to appear in the top and left panes. This is because data in the frozen panes cannot be scrolled like data in regular panes. The worksheet is already positioned appropriately in the window.

1 ■ Move to B7.

■ Choose **W**indow/**F**reeze Panes.

Your screen should be similar to Figure 3–31.

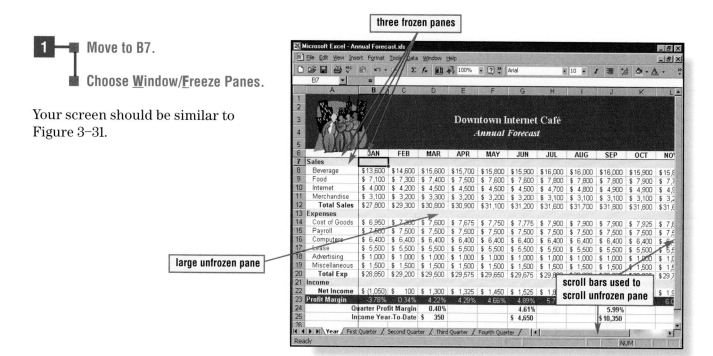

Figure 3–31

The window is divided into four panes at the cell selector location. One set of scroll bars is displayed because the only pane that can be scrolled is the larger lower-right pane. You can move the cell selector into a frozen pane, but the data in the frozen panes will not scroll. Also, there is only one cell selector that moves from one pane to another over the pane divider, making it unnecessary to click on the pane to make it active before moving the cell selector in it.

2 ■ Use the ↓ key to move the cell pointer down column B until row 21 is below row 6.

Your screen should be similar to Figure 3–32.

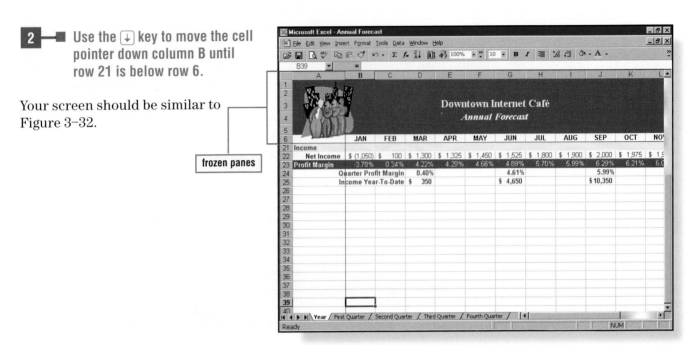

frozen panes

Figure 3–32

Now the only information visible is the title and month headings and Income data. All data in rows 7 through 20 is no longer visible, allowing you to concentrate on the Income area of the worksheet.

The company owner wants you to adjust the forecast for the second quarter to show a profit margin of at least 5 percent for each month.

Using What-If Analysis

To increase the profit margin for the second quarter, you will need to adjust the values in the second quarter sheet.

1 ■ Make the Second Quarter sheet active.

Your screen should be similar to Figure 3–33.

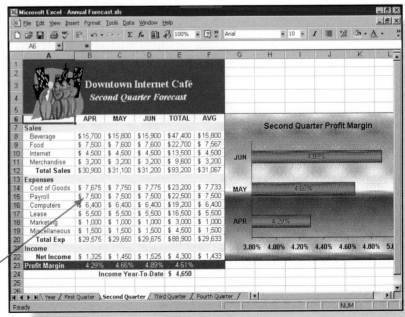

you will reduce payroll expenses to increase the profit margin

Figure 3–33

After some consideration, you decide you can most easily reduce monthly payroll expenses by carefully scheduling employee work during these three months. Reducing the monthly expense will increase the profit margin for the quarter. You want to find out what the maximum payroll value you can spend during that period is for each month to accomplish this goal.

To do this, you will enter different payroll expense values for each month and see what the effect is on that month's profit margin. The process of evaluating what effect reducing the payroll expenses will have on the profit margin is called what-if analysis.

Concept 9 What-If Analysis

What-if analysis is a technique used to evaluate the effects of changing selected factors in a worksheet. This technique is a common accounting function that has been made much easier with the introduction of spreadsheet programs. By substituting different values in cells that are referenced by formulas, you can quickly see the effect of the changes when the formulas are recalculated.

You will adjust the May payroll value first.

2 ── Enter **7300** in cell C15.

Your screen should be similar to Figure 3–34.

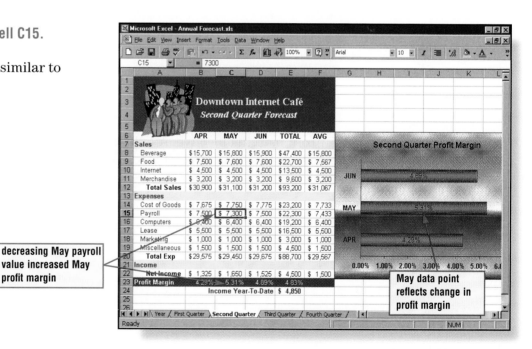

decreasing May payroll value increased May profit margin

May data point reflects change in profit margin

Figure 3–34

Now by looking in cell C23 you can see that decreasing the payroll expenses has increased the profit margin for the month to 5.31 percent. Also notice the chart has changed to reflect the change in May's profit margin. This is more than you need.

3 — Enter **7400** in cell C15.

The profit margin is now 4.98 percent. That's closer—you just need to reduce the payroll value slightly.

4 — Enter **7390** in cell C15.

— Enter **7395** in cell C15.

Your screen should be similar to Figure 3–35.

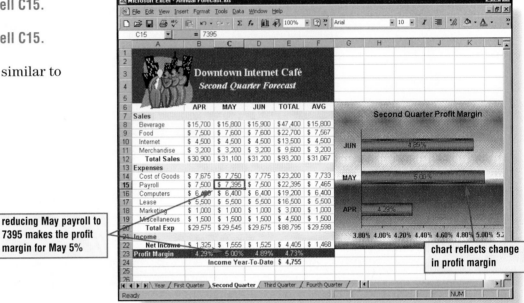

reducing May payroll to 7395 makes the profit margin for May 5%

chart reflects change in profit margin

Figure 3–35

That's it! Reducing the payroll value from 7500 to 7395 will achieve the 5% profit margin goal for the month.

Using Goal Seek

It took you several tries to find the payroll value that would achieve the profit margin objective. A quicker way to find the payroll value that will achieve the desired result is to use the Goal Seek tool.

Concept (10) Goal Seek

The **Goal Seek** tool is used to find the value needed in one cell to attain a result you want in another cell. Goal Seek varies the value in the cell you specify until a formula that is dependent on that cell returns the desired result. The value of only one cell can be changed.

You will use this method to find the payroll value for April that will produce a 5 percent profit margin for that month. The current profit margin value is 4.29 percent in cell B23.

1 Move to B23.

Choose **T**ools/**G**oal Seek.

Your screen should be similar to Figure 3–36.

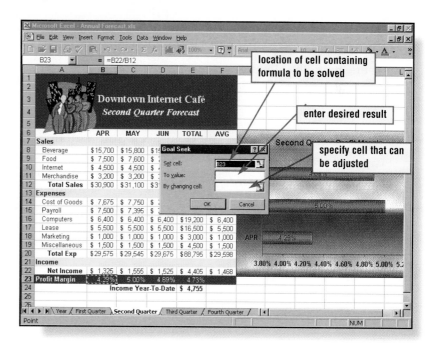

Figure 3–36

In the Goal Seek dialog box, you need to specify the location of the cell containing the formula to be solved, the desired calculated value, and the cell containing the number that can be adjusted to achieve the result. You want the formula in cell B23 to calculate a result of 5 percent by changing the payroll number in cell B15. The Set Cell text box correctly displays the current cell as the location of the formula to be solved. To complete the information needed in the Goal Seek dialog box,

2 ■ Click in the To Value text box and enter the value **5.00%**.

■ Click in the By Changing Cell text box and then click on cell B15 in the worksheet to enter the cell reference to cell B15 in the text box.

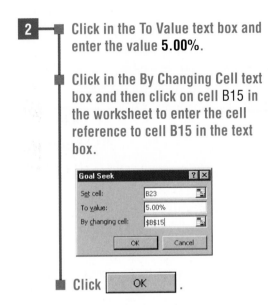

■ Click   OK   .

Your screen should be similar to Figure 3–37.

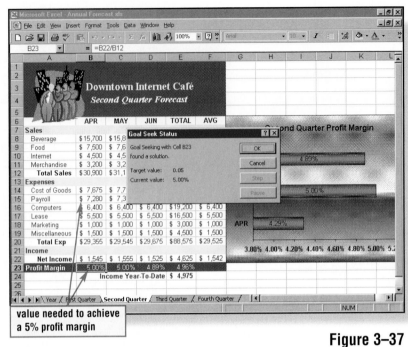

Figure 3–37

The Goal Seek Status dialog box tells you it found a solution that will achieve the 5 percent profit margin. The payroll value of 7280 that will achieve the desired result has been temporarily entered in the worksheet. You can reject the solution and restore the original value by choosing   Cancel   . In this case, however, you want to accept the solution.

3 ─■ Click [OK]

Your screen should be similar to
Figure 3–38.

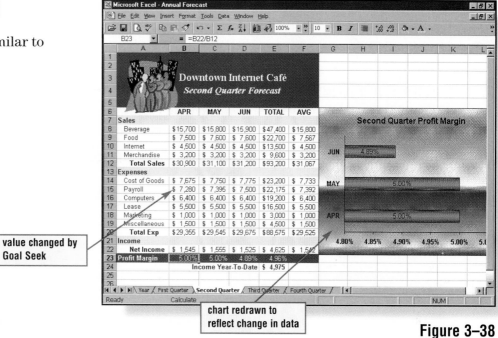

value changed by
Goal Seek

chart redrawn to
reflect change in data

Figure 3–38

The payroll value is permanently updated and the chart redrawn to reflect
the change in profit margin.

Finally, you need to adjust the June payroll value. This time you will
find the value by dragging the June chart data marker to the 5% position
on the chart. As you drag the data marker, a dotted bar line will show the
new bar length and a ChartTip will display the new profit margin value.
An indicator on the X axis also marks your location. Releasing the mouse
button with the bar at the new position specifies the new value and opens
the Goal Seek dialog box.

> The bar is surrounded by eight selection handles.

4 ■ Click on the June data series bar twice (slowly) to select the individual bar.

5 ■ Drag the middle selection handle on the right end of the bar to increase the length of the bar. When the bar ChartTip value is 0.05 or as close as your mouse will allow, release the mouse button.

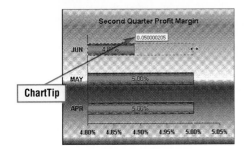

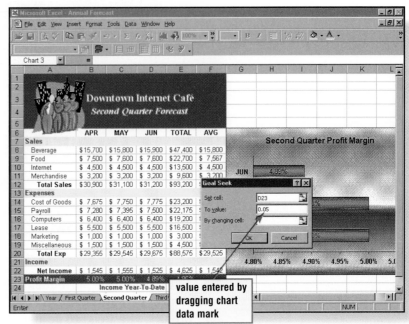

Your screen should be similar to Figure 3–39.

Figure 3–39

Dragging the data marker specifies the value you want to change to and the location of the cell containing the formula. The Goal Seek dialog box is displayed. The Set Cell location and value to attain are entered. Depending on the value you were able to attain by dragging the data mark, you may still need to adjust the value to the exact value of .05. You also need to specify the cell location of the value to change.

6 ■ If necessary, edit the To Value contents to 0.05.

■ Enter cell D15 in the By Changing Cell text box.

■ Click [OK] .

■ Click [OK] to accept the solution.

Your screen should be similar to Figure 3–40.

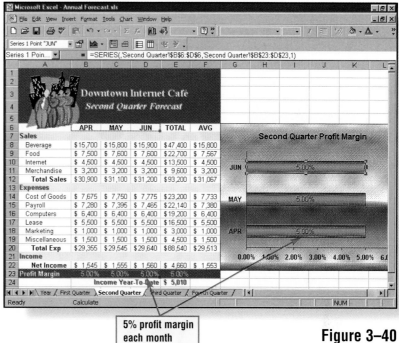

5% profit margin
each month

Figure 3–40

The second quarter values are now at the 5 percent profit margin objective.

7 ■ Make the Year sheet active and verify that the profit margin values for the second quarter have changed.

■ Choose **W**indow/Un**f**reeze Panes.

■ Update the workbook documentation by entering your name as author.

■ Save the revised forecast as **Annual Forecast Revised**.

Changing Page Orientation

Now you are ready to print the workbook. To preview all the sheets in the workbook,

1 ■ **Right-click a sheet tab and select <u>S</u>elect All Sheets from the Shortcut menu.**

The tabs of all sheets appear white indicating they are selected; the active sheet tab name is bold.

■ **Click  Print Preview**

Your screen should be similar to Figure 3–41.

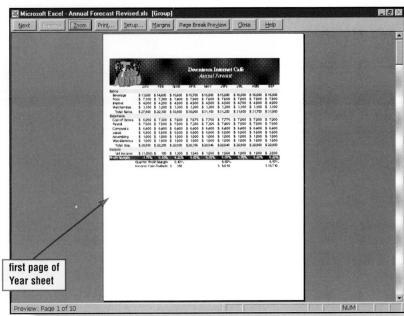

first page of Year sheet

Figure 3–41

The first page of the Year worksheet is displayed in the Preview window. Notice that the entire sheet does not fit across the width of the page. To see the second page,

2 ■ Click Next .

The last three columns of data appear on the second page. Although you could use the Fit To feature to compress the worksheet to a single page, this would make the data small and difficult to read. Instead you can change the orientation or the direction the output is printed on a page. The default orientation is **portrait.** This setting prints across the width of the page. You will change the orientation to **landscape** so that the worksheet prints across the length of the paper. Then you will use the Fit To feature to make sure it fits on one page with the new orientation.

3 ■ Click Previous .

■ Click Setup... .

■ If necessary, open the Page tab.

■ Select Landscape.

■ Select Fit to.

■ Click OK .

Your screen should be similar to Figure 3–42.

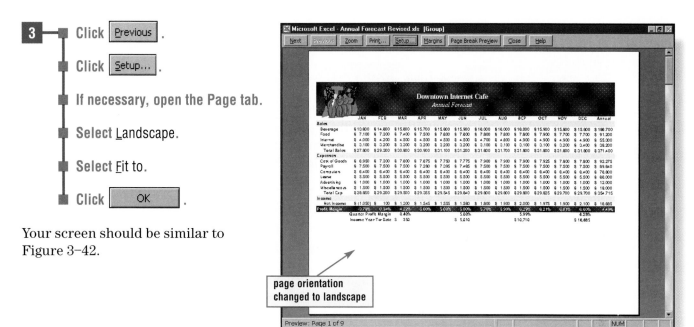

page orientation changed to landscape

Figure 3–42

The entire worksheet now easily fits across the length of the page. Because the worksheet is large, you also feel the worksheet may be easier to read if the row and column gridlines were printed. In addition, you want the worksheet to be centered horizontally on the page. To make these changes,

4 ■ Click Setup... .

■ From the Sheet tab, select **G**ridlines.

■ From the Margins tab, select Hori**z**ontally.

■ Click OK .

Your screen should be similar to Figure 3–43.

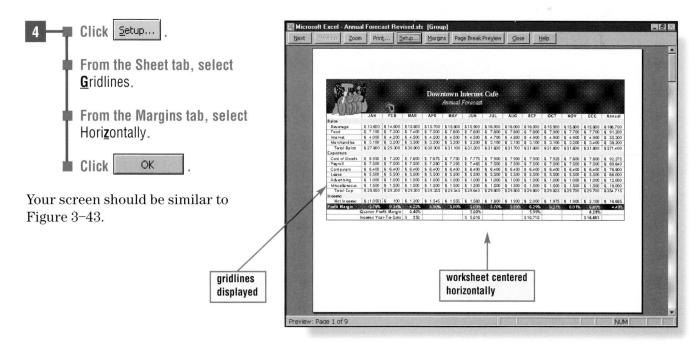

gridlines displayed

worksheet centered horizontally

Figure 3–43

The Preview screen is re-created showing how the sheet will appear centered horizontally and with gridlines.

5 ─■ Click  .

You would also like to change the orientation to landscape for the four quarterly sheets. Rather than change each sheet individually in the Preview window, you can make this change to the four sheets at the same time in the worksheet window.

6 ─■ Click  .

The five sheet tabs are still selected. To deselect the Year sheet and change the orientation to landscape for the four selected sheets,

7 ─■ Hold down Ctrl and click the Year tab.

■ Choose **F**ile/Page Set**u**p

■ Select **L**andscape from the Page tab.

■ Click  .

■ Look at the four sheets.

The four sheets are displayed in landscape orientation in the Preview window. With landscape orientation, there is more white space to the right of the chart. Before printing, you will move the chart slightly away from the worksheet data to make it look more balanced on the page.

Adding Custom Headers and Footers

You would also like to add a custom footer to all the sheets. It is faster to add the footer to all sheets at the same time. If you make changes to the active sheet when multiple sheets are selected, the changes are made to all other selected sheets. These changes may replace data on other sheets.

1

- Click <u>C</u>lose .

- Hold down Ctrl and click the Year sheet tab again to add it to the selection.

- Choose <u>F</u>ile/Page Set<u>u</u>p.

- Open the Header/Footer tab.

- Click Custom Footer... .

Your screen should be similar to Figure 3–44.

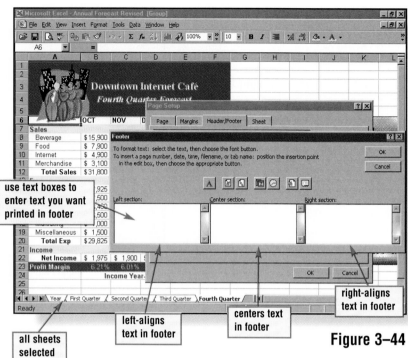

Figure 3–44

The Left Section text box will display the footer text you entered aligned with the left margin, the Center Section will center the text, and the Right Section will right-align the text. The insertion point is currently positioned in the Left Section text box. You want to enter your name, class, and the date in this box. You will enter your name and class by typing it directly in the box. Instead of typing the date, however, you will enter a code that will automatically insert the current date whenever the worksheet is printed. The buttons above the section boxes are used to enter the codes for common header and footer information. They are identified below.

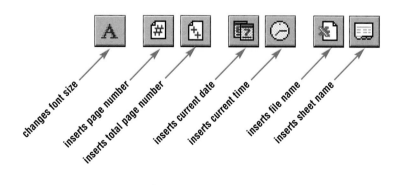

changes font size · inserts page number · inserts total page number · inserts current date · inserts current time · inserts file name · inserts sheet name

2 ■ Type **Created by [your name]**.

■ Press Tab.

■ Enter the name of your class and the section or time.

■ Press Tab.

■ Click Date.

Your screen should be similar to Figure 3–45.

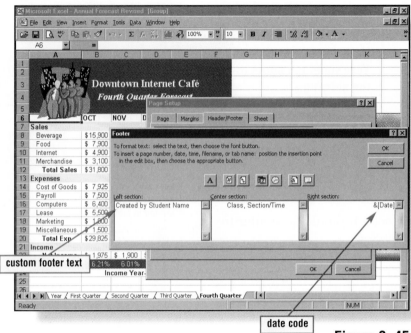

Figure 3–45

3 ■ Click OK.

■ Click Print Preview.

Your screen should be similar to Figure 3–46.

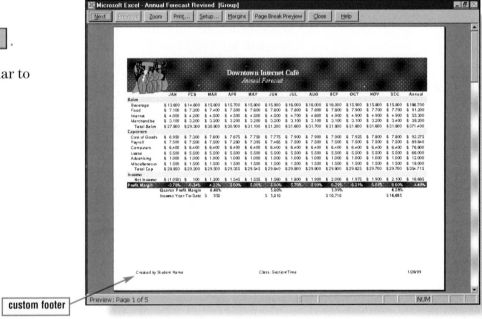

Figure 3–46

The footer as you entered it appears on the preview page for the Year sheet.

4 ■ Look at the other sheets to confirm that the footer was added to them as well.

■ Close the Preview window.

Printing Selected Sheets

You want to print the Year and Second Quarter worksheets only. First you want to adjust the placement of the chart in the Second Quarter sheet. Then you will select the two sheets you want to print.

1 ■ Make the Second Quarter sheet active.

■ Move the chart so that it is evenly balanced between the right edge of the worksheet and the right page break line.

■ Make the Year sheet active and save the file again.

■ Hold down Ctrl and click the Second Quarter Sheet tab to add it to the selection of sheets to print.

■ Click 🖨 Print.

■ Exit Excel.

> If you need to specify print settings that are different from the default settings on your system, use the Print command on the File menu to print the worksheet.

Your printed output should look like that shown in the Case Study at the beginning of this tutorial.

Concept Summary

Tutorial 3: Managing and Analyzing a Workbook

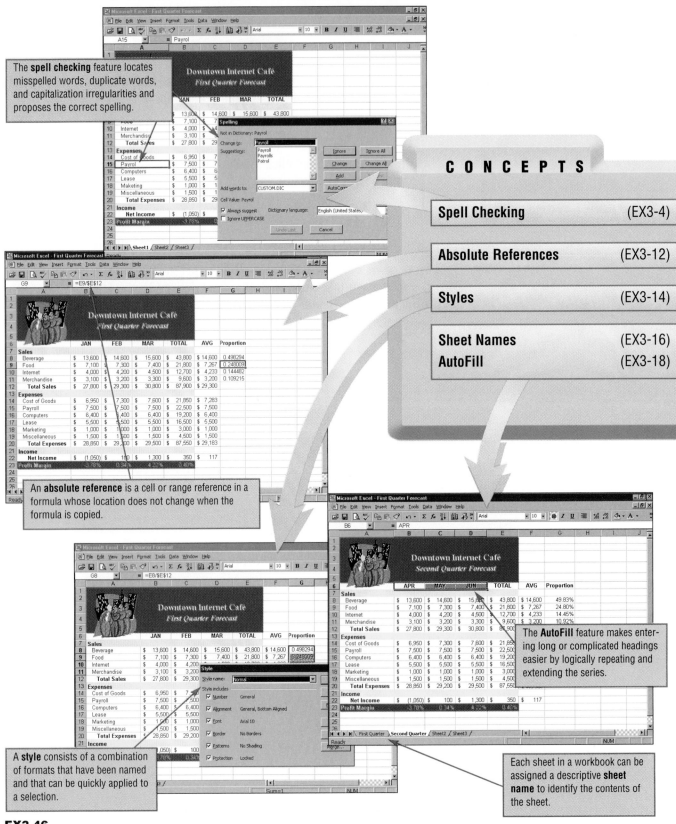

The **spell checking** feature locates misspelled words, duplicate words, and capitalization irregularities and proposes the correct spelling.

CONCEPTS

Spell Checking	(EX3-4)
Absolute References	(EX3-12)
Styles	(EX3-14)
Sheet Names	(EX3-16)
AutoFill	(EX3-18)

An **absolute reference** is a cell or range reference in a formula whose location does not change when the formula is copied.

The **AutoFill** feature makes entering long or complicated headings easier by logically repeating and extending the series.

A **style** consists of a combination of formats that have been named and that can be quickly applied to a selection.

Each sheet in a workbook can be assigned a descriptive **sheet name** to identify the contents of the sheet.

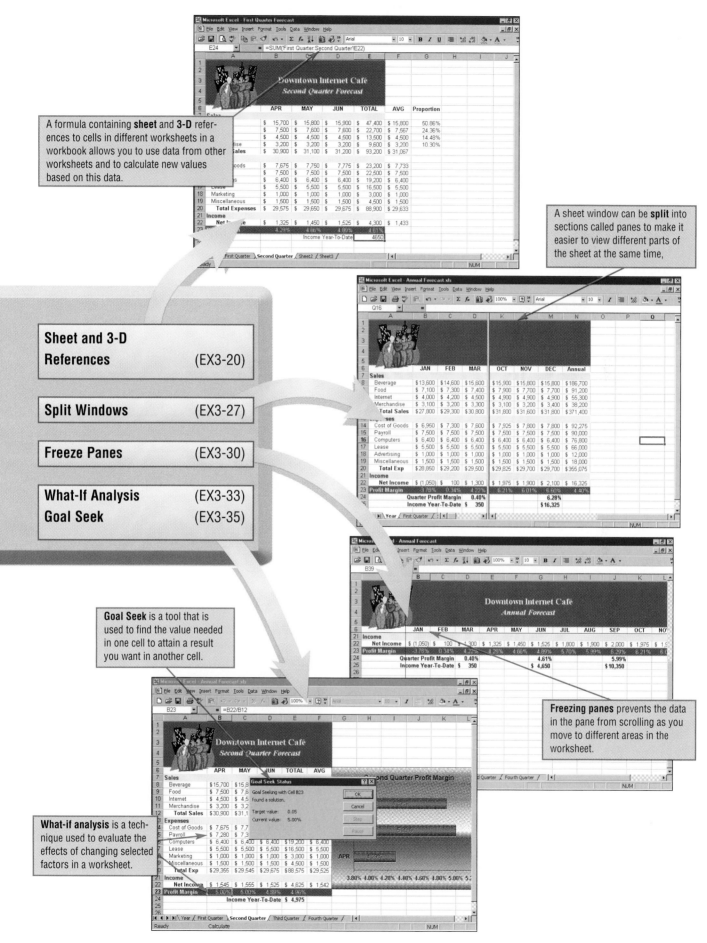

A formula containing **sheet** and **3-D** references to cells in different worksheets in a workbook allows you to use data from other worksheets and to calculate new values based on this data.

A sheet window can be **split** into sections called panes to make it easier to view different parts of the sheet at the same time.

Sheet and 3-D References (EX3-20)

Split Windows (EX3-27)

Freeze Panes (EX3-30)

What-If Analysis (EX3-33)
Goal Seek (EX3-35)

Goal Seek is a tool that is used to find the value needed in one cell to attain a result you want in another cell.

Freezing panes prevents the data in the pane from scrolling as you move to different areas in the worksheet.

What-if analysis is a technique used to evaluate the effects of changing selected factors in a worksheet.

Tutorial Review

Key Terms

3-D reference   EX3-20
absolute reference   EX3-12
active pane   EX3-28
AutoFill   EX3-18
custom dictionary   EX3-4
freeze   EX3-30

Goal Seek   EX3-35
landscape   EX3-40
main dictionary   EX3-4
mixed reference   EX3-12
pane   EX3-27
portrait   EX3-40

sheet reference   EX3-20
spell checking   EX3-4
style   EX3-14
what-if analysis   EX3-33

Command Summary

Command	Shortcut Keys	Button	Action
Edit/**M**ove or Copy Sheet			Moves or copies selected sheet
File/Page Set**u**p/**P**age/**L**andscape			Changes orientation to landscape
Insert/**F**unction	⇧Shift + F3	*f*ₓ	Inserts a function
F**o**rmat/S**h**eet/**R**ename			Renames sheet
F**o**rmat/**S**tyle/**S**tyle name/Currency		$	Applies currency style to selection
F**o**rmat/**S**tyle/**S**tyle name/Percent		%	Changes cell style to display percentage
Tools/**S**pelling	F7	ABC✓	Spell checks worksheet
Tools/**G**oal Seek			Adjusts value in specified cell until a formula dependent on that cell reaches specified result
View/**Z**oom		100% ▾	Changes magnification of window
Window/Un**f**reeze			Unfreezes window panes
Window/**F**reeze Panes			Freezes top and/or leftmost panes
Window/**S**plit			Divides window into four panes at active cell
Window/Remove **S**plit			Removes split bar from active worksheet

Screen Identification

In the following worksheet and chart, several items are identified by letters. Enter the correct term for each item in the space provided.

a. _____

b. _____

c. _____

d. _____

Matching

Match the lettered item on the right with the numbered item on the left.

1. 'Second Quarter'!A13 _____ a. prevents scrolling of information in upper and left panes of a window

2. pane _____ b. spell checks worksheet

3. freeze _____ c. tool to find the value needed in one cell to attain a desired result in another cell

4. F7 _____ d. the sections of a divided window

5. Sheet1:Sheet3!H3:K5 _____ e. sheet reference

6. #DIV/0! _____ f. mixed cell reference

7. landscape _____ g. 3-D reference

8. $M$34 _____ h. indicates division by zero error

9. Goal Seek _____ i. prints across the length of the paper

10. $B12 _____ j. absolute cell reference

Fill-In Questions

Complete the following statements by filling in the blanks with the correct terms.

1. Excel checks spelling by comparing text entries to words in a(n) _____.

2. You can create a _____ dictionary to hold words you use that are not included in the main dictionary.

3. A worksheet window can be divided into four _____.

4. A(n) _____ reference is a cell or range reference in a formula whose location does not change when the formula is copied.

5. _____ _____ varies the value in a specified cell until a formula that is dependent on that cell returns a desired result.

6. _____ panes prevents the data in the pane from scrolling as you move to different areas in a worksheet.

7. _____ analysis is a technique used to evaluate the effects of changing selected factors in a worksheet.

8. When a window is split, the _____ pane is affected by your movements.

9. Use _____ to make entering long or complicated headings easier by logically repeating and extending the series.

10. Use a _____ formula to perform a calculation using data from multiple sheets.

Multiple Choice

Circle the correct response to the questions below.

1. The spell checking feature locates:

   a. misspelled words

   b. duplicate words

   c. capitalization irregularities

   d. all of the above

2. The cell reference to adjust row 4 without adjusting column C is:

   a. $C$4

   b. C4

   c. $C4

   d. C$4

3. The number 32534 displayed with the Currency[0] style would appear as _____ in a cell.

   a. 32,534

   b. $32534

   c. $32,534

   d. $32,534.00

4. Each sheet in a workbook can be assigned a descriptive name called a:

   a. sheet name

   b. reference name

   c. content name

   d. label name

5. A _____ consists of a combination of formats that have been named and that can be quickly applied to a selection.

   a. copy reference

   b. relative reference

   c. style

   d. sheet

6. A _____ reference is a reference to the same cell or range on multiple sheets in the same workbook.

   a. copied

   b. 3-D

   c. sheet

   d. workbook

7. To make it easier to view different parts of the sheet at the same time, a sheet window can be split into _____.

   a. windows

   b. parts

   c. panes

   d. sections

8. The information in the worksheet can be _____ in the top and left panes of a window only.

   a. frozen

   b. fixed

   c. aligned

   d. adjusted

9. A common accounting function that helps evaluate data by allowing the user to adjust values to see the effect is called:

   a. auto calculate

   b. what-if analysis

   c. auto fill

   d. value analysis

10. The _____ tool is used to find the value needed in one cell to attain a result you want in another cell.

    a. AutoFill

    b. function

    c. value analysis

    d. Goal Seek

True/False

Circle the correct answer to the following questions.

1.	The main dictionary supplied with the program allows the user to add words.	True	False
2.	An absolute reference is a cell or range reference in a formula whose location does not change when the formula is copied.	True	False
3.	A style consists of a combination of formats that have been named and that can be quickly applied to a selection.	True	False
4.	A sheet name can be up to 255 characters in length.	True	False
5.	Dragging the fill handle activates the AutoFill feature if Excel recognizes the entry in the cell as an entry that can be incremented.	True	False
6.	The sheet reference consists of the name of the sheet separated from the cell reference by an exclamation point.	True	False
7.	When split horizontally, the panes scroll together when you scroll vertically.	True	False
8.	To create two horizontal panes with the left pane frozen, move the cell selector in the top row of the window and select the column to the left of where you want the split to appear.	True	False
9.	What-if analysis is a technique used to evaluate the effects of changing selected factors in a worksheet.	True	False
10.	Goal Seek varies the value in the cell you specify until a formula that is dependent on that cell returns the desired result.	True	False

Discussion Questions

1. Define, compare, and contrast relative references, sheet references, and 3-D references. Provide a brief example of each.

2. Discuss how absolute and mixed cell references can be used in a worksheet. What is an advantage of using these types of references over a relative cell reference?

3. Discuss the differences between splitting a window and freezing a window. When would it be appropriate to split a window? When would it be appropriate to freeze a window?

4. Discuss the differences between what-if analysis and Goal Seek. Under what conditions would it be more appropriate to use what-if analysis? When would it be more appropriate to use Goal Seek?

Hands-On Practice Exercises

Step by Step

Rating System	☆ Easy
	☆ ☆ Moderate
	☆ ☆ ☆ Difficult

1. John Walsh owns the Gourmet Cookie Shop. He has created a worksheet to record the shop's first quarter sales. John would like you to extend this first quarter sales worksheet to another worksheet that provides a sales forecast for the second quarter. The completed worksheets are shown here.

a. Open the workbook file Gourmet Cookie. Insert a copy of Sheet1 before Sheet2. Rename the Sheet1 tab to **1st Quarter Sales** and then rename Sheet1(2) tab to **2nd Quarter Sales**.

b. In the 2nd Quarter Sales sheet, change the monthly labels to **Apr**, **May**, and **June** using AutoFill.

c. Enter the following projected April sales figures:

Type	Number
Chocolate Chip	1900
Chocolate Chip w/Nuts	1425
White Chocolate Macadamia	1300
Butterscotch	780
Peanut Butter	950
Oatmeal Raisin	350
Gingerbread	525

Student Name
1/11/01

The Gourmet Cookie Shop

Type	Jan	Feb	Mar	Total
Chocolate Chip	$1,000.00	$1,020.00	$1,000.00	$ 3,020.00
Chocolate Chip w/Nuts	$1,430.00	$1,425.00	$1,390.00	$ 4,245.00
White Chocolate Macadamia	$1,220.00	$1,250.00	$1,295.00	$ 3,765.00
Butterscotch	$ 750.00	$ 775.00	$ 800.00	$ 2,325.00
Peanut Butter	$1,000.00	$1,050.00	$ 975.00	$ 3,025.00
Oatmeal Raisin	$ 450.00	$ 375.00	$ 415.00	$ 1,240.00
Gingerbread	$ 530.00	$ 535.00	$ 500.00	$ 1,565.00
Total	*$6,380.00*	*$6,430.00*	*$6,375.00*	*$ 19,185.00*

Student Name
1/11/01

The Gourmet Cookie Shop

Type	Projected Sales			
	Apr	May	Jun	Total
Chocolate Chip	$1,900.00	$2,090.00	$2,403.50	$ 6,393.50
Chocolate Chip w/Nuts	$1,425.00	$1,567.50	$1,802.63	$ 4,795.13
White Chocolate Macadamia	$1,300.00	$1,430.00	$1,644.50	$ 4,374.50
Butterscotch	$ 780.00	$ 858.00	$ 986.70	$ 2,624.70
Peanut Butter	$ 950.00	$1,045.00	$1,201.75	$ 3,196.75
Oatmeal Raisin	$ 350.00	$ 385.00	$ 442.75	$ 1,177.75
Gingerbread	$ 525.00	$ 577.50	$ 664.13	$ 1,766.63
Total	*$7,230.00*	*$7,953.00*	*$9,145.95*	*$ 24,328.95*

Sales Year-To-Date: $ 43,513.95

d. A new advertising campaign for May and June are expected to increase monthly sales. May sales for each type of cookie are expected to be 10 percent more than April sales and June sales are expected to be 15 percent more than May. Enter formulas to calculate May and June sales for chocolate chip cookies and then copy these formulas into the other appropriate cells.

e. Enter and bold the heading **Projected Sales** in cell C2. Center the heading over columns C and D.

f. Enter, bold, italicize, and right-align the heading **Sales Year-To-Date:** in cell D14. In cell E14 enter a formula to calculate the total sales for the first six months by summing cells E11 on both sheets.

g. Make the following changes in both sheets:

   ■ format the numbers to Accounting with two decimal places.

   ■ format the column headings to centered, bold, and underlined.

   ■ format the worksheet title to 14 pt., with a color and font of your choice.

   ■ center the title over the columns of data.

   ■ indent, bold, and italicize the Total row heading.

   ■ bold and italicize the Total row values.

   ■ add a custom header that contains your name and the date right-aligned.

h. Preview the workbook. Save the workbook file as Gourmet Cookie Revised. Print the workbook.

2. Lang's is an office supply company located in the Midwest. Their accountant, Ron, has just completed the budgeted income statement for the first quarter. You are going to use this statement to test the sensitivity of Sales to Net Income. The completed worksheet is shown here.

a. Open the file Lang's Income Statement. Examine the contents of the cells under Jan. You will notice that Sales and Fixed Costs are values while the other entries are formulas. This is also the case for the cells under Feb and Mar.

b. Ron has been told there may be a rent increase beginning in February that will increase fixed costs to 1000. Update the February and March fixed expense values to see the effect of this increase.

Student Name
1/11/01

Lang's Supply Company
Budgeted Income Statement
First Quarter

	Jan	Feb	Mar	Total
Sales	$ 40,000	$ 47,333	$ 50,667	$ 138,000
Costs of Goods Sold	$ 24,000	$ 28,400	$ 30,400	$ 82,800
Gross Profit	$ 16,000	$ 18,933	$ 20,267	$ 55,200
Variable Costs	$ 6,000	$ 7,100	$ 7,600	$ 20,700
Contribution Margin	$ 10,000	$ 11,833	$ 12,667	$ 34,500
Fixed Costs	$ 750	$ 1,000	$ 1,000	$ 2,750
Income Before Taxes	$ 9,250	$ 10,833	$ 11,667	$ 31,750
Income Tax Expense	$ 3,700	$ 4,333	$ 4,667	$ 12,700
Net Income	$ 5,550	$ 6,500	$ 7,000	$ 19,050

c. Next Ron would like to know what level of sales would be necessary to generate a February Net Income of $6500 and March of $7000. Use Goal Seek to answer this question.

d. Add a custom header that contains your name and the date left-aligned. Save the workbook file as Lang's Income Statement Revised. Print the workbook.

3. Parker Brent works for United Can Corp. He is paid $8.50 per hour plus time and a half for overtime. For example, this past Monday Parker worked 10 hours. He earned $68 (8 hours times $8.50 per hour) for regular time plus $25.50 (2 hours times $8.50 per hour times 1.5) for overtime for a total of $93.50. He has started to create a worksheet to keep track of weekly hours. You are going to complete this worksheet and create another that Parker will use to schedule next week's hours. The completed worksheets are shown here.

a. Open the workbook file Time Sheets. Enter a formula in E8 that calculates Monday's total hours by adding Monday's regular and overtime hours. Center the data. Enter formulas to calculate total hours for the other days by copying the formula in E8 down the column.

b. Using an absolute reference to the Hourly Wage in cell C15, enter a formula in cell F8 to calculate Monday's pay. Be sure to include regular and overtime pay in the formula. Enter formulas to calculate pay for the other days by copying the formula in cell F8 down the column. Calculate the total Pay. Format the Pay column to Accounting with two decimal places.

c. Parker has received his work schedule for next week and would like to record those times by extending the current worksheet to a second week. Insert a copy of Sheet1 before Sheet2. Rename the Sheet1 tab to First Week and rename the Sheet1(2) tab to Second Week.

d. In the Second Week sheet, change the title in cell B4 to Week #2 Time Sheet and enter the following work hours.

	Regular Hours	Overtime Hours
Monday	8	0
Tuesday	8	3
Wednesday	7	0
Thursday	8	4
Friday	8	1

1/11/01   Student Name

Week #1 Time Sheet

	Regular Hours	Overtime Hours	Total Hours	Pay
Monday	8	2	10	$ 93.50
Tuesday	7	0	7	$ 59.50
Wednesday	7	0	7	$ 59.50
Thursday	8	1	9	$ 80.75
Friday	8	4	12	$ 119.00
Total	38	7	45	$ 412.25

Hourly Wage $8.50

1/11/01   Student Name

Week #2 Time Sheet

	Regular Hours	Overtime Hours	Total Hours	Pay
Monday	8	0	8	$ 78.43
Tuesday	8	3	11	$ 122.55
Wednesday	7	0	7	$ 68.63
Thursday	8	4	12	$ 137.25
Friday	8	1	9	$ 93.14
Total	39	8	47	$ 500.00

Hourly Wage $9.80

Reg. Pay To-Date	$ 705.35
Overtime Pay To-Date	$ 206.90
Total Pay To-Date	$ 912.25

e. Enter, bold and right-align the following labels:

Reg. Pay To-Date: in cell D17

Overtime To-Date: in cell D18

Total Pay To-Date: in cell D19

f. Enter a formula in cell E17 to calculate the regular pay to date by multiplying the total regular hours times the hourly rate on each sheet and summing the values. Enter a similar formula in cell E18 for overtime pay to date. Calculate the total pay to-date in cell E19. Format these values to Accounting with two decimal places.

g. Parker is thinking about asking for a raise from $8.50 to $9.00 to be effective next week. To evaluate the impact of the raise, change the hourly rate in the Week 2 sheet.

h. Use Goal Seek to determine the hourly rate required to achieve a weekly total pay of $500 for Week 2.

i. Add a custom header to both sheets that contains the date centered and your name right-aligned. Preview the workbook. Save the workbook file as Time Sheets Revised. Print the workbook.

4. Kelly Young works for The Sports Company, a sporting goods retail store. She has nearly completed a six-month forecast for the store. Kelly wants to complete the six-month forecast, extend it for the next six months, and then analyze the forecasts. The completed second half worksheet is shown here.

a. Open the workbook Sports Company Forecast. Spell check and correct any errors in the workbook.

b. Use the Paste Function feature to enter the function to calculate the Average in cell I6. Copy the function down the column.

c. Profit margin is equal to Income/Total Sales. Enter a formula to calculate January's Profit margin. Format the cell to percent with 2 decimal places. Copy this formula across the row to enter the formulas for February through June's profit margins.

Sports Company Forecast Revised   1/11.01   Student Name

	JUL	AUG	SEP	OCT	NOV	DEC	TOTAL	AVG.
SALES								
Clothing	$ 188,700	$ 190,587	$ 192,493	$ 194,418	$ 196,362	$ 198,326	$ 1,160,886	$ 193,481
Hard Goods	$ 127,500	$ 128,775	$ 130,063	$ 131,363	$ 132,677	$ 134,004	$ 784,382	$ 130,730
Total Sales	$ 316,200	$ 319,362	$ 322,556	$ 325,781	$ 329,039	$ 332,329	$ 1,945,267	$ 324,211
EXPENSES								
Advertising	$ 12,648	$ 12,774	$ 12,902	$ 13,031	$ 13,162	$ 13,293	$ 77,811	$ 12,968
Cost of Goods	$ 183,396	$ 185,230	$ 187,082	$ 188,953	$ 190,843	$ 192,751	$ 1,128,255	$ 188,042
Salary	$ 27,536	$ 28,421	$ 29,316	$ 23,703	$ 24,550	$ 25,406	$ 158,932	$ 26,489
Lease	$ 21,000	$ 21,000	$ 21,000	$ 21,000	$ 21,000	$ 21,000	$ 126,000	$ 21,000
Miscellaneous	$ 18,000	$ 18,000	$ 18,000	$ 18,000	$ 18,000	$ 18,000	$ 108,000	$ 18,000
Overhead	$ 22,000	$ 22,000	$ 22,000	$ 22,000	$ 22,000	$ 22,000	$ 132,000	$ 22,000
Total Expenses	$ 284,580	$ 287,426	$ 290,300	$ 286,687	$ 289,554	$ 292,450	$ 1,730,997	$ 288,500
INCOME	$ 31,620	$ 31,936	$ 32,256	$ 39,094	$ 39,485	$ 39,880	$ 214,270	$ 35,712
Profit Margin	10.00 %	10.00 %	10.00 %	12.00 %	12.00 %	12.00 %		

The Sports Company
Projected Second Half Forecast

d. Insert a copy of Sheet1 before Sheet2. Rename the Sheet1 tab to **First Half** and rename Sheet1(2) to **Second Half**.

e. Use the AutoFill feature to replace the months JAN through JUN with **JUL** through **DEC** on the Second Half sheet. Update the title of the Second Half sheet to **Projected Second Half Forecast**.

f. Kelly expects sales of clothing and hard goods for July to increase by 2 percent over June and then to increase 1 percent per month beginning August until the end of the year. Create a formula to calculate the clothing sales for July by taking the clothing sales figure from June in the First Half sheet and multiplying it by 1.02. Copy this formula to hard goods sales for July. Create a formula to calculate August's clothing sales by taking the clothing sales in July and multiplying it by 1.01. Copy this formula down and across to calculate the remaining clothing and hard goods sales.

g. The lease will increase to 21000 effective in July and miscellaneous expenses are expected to increase to 18000 for each month. Update the Second Half sheet to reflect these monthly changes.

h. Use Goal Seek to achieve a profit margin of 10 percent for July, August, and September and 12 percent in October, November, and December by adjusting Salary.

i. Add a custom header that contains the file name left-aligned, the date centered, and your name right-aligned. Preview the workbook. Save the workbook file as Sports Company Forecast Revised. Print the Second Half worksheet using landscape orientation.

5. Alice, a travel analyst for Adventure Travel Tours, is evaluating the profitability of a planned African Safari package. She has researched competing tours and has determined that a price of $4,900 is appropriate. Alice has determined the following costs for the package.

Item	Cost
Air transport	$1,800 per person
Ground transportation	$360 per person
Lodging	$775 per person
Food	$750 per person
Tour Guides	$3,000
Administrative	$1,200
Miscellaneous	$4,000

Alice has started a worksheet to evaluate the revenues and costs for the African Safari. She wants to know how many travelers are needed to break even (revenues equal costs), how many are needed to make $5,000, and how many are needed to make $10,000. The three worksheets of the completed analysis are shown on this page and next.

a. Open the workbook file African Safari. Notice that Alice has already entered the tour price and an estimated number of travelers.

b. Spell check and correct any errors in the workbook.

c. Revenue from reservations is calculated by multiplying the tour price times the number of travelers. Enter this formula into C11.

d. Based on Alice's cost information, air transportation is $1800 times the number of travelers. Enter this formula into B14. Enter formulas into B15, B16, and B17 for the other expenses (see table above) related to the number of travelers.

e. Enter the remaining expenses into cells B18, B19, and B20.

f. Calculate total costs in cell C21. Net revenue is the difference between revenue from reservations and total costs. Enter this formula into cell C23.

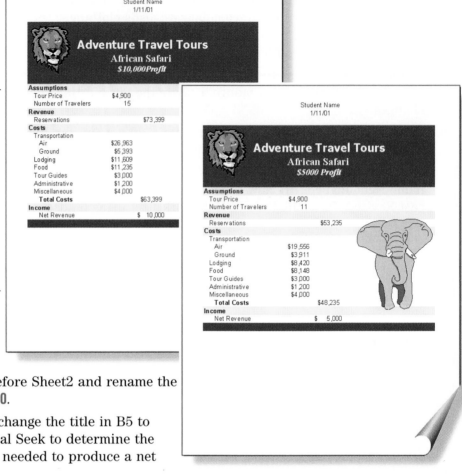

g. Format the currency values in the worksheet to Currency with no decimal places.

h. Use Goal Seek to determine the number of travelers required to just break even (Net revenue equals zero).

i. Rename the sheet tab to **Break Even**. Insert a copy of the Break Even sheet before Sheet2 and rename the tab of the copy **$5000**.

j. In the $5000 sheet, change the title in B5 to **$5,000 Profit**. Use Goal Seek to determine the number of travelers needed to produce a net revenue of $5,000.

k. Insert a copy of the $5000 sheet before Sheet2 and rename the tab of the copy to **$10,000**. Change the title in B5 to **$10,000 Profit**. Use Goal Seek to determine the number of travelers needed to produce a net revenue of $10,000.

l. Preview the workbook. Add a custom header that contains your name and the date center-aligned to the three sheets. Save the workbook file as African Safari Revised. Print the workbook with the sheets centered horizontally.

6. Amy Marino is a college student who has just completed her first two years of her undergraduate program as a business major. In this exercise, you will calculate semester and cumulative totals and GPA for each semester. The completed worksheet for Spring 2000 is shown here

a. Open the file Grade Report. Look at the four sheets. Rename the sheet tabs **Fall 2000**, **Spring 2001**, **Fall 2001**, and **Spring 2002**.

b. You need to enter the formulas to calculate the Total Points and GPA for the four semesters. You will do this for all four sheets at the same time. Select the four sheets. In the Fall 2000 sheet, multiply the Grade by the Credits Earned to calculate Total Points for Intro to Business. Copy that formula down the column. Sum the Credits Attempted, Credits Earned, and Total Points columns and display the results in the Semester Total row.

c. In cell G13, divide the Semester Total's Total Points by the Semester Total's Credits Earned to calculate the GPA for the semester. Use what-if analysis to see what Amy's GPA would be if she had earned a 3 instead of a 2 in Western Civ. Change the grade back to a 2.

d. Look at each sheet to see that the formulas were entered and the calculations performed.

Student Name
1/11/01

Spring 2002 Grades

Course	Course Title	Grade	Credits Attempted	Credits Earned	Total Points	GPA
BIO102	Biology II	3	3	3	9	
IST218	COBOL Prog II	4	3	3	12	
IST227	Systems Design	4	3	3	12	
IST299	Data Proc. Projects	4	3	3	12	
PSY101	Intro to Psychology	3	3	3	9	
	Semester Total:		15	15	54	3.60
	Cumulative Total:		60	60	189	3.15

e. Go to cell D14 in the Fall 2000 sheet. Enter the reference formula **=D13** to copy the Semester Total Credits Attempted number to the Cumulative Total row. Copy the formula to cells E14 and F14 to calculate Credits Earned and Total Points.

f. Go to the Spring 2001 sheet and calculate a Cumulative Total for Credits Attempted by summing the Spring 2001 Semester Total and the Fall 2000 Cumulative Total. (*Hint:* You can use pointing to enter the Cumulative Totals formula.)

g. Copy that formula to the adjacent cells to calculate Cumulative Totals for Credits Earned and Total Points. Repeat this procedure on the Fall 2001 and Spring 2002 sheets.

h. Go to the Fall 2000 sheet. Select all four sheets. In cell G14, calculate the GPA for the Cumulative Total. Format the Semester Total GPA and the Cumulative Total GPA to display two decimals. Look at each sheet to see the GPA for each semester. (*Hint:* Amy's GPA at the end of the Spring 2002 semester is 3.15.) Display the Sheet tab shortcut menu and ungroup the sheets.

i. Go to the Fall 2000 sheet and preview the workbook. Add a custom header that contains your name and the date center-aligned to the sheets. Save the workbook file as Grade Report Complete. Print the Spring 2002 sheet centered horizontally on the page.

On Your Own

7. In Practice Exercise 8 of Tutorial 1, you created a workbook for a six-month budget. Extend this workbook by adding two additional sheets. One sheet is to contain a budget for the next six months. The final sheet is to present a full year's summary using 3-D references to the values in the appropriate sheets.

Consider making a special purchase, such as a car or a new computer, or perhaps taking a trip. On a separate line below the total balance in the summary sheet, enter the amount you would need. Subtract this value from the total balance. If this value is negative, reevaluate your expenses and adjust them appropriately. Format the sheets using the features you have learned in the first three tutorials. Include a custom header on all sheets that includes your name. Preview, print, and save the workbook.

8. Obtain yearly income and expense data for three major sports at your college or university. In a workbook containing four sheets, record each sport's data in a separate sheet. In a fourth sheet, calculate the total income, total expenses, and net income for each sport. Also in this sheet, calculate the overall totals for income, expense, and net income. Format the sheets using the features you have learned in the first three tutorials. Include a custom header on all sheets that includes your name.

9. Select three stocks listed on the New York Stock Exchange. Using the Internet or the library, determine each stock's month-ending price for the past year. In a workbook containing four sheets, record each stock's prices in separate worksheets. In a fourth sheet, calculate the average, standard deviation, and maximum and minimum for each of the three stocks. Also, in the final sheet, chart the average data for the three stocks. Format the sheets using the features you have learned in the first three tutorials. Include a custom header on all sheets that includes your name.

10. Owning and managing a small business is a dream of many college students. Visit a local small business that interests you and ask for information showing their quarterly income and expenses over the past year. Enter the information for each quarter in separate worksheets. In a fifth sheet, show the total for the year. Include a year-to-date value in each quarterly sheet. In the last quarter sheet, select one expense and determine what value the expense would have to have been so that the net income for that quarter would have been 10 percent higher than the current level. Format the sheets using the features you have learned in the first three tutorials. Include a custom header on all sheets that includes your name.

Working Together: Linking Excel and Word

Case Study   Your analysis of sales data for the first quarter has shown a steady increase in total sales. The Café owner has asked you for a copy of the forecast that shows the growth in Internet sales if a strong sales promotion is mounted. You would like to send a memo explaining this information to the owner. In addition, you want to include the worksheet and chart of the sales forecast in the memo.

All Microsoft Office applications have a common user interface such as similar commands and menu structures. In addition to these obvious features, they have been designed to work together, making it easy to share and exchange information between applications. You will learn how to share information between applications while you create the memo. Your completed document will look like that shown below.

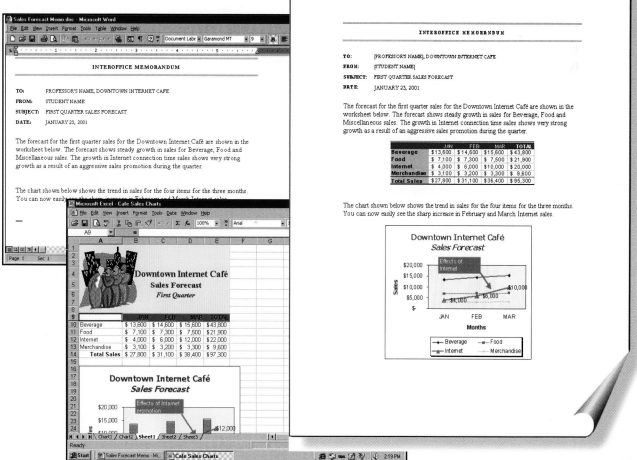

Note: This lab assumes that you already know how to use Word 2000 and that you have completed Tutorial 2 of Excel 2000. You will need the data file Café Sales Charts you created in Tutorial 2.

Copying between Applications

The memo to the manager about the analysis of the sales data has already been created using Word 2000. However, you still need to add the Excel worksheet data and charts to the memo.

1   **Start Word and open the file Sales Forecast Memo on your data disk.**

     In the memo header, replace [Professor's Name] with your instructor's name and [Student Name] with your name.

Your screen should be similar to Figure 1.

insert worksheet

insert chart

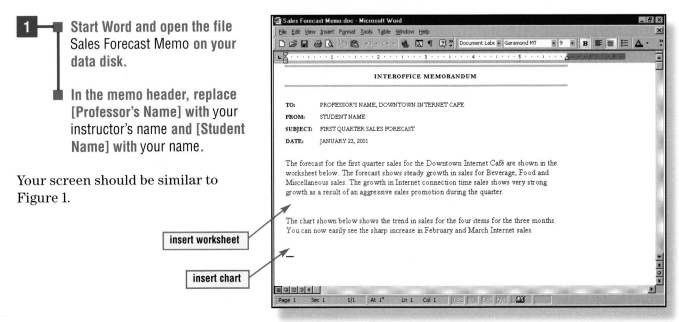

Figure 1

You will insert the worksheet data of the first quarter sales forecast below the first paragraph. Below the second paragraph, you will display the combination chart of sales by category. To insert the information from the Excel workbook file into the Word memo, you need to open the worksheet document.

2 ■ Load Excel and open the workbook file Café Sales Charts on your data disk.

■ If necessary, move to cell A9.

Your screen should be similar to Figure 2.

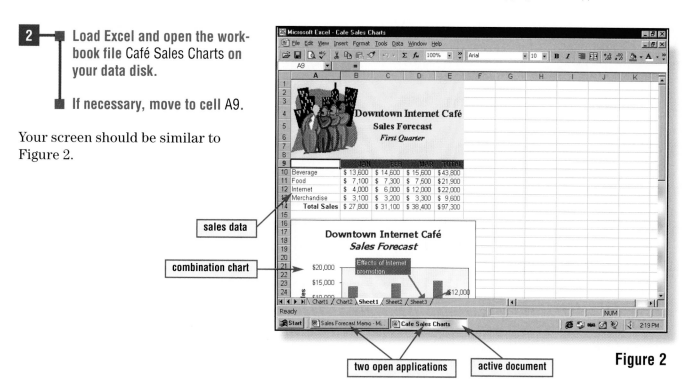

sales data

combination chart

two open applications

active document

Figure 2

There are now two open applications, Word and Excel. Word is open in a window behind the Excel application window. Both application buttons are displayed in the taskbar. There are also two open files, Cafe Sales Charts in Excel and Sales Forecast Memo in Word. Excel is the active application and Cafe Sales Charts is the active file.

First you will copy the worksheet data into the Word memo. While using the Excel application, you have learned how to move and copy information within the same document. You can also perform these operations between documents in the same application and between documents in different applications. For example, you can copy information from a Word document and paste it into an Excel worksheet. The information is pasted in a format that the application can edit, if possible.

You want to copy the worksheet data in cells A9 through E14 into the memo.

EXCEL 2000

3 ▪ Select cells A9 through E14.

▪ Click 📋 Copy.

▪ Click 📄Sales Forecast Memo.doc ... in the taskbar.

▪ Move to the second blank line below the first paragraph of the memo.

▪ Click 📋 Paste to copy the contents of the Clipboard into the memo.

Your screen should be similar to Figure 3.

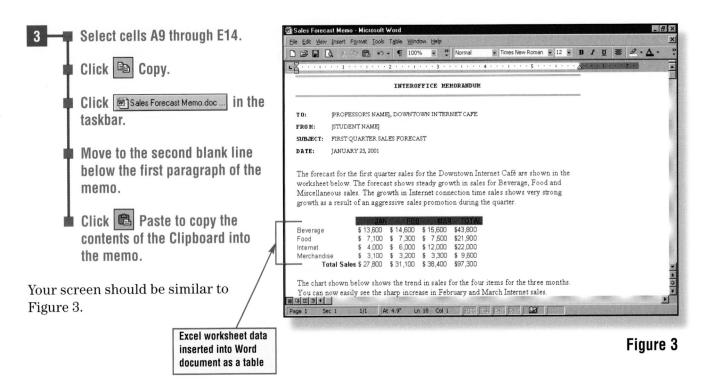

Excel worksheet data inserted into Word document as a table

Figure 3

The worksheet data has been copied into the Word document as a table that can be edited and manipulated within Word. Much of the formatting associated with the copied information is also pasted into the document. You think the memo would look better if the table was centered between the margins.

4 ▪ Select the entire table.

▪ Click ▤ Center.

▪ Clear the selection.

Your screen should be similar to Figure 4.

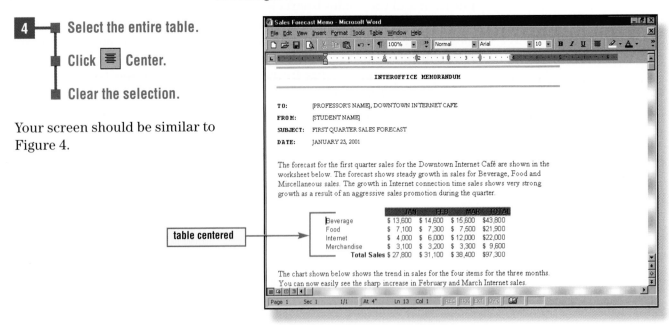

table centered

Figure 4

Linking an Object to Another Application

Next you want to display the combination chart of sales trends for the four categories below the second paragraph in the memo.

1 ■ Switch to the Excel application and select the combination chart.

■ Click 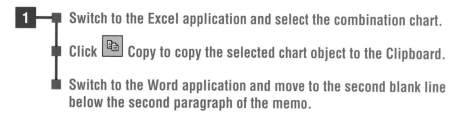 Copy to copy the selected chart object to the Clipboard.

■ Switch to the Word application and move to the second blank line below the second paragraph of the memo.

You will insert the chart object into the memo as a **linked object**. Information created in one application can also be inserted as a linked object into a document created by another application. When an object is linked, the data is stored in the **source file** (the document it was created in). A graphic representation or picture of the data is displayed in the **destination file** (the document in which the object is inserted). A connection between the information in the destination file to the source file is established by the creation of a link. The link contains references to the location of the source file and the selection within the document that is linked to the destination file.

When changes are made in the source file that affect the linked object, the changes are automatically reflected in the destination file when it is opened. This is called a **live link**. When you create linked objects, the date and time on your machine should be accurate. This is because the program refers to the date of the source file to determine whether updates are needed when you open the destination file.

By making the chart a linked object, it will be automatically updated if the source file is edited. To create a linked object,

2 ■ Choose **E**dit/Paste **S**pecial.

■ Select Paste **L**ink.

Your screen should be similar to Figure 5.

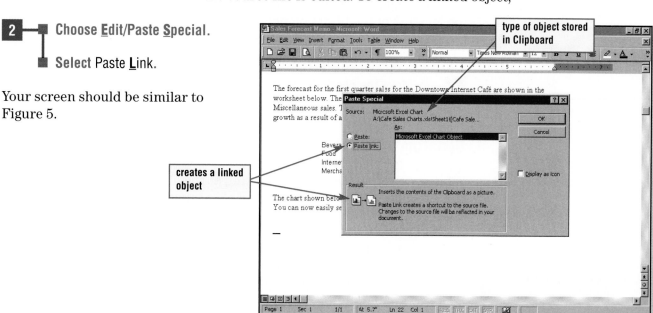

Figure 5

The Paste Special dialog box displays the type of object contained in the Clipboard and its location in the Source area. From the As list box you select the type of format in which you want the object inserted into the destination file. The only available option for this object is as a Microsoft Excel Chart Object. The Result area describes the effect of your selections. In this case, the object will be inserted as a picture and a link will be created to the chart in the source file. Selecting the Display as Icon option changes the display of the object from a picture to an icon. Double-clicking the icon displays the object picture. The default selections are appropriate.

3 ■ Click [OK].

■ Set the Zoom to 75%.

■ Position the window so you can see both the worksheet and the chart on the page.

Your screen should be similar to Figure 6.

picture of chart is linked to Excel workbook

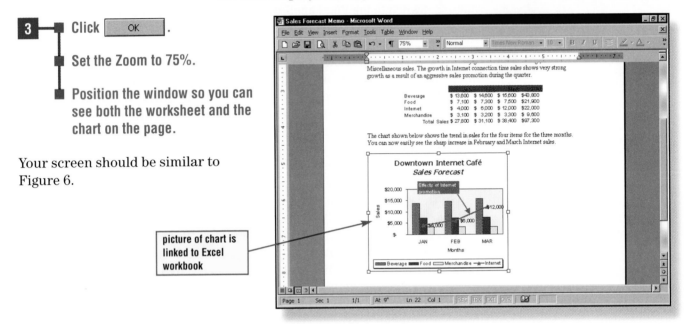

Figure 6

Word changed to Print Layout view and the chart object is displayed at the location of the insertion point aligned with the left margin. The object has been scaled to fit in the document.

4 ■ Move the chart object so it is centered horizontally on the page.

Updating a Linked Object

While reading the memo and looking at the chart, you decide to change the chart type from a combination chart to a line chart. You feel a line chart will show the sales trends for all sales items more clearly. You also decide to lower your sales expectation for Internet sales from 12,000 to 10,000 for March.

To make these changes, you need to switch back to Excel. Double-clicking on a linked object quickly switches to the open source file. If the source file is not open, it opens the file for you. If the application is not open, it both starts the application and opens the source file.

The menu equivalent is **E**dit/Linked **O**bject/**E**ditLink

1 — Double-click the chart object.

Click 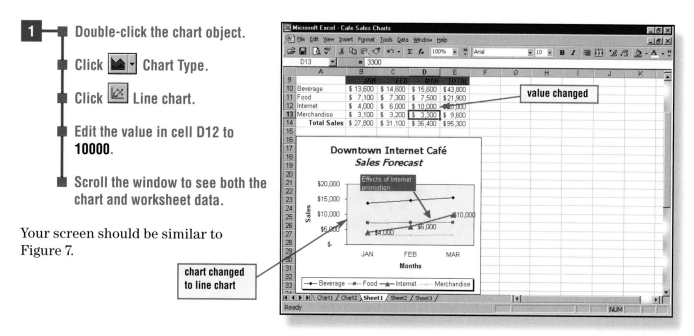 ▾ Chart Type.

Click Line chart.

Edit the value in cell D12 to **10000**.

Scroll the window to see both the chart and worksheet data.

Your screen should be similar to Figure 7.

Figure 7

The chart type has changed to a line chart and the chart data series has been updated to reflect the change in data. Now you will switch to the memo to see what changes were made to the worksheet and chart.

2 — To see the changes made in the memo, switch to Word.

Your screen should be similar to Figure 8.

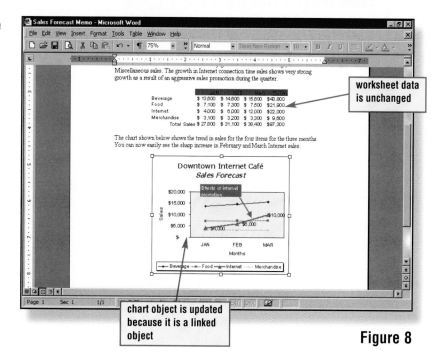

Figure 8

EXCEL 2000

The chart in the memo reflects the change in chart type and the change in data for the Internet sales. This is because any changes you make in the chart in Excel will be automatically reflected in the linked chart in the Word document. However, because the worksheet data is a word table and not a linked object, it does not reflect the change in data made in Excel. Normally you would want to link both the worksheet and the related chart so that both reflect the changes made to the data. You will delete the table and copy the worksheet into the memo as a linked object.

3

- Select the worksheet table.

- Choose T<u>a</u>ble/<u>D</u>elete/<u>T</u>able

- Switch to Excel.

- Select and copy cells A9 through E14.

- Switch to Word.

- Choose <u>E</u>dit/Paste <u>S</u>pecial/Paste <u>L</u>ink.

- Select Microsoft Excel Worksheet Object as the type.

- Click ⌈ OK ⌋.

- Center the linked worksheet object on the page.

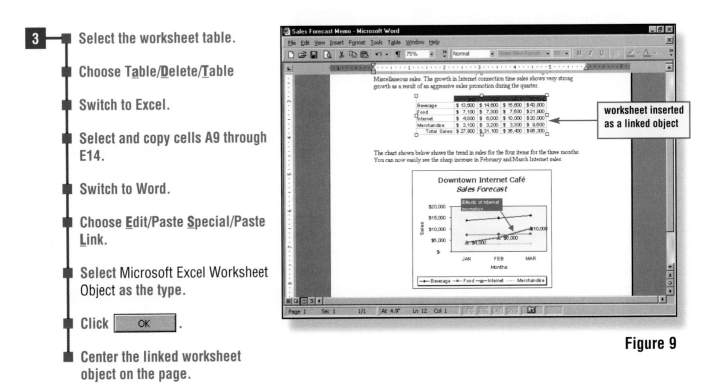

Figure 9

Your screen should be similar to Figure 9.

Applying an Autoformat

The worksheet is inserted into the memo as a linked object. However, you do not like how the formatting of the worksheet looks as a linked object in the memo. To quickly improve the appearance of the worksheet, you will apply an autoformat to the worksheet data.

An **autoformat** is a built-in combination of formats that can be applied to a range of cells. The autoformats consist of a combination of number formats, fonts and attributes, colors, patterns, borders, frames, and alignment settings.

To see both applications on your screen at the same time and watch the changes as they are made to both documents,

1 ▪ Right-click on a blank area of the taskbar to open the shortcut menu.

▪ Select Tile Windows **V**ertically.

Your screen should be similar to Figure 10.

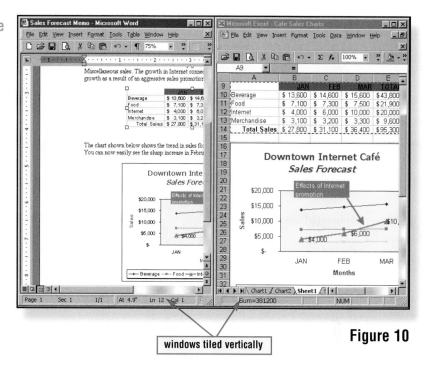

windows tiled vertically

Figure 10

To use an autoformat, you first specify the range you want affected by the formatting. In this case, you want to apply an autoformat to cells A9 through E14. You can select the range or you can let Excel select the range for you. To have Excel automatically select the range, the cell selector must be on any cell in the range. Excel determines that the range you want to autoformat is the range of cells that includes the active cell and is surrounded by blank cells.

2 ▪ Click on the Excel window to make it active.

▪ Move to any cell in the worksheet data.

▪ Choose F**o**rmat/**A**utoformat

Your screen should be similar to Figure 11.

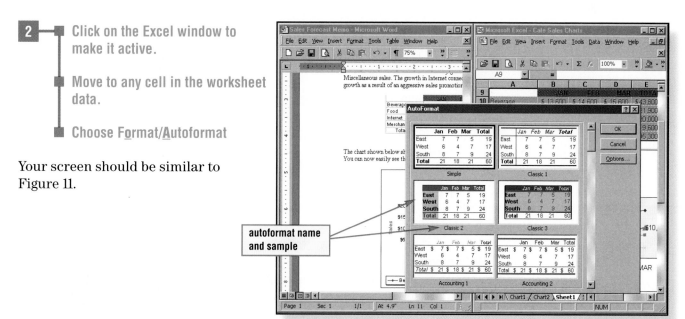

autoformat name and sample

Figure 11

EXCEL 2000

Use the None autoformat design to remove an existing autoformat.

The range A9 through E14 is correctly selected as the range to autoformat, and the AutoFormat dialog box is displayed. Samples of the 16 different autoformat designs are displayed with the names assigned to the design below the sample.

You think the Classic 2 autoformat would be appropriate for the Sales data. To format the worksheet using this layout,

3 ⬛ **Select Classic 2**

⬛ **Click** OK

Your screen should be similar to Figure 12.

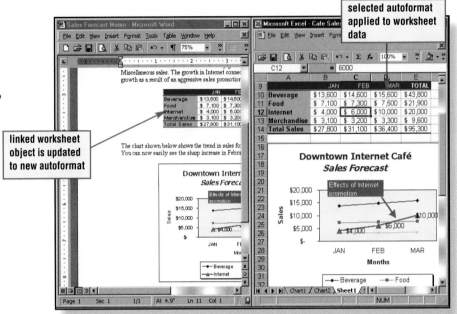

Figure 12

The Classic 2 autoformat has been applied to the worksheet range and the linked worksheet object in the memo has been updated. This format includes border lines of different weights, color, accounting number format with no decimal places, and adjustment of column widths to fit the entries in the selected range.

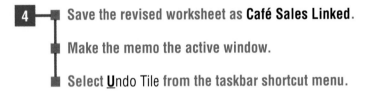

4 ⬛ Save the revised worksheet as **Café Sales Linked**.

⬛ Make the memo the active window.

⬛ Select **U**ndo Tile from the taskbar shortcut menu.

Editing Links

Whenever a document is opened that contains links, the application looks for the source file and automatically updates the linked objects. If there are many links, updating can take a lot of time. Additionally, if you move the source file to another location, or perform other operations that may interfere with the link, your link will not work. To help with situations like these, you can edit the settings associated with links. To see how you do this,

1 ■ Select the worksheet object.

■ Choose <u>E</u>dit/Lin<u>k</u>s.

Your screen should be similar to Figure 13.

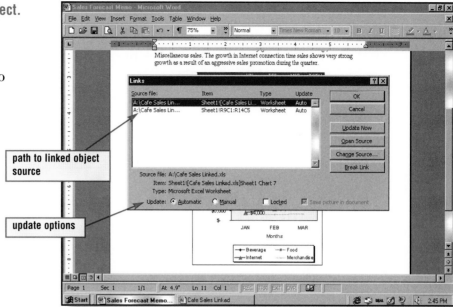

path to linked object source

update options

Figure 13

The Links dialog box displays the object path for all links in the document in the list box. The field code specifies the path and name of the source file, the range of linked cells or object name, the type of file, and the update status. Below the list box, the details for the selected link are displayed. The other options in this dialog box are described in the table below.

Option	Effect
Automatic	Updates the linked object whenever the destination document is opened or the source file changes. This is the default.
Manual	The destination document is not automatically updated and you must use the Update Now command button to update the link.
Locked	Prevents a linked object from being updated.
Open Source	Opens the source document for the selected link.
Change Source	Used to modify the path to the source document.
Break Link	Breaks the connection between the source document and the active document.

2 ■ Click [Cancel] .

■ Clear the selection and save the Word document as **Sales Forecast Memo Linked**.

■ Print the document.

■ Exit Word and Excel.

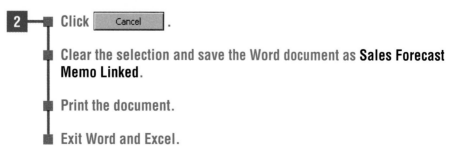

EXCEL 2000

Linking documents is a very handy feature particularly in documents whose information is updated frequently. If you include a linked object in a document that you are giving to another person, make sure the user has access to the source file and application. Otherwise the links will not operate correctly.

Key Terms

autoformat   EXW-8
destination file   EXW-5
linked object   EXW-5
live link   EXW-5
source file   EXW-5

Command Summary

Command	Action
Edit/Paste **S**pecial/Paste **L**ink	Creates a link to the source document
Edit/Lin**k**s	Modifies selected link
Edit/Linked **O**bject/**E**dit Link	Modifies selected linked object
F**o**rmat/**A**utoformat	Applies one of 16 built-in table formats to the worksheet range.

Hands-On Practice Exercises

Step by Step

Rating System

1. Adventure Travel Tours travel agency sends a monthly status report to all subsidiary offices showing the bookings for the specialty tours offered by the company. Previously the worksheet data was printed separately from the memo. Now you want to include the worksheet in the same document as the memo.

a. Load Word and open the Tour Status Report file on your data disk. Replace Student Name with **your name** on the From line in the heading.

b. Load Excel and open the Adventure Travel Monthly worksheet on your data disk.

c. Copy the worksheet as a linked object into the memo below the paragraph.

d. In Excel, enter the following data for March bookings.

Tour	March Data
Tuolumne Clavey Falls	20
Costa Rica Rainforest	4
Kilimanjaro	4
Machu Picchu	3
Himalayas	6
Tanzania Safari	6

e. Save the worksheet as Adventure Travel Monthly March. Exit Excel.

f. Center the worksheet object in the word document

g. Save the Word document as March Status Report. Print the memo.

INTEROFFICE MEMORANDUM

TO: ADVENTURE TRAVEL EMPLOYEES
FROM: STUDENT NAME
SUBJECT: TOUR STATUS REPORT
DATE: 4/1/01

The bookings to date for our upcoming specialty tours are displayed in the following table. As you can see the new white water rafting tour to below the Tuolumne Clavey Falls in California is almost full to capacity and we are considering offering a second week. Because several others are also close to capacity you may want to advise any clients who are considering one of these tours to make reservations as soon as possible.

Adventure Travel Tours
Speciality Tours Status Report

Tour	Jan	Feb	Mar	Total	Tour Capacity
Tuolumne Clavey Falls	8	14	20	22	46
Costa Rica Rainforests	5	9	4	14	36
Kilimanjaro	2	2	4	4	15
Machu Picchu	4	8	3	12	30
Himalayas	0	0	6	0	18
Tanzania Safari	4	3	6	7	21

2. Karen works for a large hotel chain in the marketing department. She has recently researched hotel occupancy rates for the Phoenix area and has created a worksheet and stacked-column chart of the data. Now Karen wants to send a memo containing the chart to her supervisor.

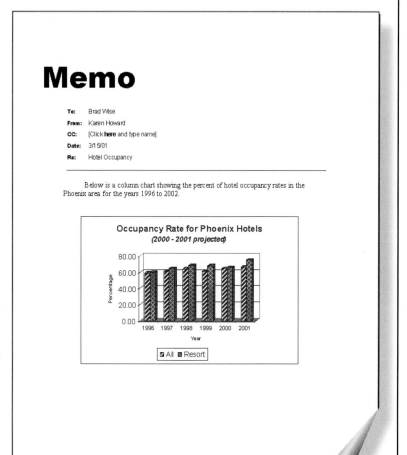

a. Load Word and open the document Hotel Memo on your data disk.

b. In the header, replace the placeholder information in brackets with the following:

TO:	**Brad Wise**
FROM:	**Karen Howard**
CC:	**[your name]**
RE:	**Hotel Occupancy**

c. Load Excel and open the workbook file Hotel Occupancy Data. Link the column chart to below the paragraph in the Word memo. Center the chart in the memo.

d. You decide you need to clarify that the data for 2000 and 2001 is projected. Add a second title line **(2001 - 2002 projected)** to the chart in 12 point, italic.

e. Save the Word document as Hotel Occupancy. Preview and print the document. Exit Word.

f. Save the Excel workbook as Hotel Data Linked. Close the Excel file.

3. To complete this exercise, you must have created the worksheet in Exercise 3 of Tutorial 2. Tyler Johnson works for Books Online. He has compiled a list of the 10 best-selling children's books and created a chart comparing their price to the list price for each book. He wants to send a memo showing this information to management.

a. Load Word and open the Children's Book Memo file on your data disk. Enter **your name** on the To line in the heading.

b. Load Excel and open the Book List Chart worksheet on your data disk.

c. Copy the worksheet range B5 through D15 as a linked object into the memo below the first paragraph. Center it on the page.

d. Copy the chart into the memo as a linked object below the second paragraph. Reduce the chart size and move it so it fits on a single page with the worksheet. Center it on the page.

e. Apply an autoformat of your choice to the worksheet range B5 through D15.

f. Save the worksheet as **Book List Linked**. Exit Excel.

g. Save the Word document as **Children's Book Memo Linked**. Print the memo.

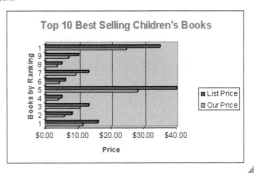

Memo

To:	Student Name
From:	Tyler Johnson
Date:	11/1/2000
Re:	Top Children's Book Price Comparison

The following table lists the top 10 best selling children's books. To increase sales in this area, we have discounted the prices of these books considerably.

Ranking	Title	Our Price	List Price
1	Today I Feel Silly	$11.17	$15.95
2	Green Eggs & Ham	$5.59	$7.99
3	Chicken Soup for the Kid's Soul	$10.36	$12.95
4	The Suspicion, Animorphs #24	$3.99	$4.99
5	The 20th Century Children's Book Treasury	$28.00	$40.00
6	Teletubbies Play Hide-And-Seek	$4.19	$5.99
7	The Hork-Bajir Chronicles	$9.07	$12.95
8	Cheerios Play Book	$3.49	$4.99
9	The Diary of Margaret Ann Brady	$6.97	$9.95
10	New Way Things Work	$24.50	$35.00

The chart shown below compares our discounted price to the list price for these books.

Using Solver, Creating Workbook Templates, Linking Workbooks, and Creating Scenarios

Competencies

After completing this tutorial, you will know how to:

1. Use Solver.
2. Create and use workbook templates.
3. Protect a worksheet.
4. Open and use multiple workbooks.
5. Link workbooks.
6. Create and use Scenarios.
7. Create a Scenario Summary.
8. Create and modify 3-D shapes.
9. Display the current date and time.

Case Study

After further discussion with Evan, the owner of the Downtown Internet Café, you continued to refine the forecast analysis. You made several suggested formatting changes to the worksheet and revised some values. You also contin-

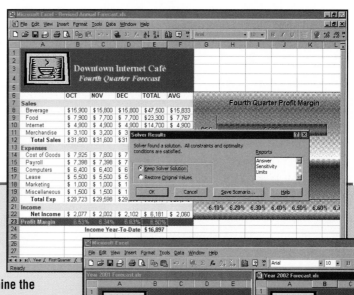

Using Solver, you can quickly determine the effect of changing values in two or more cells on another cell.

Creating links between workbooks allows changes you make in one file to be automatically reflected in the other file.

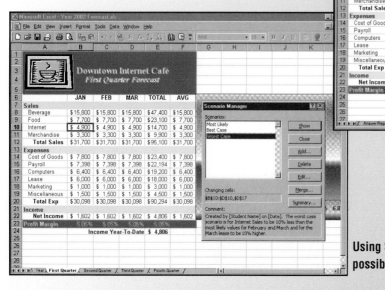

Using Scenario Manager, you can analyze various possible outcomes to help plan for the future.

ued to use Goal Seek to determine the monthly payroll expense needed to achieve monthly profit margins of 6 percent for the third quarter.

Evan wants you to further determine a fixed payroll expense for the fourth quarter that will achieve a quarterly profit margin of 6.5 percent. You will use the Solver tool to determine the values. Additionally, you have been asked to create three different scenarios that will show the best, worst, and most likely scenarios for the annual forecast.

Once the annual forecast for 2001 is complete, Evan wants you to use the same procedure to create the forecast for 2002. You will use the 2001 annual forecast worksheet to create a template for the next year's forecast, and then you will use the template to create the first quarter forecast for that year.

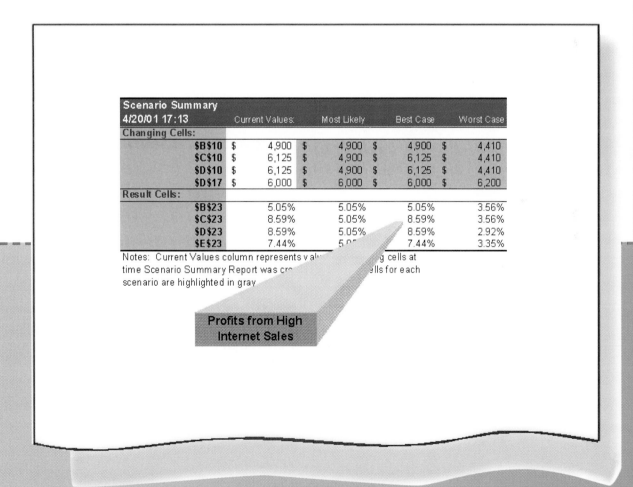

Scenario Summary		Current Values:		Most Likely		Best Case		Worst Case
4/20/01 17:13								
Changing Cells:								
$B$10	$	4,900	$	4,900	$	4,900	$	4,410
$C$10	$	6,125	$	4,900	$	6,125	$	4,410
$D$10	$	6,125	$	4,900	$	6,125	$	4,410
$D$17	$	6,000	$	6,000	$	6,000	$	6,200
Result Cells:								
$B$23		5.05%		5.05%		5.05%		3.56%
$C$23		8.59%		5.05%		8.59%		3.56%
$D$23		8.59%		5.05%		8.59%		2.92%
$E$23		7.44%		5.05%		7.44%		3.35%

Notes: Current Values column represents valu̶e̶s̶ g cells at time Scenario Summary Report was cr̶e̶ ̶ ̶ ̶ ̶ ̶ells for each scenario are highlighted in gray.

Profits from High Internet Sales

Concept Overview

The following concepts will be introduced in this tutorial:

1 **Solver**   Solver is a tool used to perform what-if analyses to determine the effect of changing values in two or more cells on another cell.

2 **Workbook Template**   A workbook template is a workbook file that contains predesigned worksheets that can be used as a pattern for creating similar worksheets in new workbooks.

3 **Worksheet Protection**   Worksheet protection prevents users from changing a worksheet's contents by protecting the entire worksheet or specified areas of it.

4 **Arrange Windows**   The Arrange Windows feature displays all open workbook files in separate windows on the screen, in a tiled, horizontal, vertical, or cascade arrangement.

5 **Link Workbooks**   A link creates a connection between files that automatically updates the data in one file whenever the data in the other file changes.

6 **Scenario**   A scenario is a named set of input values that you can substitute in a worksheet to see the effects of a possible alternative course of action. Scenarios are designed to help forecast the outcome of various possible actions.

Using Solver

After seeing how the payroll values changed each month to achieve higher second- and third-quarter profit margins, Evan would like you to do a similar analysis on the fourth-quarter. To see the current profit margin for the fourth quarter,

1 Open the workbook file Revised Annual Forecast.

Make the Fourth Quarter sheet active.

Move to cell E23.

Your screen should be similar to Figure 4-1.

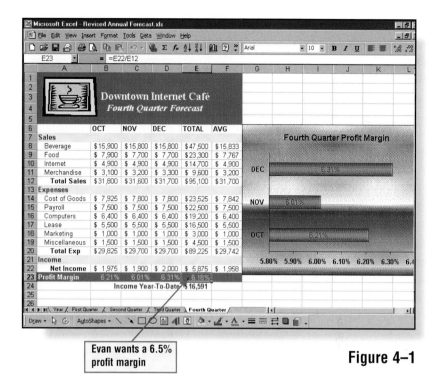

Evan wants a 6.5% profit margin

Figure 4–1

The profit margin for the fourth quarter is 6.18 percent. This time, Evan would like to keep the payroll expenses constant for the quarter while achieving a 6.5 percent quarterly profit margin. Although you could use What-If or Goal Seek to figure out these values, it would be much quicker to use the Solver tool.

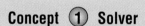
Concept 1 Solver

Solver is a tool used to perform what-if analyses to determine the effect of changing values in two or more cells, called the **adjustable cells,** on another cell, called the **target cell.** Solver calculates a formula to achieve a given value by changing one of the variables that affect the formula. To do this Solver works backward from the result of a formula to find the numbers. The cells you select must be related through formulas on the worksheet. If they are not related, changing one will not change the other.

Solver can also produce three types of reports about the solution: Answer, Sensitivity, and Limits. In an Answer report, the original and final values of the target cell and adjustable cells are listed along with any constraints and information about the constraints. Information about how sensitive the solution is to small changes in the target cell formula or in the constraints is provided in a Sensitivity report. A Limits report includes the original and target values of the target cell and adjustable cells. It also lists the lower limit, the smallest value that the adjustable cell can take while holding all other adjustable cells fixed and still satisfying the constraints and upper or greatest value.

2 —■ Choose Tools/Solver.

Your screen should be similar to
Figure 4–2.

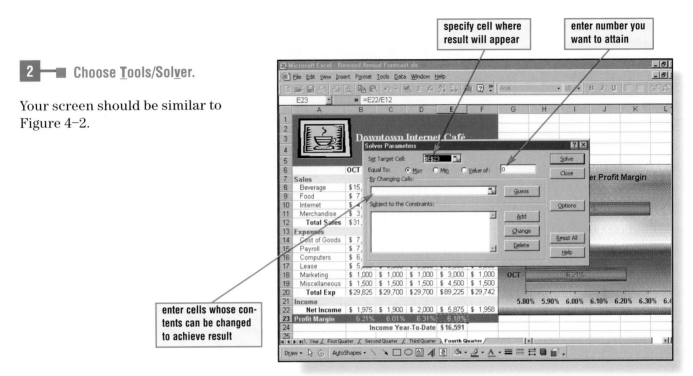

Figure 4–2

In the Solver Parameters dialog box, you need to supply three items of information: the target cell where the result will appear, the result value, and the cell or cells that will be changed to achieve the result.

The cell reference of the cell containing the formula you want to solve is entered in the Set Target Cell text box. The cell reference of the active cell, E23, is already correctly entered in this box.

The number you want as the result of the formula is entered in the Equal To text box. You can set the number to be a maximum, minimum, or an exact number. The maximum option sets the target cell to the highest possible number, while the minimum option sets the target cell for the lowest possible number.

The final information needed is the cell or cell range whose contents can be changed when the formula is computed. This range is entered in the By Changing Cells text box.

In the fourth quarter, you are looking for a value of 6.5 percent by changing the values in the range of cells B15 through D15. To specify the value and range,

3 ■ Select <u>V</u>alue of.

■ Type **.065** in the Value Of text box.

■ Specify the range B15 through D15 in the By Changing Cells text box.

> Reminder: You can minimize the dialog box using the ☒ button and select the range by highlighting it in the worksheet.

Your screen should be similar to Figure 4–3.

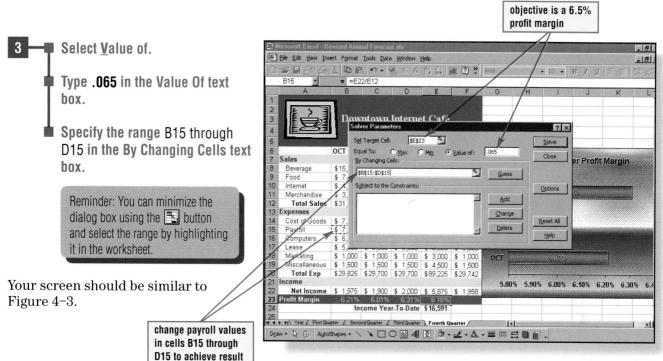

objective is a 6.5% profit margin

change payroll values in cells B15 through D15 to achieve result

Figure 4–3

To have Solver find the values to meet the parameters you specified,

4 ■ Click [<u>S</u>olve].

Your screen should be similar to Figure 4–4.

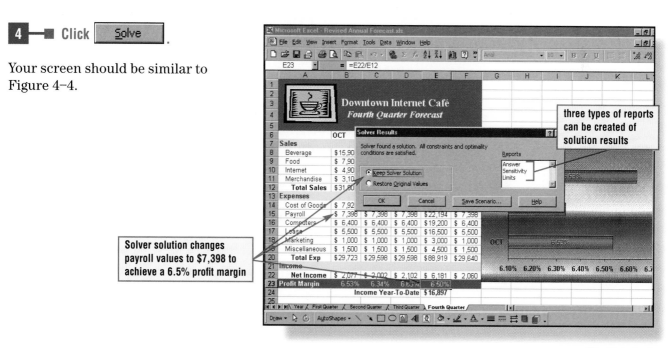

three types of reports can be created of solution results

Solver solution changes payroll values to $7,398 to achieve a 6.5% profit margin

Figure 4–4

The Solver Results dialog box is displayed, indicating that Solver found a solution. The new payroll numbers are entered in the worksheet range and the worksheet is automatically recalculated. By setting the payroll expense to $7,398, the monthly profit margins vary and the quarterly or total profit margin is 6.5 percent.

From the Solver Results dialog box you can choose whether to keep the solution or restore the original values. In addition, you can have Solver create Answer, Sensitivity, and Limits reports. You decide to keep the solution and to create an Answer report.

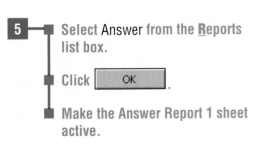

5 Select Answer from the Reports list box.

Click [OK].

Make the Answer Report 1 sheet active.

Your screen should be similar to Figure 4–5.

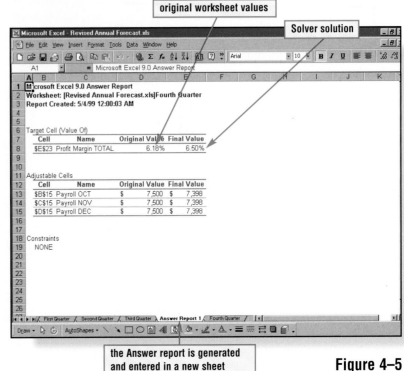

original worksheet values

Solver solution

the Answer report is generated and entered in a new sheet

Figure 4–5

The Answer Report 1 sheet displays the Answer report that was generated. The target cell section of the report shows the original profit margin value of 6.18 percent and the final value of 6.50 percent. The Adjustable Cells area shows the original and final values for each cell that was changed to achieve the profit margin of 6.50 percent. The final value entered in each adjustable cell will be the same number even if the original values were different in each cell.

Next you want to see the effect changing the payroll expenses for the fourth quarter had on the annual profit margin.

6 ■ Make the Year sheet active.

■ Move to cell N23.

Your screen should be similar to Figure 4–6.

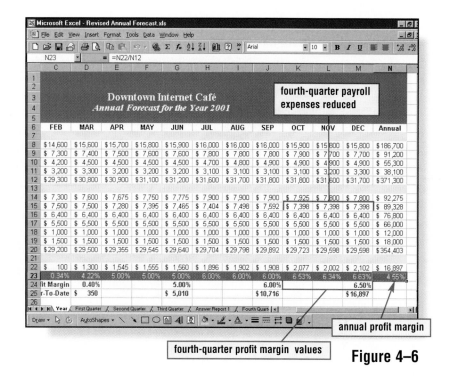

fourth-quarter payroll expenses reduced

annual profit margin

fourth-quarter profit margin values

Figure 4–6

The new fourth-quarter figures appear, along with the annual profit margin of 4.55 percent in cell N23. The profit margin for the year increased due to the reduction of payroll expenses in the fourth quarter. The forecast for 2001 is now complete.

7 ■ Press Ctrl + Home and save the current workbook file as **Year 2001 Forecast**.

Creating a Workbook Template.

After seeing the effects of your analyses on the Year sheet, Evan has found it to be a valuable tool for planning and managing operations. He has asked you to create a new workbook containing a forecast for the following year. You could create this new forecast workbook by starting all over again, specifying the formats and formulas. However, the current workbook already contains this information, so you decide to use it as a model or template for future forecasts.

Concept ② Workbook Template

A workbook **template** is a workbook file that contains predesigned worksheets that can be used as a pattern for creating similar sheets in new workbooks. Templates can contain text, graphics, formats, page layouts, headers and footers, functions and formulas, and macros.

Templates are useful in any application where input and output are required using the same format. By not having to redesign the worksheet form each time the report is needed, you save time. You can go back to the original design repeatedly by saving the workbook containing the data under a different file name than the one you used to save the workbook template.

Excel saves a workbook template using a special file format with the file extension .xlt. Workbook templates are also stored in a special Templates folder. To use a workbook template, you select the template file name from the General tab of the New File dialog box. When you save the workbook after entering data in the template, Excel automatically displays the Save As dialog box so you can specify the new file name. It also changes the file type to an Excel workbook (.xls). This ensures that you do not unintentionally save over the template file.

A well-designed template allows you to enter information into the appropriate locations while protecting formulas and basic format. Since the basic workbook design that you want to use for your template is already in place, the first steps are to eliminate the Answer Report 1 sheet and to change the current values in the remaining sheets without changing any of the underlying formulas.

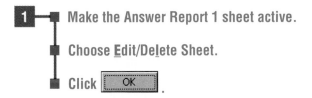

1 — ■ Make the Answer Report 1 sheet active.

■ Choose <u>E</u>dit/De<u>l</u>ete Sheet.

■ Click ⬚ OK ⬚ .

Next you will modify the subtitle in the Year sheet by removing the year, and then you will replace all of the monthly values in the quarter sheets with zeros.

2 ■ Make the Year sheet active.

■ Delete the year 2001 from the subtitle in cell D4.

■ Select the First Quarter through Fourth Quarter sheets.

> Reminder: Hold down
> ⟨⇧Shift⟩ to extend the sheet selection.

■ Enter **0** in cells B8 through D11 and cells B15 through D19 in the First Quarter sheet.

■ Move to cell A23.

Your screen should look like Figure 4–7.

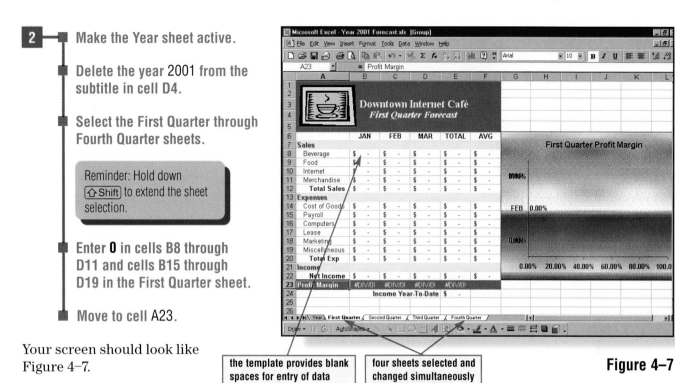

the template provides blank spaces for entry of data

four sheets selected and changed simultaneously

Figure 4–7

The selected cell format displays cells containing zero values with a dash symbol.

3 ■ Look at each of the three other quarter sheets to verify that the values have been replaced.

■ Make the Year sheet active

Protecting the Worksheet

Because the Year sheet contains formulas that link to the values in the quarter sheets, this sheet also displays zero values. Now that all the values have been removed, you want to prevent unwanted changes to the worksheet that would cause headings and formulas to be altered or cleared. To do this, you can protect the worksheet.

EXCEL 2000

Concept ③ Protection

Protection prevents users from changing a worksheet's contents by protecting the entire worksheet or specified areas of it. When a worksheet is protected, all cells and graphic objects on it are locked. The contents of a locked cell cannot be changed. If you want to leave some cells unlocked for editing, such as in a worksheet you use as an entry form, you can lock cells containing labels and formulas but unlock the entry fields so that others can fill them in. This type of protection prevents you from entering or changing an entry in any locked cells.

You can also protect an entire workbook from unauthorized changes in two ways. First, you can protect the structure of a workbook so that sheets cannot be moved or deleted or new sheets inserted. Second, you can protect a workbook's windows. This prevents changes to the size and position of windows and ensures that they appear the same way each time the workbook is opened.

In addition, you can include a **password** that prevents any unauthorized person from turning off protection and changing the worksheet. If you use a password, you must remember the password in order to turn protection off in the future.

Initially all cells in a worksheet are locked. However, you can enter data in the cells because the worksheet protection feature is not on. When protection is turned on, all locked cells are protected. Therefore, before protecting this sheet, you need to unlock the range of cells where the data will be entered.

The only area of the Year sheet that needs to be unprotected is the subtitle where the year will be entered when the template is used. To unlock the cell containing the subtitle and to protect rest of the worksheet,

1 ● Move to cell D4.

● Choose Format/Cells.

● Open the Protection tab.

● Clear the Locked option box.

Your screen should be similar to Figure 4–8.

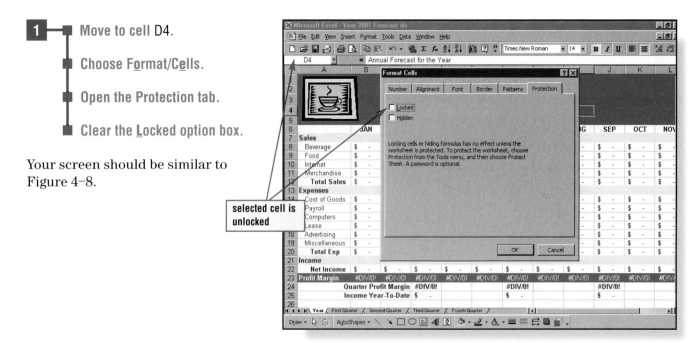

Figure 4–8

Once the cells you want to change in a protected worksheet are unlocked, you can add protection.

2 ■ Click [OK].

■ Choose **T**ools/**P**rotection/**P**rotect Sheet.

Your screen should be similar to Figure 4–9.

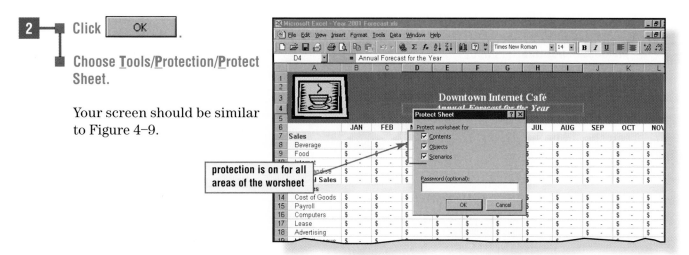

protection is on for all areas of the worsheet

Figure 4–9

The three protection options are selected by default and provide complete protection for the worksheet. Clearing an option removes protection for the features covered by that option.

3 ■ Click [OK].

Next, you will unprotect the data-entry areas of the quarter sheets and then turn on protection for the sheets.

4 ■ Select the First through Fourth Quarter sheets.

■ Select cells B8 through D11 and B15 through D19.

■ Choose F**o**rmat/C**e**lls.

■ Clear the **L**ocked option box in the Protection tab.

■ Click [OK].

When protecting worksheets, you must protect each sheet individually. You will ungroup the sheets and protect each sheet.

> You can also hold down ⇧ Shift while clicking a sheet tab to un-group sheets.

5 ■ Select **U**ngroup sheets from the sheet tab shortcut menu.

■ If necessary, make the First Quarter sheet active.

■ Choose **T**ools/**P**rotection/**P**rotect Sheet.

■ Click [OK].

■ In a similar manner protect the other three quarter sheets.

Now all locked cells in the sheet are protected. Only those cells you un-locked prior to turning on protection can be changed. To test this out, you will try to make an entry in a protected cell.

6 ■ Make the First Quarter sheet active.

■ Type any character in cell B6.

Your screen should be similar to Figure 4–10.

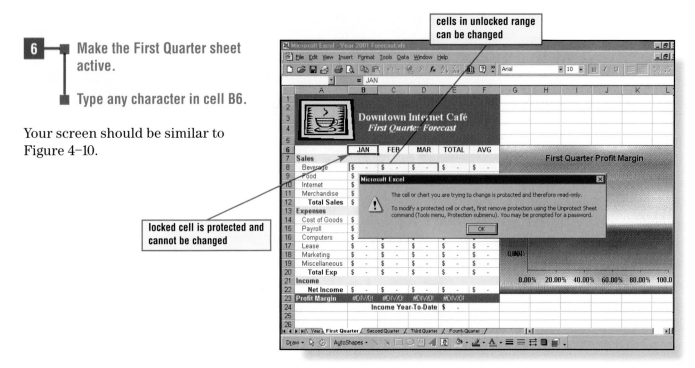

Figure 4–10

The warning dialog box informs you that you cannot change entries in locked cells. Next you will enter a value in an unlocked cell.

7 ■ Click OK to clear the message.

■ Type any value in cell B8 and press ⏎Enter .

The entry is accepted because the cell was unlocked before protection was applied to the sheet.

8 ■ Click ↶ ▾ to clear the entry.

Now that the sheets are protected, you will save this workbook as a template file.

9 ■ Make the Year sheet active.

■ Choose File/Save As.

Additional Information

You cannot save a workbook as a template by typing the file extension .xlt in a file name. You must select the Template (.xlt) file type from the Save As Type list box.

■ Enter the new name, **Forecast Template**, in the File Name text box.

■ From the Save As Type list box select Template (*.xlt).

■ Click 💾 Save .

■ Close the Forecast Template file.

The Forecast Template is now ready to use.

Using a Workbook Template

Now you will use the Forecast Template file to create a new 2002 forecast workbook for the Downtown Internet Café.

1 ■— Choose File/New.

■ If necessary, open the General tab.

Your screen should be similar to Figure 4–11.

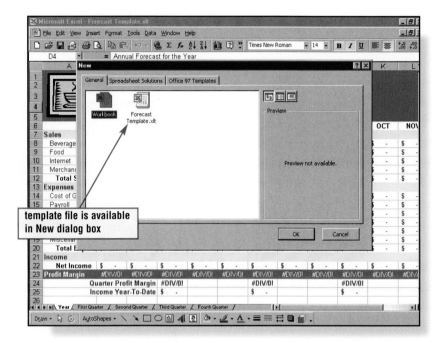

template file is available in New dialog box

Figure 4–11

The Forecast Template file appears in the New dialog box as an icon. To use the template,

Additional Information

Your General tab may display additional icons depending on how many and what kind of templates have been created and saved in Excel.

2 ■— Select Forecast Template.xlt.

■ Click ☐ OK ☐.

The workbook template appears just as it did when you saved it. The first thing you will do in the year worksheet is change the subtitle to display the year.

3 ■— Change the subtitle in cell D4 of the Year sheet to **Annual Forecast for the Year 2002**.

Before continuing, you want to save the revised template file as a workbook file for the 2002 forecast data. When using a template to create a new workbook file, use the Save command and Excel automatically displays the Save As dialog box so you can specify the new file name. This prevents you from accidentally overwriting the template with another file.

To ensure that you don't unintentionally save over the template file, Excel automatically assigns the .xls workbook extension as the file type.

4 ■— Click 🖫.

■ Enter the new name, **Year 2002 Forecast**, in the File Name text box.

■ Click 🖫 Save ☐.

Working with Multiple Workbooks

Evan wants you to focus on the 2002 first-quarter forecast. Because he expects all sales and expenses to remain the same as the December 2001 values, you can obtain the data from the Year 2001 Forecast workbook you saved previously. You do not need to close the workbook that is currently displayed in order to open a second workbook. Instead, you will open the workbook that contains the data you need and arrange the workbook windows so you can see them both simultaneously.

1 ▬ Open the Year 2001 Forecast workbook file.

Your screen should be similar to Figure 4–12.

active workbook contains cell selector

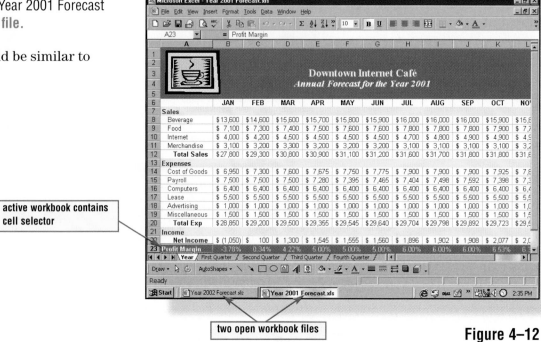

two open workbook files

Figure 4–12

Excel displays the Year 2001 Forecast workbook file in a second window on top of the Year 2002 Forecast workbook file window. There are now two open workbook files. The newly opened file is the **active workbook** file. It is the file that will be affected by changes and that contains the cell selector.

The way the workbooks are currently displayed makes it difficult to work with both files simultaneously. To make it easier to work with both files at the same time, you'll change the arrangement of the windows so that they appear next to each other.

Concept (4) Arrange Windows

The **Arrange Windows** feature displays all open workbook files in separate windows on the screen. The following window arrangement options are available:

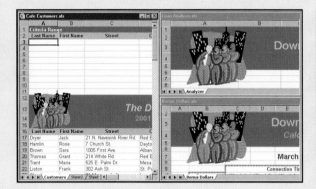

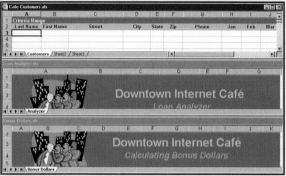

Tiled: The windows are displayed one after the other in succession, across and down the screen.

Horizontal: The windows are displayed one above the other.

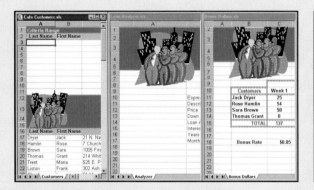

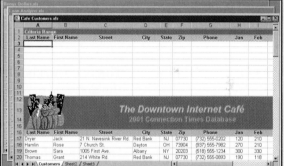

Vertical: The windows are displayed side-by-side.

Cascade: The windows are displayed one on top of the other, cascading down from the top of the screen.

You can also use this feature to display multiple sheets of a workbook on the screen at the same time.

You decide that the easiest way to work with the two files would be to tile them.

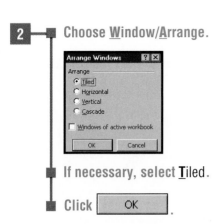

2 ■ Choose <u>W</u>indow/<u>A</u>rrange.

■ If necessary, select <u>T</u>iled.

■ Click OK.

Your screen should be similar to Figure 4–13.

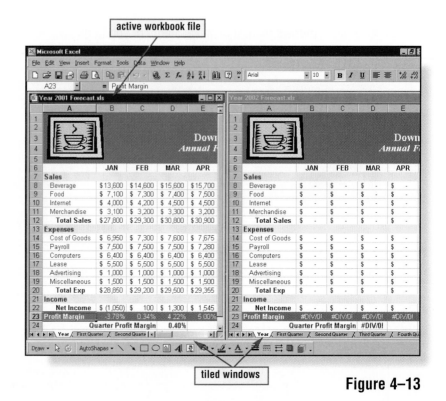

Figure 4–13

The two workbook file windows appear next to each other. The title bar of the active workbook file is highlighted. To see the December values in the Fourth Quarter sheet of the 2001 forecast and to display the First Quarter sheet from the 2002 forecast,

3 ■ Display the Fourth Quarter sheet in the Year 2001 Forecast workbook.

■ Display the First Quarter sheet in the Year 2002 Forecast workbook.

Your screen should be similar to Figure 4–14.

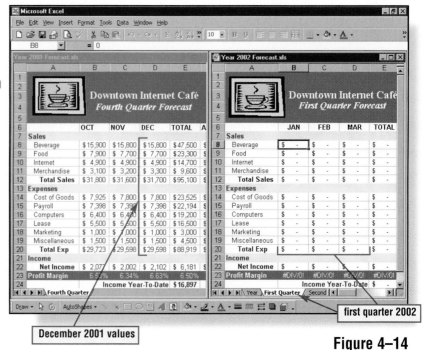

Figure 4–14

Linking Workbooks

You want to use the December data from the 2001 forecast workbook in the 2002 forecast workbook. Additionally, you want the data in the 2002 forecast to update automatically if the data in the 2001 forecast changes. To do this, you will create a link between the two workbook files.

Concept (5) Link Workbooks

A **link** creates a connection between files that automatically updates the linked data in one file whenever the data in the other file change. The link between the workbook files is formed by entering an **external reference formula** in one workbook that refers to a cell in another workbook. When data in a linked cell change, the workbook that is affected by this change is automatically updated when it is opened.

The formula is entered in the workbook that receives the data. This workbook file is called the **dependent workbook**. The workbook that supplies the data is called the **source workbook**. The cell containing the external reference formula (the **dependent cell**) refers to the cell (the **source cell**) in the source file that contains the data to be copied.

An external reference formula uses the following format:

= [workbook file reference]sheet reference!cell reference

The file reference consists of the file name of the source file followed by the name of the worksheet. The cell reference of the cell or range of cells containing the number to be copied into the dependent workbook follows the file reference. The two parts of the formula are separated by an exclamation point.

You will create a link between the two workbook files by entering external reference formulas in the Year 2002 First Quarter worksheet that reference the cells containing the values in the Fourth Quarter sheet of the Year 2001 Forecast workbook. The Year 2001 Forecast workbook is the source workbook, and the Year 2002 Forecast workbook is the dependent workbook.

The first external reference formula you will enter will link the beverage sales numbers. To create an external reference formula, you copy the contents of the source cell to the Clipboard, switch to the dependent workbook, and then use the Edit/Paste Special command to create the external reference formula link in the specified cell of the dependent workook.

The source cell is cell D8 of the Fourth Quarter sheet in the Year 2001 Forecast workbook. To copy this source cell and paste it into the dependent cell,

1 ■ Select cell D8 of the Fourth Quarter sheet in the Year 2001 Forecast workbook.

■ Click 🖺 Copy.

■ Select cell B8 in the First Quarter sheet of the Year 2002 Forecast workbook.

■ Choose **E**dit/Paste **S**pecial.

Your screen should be similar to Figure 4–15.

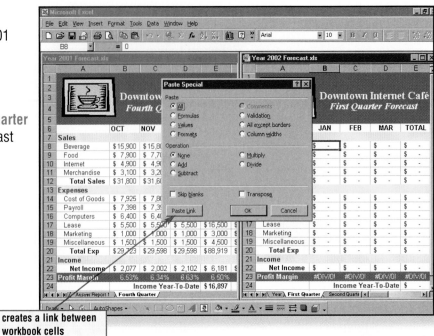

creates a link between workbook cells

Figure 4–15

From the Paste Special dialog box, you specify how much of the cell contents you want pasted. You can paste either the entire cell contents (including formatting), or selected attributes associated with the cell, such as only the formula, value, format, comments, validation, or column width of the cell. You can also perform an addition, subtraction, multiplication, or division operation on the pasted cell.

You can also create a link to the source cell contents so that when the source cell is changed, the linked cell is automatically changed as well.

2 ■ Click  .

Your screen should be similar to Figure 4–16.

external reference formula

absolute reference

value from D8 of the 2001 workbook file pasted as a link

Figure 4–16

The link has been established and an external reference formula has been entered into the selected cell of the dependent workbook. The formula is displayed in the formula bar, and the number in cell D8 of the source workbook is entered into the dependent workbook and displayed in cell B8. Notice that Excel uses absolute references in the external reference formula.

Next you want to create a link between the other December values in the source workbook. To do this quickly, you can copy the external reference formula down the column and across the rows. However, you must first change the cell reference $D$8 in the external reference formula to a mixed reference of ($D8) so that it will adjust appropriately as the formula is copied.

3 ■ Change the reference in the formula in cell B8 of the Year 2002 Forecast workbook. to **$D8**.

■ Copy the external reference formula in cell B8 into cells C8 and D8 and cells B9 through D11.

■ Copy the external reference formula in cell B8 into the range B15 through D19.

■ Click cell D19 to clear the selection.

Your screen should be similar to Figure 4–17.

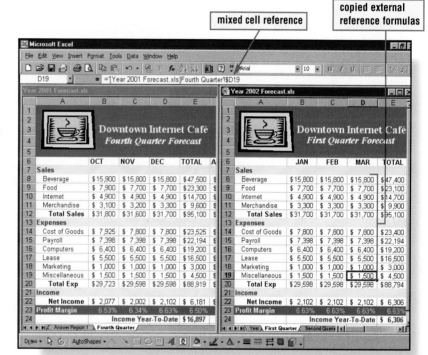

Figure 4–17

Evan advises you that the lease for the café will increase to $6,000 a month beginning in October of 2001. To observe the effect of this change,

4 ▪— Enter **6,000** into cells B17, C17, and D17 in the Fourth Quarter sheet of the Year 2001 Forecast workbook.

Your screen should be similar to Figure 4–18.

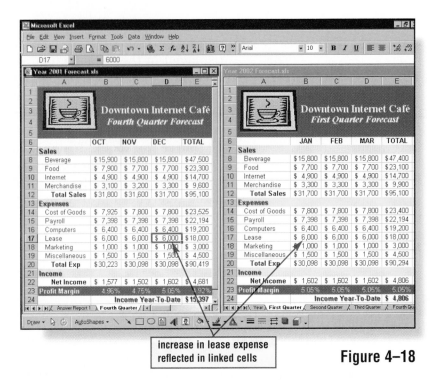

increase in lease expense
reflected in linked cells

Figure 4–18

All affected formulas are recalculated. Because the workbooks are linked, the change in the Year 2001 Forecast is automatically reflected in the Year 2002 Forecast, where the Total Profit Margin dropped from 6.63 percent to 5.05 percent.

Once an external reference formula is entered in a worksheet, whenever the data in the cell referenced in the source file change, the dependent file is automatically updated if it is open. However, if the dependent file is not open, it is not updated. To ensure that a dependent file gets updated when you open the source file Excel displays an alert message asking if you want to update references to unopened documents. If you respond Yes, Excel checks the source documents and updates all references to them so that you will have the latest values from the source worksheet.

You do not need to obtain any further data from the Year 2001 Forecast workbook at this time, so you can close it and enlarge the 2002 Forecast window to make it easier to work with.

5 ■ Close the Year 2001 Forecast workbook, saving the changes.

■ Maximize the Year 2002 Forecast window.

Your screen should be similar to Figure 4–19.

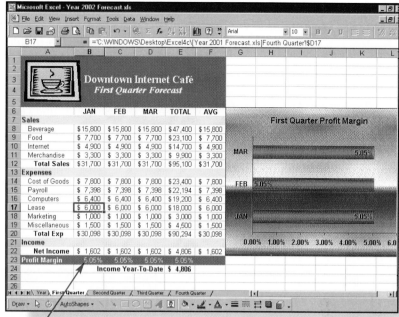

First Quarter worksheet reflects most likely sales and expenses

Figure 4–19

Creating Scenarios

- -

Evan has reviewed the First Quarter Forecast and is comfortable with it. While he realizes that sales and costs may be higher or lower than those presented, Evan believes the most likely scenario, or set of values, is reflected in the First Quarter worksheet. He has asked you to evaluate a best-case scenario and a worst-case scenario.

Concept ⑦ Scenario

A **scenario** is a named set of input values that you can substitute in a worksheet to see the effects of a possible alternative course of action. Scenarios are designed to help forecast the outcome of various possible actions. You can create and save different groups of scenario values on a worksheet and then switch to any of these scenarios to view the results.

For example, if you want to create a budget forecast based on various revenue values, you could define the potential values and then switch between the scenarios to perform what-if analyses.

You can also create reports in separate sheets that summarize the scenarios you create.

The current workbook reflects the most likely scenario. Evan has identified the best case scenario as one where sales from Internet use increases 25 percent above the current estimate of $4,900 to $6,125 in February and March and all other values remain unchanged. His worst-case scenario is if Internet sales decrease 10 percent below the current estimate to $4,410 for the entire quarter and the lease in March increases from $6,000 to $6,200. You are going to use the Scenario tool to evaluate the alternative scenarios by changing the values for Internet Sales for January (cell B10), February (cell C10), and March (cell D10) and for March Lease Expense (cell D17).

You could create separate worksheets to evaluate each scenario. However, using the Scenario Manager tool, you can create different scenarios and insert these scenarios directly into the workbook to see how each affects the worksheet.

1 ■ Move to cell B10.

■ Choose **T**ools/Sc**e**narios.

■ Move the Scenario Manager dialog box to the right of column F.

Your screen should be similar to Figure 4–20.

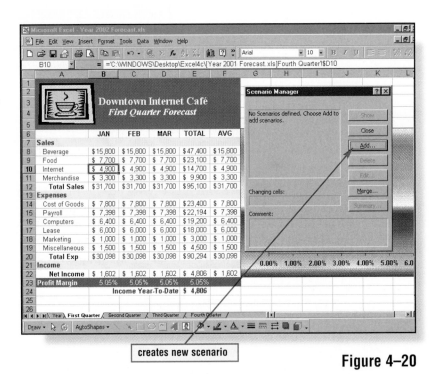

creates new scenario

Figure 4–20

The Scenario Manager dialog box is used to add, delete, and edit scenarios. There are no scenarios named yet. First you will define the most likely scenario.

2 ■ Click [Add...].

Your screen should be similar to Figure 4–21.

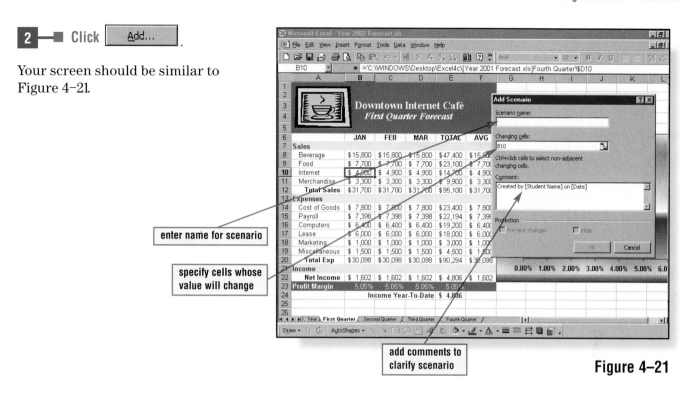

enter name for scenario

specify cells whose value will change

add comments to clarify scenario

Figure 4–21

In the Add Scenario dialog box you enter a name for the first scenario and the range of cells that will contain the changing values in the Changing Cells text box.

3 ■ Type **Most Likely** in the Scenario **N**ame text box.

■ Specify the range B10 through D10 and cell D17 as the changing cells in the Changing Cell text box.

> Click 🔳 to reduce the dialog box and select the range from the worksheet. Click on cell D17 while holding down Ctrl to select the nonadjacent cell.

Your screen should be similar to Figure 4–22.

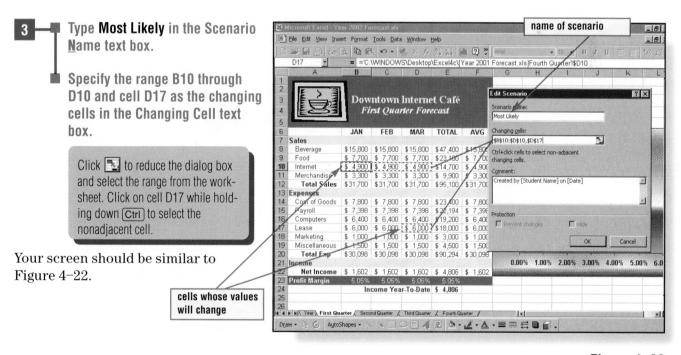

name of scenario

cells whose values will change

Figure 4–22

It is often helpful to add a comment to clarify the data included in the scenario. The default comment in the Comment text box displays the text "Created by [name] on [date]." To add a comment,

4 ■ Click in the Comment text box.

■ If necessary, replace the name with your name. Add the following text after the date: **The most likely scenario is for first quarter sales and expenses to be the same as December 2001.**

■ Click [OK].

■ Click [OK] to accept that formulas will be replaced by values.

Your screen should be similar to Figure 4-23.

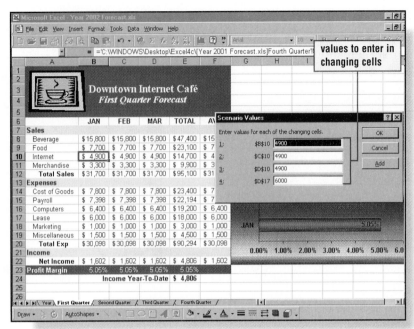

Figure 4-23

The Scenario Values dialog box is used to enter the values to be varied for the different scenarios. To accept the current worksheet values for the Most Likely scenario,

5 ■ Click [OK].

Your screen should be similar to Figure 4-24.

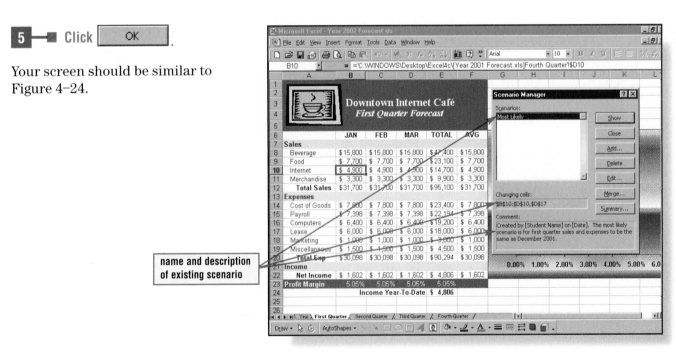

Figure 4-24

You are returned to the Scenario Manager dialog box and the name of the new scenario is displayed in the Scenarios list box. Next you will create the best-case scenario.

6 ■ Click [Add...].

■ In the Scenario Name text box, type **Best Case**.

■ In the Comment text box, change the name if necessary and enter the following: **The best-case scenario is for Internet Sales to be 25% above the most likely values for February and March and for the March lease expense to remain the same.**

■ Click [OK] twice.

■ Enter the value **6125** into the changing cells $C$10 and $D$10 text boxes.

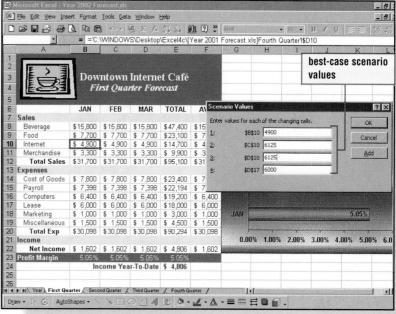

Your screen should be similar to Figure 4-25.

Figure 4-25

Next you will create the worst-case scenario.

7 ■ Click [OK].

■ Click [Add...].

■ In a similar manner, define the worst-case scenario using the following settings:

Scenario name	**Worst Case**
Comment	**The worst case scenario is for Internet Sales to be 10% less than the most likely values for January, February and March and for the March Lease to be 10% higher.**
$B$10, $C$10, and $D$10 changing cell value	**4410**
$D$17 changing cell value	**6200**

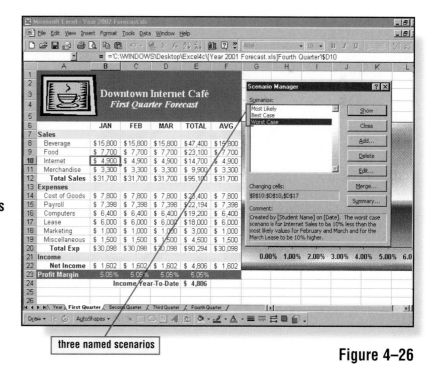

three named scenarios

Figure 4-26

Your screen should be similar to Figure 4-26.

Using Scenarios

There are now three different scenarios. Now you want to see the effect of the worst-case scenario on the worksheet.

1 In the Scenario Manager dialog box, select Worst Case, if it is not already selected.

Click **Show**.

Move the Scenario Manager dialog box down to row 23 so you can see the graph.

Your screen should be similar to Figure 4–27.

worst-case scenario values

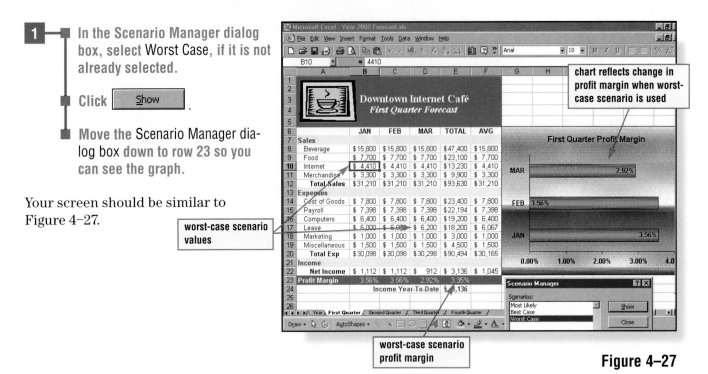

chart reflects change in profit margin when worst-case scenario is used

worst-case scenario profit margin

Figure 4–27

The worksheet displays the worst-case values. These values result in a total profit margin of 3.35 percent and the chart reflects the change in monthly profit margins.

If Excel did not update the chart, move the Scenario Manager box slightly to refresh the window.

2 In a similar manner, display the Best Case scenario.

The total profit margin is now 7.44 percent.

Creating a Scenario Report

Another way to evaluate the scenarios is to create a summary report that will display the effect on the profit margins for each scenario.

1 Move the Scenario Manger dialog box up to row 5.

Click Summary....

Specify the range B23 through E23 (containing the profit margin values) as the range of cells whose results you want summarized.

Click OK

Your screen should be similar to Figure 4-28.

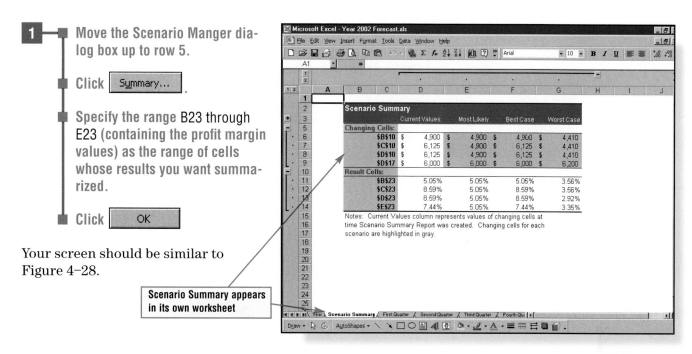

Scenario Summary appears in its own worksheet

Figure 4-28

The Scenario Summary report is created and displayed in a separate sheet. It displays the values for the three scenarios and the results on the profit margin for each scenario. As you can see from the summary, the most likely scenario yields a constant 5.05 percent profit margin. The best case scenario yields higher profit margins, with an average of 7.44 percent for the quarter. The worst case scenario yields lower profit margins, with an average of 3.35 percent.

You have now completed best- and worst-case scenarios for the year 2002, as Evan requested. However, before printing the Scenario Summary worksheet and giving it to Evan, you want to add some 3-D graphics to the Scenario Summary worksheet to emphasize the best-case profit margin scenario.

2 Save the workbook.

Creating and Modifying 3-D Shapes

To emphasize the impact of Internet sales, you want to add a three-dimensional (3-D) shape to the Scenario Summary report to draw attention to the rising profits. A **3-D shape** is a line, AutoShape, or free-form drawing object that has a three-dimensional effect applied to it. The first object you want to create is a text box that identifies the Internet promotion as the focus of the high-sales scenario. To create the text box,

1 Click 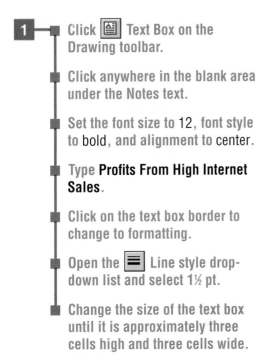 Text Box on the Drawing toolbar.

Click anywhere in the blank area under the Notes text.

Set the font size to 12, font style to bold, and alignment to center.

Type **Profits From High Internet Sales**.

Click on the text box border to change to formatting.

Open the ≡ Line style drop-down list and select 1½ pt.

Change the size of the text box until it is approximately three cells high and three cells wide.

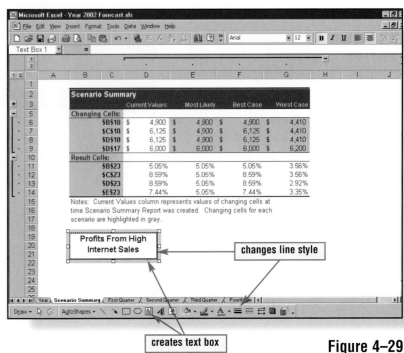

Figure 4–29

Your screen should be similar to Figure 4–29.

Now you want to apply a 3-D effect to the text box. Excel includes many 3-D options you can use to change the depth (the extrusion) of the object and its color, rotation, angle, direction of lighting, and surface texture. When you change the color of a 3-D effect, only the 3-D effect of the object is changed, not the object itself.

2 Click 3-D on the Drawing toolbar.

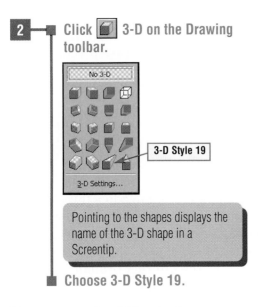

Pointing to the shapes displays the name of the 3-D shape in a Screentip.

Choose 3-D Style 19.

Your screen should be similar to Figure 4–30.

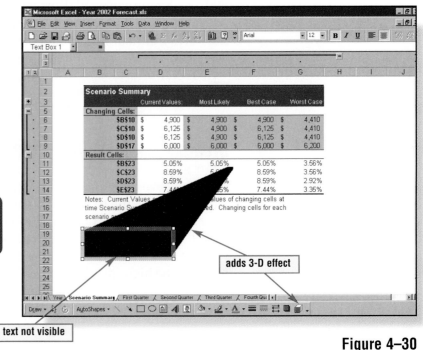

Figure 4–30

The 3-D shape is added to the text box, but the text is no longer visible. This is because the text color is black and 3-D style you selected uses black to fill its boxes as well. To remedy this, you'll change the fill color.

3 — Open the [🪣 ▾] Fill Color drop-down menu and select a color of your choice.

Your screen should look like Figure 4–31.

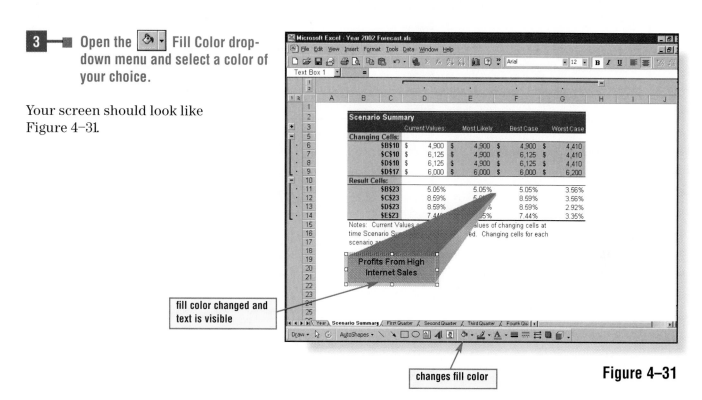

fill color changed and text is visible

changes fill color

Figure 4–31

You would also like to see how the 3-D effect would look with different settings applied to it, such as a different lighting effect and box color.

4 — Open the [▨] 3-D drop-down menu and select 3-D Settings.

The 3-D Settings toolbar buttons (identified below) are used to modify the depth (the extrusion) of the 3-D effect and its color, rotation, angle, direction of lighting, and surface texture.

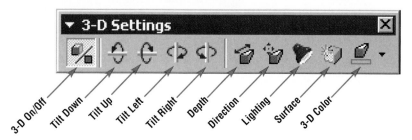

5 ■ Open the 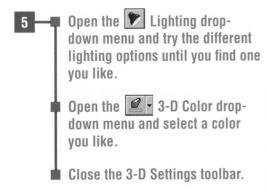 Lighting drop-down menu and try the different lighting options until you find one you like.

■ Open the 3-D Color drop-down menu and select a color you like.

■ Close the 3-D Settings toolbar.

Your screen should be similar to Figure 4–32.

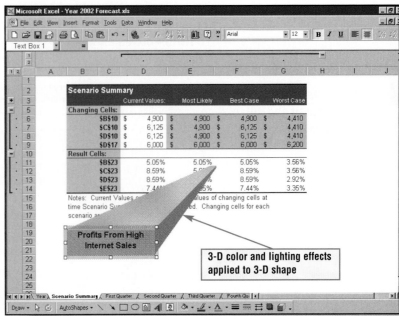

Figure 4–32

Deleting and Moving Objects

After looking at the 3-D text box you've created, you are not sure it is very effective and you decide to delete the object.

1 ■ If necessary, click on the object to select it.

■ Press Delete.

The entire 3-D text box is deleted. However, now you decide that the graphic may be effective after all if it points to the area of the report displaying the best-case results. To restore the deleted object,

2 ■ Click .

You want to move the 3-D text box so that it points to the best-case result cells.

3 Drag the text box until it points to the center of the best-case result column.

Your screen should be similar to Figure 4-33.

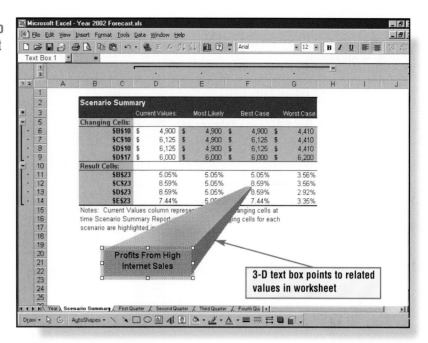

Figure 4-33

Now the 3-D text box is more effective.

Displaying the Current Date and Time

You would also like to include a date and time stamp on the Scenario Summary worksheet to identify when the values were entered and the scenarios applied. You could just enter the current date and time on the worksheet, but you want to ensure that it reflects exactly when the most recent changes and analyses are done. To have the date and time automatically update whenever a worksheet is recalculated, you'll use the NOW date function.

1 Move to cell B3 on the Scenario worksheet.

Click 𝒇𝓍 Paste Function.

From the Date & Time category, select NOW.

Click **OK**.

Your screen should be similar to Figure 4-34.

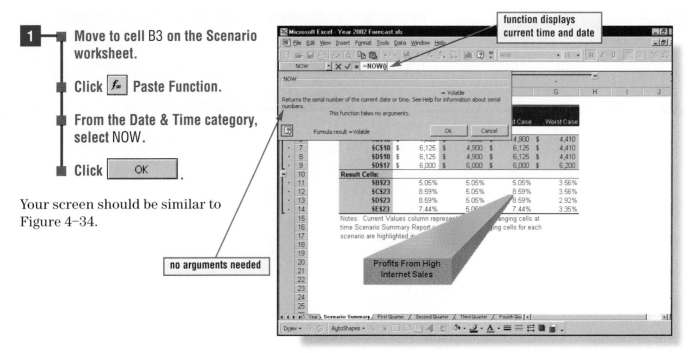

Figure 4-34

The Paste Function dialog box displays a message telling you that this function displays the current date and time, and requires no arguments. To complete the function,

2 Click **OK**.

Your screen should be similar to Figure 4-35.

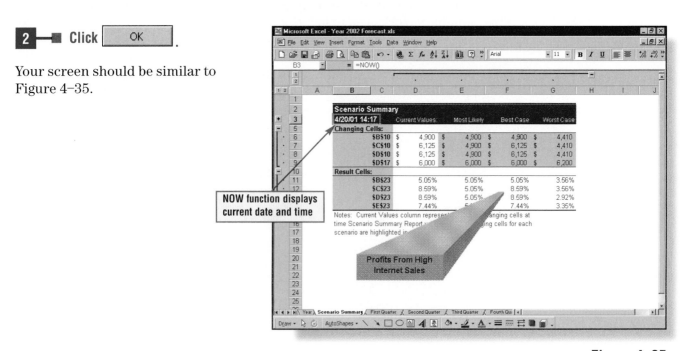

Figure 4-35

The current date and time are displayed in cell B3. Now you'd like to print the Scenario Summary to show it to Evan.

3 Enter your name and the worksheet name in a footer.

Print the Scenario Summary worksheet.

Save the file and exit Excel.

Concept Summary

Tutorial 4: Using Solver, Creating Workbook Templates, Linking Workbooks, and Creating Scenarios

Solver is a tool used to perform what-if analyses to determine the effect of changing values in two or more cells on another cell.

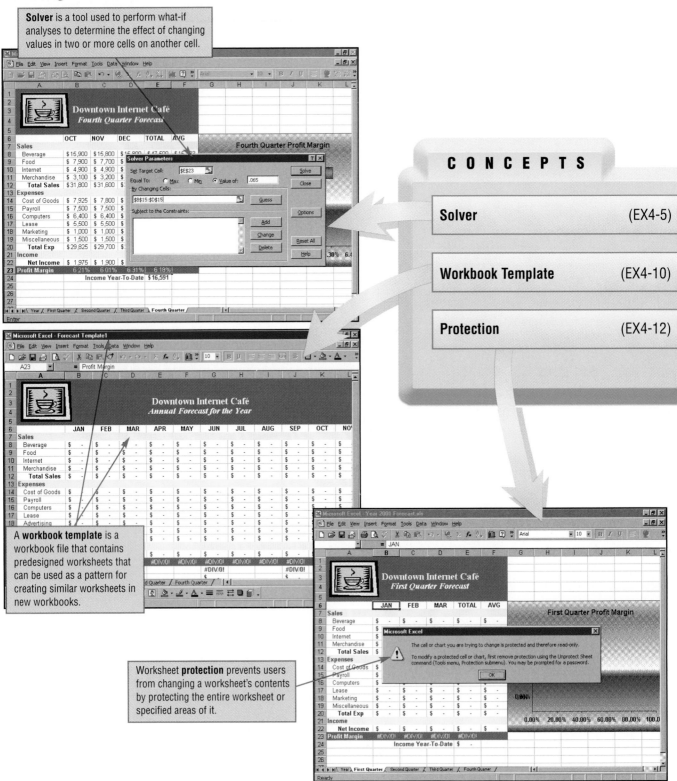

A **workbook template** is a workbook file that contains predesigned worksheets that can be used as a pattern for creating similar worksheets in new workbooks.

Worksheet **protection** prevents users from changing a worksheet's contents by protecting the entire worksheet or specified areas of it.

CONCEPTS

Solver	(EX4-5)
Workbook Template	(EX4-10)
Protection	(EX4-12)

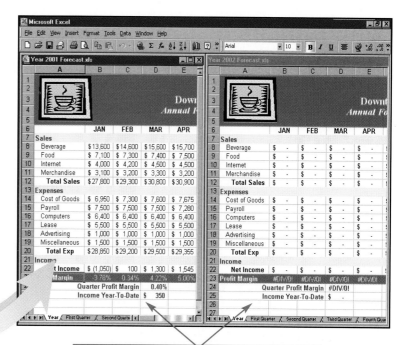

The **Arrange Windows** feature displays all open workbook files in separate windows on the screen in a tiled, horizontal, vertical, or cascade arrangement.

Arrange Windows	(EX4-17)
Link Workbooks	(EX4-19)
Scenario	(EX4-23)

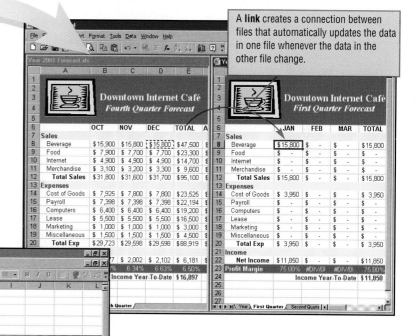

A **link** creates a connection between files that automatically updates the data in one file whenever the data in the other file change.

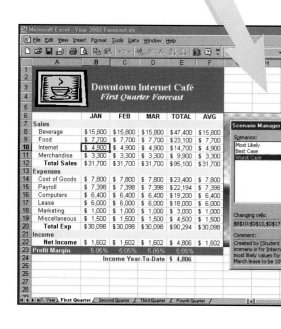

A **scenario** is a named set of input values that you can substitute in a worksheet to see the effects of a possible alternative course of action. Scenarios are designed to help forecast the outcome of various possible actions.

Tutorial Review

Key Terms

3-D shape   EX4-29
active workbook   EX4-16
adjustable cells   EX4-5
Arrange Windows   EX4-17
cascade   EX4-17
dependent cell   EX4-19
dependent workbook   EX4-19

external reference
    formula   EX4-19
horizontal   EX4-17
link   EX4-19
password   EX4-12
protection   EX4-12
scenario   EX4-23

Solver   EX4-5
source cell   EX4-19
source workbook   EX4-19
target cell   EX4-5
template   EX4-10
tiled   EX4-17
vertical   EX4-17

Command Summary

Command	Shortcut Keys	Button	Action
Edit/De**l**ete Sheet			Deletes selected worksheets from a workbook
Tools/**P**rotection/**P**rotect Sheet			Prevents unauthorized users from changing a worksheet's contents
Tools/**S**cenarios			Creates and saves sets of data used to perform what-if analyses
Tools/Sol**v**er			Calculates a formula to achieve a given value by changing one of the variables that affects formulas
Window/**A**rrange			Arranges open windows side-by-side, vertically, horizontally, or tiled

Screen Identification

In the following worksheet, several items are identified by letters. Enter the correct term for each item in the spaces that follow.

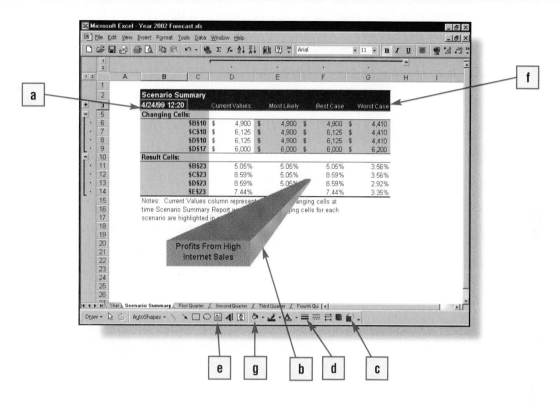

a. _____   f. _____

b. _____   g. _____

c. _____

d. _____

e. _____

Matching

Match the letter on the right to the item in the numbered list on the left.

1. =[ANNUAL.xls]YEAR!$B$12 _____   **a.** arranges worksheet windows side-by-side

2. scenario _____   **b.** creates a data connection between files

3. tiled _____   **c.** achieves a given value by changing formula variables

4. link _____   **d.** an external reference formula

5. dependent workbook _____   **e.** worksheet that supplies data in a linking formula

6. template _____   **f.** worksheet that receives data in a linking formula

7. NOW _____   **g.** used to perform what-if analyses

8. Solver _____   **h.** used as a pattern for creating new workbooks

9. source workbook _____   **i.** function that displays current date and time

10. target cell _____   **j.** cell containing value you want to solve for

Fill-In

Complete the following statements by filling in the blanks with the correct terms.

a. Tiling displays _____ side-by-side.

b. Use _____ to change the settings of a 3-D shape.

c. _____ receives linked data.

d. The _____ function automatically updates the date and time whenever a worksheet is recalculated.

e. Before protecting a worksheet, _____ those cells whose contents you want to change.

f. The Excel workbook template file extension is _____.

g. _____ contains predesigned worksheets that can be used as a pattern for creating similar worksheets in new workbooks.

h. The Paste Special command _____ or _____ a cell that's on the Clipboard in a specific format.

i. The cell containing a formula you want to solve is called the _____

j. When using Solver the cells you select must be related through _____ on this worksheet.

Multiple-Choice

Circle the correct response to the questions below.

1. A workbook file containing predesigned worksheets is called a _____ workbook.

    a. sheet

    b. model

    c. template

    d. form

2. In the external reference formula [Forecast.xls]Year$N$8, the name in brackets is _____.

    a. the source file

    b. the destination file

    c. the active file

    d. the current worksheet

3. The Solver Results dialog box lets you _____.

    a. restore original values

    b. keep the Solver solution

    c. create a report

    d. any of the above

4. The Paste Special command enables you to paste the _____ of one cell into another cell.

    a. contents

    b. comments

    c. column width

    d. all of the above

5. The _____ tool lets you view varying values applied to a worksheet:

    a. Scenario

    b. Solver

    c. What-If

    d. Goal-Seek

6. To display the current system date and time, you use the _____.

    a. DATE function

    b. TODAY function

    c. TIME function

    d. none of the above

7. _____ prevents user from changing the contents of worksheet.

    a. Locking cells

    b. Protecting a worksheet

    c. Unlocking cells

    d. A password

8. The _____ command permanently deletes a selected worksheet.

    a. Clear Sheet

    b. Remove Sheet

    c. Delete Sheet

    d. Clear Contents

9. The workbook file that receives linked data is called the _____.

    a. source workbook

    b. reference workbook

    c. dependent workbook

    d. external workbook

10. The _____ tool is used to find the value needed in one cell by changing the values in one or more other cells in the worksheet.

    a. Query

    b. Solver

    c. Value Analysis

    d. Look Up

True/False

Circle the correct answer to the following questions.

1.	A worksheet that is deleted can be retrieved.	True	False
2.	You can apply both a 3-D effect and shadowing to an object.	True	False
3.	Cells you select as variables in Solver must be related through formulas on a worksheet.	True	False
4.	You must use Save As to save a workbook that you create from a template.	True	False
5.	To cascade worksheet windows means to display them side-by-side on the screen.	True	False
6.	Whenever data containing an external reference formula are changed in the dependent workbook, data in the linked cell in the source workbook are automatically changed as well.	True	False
7.	A Scenario Summary shows the results of all scenarios created for a worksheet.	True	False
8.	The horizontal window arrangement displays windows side by side.	True	False
9.	A cell that is linked only changes when the workbook is reopened.	True	False
10.	A password prevents users from changing the contents of a worksheet	True	False

Discussion Questions

1. Discuss how templates can be used to make workbook creation easier. What types of templates do you think would be most helpful, and what should these templates contain?

2. Discuss what happens to formulas that are linked to another workbook when the original workbook is updated. When would it be appropriate to link data between workbooks?

3. Discuss the differences between Paste and Paste Special. Under what conditions would it be more appropriate to use Paste Special?

4. Discuss how Solver and scenarios are used in a worksheet. How can they help with the analysis of data?

Hands-On Practice Exercises

Step by Step

☆

1. Adventure Travel has a six-month income worksheet that it uses to track the amount of income from different sources. The company would like to create a template that not only tracks the information but analyzes future revenue based on past performance. Your completed worksheet will be similar to the one shown here.

a. Open the file Adventure Travel Analysis on your data disk.

b. Make a copy of Sheet1(2). Rename sheet1 **First Six Months** and Sheet2 **Second Six Months**.

Adventure Travel
Sources of Income

	Jan	Feb	Mar	Apr	May	Jun	Total
Hotels	$16,581	$15,151	$17,854	$15,154	$15,412	$15,454	$ 95,606
Airlines	$27,584	$24,844	$24,587	$25,484	$25,458	$26,585	$154,542
Bus Tours	$ 1,540	$ 1,625	$ 1,254	$ 1,525	$ 1,558	$ 1,452	$ 8,954
Car Rentals	$ 787	$ 732	$ 844	$ 645	$ 932	$ 520	$ 4,460
Tour Packages	$ 1,548	$ 1,558	$ 1,254	$ 1,365	$ 1,475	$ 1,548	$ 8,748
Hiking Tours	$ 253	$ 248	$ 458	$ 214	$ 597	$ 425	$ 2,195
Cruse Packages	$ 1,854	$ 1,125	$ 1,452	$ 1,259	$ 1,574	$ 1,597	$ 8,861
Total	$50,147	$45,283	$47,703	$45,646	$47,006	$47,581	$283,366

Student Name
4/20/01 15:15

c. Delete the other blank sheets from the workbook.

d. Modify the month column labels in the Second Six Months sheet to reflect the last six months of the year.

e. Select both sheets. Select cells B5 through G11 and unlock the cells.

Adventure Travel
Sources of Income

	Jul	Aug	Sep	Oct	Nov	Dec	Total
Hotels	$17,854	$15,154	$15,412	$15,454	$17,832	$19,432	$101,138
Airlines	$24,587	$25,484	$25,458	$26,585	$24,587	$26,590	$153,291
Bus Tours	$ 1,254	$ 2,525	$ 2,558	$ 2,452	$ 2,232	$ 1,944	$ 12,965
Car Rentals	$ 944	$ 845	$ 732	$ 720	$ 832	$ 932	$ 5,005
Tour Packages	$ 2,254	$ 2,365	$ 2,475	$ 2,548	$ 3,332	$ 3,132	$ 16,106
Hiking Tours	$ 458	$ 214	$ 597	$ 425	$ 532	$ 542	$ 2,768
Cruse Packages	$ 1,452	$ 1,259	$ 1,574	$ 1,597	$ 1,232	$ 1,324	$ 8,438
Total	$48,803	$47,846	$48,806	$49,781	$50,579	$53,896	$299,711

Student Name
4/20/01 15:15

f. Ungroup the worksheets.

g. Save the workbook as a template with the name **AT Analysis Template**. Close the workbook and open a new workbook with the template.

h. Enter sample data in both worksheets.

i. Enter your name and the current date using the NOW function in cells A15 and A16 respectively, of both sheets.

j. Save the workbook as **Revenue Analysis**. Print the workbook.

2. You have been hired as the office manager for a department at the university. Part of your job is to keep track of the hours worked by student employees and funds available for their pay. You are working on creating an Excel template that you can use to track this information each semester. Your completed template will be similar to the one shown here.

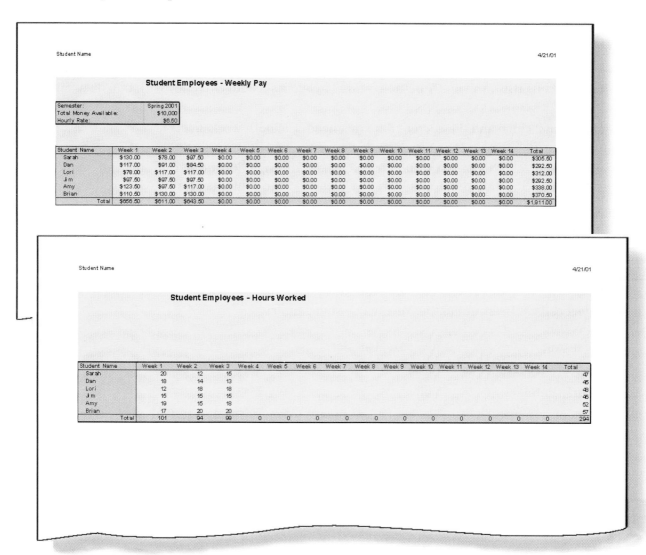

a. Open the file Student Workers on your data disk. You still need to create a second worksheet to record the weekly hours worked and enter a formula to calculate weekly pay.

b. Make a copy of the Weekly Pay sheet. Name the new sheet **Hours Worked**. Change Weekly Pay in the title to Hours Worked. Clear the contents and the format from cells A4 through C6. Apply the same yellow fill to the ranges in surrounding cells.

c. In the Weekly Pay sheet enter the formula **=$C$6**＊**'Hours Worked'!B11** to calculate weekly pay in cell B11. Copy the formula from B11 to complete the remaining weeks for the six students.

d. To test the template for the upcoming semester enter the following sample data in both sheets:

Semester:	**Enter your current semester (Fall 2001)**
Total Money Available:	**8000**
Hourly Rate:	**6.00**
Student Name:	[Enter six first names to represent the student workers. Enter sample data in the Hours Worked worksheet for the first week. Each student can work up to 20 hours per week.]

e. Format cells B11 through P17 in the Weekly Pay worksheet to currency with two decimal places.

f. Enter your name and the current date in a header of both worksheets

g. Now that the workbook gives you the information you want, you will create a template to use for any semester. Remove the data from cells C4 through C6, and A11 through A16 of the Weekly Pay Sheet. In the Hours Worked sheet clear the contents of cells A11 through B16.

h. Unlock cells C4 through C6, and A11 through A16 of the Weekly Pay sheet. Unlock cells A11 through O16 of the Hours Worked sheet.

i. Protect the worksheets.

j. Save the workbook as a template. Close the workbook and open a new workbook using the template.

k. Select cells A11:A16 and in the Weekly Pay sheet enter:

Semester:	**Your next semester**
Total Money Available:	**10000**
Hourly Rate:	**6.50**
Student Name:	[Enter six first names to represent the student workers in both sheets.]

l. Enter hours worked for the first three weeks for each student. Save the workbook. Print both worksheets to fit on one page in landscape orientation.

3. You have just graduated from college, started your first professional job, and purchased a new car and a house. With all the new financial obligations you have, you decide to create an annual budget to help you meet your obligations as well as save to purchase new furniture for your home. You have already started a worksheet containing the labels and the monthly expenses. Your completed budget will be similar to the one shown here.

Student Name Budget

		Jul	Aug	Sep	Oct	Nov	Dec	Jan	Feb	Mar	Apr	May	Jun	Total
Base Salary:	$35,000													
Retirement Contribution	$3,500													
Insurance Contribution	$456													
Tax Bracket	29%													
Income														
Monthly Take Home Pay		$1,741	$1,741	$1,741	$1,741	$1,741	$1,741	$1,741	$1,741	$1,741	$1,741	$1,741	$1,741	$20,894
Signing Bonus		$5,500												$5,500
December Bonus							$3,000							$3,000
Total Income		$7,241	$1,741	$1,741	$1,741	$1,741	$4,741	$1,741	$1,741	$1,741	$1,741	$1,741	$1,741	$29,394
Fixed Expenses														
House Payment		$650	$650	$650	$650	$650	$650	$650	$650	$650	$650	$650	$650	$7,800
Auto Payment		$324	$324	$324	$324	$324	$324	$324	$324	$324	$324	$324	$324	$3,888
Student Loan		$210	$210	$210	$210	$210	$210	$210	$210	$210	$210	$210	$210	$2,520
Estimated Expenses														
Phone Bill		$35	$35	$35	$35	$35	$35	$35	$35	$35	$35	$35	$35	$420
Cable Company		$31	$31	$31	$31	$31	$31	$31	$31	$31	$31	$31	$31	$372
Auto Insurance				$325	$326					$325	$326				$1,302
Homeowners Insurance		$325						$325							$650
Daily Newspaper		$34			$34			$34			$34				$136
Auto Registration				$122											$122
Electric Bill		$90	$90	$90	$90	$90	$90	$90	$90	$90	$90	$90	$90	$1,080
City Water/Trash Collectio		$32	$32	$32	$32	$32	$32	$32	$32	$32	$32	$32	$32	$384
Property Tax					$450					$450					$900
Automobile Gas		$30	$30	$30	$30	$30	$30	$30	$30	$30	$30	$30	$30	$360
Clothing		$141	$141	$141	$141	$141	$141	$141	$141	$141	$141	$141	$141	$1,689
Food		$141	$141	$141	$141	$141	$141	$141	$141	$141	$141	$141	$141	$1,689
Entertainment		$141	$141	$141	$141	$141	$141	$141	$141	$141	$141	$141	$141	$1,689
Total Expenses		$2,183	$1,824	$2,271	$2,634	$1,824	$1,824	$2,183	$1,824	$2,599	$2,184	$1,824	$1,824	$25,000
Available Funds		$5,058	-$83	-$530	-$893	-$83	$2,917	-$442	-$83	-$858	-$443	-$83	-$83	$4,394

a. Open the file First Year Budget on your data disk.

b. Add your name followed by **Budget** as the title at the top of the worksheet. Center and merge the title over the worksheet. Increase the font size to 14.

c. Calculate and enter the monthly take home pay for row 11. =($B$4-$B$5-$B$6-($B$4*$B$7))/12)

d. Calculate the total expenses and available funds for rows 31 and 32.

e. After doing all the calculations, you realize that you are going to be short of funds for this year. Using Solver, reduce the clothing, food, and entertainment expenses to achieve a target value (cell N31) equal to your income. Keep the Solver solution in the worksheet. Looking over the solution, you realize that the values for these three categories are inappropriate and you would never be able to stay on budget. However, you know that, as part of your employment negotiations, you are going to receive a $5,500 signing bonus and a December bonus of $3,000.

f. Insert three rows below the Monthly Take Home Pay row. Label the new rows **Signing Bonus**, **December Bonus**, and **Total Income**. Enter **5,500** in July for the signing bonus and **3,000** in December. Enter formulas to calculate totals for N12, N13, and B14 through N14.

g. Adjust the formula in row 35 to calculate the new available funds.

h. Use Solver again to calculate the amount you can spend to equal your income. The solution gives you more than enough each month to meet your expenses. However, you would like to calculate a more realistic value for these cells. To do this, restore the original values and solve for $25,000. Keep the Solver solution.

i. Apply fill colors, font colors, and other features of your choice to enhance the worksheet.

j. Save the workbook. Print the worksheet in landscape orientation on one page.

4. You are working in the university's registration office. As part of your job you have been asked to create a worksheet comparing college enrollments for the past four years. Additionally, you need to project best- and worst-case scenarios for enrollments for the next year. Your completed worksheet will be similar to the one shown here.

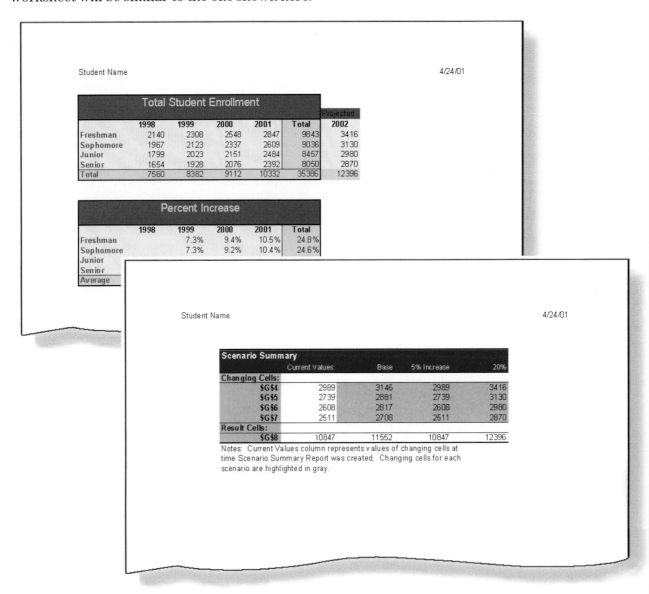

a. Open the file School Enrollment on your data disk.

b. Move to cell B4 in the Total Enrollment worksheet. Enter the formula **='Business'!B4+ 'Education'!B4+'Fine Arts'!B4+'Engineering'!B4** to calculate the total freshman class enrollment for the four colleges for 1998.

c. Copy the formula to cells C4 through E4. Copy the formulas from B4 through E4 to B5 through E7.

d. Next you want to calculate the percent change for each class over the 4 years. Copy the worksheet from cells A1 through F8 to cells A11 through F18. Change the title to **Percent Increase** in cell A11. Delete the 1998 data in B14 through B18.

e. Enter the formula **=(C4−B4)/C4** in cell C14 to calculate the percent change from 1998 to 1999 for the freshman class. Format the cell to Percent with One Decimal Place. Copy the formula to calculate the percentages for the rest of the data (C14:E17).

f. Change the label in cell A18 to Average and enter functions in cells C18 through F18 to calculate the average. Format C18 to F18 as Percent with One Decimal Place.

g. Enter the formula **=(E4-B4)/E4** in cell F14 to calculate the total percent change over the four years. Apply the percent format with one decimal place. Copy the formula down the column through row 17.

h. In cell G2, enter the title **Projected** and in cell G3 enter **2002**. Make the titles bold and center them. Apply the yellow fill color to cells G2 through G7.

i. To calculate a steady increase as the base for your scenario, enter the formula **=E4+(E4*E14)** in cell G4. Copy the formula to cells G5 through G7. Enter a function in G8 to sum the projected column.

j. Apply the same fill color as in adjacent cells to the left to the new column to complete the worksheet format.

k. Create a scenario for the base values. Label this the **Base** scenario and use cells G4 through G7 as your changing cells. Add the comment **Base scenario with growth equal to previous year.** (Choose [OK] when the message to convert formula to fixed values appears.)

l. Create a scenario for a 5 percent increase and another for a 20 percent increase. Label and comment the scenarios appropriately. Use the data in the following table for changing the cell values.

5% Increase	20% Increase
2,989	3,416
2,739	3,130
2,608	2,980
2,511	2,870

m. Create a Scenario Summary report using cell G8 as the result cell.

n. Add your name and the current date to a header in the Total Enrollment worksheet and the Scenario Summary worksheet.

o. Save the workbook. Print the Total Enrollment worksheet with the scenario values for a 20 percent increase. Print the Scenario Summary worksheet.

5. Animal Angels, a nonprofit animal rescue agency, relies on donations to cover all of its expenses. You would like to do some analysis on the data and project the amount that will be needed for next year based on scenarios that the committee feels are likely. Your completed income analysis will be similar to the one shown here.

Student Name   2/10/2001

Animal Angels
Analysis of 2001 and Projections for 2002

	2001 Income	5% Increase	10% Increase	10% Decrease	5% Decrease	Current Scenario
Annual Memberships	$54,834	$57,576	$60,317	$49,351	$52,092	$60,317
Phone Solicitation	6,400	6,720	$7,040	5,760	$6,080	6,400
Corporate Donations	45,000	47,250	$49,500	40,500	$42,750	44,888
Raffle Tickets	2,894	3,039	$3,183	2,605	$2,749	2,894
Pet Shows	16,000	16,800	$17,600	14,400	$15,200	16,000
Other	24,000	25,200	$26,400	21,600	$22,800	24,000
Total	$149,128	$156,584	$164,041	$134,215	$141,672	$154,499

Student Name   2/10/2001

Scenario Summary

	Current Values:	Most Likely	Least Likely	Ideal
Changing Cells:				
$G$5	$54,834	$60,317	$49,351	$60,317
$G$6	6,400	6,400	6,400	7,040
$G$7	45,000	42,750	40,500	49,500
$G$8	2,894	2,894	2,894	3,183
$G$9	16,000	16,000	16,000	17,600
$G$10	24,000	24,000	21,600	26,400
Result Cells:				
$G$11	$149,128	$152,361	$136,74	$164,040

Notes: Current Values column represents values of changing c___ ___ time Scenario Summary Report was created. Changing cell___ ___ch scenario are highlighted in gray.

Ideal scenario includes a 10% increase in all areas.

a. Open the file Animal Angels Contributions to see last year's income.

b. Copy the Fall-Winter sheet to a new sheet and rename the tab for the new sheet Analysis. Delete column H.

c. Merge cells A3 through G3 when you center the new title Analysis of 2001 and Projections for 2002.

d. Enter the labels 2001 Income, 5% Increase, 10% Increase, 10% Decrease, 5% Decrease, and Current Scenario in cells B4 through G4. Adjust the size of the columns to fully display the labels.

e. Enter the reference formula ='Spring-Summer'!H5+'Fall-Winter'!H5 in cell B5. Copy the formula down the column to cell B10.

f. Use the number in cell B5 to calculate the values for cells C5 through F5. Copy the formulas down the columns to row 10.

g. Copy and paste just the values from column B to column G. *Hint*: Use Edit/Paste Special and choose Values.

h. Create the following scenarios using cells G5 through G10 as the changing cells and the following calculated values in the worksheet:

Most Likely

Annual Memberships	10% increase
Phone Solicitation	Current
Corporate Donations	5% decrease
Raffle Tickets	Current
Pet Shows	Current
Other	Current

Least Likely

Annual Memberships	10% decrease
Phone Solicitation	Current
Corporate Donations	10% decrease
Raffle Tickets	Current
Pet Shows	Current
Other	10% decrease

Ideal

Annual Memberships	10% increase
Phone Solicitation	10% increase
Corporate Donations	10% increase
Raffle Tickets	10% increase
Pet Shows	10% increase
Other	10% increase

i. Create a Scenario Summary displaying the results for cell G11.

j. Create a 3-D object that highlights the Ideal scenario in the Scenario Summary worksheet.

k. Enter your name and the current date in a header of the Analysis and Scenario Summary worksheets.

l. Save the workbook. Print the Analysis worksheet in landscape orientation on one page with the most likely scenario displayed. Print the Scenario Summary worksheet.

On Your Own

6.   As the accounting manager of the Lifestyle Fitness Club, you have decided to create a workbook template to track the revenues from memberships, classes, equipment and clothing sales, and special events for each quarter. Create a worksheet for the first quarter with row labels that reflect revenue sources. Include a title and column labels for the months in the first quarter. Calculate totals where appropriate. Copy the worksheet to three other sheets to be used for the next three quarters, and appropriately adjust the column labels and title. Unlock the cells that will be used for value inputs. Enter your name and the current date as a footer for each sheet. Add worksheet protection and save it as a template. Use the template to enter sample data in the First Quarter sheet. Save and print the worksheet.

7.   You have been hired as a consultant by a local Internet service provider (ISP) to help the ISP project expected growth over the next five years based on its research. Assume that the company currently has 15 percent of the local market. The current number of customers is 3,500, and available research estimates an increase of 2 percent in year 2; 4 percent in year 3; 7 percent in year 4; and 12 percent in year 5. Create a worksheet that shows the current customer figure and the projected increases for the next five years. Use these numbers to create revenue figures based on a yearly profit of $75 per customer. Create scenarios with the calculated values as the baseline, a 2 percent decrease in customers and revenue per year as the worst case, and an additional 4 percent increase per year as the best case. Create a Scenario Summary report. Enter your name and the current date in all the worksheets. Print the worksheets.

8.   Create and evaluate your yearly budget to determine whether you will have enough money to pay for your school expenses for next year. Assume that you work part-time, earning $7.00 per hour. You have a scholarship for tuition. In addition, your parents contribute $300 per month for living expenses. Use Solver to determine the number of hours you need to work to get enough money for the rest of your expenses. Create three scenarios: one showing the current values, a second showing a 5 percent increase in rent and travel expenses, and a third showing a decrease in one of your other expenses with a raise in your wages. Create a Scenario Summary. Enter your name and the current date in a header for all the worksheets. Print the worksheets.

9.   You have been studying the stock market in your economics class and would like to evaluate a portfolio of four different stocks. Using the Web or other news source, choose four stocks listed on the New York Stock Exchange and enter the following information about each stock in separate sheets of a workbook: stock exchange number, cost per share, brokerage fee, total cost per share, price/earnings ratio, dividend return percentage, and week-ending price. Track your stocks (or use historical values) for a month. Create scenarios of good, bad, and expected market changes in the current month-ending price over the next month. Enter your name and the current date in headers in the worksheets and print the workbook.

 ☆ ☆ ☆

10. Create a workbook to evaluate your grade status as you are going into final exams—Sheet 1 should contain all the current courses and a column to display the letter grade and percentage for each course. In the following sheets, create a worksheet for each class that contains all the columns necessary to calculate your grade—list homework grades, project grades, quiz grades, and exam grades (not including final exam). Depending on the structure of the course, total the points to date or add the percentage earned to date. Link the individual sheets for each class to sheet1. Develop scenarios to project your final grades for all courses based on what you feel is the most likely outcome, the least likely outcome, and the optimal outcome (grade you want to earn) to help you decide which course(s) you should focus on when studying for finals. Create a Scenario Report for each. Enter your name and the current date in a header of all worksheets. Print Sheet 1 of the workbook showing the results from the most likely scenarios for each course and print one of the Scenario Reports.

Using Data Tables, Creating Macros, and Designing Onscreen Forms

Competencies

After completing this tutorial, you will know how to:

1. Use the PMT function.
2. Use a data table.
3. Add controls.
4. Create a macro with the Visual Basic Editor.
5. Create a macro with the Macro Recorder.
6. Create a form.
7. Name a range.
8. Use the IF function.
9. Add cell comments.
10. Document a file.

Case Study

Evan, the owner of the Downtown Internet Café, has been impressed with your use of Excel to forecast the café's future through 2002. He has two more projects for you. First, he is considering the purchase of a new espresso/cappuccino machine to replace the current one, which is leased. Evan plans

Using a data table is another way to perform what-if analysis.

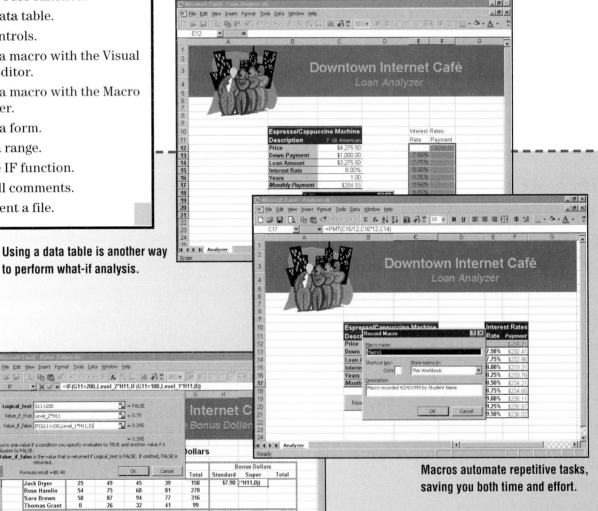

Macros automate repetitive tasks, saving you both time and effort.

Using an IF function allows different calculations to be performed if certain conditions are met.

to finance the purchase and would like you to evaluate several different loan options. You will create a loan analysis spreadsheet that incorporates Excel's PMT function, macros, and Data Table feature.

Next, Evan would like you to develop a spreadsheet to calculate and record customer Bonus Dollars. Bonus Dollars are awarded to customers based on their monthly Internet connection-time usage and can be redeemed for more connection time or other merchandise at the café. They are an incentive for customers to extend their stay at the café and, of course, spend more money while they're there. You will create an electronic form that uses the IF and Index functions to calculate and record customer Bonus Dollars.

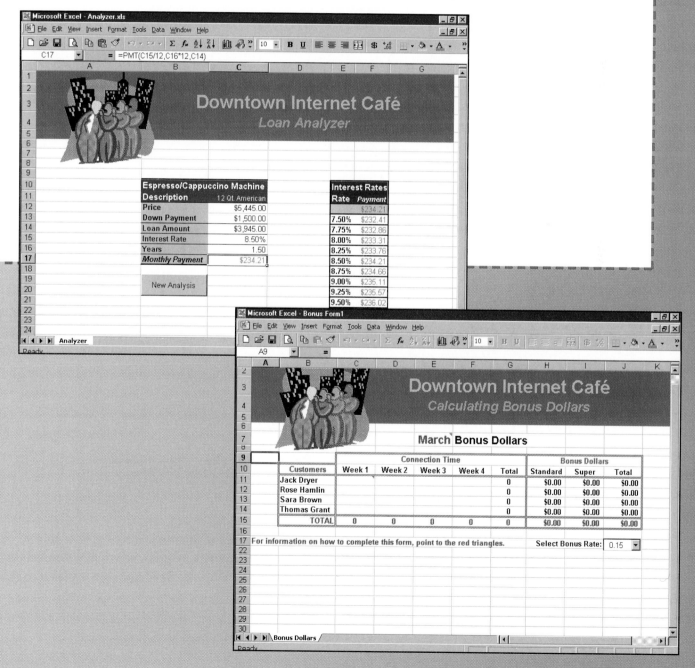

Concept Overview

The following concepts will be introduced in this tutorial:

1 **Data Table**   A data table is a type of what-if analysis in which one or more variables are changed to see the effect on the formulas that include these variables.

2 **Macro**   A macro is a stored series of keystrokes and commands that are executed automatically when the macro is run.

3 **Controls**   Controls are graphic objects that are designed to help the user interact with the form.

4 **Visual Basic Editor**   The Visual Basic Editor is a tool used to write and edit macros attached to Excel workbooks.

5 **Macro Recorder**   The Macro Recorder tool automatically creates a macro by recording a series of actions as macro commands.

6 **Form**   A form is a formatted worksheet with blank spaces that can be filled in online or on paper.

7 **Range Name**   A range name is a description of a cell or range of cells that can be used in place of cell references.

8 **IF Function**   The IF function checks to see if certain conditions are met and then takes action based on the results of the check.

9 **Comments**   Comments are notes attached to cells that can be used to clarify the meaning of the cell contents, provide documentation, or ask a question.

Using the PMT Function

Evan has researched different kinds of commercial espresso/cappuccino machines and would like to see an analysis of what the monthly loan payments would be for different down payments, interest rates, and repayment periods for each kind. You have already started to create the analysis by entering some descriptive labels and formats. To open the workbook,

1 Load Excel and open the work-book file Loan Analyzer.

If necessary, maximize the application and worksheet windows.

Your screen should be similar to Figure 5–1.

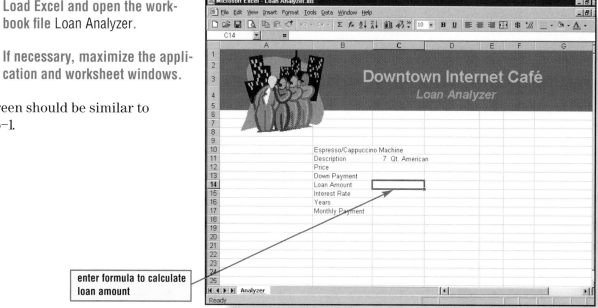

enter formula to calculate loan amount

Figure 5–1

Much of the structure for the Loan Analyzer worksheet has already been started. To continue to create the worksheet, you need to enter a formula to calculate the loan amount. (The amount of the loan is the price of the item minus the down payment.) Then you will enter the data for the first espresso/cappuccino machine Evan has selected.

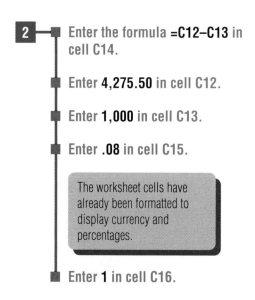

2 Enter the formula **=C12–C13** in cell C14.

Enter **4,275.50** in cell C12.

Enter **1,000** in cell C13.

Enter **.08** in cell C15.

The worksheet cells have already been formatted to display currency and percentages.

Enter **1** in cell C16.

Your screen should be similar to Figure 5–2.

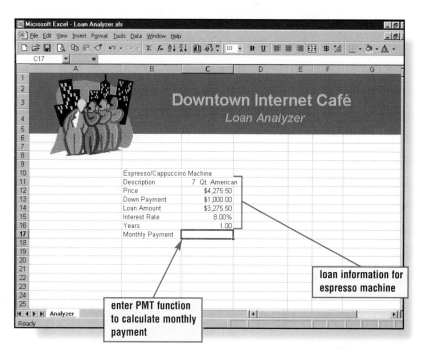

loan information for espresso machine

enter PMT function to calculate monthly payment

Figure 5–2

The next thing that needs to be entered is the monthly payment. To calculate this value, you use the PMT function. The PMT function calculates a periodic payment on a loan. The value returned includes the loan amount and interest but no taxes, reserve payments, or fees sometimes associated with loans. The PMT function uses the following syntax:

PMT(rate, nper, pv)

This function contains three arguments: rate, nper, and pv. The **rate** argument is the interest rate of the loan. The **nper** argument is the total number of payments for the loan. The **pv** argument is the amount of the loan, also referred to as the **principal.**

The rate in the PMT function you will use to calculate the monthly loan payment for the espresso machine is the yearly interest rate (C15) divided by 12. This converts the yearly rate to a monthly rate. The nper argument is the length of the loan in years (C16) multiplied by 12 to calculate the number of monthly payments. The pv argument is the loan amount in cell C14.

> When using the PMT function it is important to use consistent units for specifying rate and nper.

3 ▬ Enter the function
=PMT(C15/12,C16*12,C14)
in cell C17.

Additional Information

You can use the Paste Function feature to help enter this function.

Your screen should be similar to Figure 5–3.

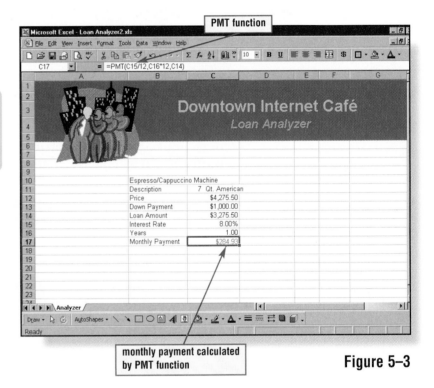

PMT function

monthly payment calculated by PMT function

Figure 5–3

Excel calculates the monthly payment and displays it in cell C17. To improve the appearance of the worksheet, you will format it.

4 Select the range B10 through C17.

Choose F<u>o</u>rmat/<u>A</u>utoFormat.

Select Classic 2 from the AutoFormat dialog box.

Click [OK]

Clear the selection.

Your screen should be similar to Figure 5–4.

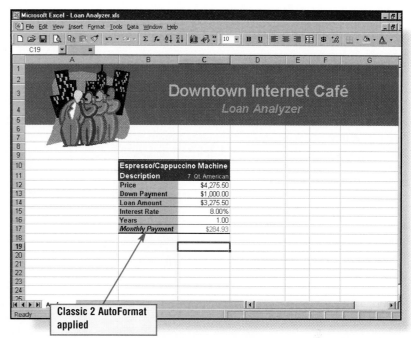

Figure 5–4

Creating a Data Table

You used an 8 percent interest rate to calculate the loan payments for the espresso/cappuccino machine, but you are aware that interest rates will vary, depending on what loan institution finances the purchase and when the loan is obtained. Therefore, you want to set up a data table that shows the effect of different interest rates on the monthly loan payment amount.

Concept ① Data Table

A **data table** is a type of what-if analysis in which one or more variables are changed to see the effect on the formulas that include these variables. Data tables allow you to quickly calculate multiple what-if versions in one operation and to view the results of all variations together in the worksheet.

A **one-variable data table** can contain one or more formulas, and each formula refers to one input cell. An **input cell** is a cell in which a list of values is substituted to see the resulting effect on the related formulas. Input values can be listed down a column (**column-oriented**) or across a row (**row-oriented**).

Espresso/Cappuccino Machine	
Description	12 Qt. American
Price	$5,445.00
Down Payment	$1,500.00
Loan Amount	$3,945.00
Interest Rate	8.50%
Months	18
Monthly Payment	$234.21

One Way Table Varying Interest Rate Only			Two Way Table Varying Interest Rates and Length of Loan			
	$234.21			$234.21	18	36	48
7.50%	$232.41		7.50%	$232.41	$122.71	$95.39
7.75%	$232.86		7.75%	$232.86	$123.17	$95.85
8.00%	$233.31		8.00%	$233.31	$123.62	$96.31
8.25%	$233.76		8.25%	$233.76	$124.08	$96.77
8.50%	$234.21		8.50%	$234.21	$124.53	$97.24
8.75%	$234.66		8.75%	$234.66	$124.99	$97.70
9.00%	$235.11		9.00%	$235.11	$125.45	$98.17
9.25%	$235.57		9.25%	$235.57	$125.91	$98.64
9.50%	$236.02		9.50%	$236.02	$126.37	$99.11

A **two-variable data table** uses only one formula that refers to two different input cells, one column-oriented and one row-oriented. The purpose of this table is to show the resulting effect on the formula when the values in both of these cells are changed.

Since you are interested in seeing the effects of changing the interest rate only, you will create a one-variable data table. When designing a one-way data table, the input values and formulas must be in contiguous rows or columns. First, you need to set up the data table in an unused portion of the worksheet by entering a title and column headings and a series of interest rate percentages.

1 ■ Enter the title **Interest Rates** in cell E10.

■ Enter the column heading **Rate** in cell E11.

■ Enter the column heading **Payment** in cell F11.

■ Enter **7.5%** in cell E13 and **7.75%** in cell E14.

■ Select the range E13 through E14 and drag the fill handle through cell E21.

Your screen should be similar to Figure 5–5.

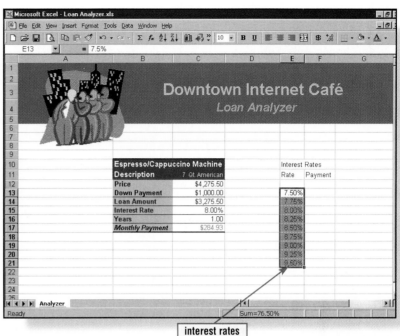

interest rates

Figure 5–5

Excel has filled column E with interest rates that range from 7.5 percent to 9.5 percent in 0.25 percent increments. Next, you enter the monthly payment formula to be used in calculating the various payments in cell F12. The formula is entered in the row above the first input value and one cell to the right of the column of values. Rather than just copying this formula from the monthly payment cell in the loan analysis section of the worksheet, you'll define the new formula as equal to that cell. This way, the data table formula will be automatically updated if the original formula (the one in the loan analysis section of the worksheet) is changed.

Additional Information

If the input values are listed across the row, the formula is entered in the column to the left of the first value and one cell below the row of values.

2 ■ Enter **=C17** in cell F12.

Finally, you need to define the range of cells that comprise the data table. In this case, the data table range consists of all cells except the ones containing the title and headings. To define the data table range,

3 ■ Select the cells **E12** to **F21**.

■ Choose **D**ata/**T**able.

Your screen should be similar to Figure 5–6.

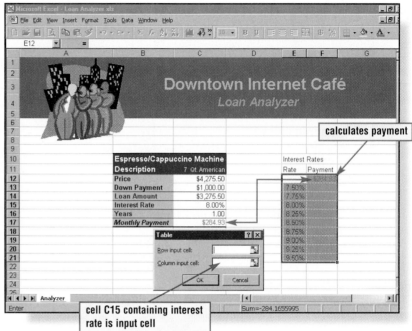

Figure 5–6

You use the Table dialog box to define the input cell in which values from the data table are substituted. Because the values in the data table are listed down a column, the input cell is entered as a Column Input Cell. In this case, the input cell is the Interest Rate cell from the loan analysis in cell C15.

4 ■ Enter **C15** in the Column Input Cell text box.

> You can also define the input cell by reducing the dialog box and selecting the input cell in the worksheet.

■ Click OK .

■ Clear the selection.

Your screen should be similar to Figure 5–7.

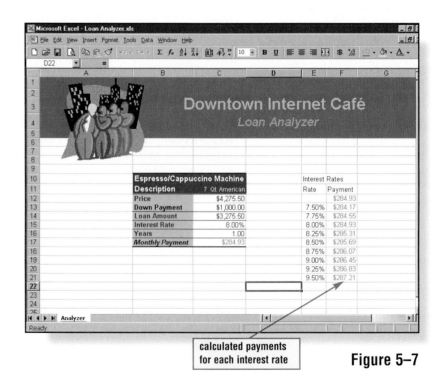

Figure 5–7

The monthly payments are calculated based on each listed interest rate.

5 ——■ **Select the range** E10 through F21 **and apply the Classic 3 AutoFormat to the range.**

> The data table area of the worksheet was also preformatted to display as Currency.

Automating Tasks with Macros

You now have the analysis worksheet for the espresso/cappuccino machine that Evan requested with a data table that calculates different interest rates for the loan. After you show the worksheet to Evan, he says he would like to see the same loan analysis and data table applied to other espresso/cappuccino machines he either is currently considering or may come across between now and the time he actually decides to purchase one. Rather than entering the necessary loan calculations for each machine, you decide to create a macro that will automate some of the data entry.

Concept Macro

A **macro** is a stored series of keystrokes and commands. When the macro is executed, or **run**, the stored actions are performed automatically. Macros are very useful for replacing a series of commands that are performed repeatedly. Instead of performing the same actions every time you need to perform a task, you use the macro, which performs the task automatically for you.

Some macros are very simple and are merely a duplicate of a series of keystrokes. For example, a macro can be written that selects a range of cells. A more complex macro may perform a command, such as copying data from one cell to another or changing column widths. Even more complex macros can be written that let you create customized functions that combine math expressions, Excel functions, and programming code to perform special calculations. Other macros can be used to create your own customized menus and dialog boxes.

A macro for your loan analysis worksheet will not only help you but will also come in handy if someone else needs to use this worksheet to enter loan information, especially if that person does not know what cells to select in order to obtain the necessary data.

Creating a Command Button

> **Additional Information**
>
> Toolbar buttons are simply macro statements that are executed when the button to which they are assigned is selected.

One of the most common ways to run a macro is to create a command button in the worksheet that, when clicked, runs the macro instructions. You will create the command button before creating the macro so that the macro instructions can be assigned to the button. A command button is one of many different controls that can be added to a worksheet.

Concept ③ Controls

Controls are graphic objects that are designed to help the user interact with the form. They can be used to display or enter data, perform an action, or make the sheet easier to read. Controls include property settings that affect how they behave and work. The properties associated with many controls can be changed to customize the control for your own use. Examples of controls are check boxes, list boxes, option buttons, and command buttons.

Excel includes two ways to add controls to a worksheet: the Forms toolbar or the Control Toolbox toolbar. The controls on the Forms toolbar are for use with existing Excel macros and work best on worksheets that will be used only in Excel. The Control Toolbox controls are ActiveX controls that allow you to make the controls "active" by writing a macro using Microsoft Visual Basic or scripts in Microsoft Script Editor that customize the behavior of the control. The Control Toolbox controls are for when the worksheet will be used in interaction with other Office programs, or on an Internet location.

You decide that a good location for the command button would be just below the first table.

1 ■ Display the Control Toolbox toolbar and move it to column A.

■ Click  Command Button.

■ Click on cell B19 to create the button.

■ Move and size the command button to cover cells B19 and B20.

Your screen should look similar to Figure 5–8.

design mode is active

creates a command button

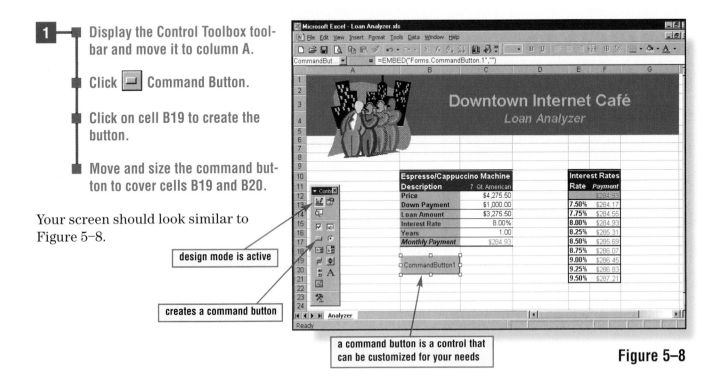

a command button is a control that can be customized for your needs

Figure 5–8

> The ☑ button appears recessed when design mode is active.

When you first create a control, Excel automatically changes to design mode so you can modify the control. You now need to change the default button name to a more descriptive name. You decide to name it New Analysis.

2
■ Right-click the command button to open the shortcut menu.

■ Choose CommandButton Object/Edit.

■ Select the default button name and replace it with **New Analysis**.

■ Click outside the button object to deselect it.

Additional Information

You can also change a command button's font attributes by selecting **P**roperties from the button's shortcut menu and selecting font and color settings.

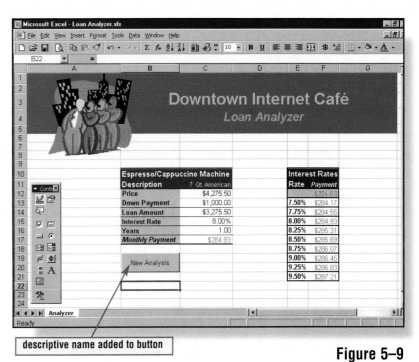

Figure 5–9

Your screen should look similar to Figure 5–9.

Create a Macro Using the Visual Basic Editor

Now that the command button is created, you can use the Visual Basic Editor to create the macro to automate the process of entering the loan data.

Concept ④ Visual Basic Editor

The **Visual Basic Editor** is a tool used to write and edit macros attached to Excel workbooks. Although Visual Basic is a programming language, you can enter information into the Visual Basic Editor just as you would in a word processor–by typing to enter text, pressing ⏎Enter to end a line, using the arrow keys to move around the screen, and pressing Delete and Backspace to remove and correct text.

The types of information you enter into the Visual Basic Editor are called **statements.** Visual Basic statements tell Excel to execute a specific task, or **Sub procedure.** A Sub procedure begins with a statement that starts the macro (when the command button is pressed) and ends with one that closes the macro (an End Sub statement). Sub procedures can also include remarks about the macro (such as its name and purpose) and functions (such as returning values to the procedure).

The **syntax,** or rules of grammar of a Sub procedure statement, is as follows:

Object ("x").Property

The **object** is the item that the statement will affect (such as a cell, cell range, worksheet, or workbook). The object is enclosed in parentheses and surrounded by quotes.

The **property** is what you want to do to the object. The property consists of reserved words that have special meaning and direct Excel to perform the specified action. The object is separated from the property by a period. For example, the statement to tell Excel to select the range C2 through C10 is:

Range("C2:C10").Select

It is very important to plan a macro before creating it to ensure that the Visual Basic statements are in the exact order in which you want them to be executed. It is often helpful to write out the macro steps and then try them out manually in Excel before entering them in the Visual Basic Editor. You want this macro to perform the following actions:

1. Select the Analyzer sheet.

2. Clear the cell ranges C11 through C13 and C14 through C15.

3. Display an input box for entry of values for cells C11, C12, C13, C15, and C16.

4. Move to cell C17.

To start the Visual Basic Editor and create the command button macro,

1 Double-click New Analysis .

If necessary, close the Project Explorer and Properties windows along the left side of the Editor window and maximize the Code window on the right.

Your screen should look similar to Figure 5-10.

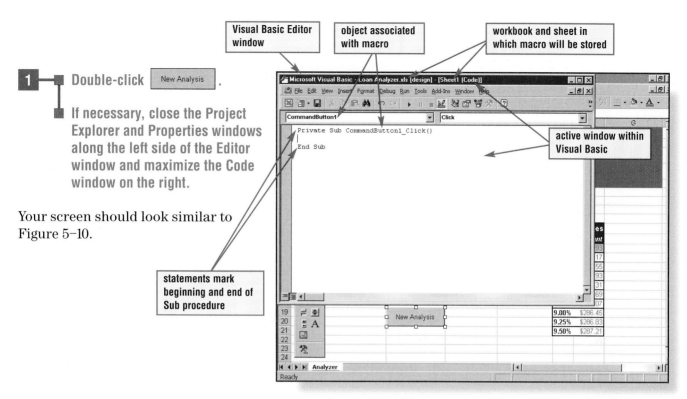

Figure 5-10

The Visual Basic Editor window already contains the Sub and End Sub statements for the command button macro. You will enter the macro statements between the Sub statements. First, however, you want to include several remark statements that describe the macro and include overall procedural documentation. Remark statements always begin with an apostrophe, which tells Excel to ignore the information on that line.

2 Enter a blank line above the Private Sub line in the window.

Type '**New Analysis Button Macro** on the newly inserted blank line.

Press ←Enter.

> If you forget to enter the apostrophe, a Compile error message is displayed. Click [OK] to clear the message and edit the line.

Your screen should look similar to Figure 5-11.

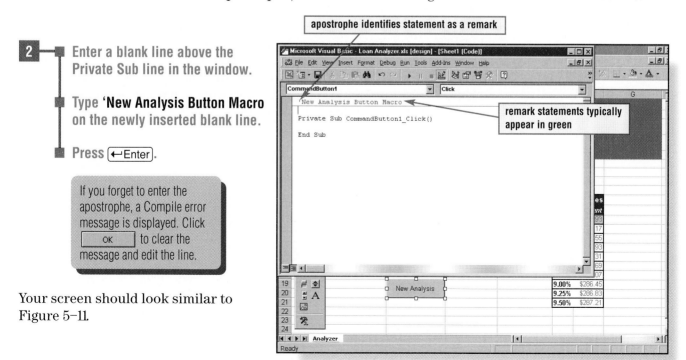

Figure 5-11

Remark lines generally appear in green type to distinguish them from the procedure statements.

3 In the same manner, enter the following three additional remarks:

> Remember to begin each remark statement with an apostrophe and press ⟨⏎Enter⟩ to move to the next line to type the next statement.

'**Date Created:** [insert today's date]
'**Run From:** Analyzer worksheet by clicking the New Analysis button.
'**Purpose:** To accept loan data and calculate a new monthly payment.

Your screen should look similar to Figure 5–12.

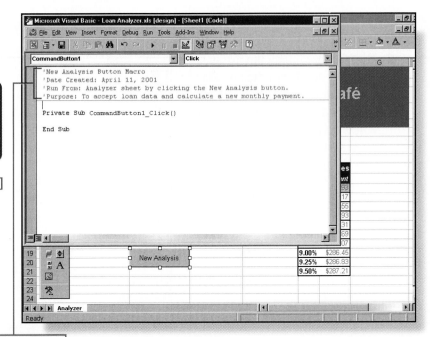

remark statements provide documentation and instructions

Figure 5–12

Next, you will enter the Sub procedure statements. To differentiate the Sub statements from the rest of the code, you should indent them using ⟨Tab⇥⟩. Once you indent the first Sub statement line, the subsequent lines are automatically indented the same number of spaces. If Visual Basic statements are not entered using the correct syntax, an error message box is displayed and the error is identified in red. You must correct the error before you can move to the next line. As you are typing, the Visual Basic Editor displays a list of acceptable statement properties. You can select the property you want from the list or continue typing it yourself. Additionally, the first letter of reserved words that are not inside parenthesis will be automatically capitalized.

4 Move the insertion point to the blank line between the Private Sub and End Sub statements.

■ Press Tab.

■ Type **Sheets("Analyzer").Select**.

■ Press ←Enter.

■ In the same manner, enter the following Sub statements:

> Remember to press ←Enter to begin a new statement on a new line.

Range("C11:C13").Select
Selection.ClearContents
Range ("C15:C16").Select

> You can also copy statements and then edit them.

Selection.ClearContents
Range("C11").Value = InputBox("What type of machine?", "Enter")
Range("C12").Value = InputBox("What is the price?", "Enter")
Range("C13").Value = InputBox("What is the down payment?", "Enter")
Range("C15").Value = InputBox("What is the interest rate?", "Enter")
Range("C16").Value = InputBox("How many years to repay the loan?", "Enter")
Range("C17").Select

Your screen should look similar to Figure 5–13.

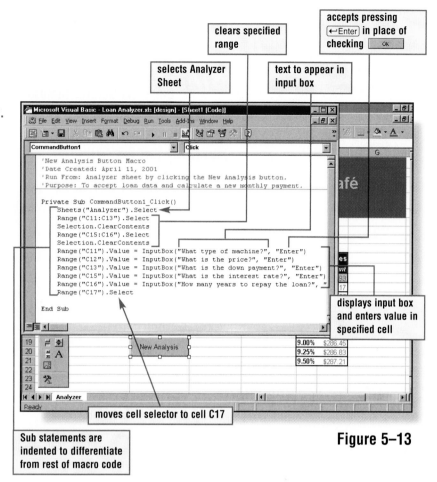

Figure 5–13

The text in parentheses following InputBox is the text that will appear when the InputBox is displayed. The "Enter" statement allows the user to press ←Enter as an alternative to clicking OK.

You are finished creating the command button macro and you can now close the Visual Basic window and return to the worksheet.

> The menu equivalent is **F**ile/**C**lose and Return to Microsoft Excel. The keyboard shortcut is Alt + Q.

5 ■ Click ❌ in the title bar of the Visual Basic window to close it.

■ Click 📝 Exit Design Mode on the Control Toolbox toolbar.

■ Close the Control Toolbox toolbar.

Running the Macro

The next step is to test the macro by running it. Before testing a new macro, it is a good idea to save the workbook file first in case the macro performs some unexpected actions.

1 ■ Save the workbook as **Analyzer**.

To test the macro, you will enter a new loan analysis for another espresso/cappuccino machine that Evan is considering. The machine type is 12 Qt. American. It costs $5,445. Evan plans to make a down payment of $1,500 and to borrow the rest at 8.5 percent for 1.5 years. To execute the macro,

2 ■ Click [New Analysis].

■ Type **12 Qt. American** in the input box.

> **Additional Information**
>
> You can interrupt the execution of a macro at any time by pressing Esc.

Your screen should look similar to Figure 5–14.

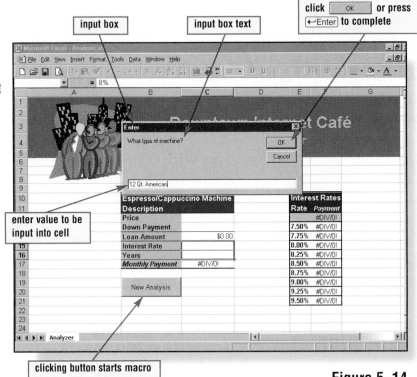

Figure 5–14

3 Using the following information, enter the remaining requested information in the input boxes.

Price: **$5,445**

Down Payment: **$1,500**

Interest Rate: **8.5%**

> You do not need to enter the values as currency, because they will format automatically. Enter the interest rate as 8.5% or .085.

Loan Length: **1.5**

Your screen should look similar to Figure 5–15.

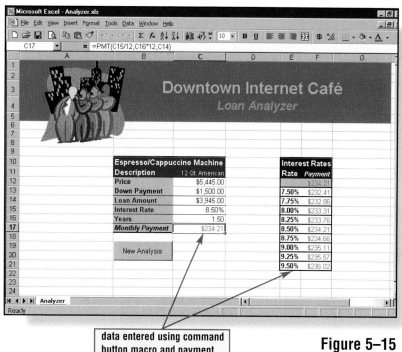

data entered using command button macro and payment calculated

Figure 5–15

The worksheet now shows the new loan analysis. Notice that the data table has also been recalculated based on the new monthly payment.

> If your macro did not run correctly, you will need to correct or debug any statement errors.

Using the Macro Recorder

Next, you will use the Macro Recorder to create a separate macro that prints the worksheet in landscape mode.

Concept ⑤ Macro Recorder

The **Macro Recorder** tool automatically creates a macro by recording a series of actions as macro commands. When the recorder is on, Excel automatically records every action you perform and stores it as a Visual Basic statement. You can then easily select the recorded macro by name and play it back, or execut it, as often as you like.

The Macro Recorder method of creating macros is much easier than the Visual Basic Editor method, and both types of macros can be viewed and changed via the editor. However, it is recommended that the Macro Recorder method be used for short procedures only (such as basic worksheet functions like formatting and printing), because it can be difficult to decipher and troubleshoot complex Visual Basic statements after they have been recorded.

> The worksheet will print when you are finished recording the macro, so make any needed printer setup preparations before you begin.

To start the Macro Recorder,

1 ■ Choose **T**ools/**M**acro/**R**ecord New Macro.

Your screen should look similar to Figure 5–16.

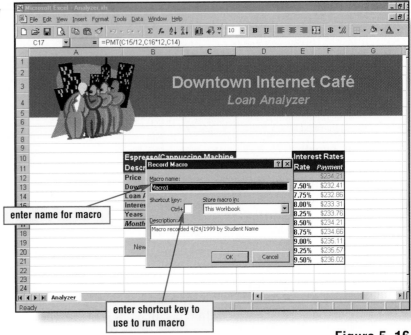

enter name for macro

enter shortcut key to use to run macro

Figure 5–16

You use the Record Macro dialog box to name the macro, assign a shortcut key that will start the macro, select a location where it will be stored if other than the active workbook, enter a description of the macro, and start the recording. You decide to name your macro Printer and assign a shortcut key of Ctrl + ⇧Shift + P to it. You will leave the rest of the selections as they are.

2 ■ Type **Printer** in the Macro name box.

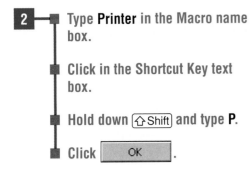

■ Click in the Shortcut Key text box.

■ Hold down ⇧Shift and type **P**.

■ Click OK .

Your screen should look similar to Figure 5–17.

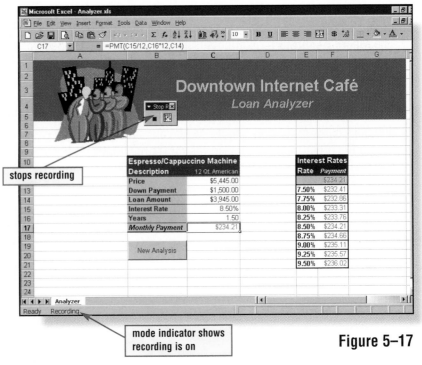

stops recording

mode indicator shows recording is on

Figure 5–17

The message "Recording" is displayed in the status bar, and the Stop Recording toolbar appears on your screen. Now any action you perform will be recorded as a macro.

3 — ■ Choose **F**ile/Page Set**u**p.

■ Open the Page tab.

■ Select **L**andscape.

■ Click [Print...].

■ Click [OK].

Your worksheet should be printing. Next, you want to stop recording.

4 — ■ Click [■] Stop Recording.

> The menu equivalent is **T**ools/**M**acro/Stop **R**ecording.

To see the macro that was created,

5 — ■ Choose **T**ools/**M**acro/**M**acros.

■ Select Printer.

■ Click [Edit].

Your screen should be similar to Figure 5–18.

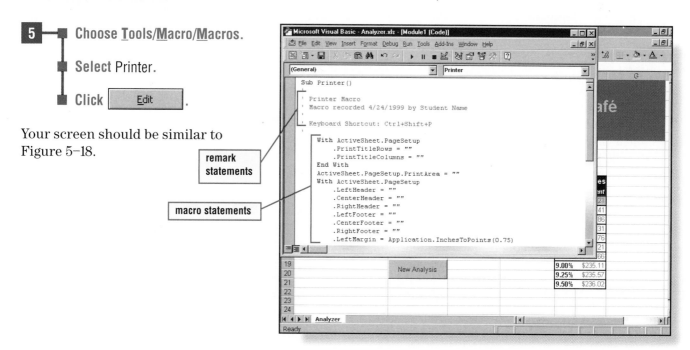

remark statements

macro statements

Figure 5–18

The macro is displayed in the Visual Basic Editor window. It contains macro instructions for all settings that are on by default in the page setup dialog box as well as those you changed.

6 — ■ Scroll the window to look at the entire macro contents.

■ Close the Visual Basic Editor window.

You can now test the macro by executing it with the shortcut key you assigned. Because you have already performed the actions in order to create the macro, you will first reverse the page setup.

The menu equivalent is **T**ools/**M**acro/**M**acro/Printer/**R**un.

7 ■— Choose **F**ile/Page Set**u**p/Po**r**trait/ .

■ Press Ctrl + ⇧Shift + P.

The macro is executed, and the worksheet is printed a second time in landscape orientation. The worksheet blinks while the macro is in progress.

8 ■— Save the workbook again.

■ Close the workbook file.

Creating a Form to Calculate Bonus Dollars

Your second project is to create a form that records customer monthly connection times and calculates Bonus Dollars earned by each customer.

Concept ⑥ Form

A **form** is a formatted worksheet with blank spaces that can be filled in online on an individual computer or on a network, or printed and completed on paper. The steps in creating a form are the same for both purposes. However, certain elements are more appropriate for one than for the other. For example, color and shading are more effective on online forms, while simplicity of design and layout is very important in printed forms. In addition, online forms can contain formulas that immediately calculate results such as totals, whereas printed forms would need to include blank spaces where the calculations would be entered manually.

Using controls makes it easier to fill out a form and increases the accuracy of the information entered in it. This is because many of the controls can include a list of options from which the user selects. Although controls are most effectively used in online forms, they can also be used in printed forms. For example, controls such as buttons and check boxes can be printed blank and then filled in by the user.

The first step when creating a form is to decide what should appear on the form and what information will be entered into the form. When customers sign on to the computers, they enter their names, and the system tracks the time between sign-on and sign-off. Obtaining connection times for each customer is just a matter of checking the computers' logs. The Bonus Dollar form needs to be designed to accept input of customer connection times and to calculate Bonus Dollars earned. Although Evan wants the form to be electronic, he also wants to be able to print it out for reference.

You have already started designing the form by entering much of the text, many of the formulas, some formatting to improve the appearance, and some sample data. To see what has been done so far,

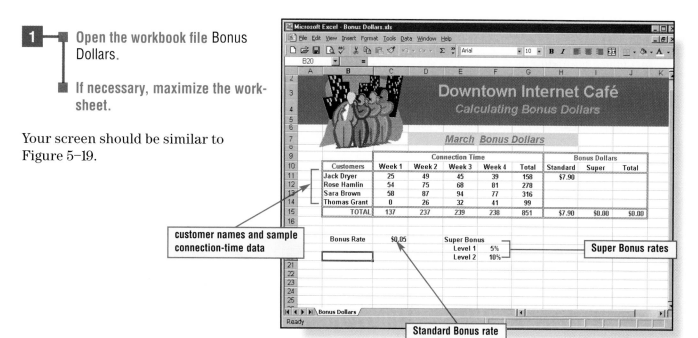

1 Open the workbook file Bonus Dollars.

■ If necessary, maximize the worksheet.

Your screen should be similar to Figure 5–19.

customer names and sample connection-time data

Super Bonus rates

Standard Bonus rate

Figure 5–19

This sample form displays the names of four customers and their connection time in minutes for each week in columns C through F.

The last three columns will be used to calculate and display customer Bonus Dollars. The Downtown Internet Café awards Bonus Dollars based on total connection time. A Standard Bonus is applied to every customer at a rate of $.05 per minute of connection time. An additional Super Bonus is awarded at two different levels for those customers who stay connected more than 100 minutes. The bonus awards are explained in the following table.

Bonus	Award
Standard Bonus	Total connection time multiplied by $.05
Super Bonus Level 1	If total connection time is greater than 100 minutes but less than or equal to 200 minutes, Standard Bonus + 5%
Super Bonus Level 2	If total connection time is greater than 200 minutes, Standard Bonus + 10%

Adding Cell Borders

The worksheet has already been formatted with colors and cell formats for currency. In addition, cell borders have been added to many areas of the worksheet to identify the different sections. You are still working on formatting the worksheet title in row 7 that identifies the month and want to see how adding the same style cell border as used in the worksheet would look around the title.

1 ■ Select cells D7 through H7.

■ Choose Format/Cells.

■ Open the Border tab.

■ Select [========] border from the Line Style list.

■ Select Dark Red from the Color drop-down menu.

■ Click [Outline] to apply the border around the entire edge of the selected cell range.

Your screen should be similar to Figure 5–20.

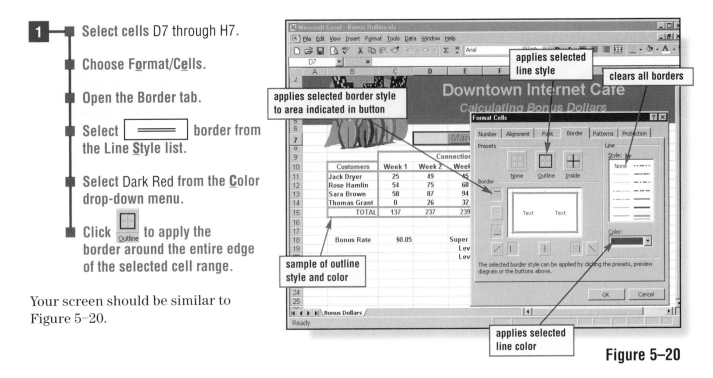

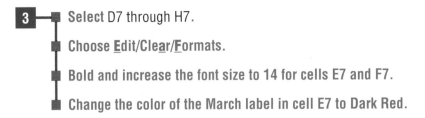

Figure 5–20

To apply the border settings,

2 ■ Click [OK].

■ Clear the selection.

Unfortunately, the title now has too many formats and does not look good. Sometimes, it is just easier to start over from scratch by clearing all the formats. Clearing cell formats leaves the content intact and reapplies the default General format to the cells. To clear the formats only from the cells and apply new ones,

3 ■ Select D7 through H7.

■ Choose Edit/Clear/Formats.

■ Bold and increase the font size to 14 for cells E7 and F7.

■ Change the color of the March label in cell E7 to Dark Red.

Sometimes simpler is better.

Naming Ranges

- -

The formula to calculate the Standard Bonus for Jack Dryer has already been entered. To see this formula,

1 ■ Move to H11.

The formula references cell C18. This cell contains the Standard Bonus rate amount of $.05 per minute. To make the formula easier to read and understand, you will assign a descriptive range name to this cell.

Concept ⑦ Range Name

A **range name** is a description of a cell or range of cells that can be used in place of cell references. The name can be used anytime a cell or range is requested as part of a command or in a formula or function.

Excel automatically proposes a name for the cell or range using the contents of the active cell if it contains text, or the cell above or to the left of the active cell if the active cell does not contain text. If the active cell or the cells above or to the left of the active cell do not contain text, or if you do not want to use the proposed name, you can type in a name of your choice. The name can be up to 255 characters long. It can include letters, numbers, underlines, periods, backslashes, and question marks. It cannot contain spaces. The first character must be a letter, underline, or backslash. A name that resembles a cell reference is not allowed.

2 ■ Move to C18.

   ■ Choose **I**nsert/**N**ame/**D**efine.

Your screen should be similar to Figure 5–21.

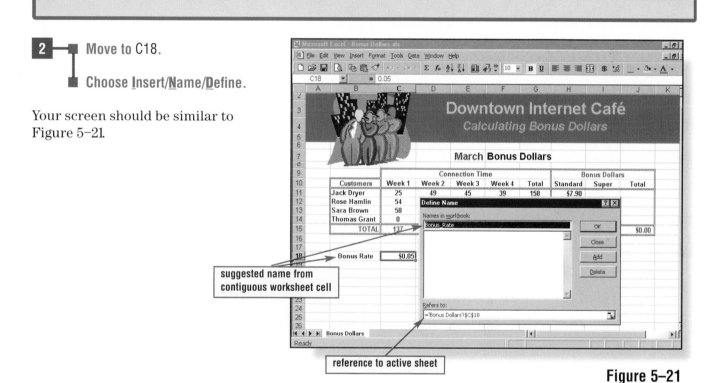

Figure 5–21

Additional Information

You can also name a range by selecting the range and typing the name into the Name box.

The Define Names dialog box is used to name, modify, and delete range names. In the Names in Workbook text box, Excel has proposed the name Bonus_Rate. The proposed name is the contents of the cell to the left of the active cell. Excel replaced the blank space between the words with an underline character because a name cannot contain spaces.

The Refers To text box displays the reference for the active cell. The reference includes the sheet name and cell reference. By default Excel makes named cell references absolute. The Names in Workbook list box is empty because this worksheet does not contain any names yet. Since both the name and the cell reference are acceptable, to complete the command,

3 — ■ Click [OK] .

Your screen should be similar to Figure 5–22.

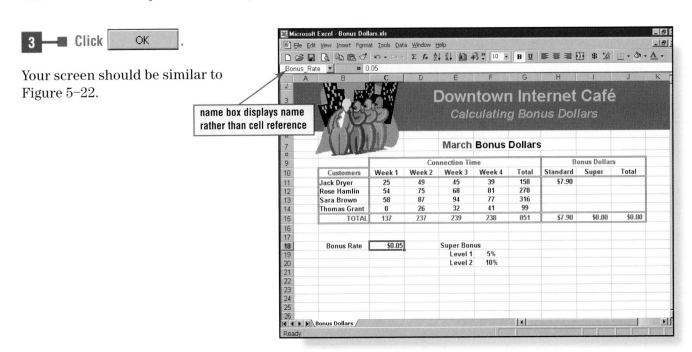

name box displays name rather than cell reference

Figure 5–22

Additional Information

You can toggle between temporarily displaying the cell reference and the name by holding down the left mouse button on the cell.

In place of the cell reference in the Name box of the formula bar, the name is displayed.

Now you need to replace the cell reference in the formula in cell H11 with the name.

4 — ■ Move to H11.

■ Change to Edit mode.

Notice that the Range Finder has highlighted the cells in the formula.

■ Select (highlight) the cell reference C18 in the formula.

■ Choose <u>I</u>nsert/<u>N</u>ame/<u>P</u>aste.

Your screen should be similar to Figure 5–23.

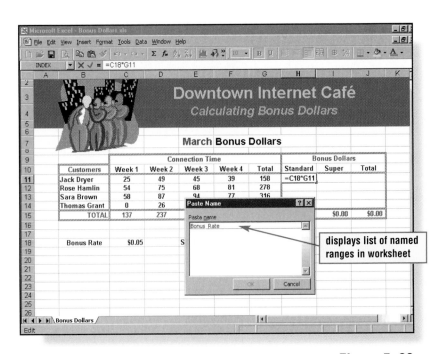

displays list of named ranges in worksheet

Figure 5–23

You need to select the name you want to use from the Paste Name dialog box.

5 Select Bonus_Rate.

■ Click OK .

Your screen should be similar to Figure 5–24.

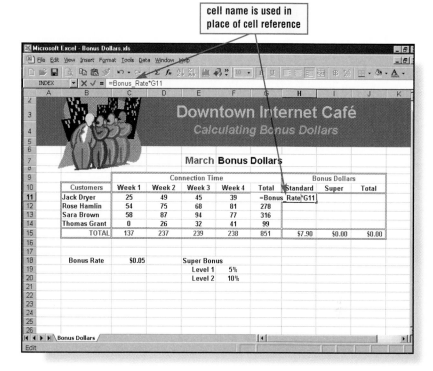

Figure 5–24

The name Bonus_Rate has replaced the reference to cell C18 in the formula. Using a name makes the formula easier to understand. To complete the edit,

6 ■ Press ←Enter .

Next you will name the Super Bonus levels in cells F19 and F20 that will be used in the formula to calculate the Super Bonus. You will name both cells at the same time using the labels in E19 and E20 as the names.

7 ■ Select E19 through F20.

■ Choose Insert/Name/Create.

Your screen should be similar to Figure 5–25.

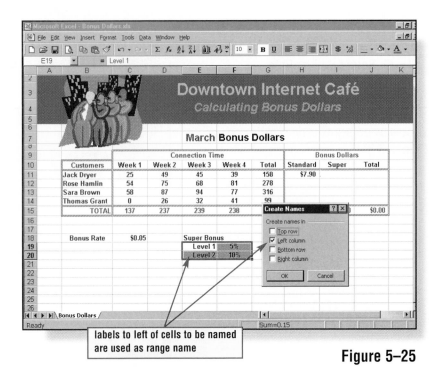

labels to left of cells to be named
are used as range name

Figure 5–25

The Create Names dialog box lets you specify the location of the labels in relation to the cells to be named. In this case, you want the labels in the column to the left (E) to be used, which is the default. To accept the default selection,

8 ■ Click  .

To verify that the names have been created,

9 ■ Move to F19 and note that Level_1 is displayed in the Name box.

■ Move to F20 and note that Level_2 is displayed in the Name box.

Using the IF Function

Now you are ready to enter a formula in cell I11 to calculate the Super Bonus. For any customer with more than 100 minutes of connection time, the Super Bonus is calculated using one of two levels. The highest level is for those with more than 200 minutes. Those customers receive a Super Bonus equal to 10 percent of their Standard Bonus. The other level is for those with less than or equal to 200 minutes who receive a Super Bonus equal to 5 percent of their Standard Bonus. To calculate the Super Bonus, you will use the IF function.

Concept (8) IF Function

The **IF function** checks to see if certain conditions are met and then takes action based on the results of the check. The syntax for this function is:

IF(logical_test,value_if_true,value_if_false)

This function contains three arguments: logical_test, value_if_true, and value_if_false. The logical_test argument is an expression that makes a comparison using logical operators. **Logical operators** are used in formulas and functions that compare numbers in two or more cells or to a constant. The result of the comparison is either true (the conditions are met) or false (the conditions are not met).

The logical operators are:

Symbol	Meaning
=	Equal to
<	Less than
>	Greater than
<=	Less than or equal to
>=	Greater than or equal to
<>	Not equal to
NOT	Logical NOT
AND	Logical AND
OR	Logical OR

The logical test argument asks the question, "Does the entry in this cell meet the stated conditions?" The answer is either True (Yes) or False (No). The second argument, value_if_true, provides directions for the function to follow if the logical test result is true. The third argument, value_if_false, provides directions for the function to follow if the logical test result is false.

First you will enter the formula to calculate the discount earned for a connection time of 200 minutes or more. Then you will modify the function to include the other conditions. You will enter the IF function using the Paste Function feature.

1 Click cell I11.

Click f_x Paste Function.

Select **IF** from the Logical Function category.

Click OK.

Your screen should be similar to Figure 5–26.

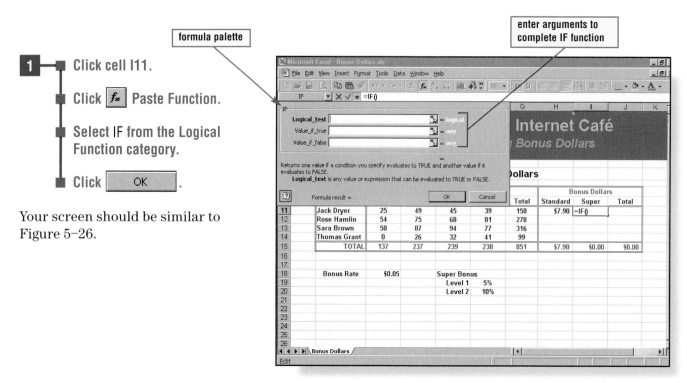

Figure 5–26

The IF formula palette contains three text boxes, one for each IF statement argument. The logical test is whether the total connection time for a customer is greater than 200 and the value_if_true argument provides directions for what to do if the logical test is true. In this case, the value_if_true directions are to multiply the value in cell H11 times the value in the cell named Level_2. To enter these arguments,

2 Enter **G11>200** in the Logical_test text box.

Enter **Level_2*H11** in the Value_if_true text box.

Your screen should be similar to Figure 5–27.

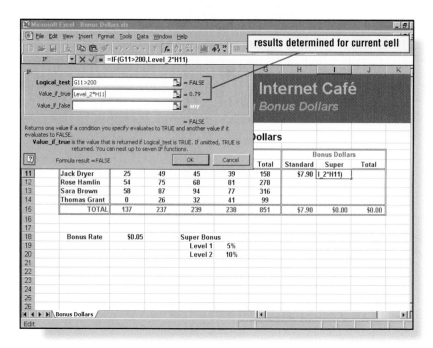

Figure 5–27

Notice that the Formula palette is already determining whether the conditions are true or false for the current customer based on the values in the referenced cells. In this case, because the value in G11 is less than 200, the logical test result is false and a Level 2 bonus would be 0.79 if true.

Next, you need to enter the value_if_false argument. It contains instructions that are executed if connection time is less than or equal to 200 minutes. If that connection time is greater than 100, then the Level_1 amount is used to calculate the Super Bonus, otherwise connection time is less than or equal to 100 and the Super Bonus is 0. To enter this condition you include a second IF statement that will apply the Level 1 bonus. The arguments for the second IF statement are enclosed in their own set of parentheses. This is called a **nested function**.

3 ■ Enter **IF(G11>100,Level_1*H11,0)** in the Value_if_false text box.

Your screen should be similar to Figure 5-28.

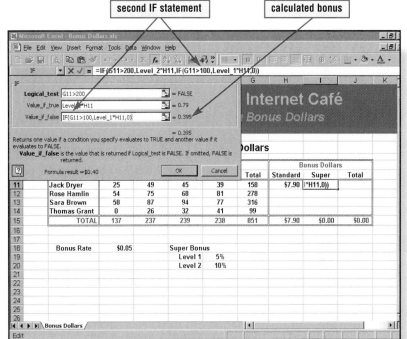

Figure 5-28

4 ■ Click  .

The Super Bonus for Jack Dryer is $0.40. The IF function determined that the number in cell G11 was less than 200 but greater than 100. Therefore, the Super Bonus was calculated using Level_1, or 5 percent. To enter the formula to calculate the Total bonus (J11) and to make these same calculation for the other three customers,

5 ■ Enter the formula =H11+I11 into cell J11.

■ Copy cells H11 through J11 to the range H12 through J14.

■ Click cell H12 to clear the selection.

Your screen should be similar to Figure 5–29.

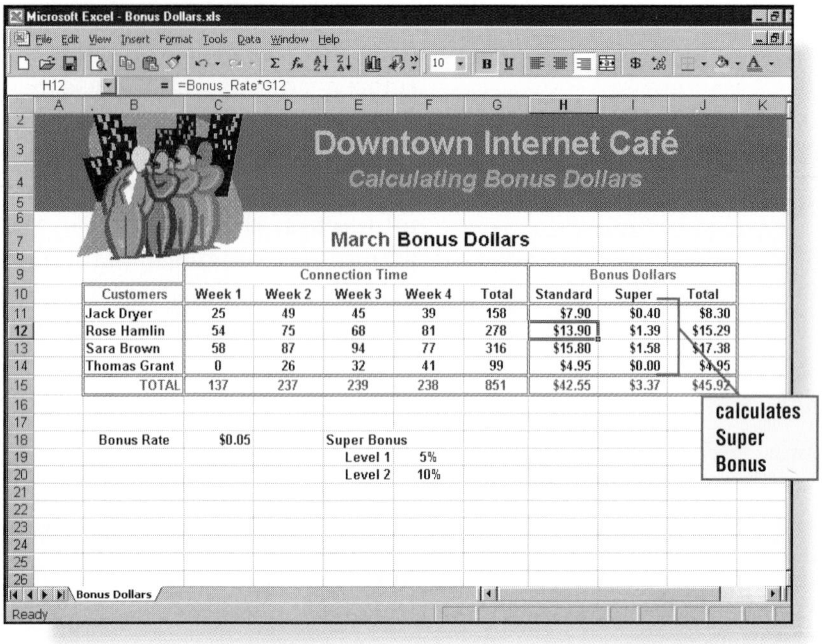

Figure 5–29

Because the named references in the copied formulas are absolute, they copied correctly. Both Rose and Sara earned Super Bonus awards of 10 percent because the values in cells G12 and G13 are greater than 200. Thomas, however, did not earn any Super Bonus, because the value in cell G14 is less than 100.

Adding a Combo Box Control

Evan really likes the layout of the form. A change needs to be made, however, to the Standard Bonus rate. During some months the bonus rate may be raised to $0.10 or $0.15 per minute. The formulas to calculate the bonuses will need to be adjusted to use the other two bonus rates during those months. You could create two additional forms that would each have a different bonus rate in cell C18. This would require that the correct form be used for that month's input based on the bonus rate for that month. A simpler way to deal with this problem is to add a combo box control to the form.

The first step is to enter the three bonus rates in a columnar range.

1 Enter **Rates** in cell H18 to identify the values in the column.

In cells H19 through H21 enter the numbers **.05**, **.10**, and **.15**.

> Cells H19:H21 were preformatted to currency.

Display the Control Toolbox toolbar.

If necessary, move the toolbar to the left side of your screen.

Your screen should be similar to Figure 5–30.

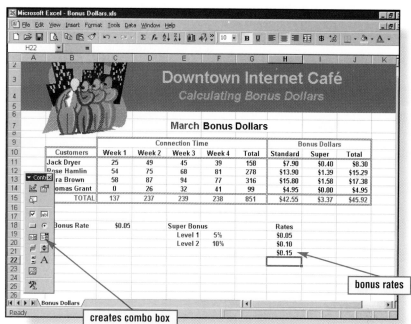

Figure 5–30

Next, you will add a combo box control to the form. This control creates a text box and button that will display a drop-down list with the three bonus amounts as options that can be selected.

2 Click [icon] Combo Box on the Control Toolbox toolbar.

Drag to create a combo box over cell J17.

> The combo box is a selected object that can be sized or moved like any other object.

Your screen should be similar to Figure 5–31.

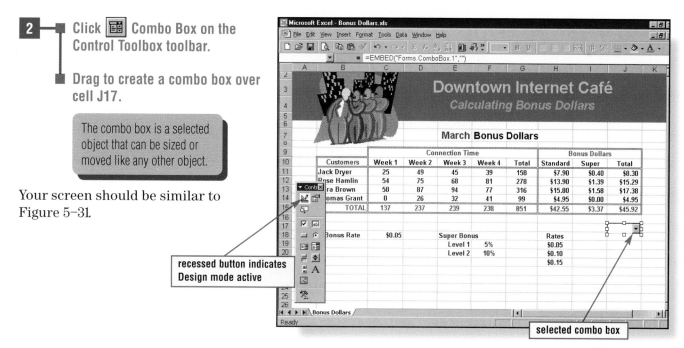

Figure 5–31

Design mode is active, so you can modify the settings associated with the selected control.

Next you need to specify the information to be displayed in the combo box drop-down list and the location of the cell to link the selection to. You do this by setting the properties of the combo box.

3 ■ Click 🖼 Properties.

■ If necessary, open the Alphabetic tab.

> You can also select Properties from the object's Shortcut menu to modify the properties.

Your screen should look similar to Figure 5–32.

> properties for selected control are listed in alphabetic order

> opens Properties dialog box

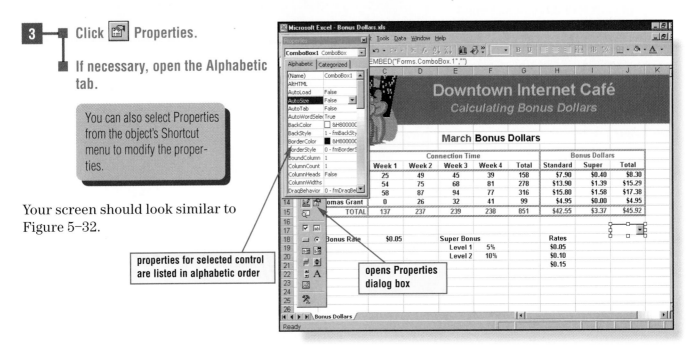

Figure 5–32

The Alphabetic tab displays the properties for the selected control in alphabetical order. The ListFillRange option is used to specify the location of the cells containing the information to be displayed in the combo box drop-down list, and the LinkedCell option is used to specify the cell to receive the selection.

4

Scroll the list to locate the ListFillRange property box.

Enter the range **H19:H21** as the ListFillRange.

Enter cell **C18** as the LinkedCell.

Click ⊠ to close the Properties dialog box.

If necessary, adjust the size of the combo box to fully display the value.

Enter the label **Select Bonus Rate:** in cell I17 to identify the combo box.

> Cell I17 was preformatted to be right aligned.

Your screen should be similar to Figure 5–33.

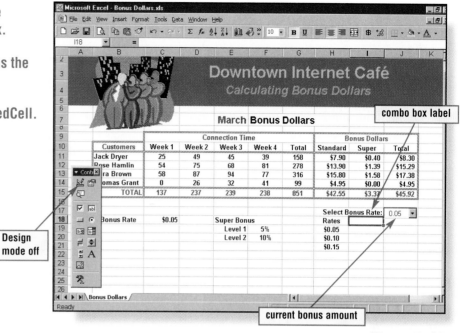

Figure 5–33

5 ■ Click  Exit Design mode to turn off design mode.

■ Close the Control Toolbox toolbar.

■ Open the combo box drop-down list and select $0.10.

Your screen should be similar to Figure 5–34.

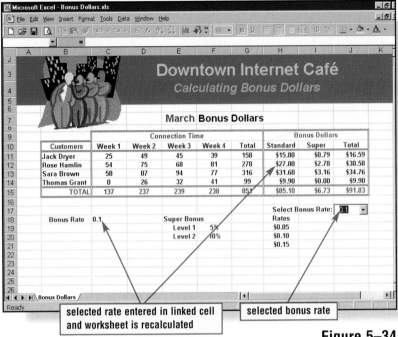

selected rate entered in linked cell and worksheet is recalculated

selected bonus rate

Figure 5–34

The selection you made from the combo box is entered in the bonus rate cell, C18, and the worksheet is recalculated using the new bonus rate. To set the bonus rate to $0.15,

6 ■ Select $0.15 from the combo box drop-down list.

Adding Comments

A well-designed form contains instructions on how to use it. Typically, these instructions are a combination of text entries and comments.

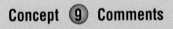

Concept **9** Comments

Comments are notes attached to cells that can be used to help clarify the meaning of the data, provide documentation, or ask a question. Using comments is a good method of adding instructions that do not interfere with the appearance of the worksheet.

A comment appears as note box attached to the cell. You can move and resize a comment box just as you would any other type of graphic object. If you move the cell that contains a comment, the associated comment box moves with it.

You will add one text entry and two cell comments that will provide the instructions for this form. To add the text entry,

1 ● Move to cell A17.

● Enter **For information on how to complete this form, point to the red triangles.**

● Format A17 to a font color of Dark Red and bold.

Your screen should be similar to Figure 5–35.

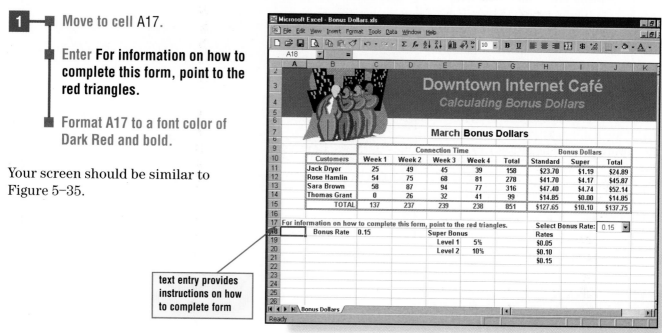

text entry provides instructions on how to complete form

Figure 5–35

Next you will add the cell comments using the Reviewing toolbar. The first comment will appear in cell E7 and will direct users to update the form's title by entering in the month.

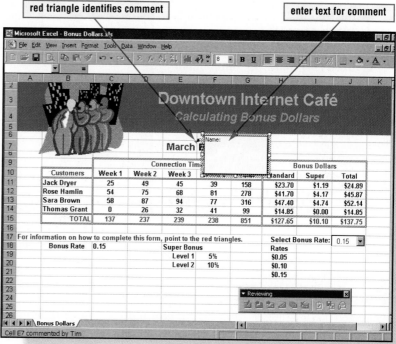

red triangle identifies comment

enter text for comment

2 ● Display the Reviewing toolbar.

● If necessary, move the toolbar to the lower right corner of the worksheet.

● Move to E7.

● Click 🔲 New Comment in the Reviewing toolbar.

The menu equivalent is Insert/Comment.

Your screen should be similar to Figure 5–36.

Figure 5–36

3 ▪ Replace any existing text in the box with **Enter the month here.**

▪ Resize the comment box to fit the text.

▪ Click in any other cell to clear the selection and point to the red triangle in cell E7.

Your screen should be similar to Figure 5–37.

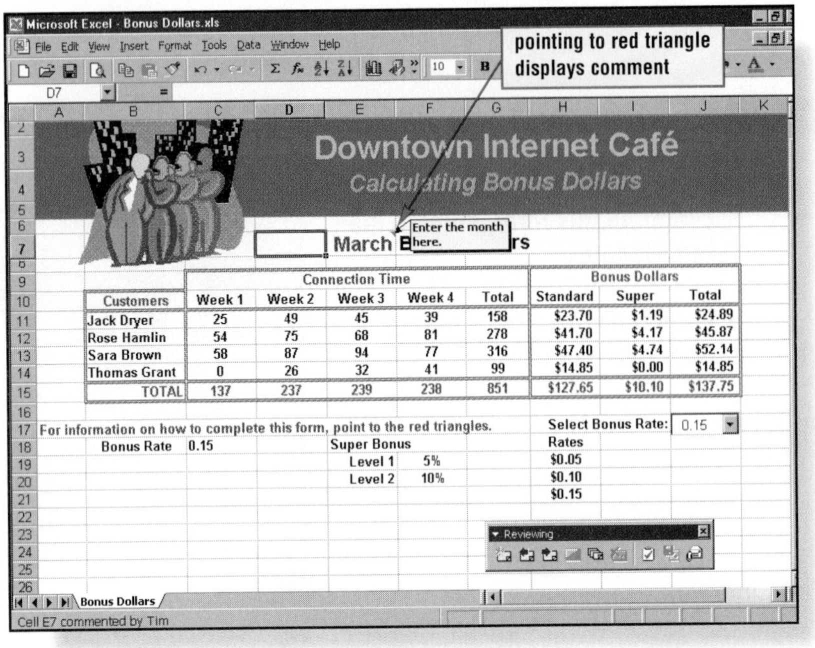

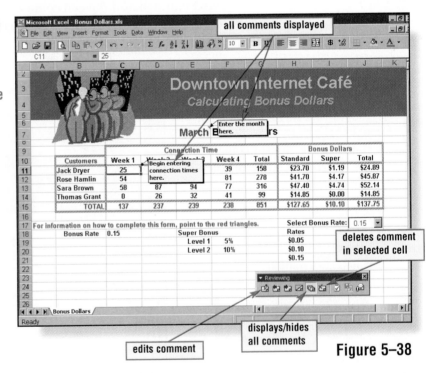

You can edit a comment using **I**nsert/**E**dit Comment or 🖻 or delete a comment using **E**dit/Cle**a**r/Co**m**ments or 🖾 .

Figure 5–37

The comment is displayed in a comment text box. The second comment will be entered in cell C11.

4 ▪ Move to C11 and add a comment containing the text **Begin entering connection times here.**

▪ Resize the comment box to fit the entered text.

▪ Click 🖼 **Show All Comments.**

Your screen should be similar to Figure 5–38.

Figure 5–38

Additional Information

You can also print comments where they appear on the worksheet or in a list at the end of the worksheet by selecting the appropriate option from the Print dialog box.

Both comments you entered are displayed. If comments overlay one another, you can move them around just like any other graphics object.

The menu equivalent, **V**iew/**C**omments, will display all comments or hide all displayed comments.

5 ■ Click  **Hide All Comments.**

■ **Close the Reviewing toolbar.**

Hiding Rows

A well-designed form is simple, uncluttered, and easy to use. To simplify the entry of data and to protect formulas and format features, appropriate areas of the worksheet should be unlocked and other areas protected.

First, you will unlock appropriate cells in the worksheet. Finally, you will protect the worksheet's format and functions.

1 ■ **Unlock the cell that displays the month (cell E7).**

■ **Unlock the cells for weekly connection times (cells C11 through F14).**

■ **Unlock cell C18 that displays the selected bonus rate.**

Before turning protection on, there are several nonessential items in the worksheet that can be hidden. For example, users of this electronic form do not need to see the list of rates and the two bonus levels. To hide this information,

2 ■ **Select** rows 18 through 21.

Click the row number to quickly select an entire row.

■ **Choose F**ormat/**R**ow/**H**ide.

To redisplay hidden rows, select the rows above and below the hidden rows and use F**o**rmat/**R**ow/**U**nhide.

Your screen should be similar to Figure 5–39.

rows 18 through 21 hidden

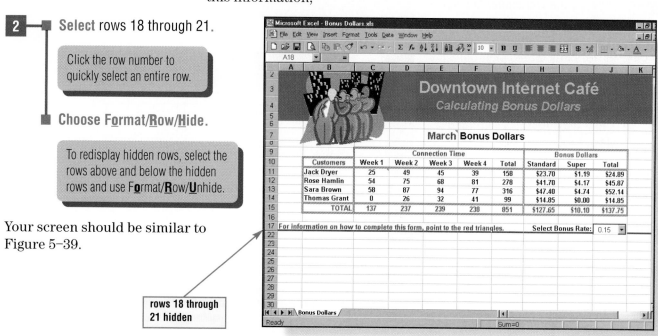

Figure 5–39

3 ■ **Choose T**ools/**P**rotection/**P**rotect Sheet/ OK .

Now all locked cells in the worksheet are protected. Any cells you unlocked prior to turning protection on can be changed.

Documenting, Printing, and Saving the Form

Next, you will enter basic documentation regarding the worksheet file.

1 — Choose **File/Properties**.

— If necessary, open the Summary tab.

— Type **Bonus Dollars** in the Title text box.

— Type **Monthly record of connection times and bonuses** in the Subject text box.

— Enter your name into the Author text box.

— Type **Point to the red triangles for instructions. Select the bonus amount from the Bonus Rate button.** in the Comments text box.

— Click [OK].

You are now ready to print and save the form.

2 — Preview the worksheet and specify the following print settings landscape orientation, centered horizontally on the page. Include a footer that displays your name and date only.

— Zoom the sheet to a full-page view.

Your screen should look similar to Figure 5–40

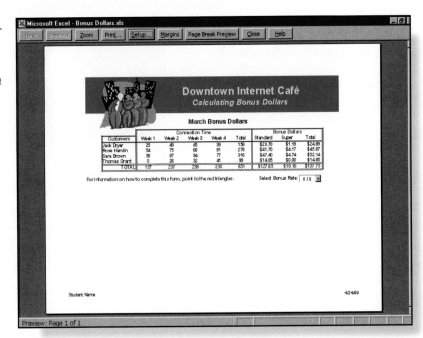

Figure 5–40

3 Print the form.

Save the completed March form as **March Bonus Dollars** to your data disk.

Because this information will be entered in a different workbook file for each month's data, you will also save it as a workbook template.

4 Clear the contents of cell E7 and cells C11 through F14.

Move to cell A9.

Choose <u>F</u>ile/Save <u>A</u>s.

Enter the new file name, **Bonus Form**, in the File Name text box.

Select Template (*.xlt) from the Save As Type list box.

Change the location to your data disk.

Click 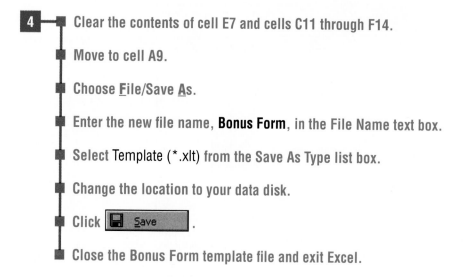 .

Close the Bonus Form template file and exit Excel.

Concept Summary

Tutorial 5: Using Data Tables, Creating Macros, and Designing Onscreen Forms

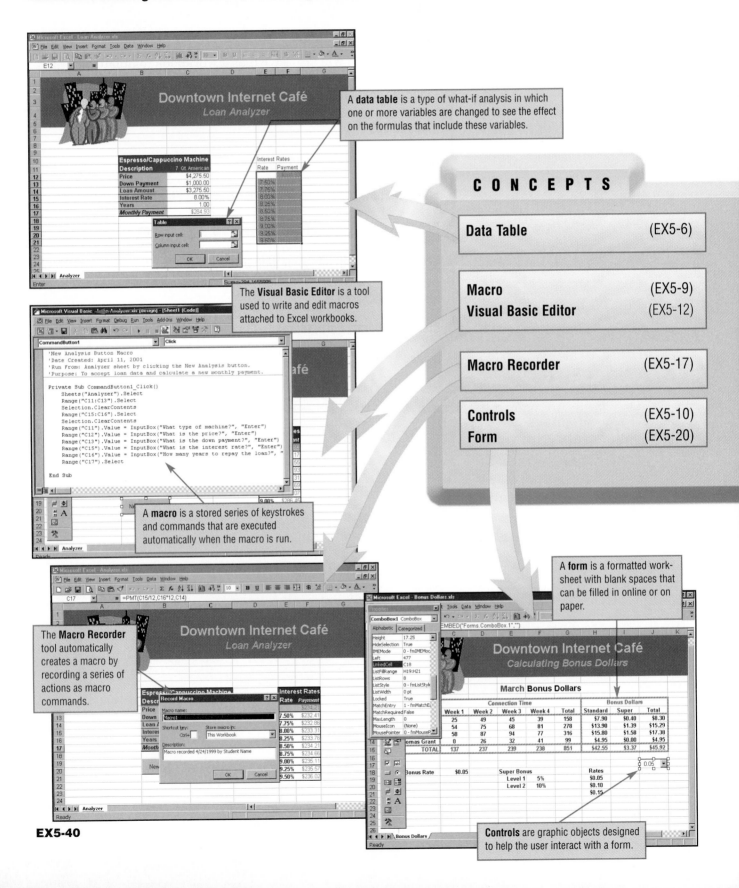

A **data table** is a type of what-if analysis in which one or more variables are changed to see the effect on the formulas that include these variables.

The **Visual Basic Editor** is a tool used to write and edit macros attached to Excel workbooks.

A **macro** is a stored series of keystrokes and commands that are executed automatically when the macro is run.

The **Macro Recorder** tool automatically creates a macro by recording a series of actions as macro commands.

A **form** is a formatted worksheet with blank spaces that can be filled in online or on paper.

Controls are graphic objects designed to help the user interact with a form.

C O N C E P T S

Data Table	(EX5-6)
Macro	(EX5-9)
Visual Basic Editor	(EX5-12)
Macro Recorder	(EX5-17)
Controls	(EX5-10)
Form	(EX5-20)

A **range name** is a description of a cell or range of cells that can be used in place of cell references.

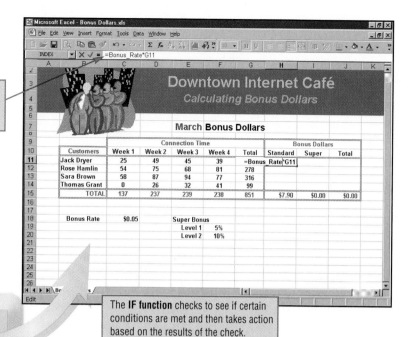

The **IF function** checks to see if certain conditions are met and then takes action based on the results of the check.

Range Name	(EX5-23)
IF Function	(EX5-27)
Comments	(EX5-34)

Comments are notes attached to cells that can be used to clarify the meaning of the cell contents, provide documentation, or ask a question.

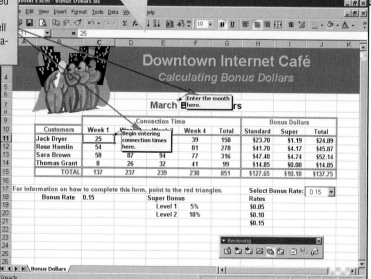

Tutorial Review

Key Terms

column-oriented EX5-6
comments EX5-34
controls EX5-10
data table EX5-6
form EX5-21
IF function EX5-27
input cell EX5-6
logical operators EX5-27
macro EX5-9

Macro Recorder EX5-17
nested function EX5-29
nper EX5-4
object EX5-12
one-variable data table EX5-6
principal EX5-4
property EX5-12
pv EX5-4
range name EX5-23

rate EX5-4
row-oriented EX5-6
run EX5-9
statement EX5-12
Sub procedure EX5-12
syntax EX5-12
two-variable data table EX5-6
Visual Basic Editor EX5-12

Command Summary

Command	Shortcut Key	Button	Action
File/**C**lose and Return to Microsoft Excel		[X]	Closes the Visual Basic Editor window and returns to the active Excel worksheet
File/Properties			Documents the workbook
Edit/Cle**a**r/Co**m**ments		[button]	Deletes comment in selected cell
View/**C**omments		[button]	Displays all comments or hides all displayed comments
Insert/**N**ame/**D**efine			Assigns a name you specify to a cell or range of cells
Insert/**N**ame/**P**aste			Places the selected cell or cell range name in the formula bar or lists names in the worksheet
Insert/**N**ame/**C**reate			Creates a range name using the text in cells
Insert/Co**m**ment		[button]	Inserts a new comment in selected cell
Insert/**E**dit Comment		[button]	Edits comment in selected cell
F**o**rmat/**R**ow/**H**ide			Hides selected rows
F**o**rmat/**R**ow/**U**nhide			Displays rows that were previously hidden
Tools/**M**acros/**M**acros/<Macro name>/**R**un			Runs selected macro
Tools/**M**acros/**M**acros/<Macro name>/**E**dit			Opens selected macro in Visual Basic Editor for editing
Tools/**M**acro/**R**ecord New Macro			Records a series of actions as a macro
Tools/**M**acro/Stop **R**ecording			Stops the recording of a macro
Data/**T**able			Creates a data table based on specified input values and formulas

Screen Identification

In the following worksheet, several items are identified by letters. Enter the correct term for each item in the spaces that follow.

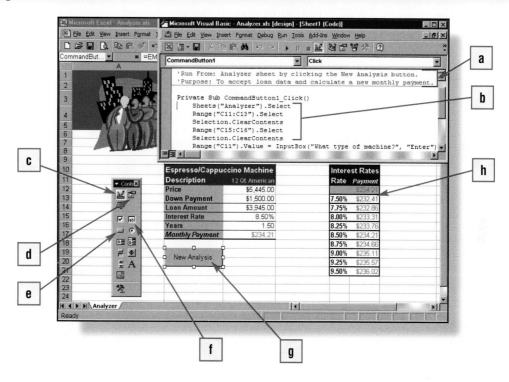

a. _____   d. _____   g. _____

b. _____   e. _____   h. _____

c. _____   f. _____

Matching

Match the letter on the right to the item in the numbered list on the left.

1. <
_____ a. information supplied to a function for calculation

2. IF
_____ b. a note attached to a cell

3. comment
_____ c. logical operator

4. arguments
_____ d. evaluates condition and takes one of two actions

5. nested function
_____ e. a function within another function

6. PMT
_____ f. a stored series of keystrokes and commands

7. data table
_____ g. information in the Visual Basic Editor

8. macro
_____ h. calculates periodic payments on a loan

9. statement
_____ i. a graphic object used on forms

10. control
_____ j. a what-if analysis in which variables are used to see the effect on formulas

Fill-In

Complete the following statements by filling in the blanks with the correct terms.

a. _____ are used in formulas and functions that compare values in two or more cells.

b. The _____ automatically records the actions you take in a worksheet for later use.

c. A _____ data table can contain one or more formulas that refers to one input cell.

d. A range _____ can consist of any combination of 255 characters.

e. A _____ appears as note box attached to a cell.

f. Excel uses the _____ computer programming language for macros.

g. The _____ in a macro is the item that the statement will affect.

h. An _____ is a cell in which a list of values is substituted to see the resulting effect on the related formulas.

i. Excel automatically displays a payment as a _____ number.

j. A _____ statement in a macro always begins with an apostrophe.

Multiple-Choice

Circle the correct response to the questions below.

1. The PMT function calculates _____.
   a. annual income
   b. annual expenses
   c. periodic payments
   d. periodic income

2. A _____ data table can be row- or column-oriented.
   a. two-variable
   b. multivariable
   c. one-variable
   d. single-variable

3. A macro can record _____.
   a. keystrokes
   b. menu selections
   c. commands
   d. all of the above

4. The item that a Sub statement in a macro will affect is called a(n) _____.
   a. property
   b. graphic
   c. object
   d. variable

5. A macro created with the Visual Basic Editor must be attached to a(n) _____.
   a. command button
   b. cell
   c. object
   d. control box

6. When a macro is _____, the actions within it are performed automatically.
   a. recorded
   b. executed
   c. stored
   d. opened

7. An Excel form can contain _____.
   a. text
   b. graphics
   c. cell comments
   d. all of the above

8. A range name must start with _____.

   a. a letter

   b. a number

   c. a backslash

   d. any of the above

9. A(n) _____ argument is an expression that makes a comparison using logical operators.

   a. if_then

   b. logical_test

   c. and_or

   d. logical_if

10. A _____ displays a drop-down list of options.

    a. text box

    b. list button

    c. scroll bar

    d. combo box

True/False

Circle the correct answer to the following questions.

1.	The value returned by PMT includes the loan amount, interest, taxes, and fees.	True	False
2.	A two-variable data table is made up of one or more formulas that refer to two input cells.	True	False
3.	A range name can include letters, numbers, or spaces.	True	False
4.	A form created in Excel can only be used online.	True	False
5.	The result of an IF argument is either true or false.	True	False
6.	Macros are used to automate repetitive tasks.	True	False
7.	Comments are attached to worksheets.	True	False
8.	An apostrophe identifies a statement as a remark.	True	False
9.	The IF function requires three arguments.	True	False
10.	The only way to execute a macro is to use a command button.	True	False

Discussion Questions

1. Discuss different ways in which a data table can be used. When would you use a one-variable data table? When would a two-variable table be more appropriate?

2. Discuss some spreadsheet functions that you could automate with a macro. Would it be more appropriate to use the Visual Basic Editor or the Macro Recorder to create each of these macros?

3. Discuss what range names are and when it is appropriate to use them. Give some examples.

Hands-On Practice Exercises

Step by Step

Rating System	
☆	Easy
☆☆	Moderate
☆☆☆	Difficult

1. The Animal Angels animal rescue agency works with limited financial resources. To operate it depends on a large volunteer base. To help repay the volunteers for their time and thank them for their support, Animal Angels gives small gifts and awards. The awards vary with the number of hours volunteered. You have been asked to create a worksheet to track the number of hours people volunteer and determine their award level.

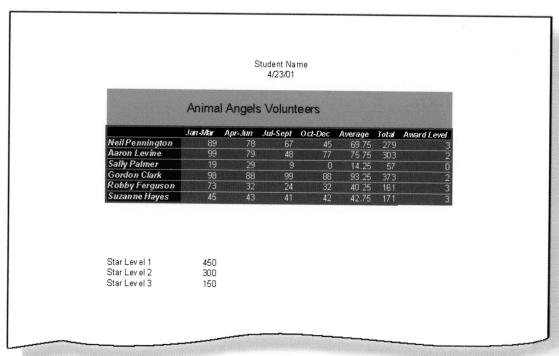

Student Name
4/23/01

Animal Angels Volunteers

	Jan-Mar	Apr-Jun	Jul-Sept	Oct-Dec	Average	Total	Award Level
Neil Pennington	89	78	67	45	69.75	279	3
Aaron Levine	99	79	48	77	75.75	303	2
Sally Palmer	19	29	9	0	14.25	57	0
Gordon Clark	98	88	99	88	93.25	373	2
Robby Ferguson	73	32	24	32	40.25	161	3
Suzanne Hayes	45	43	41	42	42.75	171	3

Star Level 1	450
Star Level 2	300
Star Level 3	150

a. Open the workbook file Animal Angels Volunteers. Enter the sample data shown below into the worksheet.

	Jan-Mar	Apr-Jun	Jul-Sep	Oct-Dec
Neil Pennington	89	78	67	45
Aaron Levine	99	79	48	77
Sally Palmer	19	29	9	0
Gordon Clark	98	88	99	88
Robby Ferguson	73	32	24	32
Susanne Hayes	45	43	41	42

b. Enter formulas to calculate the average hours for the year and the totals.

c. Apply the Colorful 1 AutoFormat to the worksheet data. Format the worksheet title appropriately.

d. Enter the labels **Star Level 1, Star Level 2,** and **Star Level 3** in cells A16 through A18. In cells B16, B17, and B18 enter **300, 200, 100,** respectively.

e. Use the Name Range command to name the values for the star levels.

f. Enter the following if statement to calculate the award level for the volunteers:
=IF(G5>=Star_Level_1,1,IF(G5>=Star_Level_2,2,IF(G5>=Star_Level_3,3,0))).

g. Change the values in cell B16, B17, and B18 to **450, 300,** and **150.** How do these numbers affect the worksheet?

h. Enter cell comments to inform the user how to use the worksheet.

i. Enter your name and the current date in a header, center the worksheet horizontally and print the worksheet.

j. Save the file as Volunteer Hours.

2. You are a graduate assistant and have been assigned to work for a university professor. You are responsible for maintaining the gradebook and have decided to create a worksheet that will calculate the students' final grades. You started the worksheet by entering the row and column labels and the points earned for a sample set of students. You need to add formulas to calculate the percentage of each point category, and you also want to add an IF statement to calculate the letter grade. The completed gradebook worksheet will be similar to the one shown here.

Gradebook for Fall 2002

ID #	Last Name	First Name	HW Points 100	HW Percent 20%	Project Points 200	Project Percent 30%	Quiz Points 100	Quiz Percent 20%	Exam Points 200	Exam Percent 30%	Final Percent 100%	Letter
272458476	Kendell	Mindy	89	17.80%	180	27.00%	95	19.00%	180	27.00%	90.80%	A
300323601	Kirk	Andrew	43	8.60%	194	29.10%	65	13.00%	165	24.75%	75.45%	C
196918993	Matthews	Scott	75	15.00%	173	25.95%	75	15.00%	194	29.10%	85.05%	B
982305399	Maurer	Nicholas	90	18.00%	195	29.25%	90	18.00%	173	25.95%	91.20%	A
714930526	Meese	Lindsay	75	15.00%	168	25.20%	67	13.40%	155	23.25%	76.85%	C
914576527	Mittelstadt	Jennifer	32	6.40%	132	19.80%	43	8.60%	166	24.90%	59.70%	E
614608549	Oestreich	Stephen	54	10.80%	155	23.25%	54	10.80%	132	19.80%	64.65%	D
682035222	Pawlowski	Vanessa	88	17.60%	165	24.75%	75	15.00%	155	23.25%	80.60%	B
459579229	Reboton	Leslie	92	18.40%	190	28.50%	88	17.60%	185	27.75%	92.25%	A
152260554	Rice	Trent	84	16.80%	173	25.95%	84	16.80%	190	28.50%	88.05%	B

Student Name
Date

a. Open the file Gradesheet on your data disk. Select cells D5 through L6. Create a name range using the top row as the labels.

b. In cell E7 enter the formula =(D7/HW_Points)*HW_Percent. Copy the formula down the column for the other students. In a similar manner, calculate the percentages for the Project, Quiz, and Exam columns.

c. To calculate the final grade percentage in column L, enter the formula =E7+G7+I7+K7. Copy the formula down the column.

d. Enter the IF statement =IF(L7>0.899,"A",IF(L7>0.799,"B",IF(L7>0.699,"C",IF(L7>0.599,"D","E")))) in cell M7. You can use the insert function command or type the IF statement directly into the cell. Copy the IF statement down the column for the other students.

e. Enter your name and the current date using the NOW function below the worksheet data.

f. Preview the worksheet. Remove the header and footer from the worksheet.

g. Set the page layout to landscape and adjust the left and right page margins to 0.5. Fit the worksheet to one page. Save and print the worksheet.

3. You are considering buying a new car. You have a limited budget and would like to create a worksheet that will help you analyze three makes and models and then do some what-if analysis on the terms of the loan you could get. The completed loan analyzer worksheet will be similar to the one shown here.

a. Open the file Auto Loan on your data disk. In columns B, E and H enter the following information for make, model and price.

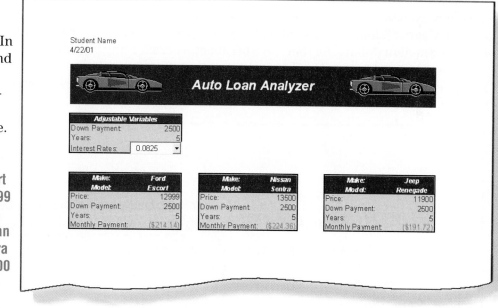

Make:	Ford
Model:	Escort
Price:	12,999

Make:	Nissan
Model:	Sentra
Price:	13,500

Make:	Jeep
Model:	Renegade
Price:	11,900

b. Enter the down payment of $1,500 in cell B7, 3 for the years in cell B8, and .0725 for the interest rate in cell B9.

c. Link the down payment amount from B7 to cells B15, E15, and H15. In a similar manner, link the years from cell B8 to cells B16, E16, and H16.

d. Enter the payment function =PMT($B$9/12,$B$8*12,B14–B15) in cell B17. Copy the formula to cells E17 and H17.

e. Since interest rates change frequently you would like to create a combo box that displays different interest rates. Enter **7.25** in cell K6 and **7.35** in cell K7. Format cells K6 and K7 to percent with two decimal places. Select K6 through K7. Copy the range down the column to cell K23.

f. Using the Forms toolbar Combo Box button, create a combo box below cell B9. Insert the input range **K6 through K23**. Set the Linked Cell to J6. Format K6:K23 as a percent.

g. Move to cell B9 and enter the index formula **=INDEX(J6,K6:K23)**.

h. Adjust the size and placement of the combo box to cover cell B9.

i. Hide columns J and K.

j. Apply an AutoFormat of your choice to the adjustable values and the three auto calculations.

k. Adjust the column widths and layout as necessary.

l. Add cell comments to inform the user how to use the worksheet.

m. To see how the worksheet recalculates the monthly payments, enter the following for changing variable values:

Down payment:	**2,500**
Years:	**5**
Interest Rate:	**8.25**

n. Save the worksheet as Auto Loan Calculator. Include your name and the current date in a header and print the worksheet using landscape orientation.

☆☆

4. You work for a company that handles a lot of foreign accounts and consequently does a lot of currency exchanging. You would like to create a worksheet that will help employees calculate the currency conversion. You have already created a worksheet that has the calculations for U.S. dollars to Canadian dollars. So that the worksheet works for any type of foreign currency, you will create a command button to ask the user to input the country's currency, the current exchange rate, and the U.S. dollar amount. The completed Exchange Rate worksheet and Visual Basic code window will be similar to the ones shown here.

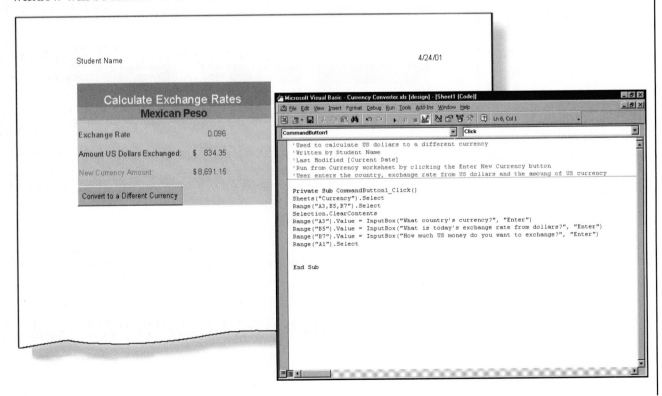

a. Open the Currency Exchange file on your data disk. Open the Control Toolbox toolbar and create a command button to cover A11 and A12. Edit the command button to display the words Convert to a Different Currency.

b. Start the Visual Basic Editor to create the Command Button macro.

c. Enter the following remarks above the Sub procedure header:

'Used to calculate US dollars to a different currency

'Written by [Student Name]

'Last Modified [Current Date]

'Run From Currency worksheet by clicking the Convert to a Different Currency button

'User selects the country, and enters the exchange rate from US dollars and the amount of US currency

d. Inside the Sub and End Sub statements enter the following:

Sheets("Currency").Select

Range("A3,B5,B7").Select

Selection.ClearContents

Range("A3").Value = InputBox("What country's currency?", "Enter")

Range("B5").Value = InputBox("What is today's exchange rate from dollars?", "Enter")

Range("B7").Value = InputBox("How much US money do you want to exchange?", "Enter")

Range("A1").Select

e. Print the text in the code window. Exit design mode and close the Control Toolbox toolbar.

f. Click the command button and enter the following to check the accuracy of your command button.

Country:	Australian Dollar
Rate:	$0.56
US Money:	$450.00

g. Use the business section of your local paper or the Internet to get the current exchange rates and calculate the number of French francs, Japanese yen, and Mexican pesos you would get if you exchanged $834.35.

h. Enter your name and the current date in a header and print the worksheet showing the exchange of Mexican pesos.

i. Save the workbook as Currency Converter.

✫ ✫ ✰

5. Adventure Travel Tours agents work closely with different airlines. To give their customers the best possible fares, ATT agents buy group seating on selected flights. Because the number of seats is calculated as a percentage of the previous year's sales and set by the airline industry, you would like to create a worksheet that will show the effects of increases from 0 to 10 percent. The com-

pleted Adventure Travel Tours Seating worksheet will be similar to the one shown here.

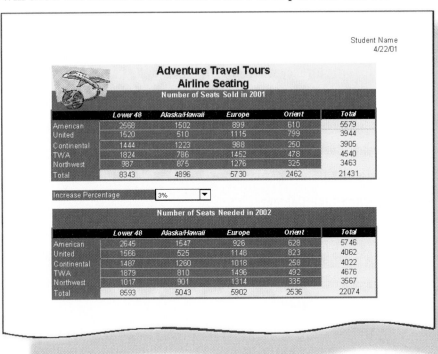

    a. Open the file Adventure Travel Seating on your data disk. Use the formatting features you have learned to make the worksheet look more attractive. Add an appropriate clip-art graphic to the worksheet. Enter functions to calculate the totals.

    b. Enter the values 0% to 10% starting in K4 to be used for the values in a combo box..

    c. Create a combo box that contains these values and display the combo box over cell C13. Link the combo box to cell J5. Enter the label Increase Percentage in cell A13.

    d. Copy cells A3 to F11 to cell A15. Change the title in row 15 to Number of Seats Needed in 2002.

    e. In cell B18 enter the formula =B6*(1+$J$5). Copy cells C18 through E18 and down to row 22.

    f. Adjust the formatting as needed to make the worksheet attractive.

    g. Enter comments to tell the user how to use the worksheet.

    h. Hide columns J and K. Set the percentage increase to 3%.

    i. Enter your name and the current date in a header, center the worksheet horizontally and print the worksheet.

    j. Save the workbook as Airline Seating.

On Your Own

✰

6. The company you work for will contribute 3 percent of your gross pay to an individual retirement account (IRA). You can add up to another 15 percent of your gross pay to the same IRA. Create a worksheet with the following columns: Gross Wages, Employer Contribution, My Contribution, and Total Contribution. Enter your gross wages and create a formula to calculate the company contribution. In a column to the right enter the numbers 0 to 10. Format them as percentages. Create a combo box that uses the percentages and calculates your contribution for the My Contribution column. Total the contributions. Use the combo box to see how much of your gross pay you can contribute to the IRA. Select the value you think is most appropriate for you. Enter your name and the current date in the worksheet. Save and print the worksheet.

7. In a blank new worksheet, use the Macro Recorder to record five macros for procedures that you use frequently and for which using a macro would save you time. For example, you may want to create a macro to modify the contents of the selected cell to 16 points, a selected font style, bold, and centered. Make sure that the macros are available to other open worksheets by using the Tools/Macros/Macros command. Add descriptions of the macros in the worksheet. Put the macro shortcut keys you assigned in cell comments. Enter your name and the current date in the worksheet. Test your macros by opening a new workbook and running the macros. Save and print both the macro and new worksheet.

8. You are interested in buying a computer. Visit a local computer store or use the Internet to find prices for similar features for computers manufactured by different companies. Using the features you learned in this tutorial, create a worksheet that allows you to compare multiple computers on the same worksheet. Use a combo box to change the loan interest rate you have to pay for financing the purchase. Link the down payment, number of years, and interest rates to cells that can vary. Format the worksheet in an attractive manner. Enter your name and the current date in a header and print the worksheet. Save the workbook.

9. The Sports Company has decided to offer its own credit card. As an incentive to get employees to promote the card, the company offers to give employees $1.00 for each card application they file. If an employee files 25 or more applications, a bonus is added. Create a worksheet for four employees that tracks the number of applications filed per week. Total the number of applications by employee and for the month. Calculate the amount the employee earned by multiplying the total by $1.00. Use a linking cell for the $1.00 bonus value so you can increase or decrease it to see the effect. Use an IF statement to calculate a 10 percent bonus for employees who file 25 applications, and a 20 percent bonus for employees who file 50 or more applications. Create a combo box with $1.00, $1.50, and $2.00 in it. Unlock the data entry cells in the worksheet. Protect the worksheet. Select the $2.00 bonus amount. Enter your name and the current date in a header of the worksheet. Save and print the worksheet.

10. You have been hired to work for the local traffic court. Create a worksheet that the clerks can use to calculate the amount of a speeding ticket. The worksheet should contain the following information: actual speed limit, speed offender was traveling, and number of tickets offender has received. The worksheet should calculate miles above speed limit, cost of ticket ($10.00 for each mile), court costs ($53.20), and additional charges ($20.00 for each offense). Use the Visual Basic Editor window and write the statements to ask the clerk to enter the actual speed limit, speed offender was traveling, and number of tickets. Calculate the cost of the speeding ticket. Enter your name and the current date in a header of the worksheet. Save and print the worksheet.

Creating and Using an Excel Database

Case Study   The form you created to track the Downtown Internet Café's customer Internet connection times and apply discounts based on those times is working quite well. However, Evan would like to have a separate database that contains the café customers' contact information so that he can use it to send

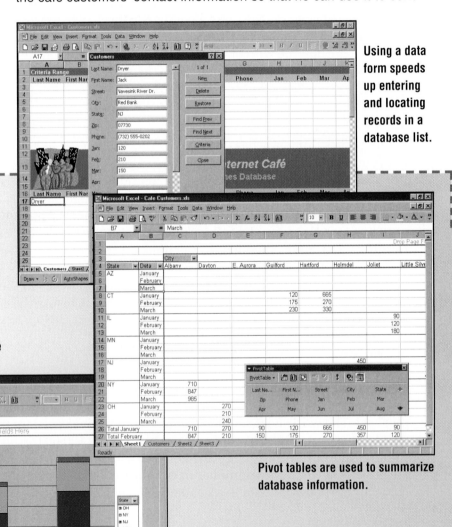

Using a data form speeds up entering and locating records in a database list.

A pivot chart visually displays the information in a pivot table.

Pivot tables are used to summarize database information.

out the discount coupons. He would also like this database to summarize the monthly connection times so he can keep track of the computer usage at the café, analyze seasonal trends, and plan marketing campaigns.

Another feature you tell Evan about is Excel's ability to create a data map based on the information in the database. Because the café is in a major city with a warm climate and a large university, it brings in people from all over the country. A data map would illustrate the diversity of the café's clients by highlighting their home states on a U.S. map, which Evan thinks would be an excellent marketing tool.

While using Excel to create the database (shown below), you will learn about entering records as well as locating, modifying, sorting, and filtering. You will also learn how to create a pivot table and pivot chart to summarize and view the data in different ways, and a data map to view geographical data.

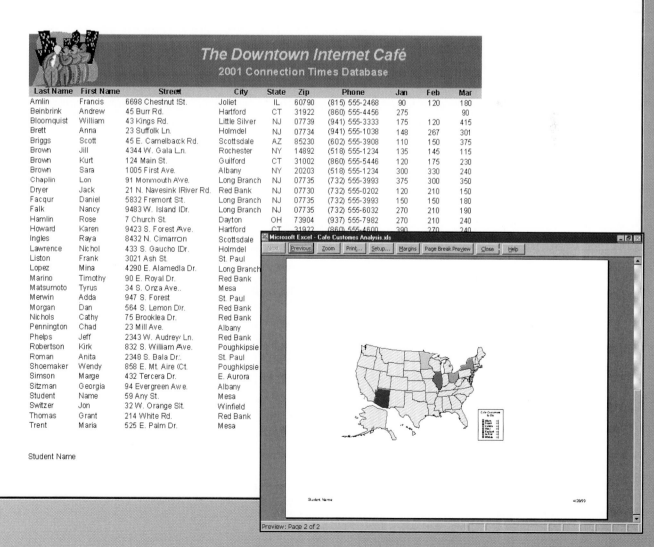

Concept Overview

The following concepts will be introduced in this tutorial:

1 **Database**   A database is an organized collection of related information consisting of records (rows) and fields (columns).

2 **Data validation**   Data validation defines the type or types of entries that are acceptable for a particular cell or range of cells.

3 **Find and Replace**   The Find and Replace feature helps you quickly find specific information and automatically replace it with new information.

4 **Sort**   You can sort data in a specified sequence, alphabetically, numerically, or by date.

5 **Automatic Subtotal**   The automatic subtotal feature displays a running subtotal for selected numeric fields.

6 **Filter**   A filter is a restriction you place on records in a list to quickly isolate and display a subset of records.

7 **Pivot Table**   A pivot table is an interactive table that can be used to summarize and manipulate worksheet data.

8 **Pivot Chart**   A pivot chart is an interactive chart that can be used to view and rearrange data.

9 **Data Map**   The data map feature is used to illustrate and analyze data by geographic region.

Creating the Database List

You want to create an Excel worksheet that will contain the café's customer contact information and Internet connection times. In order to manipulate the data the way you want to, you decide to format this worksheet as a database.

Concept ① Database

A **database** is an organized collection of related information. Typically, the information in a database is stored in a table consisting of vertical columns and horizontal rows. Each row contains a **record,** which is all the information about one person, thing, or place. Each column is a **field,** which is the smallest unit of information about a record.

In Excel, a database is created in a worksheet where the columns are the database fields and the rows are the database records. The column labels serve as field names in the database. A **field name** is a descriptive label used to identify the data stored in the field.

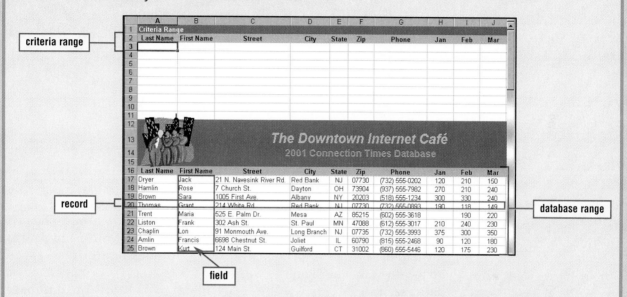

An Excel database worksheet is divided into two separate areas: one is the **database range,** or **list,** where the fields and records are entered; the other is the **criteria range,** where search conditions are entered that are used to locate and analyze the information contained in the database. The first row of the database range must contain the field names. All other contiguous rows contain the database records. The criteria range consists of at least two contiguous rows. The first row contains the same field names as in the database, and the second row is used to define the search conditions.

You have already started to create the database worksheet structure and have saved it in a file named Customers.

 Load Excel and open the workbook file Customers.

Your screen should be similar to Figure 6-1.

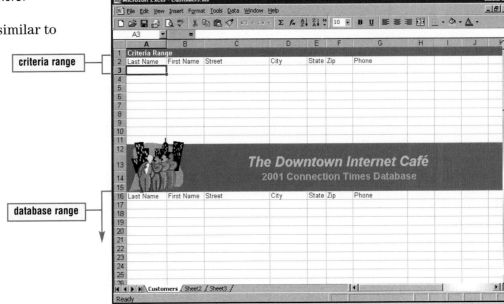

Figure 6-1

The Customers worksheet has been divided into two areas. The criteria range area is located at the top of the worksheet beginning in row 2, and the database range area begins at row 16. Although the criteria range can be located anywhere on the worksheet, it is best if it is placed above the database range. This way there are blank rows below the database list where new records can be added. If there are no blank rows below the list, Excel cannot add the new information.

Rows 2 and 16 contain the field names for the customer information that will be entered in the database. However, you still need to add field names for the months that will be used to record the monthly connection times for each customer. In addition, it is a good idea to use formatted column labels for field names to help differentiate the labels from the data in the list. You will center, bold, and add a blue fill color to all the field name labels.

Additional Information

If you use the same combination of formats frequently, you may want to define the combination as a style by assigning it a name using Format/Style. Then it can be quickly applied like any other style. Styles can be deleted just as easily by selecting the style name and clicking Delete.

2 ■ Enter **Jan** in cell H16.

■ Drag the fill handle of cell H16 to extend the range through December (cell S16).

■ Center, bold and add the Pale Blue fill to the entire range A16 through S16.

■ Copy the new format and labels in cells A16 through S16 into A2 through S2 to complete the criteria range.

Your screen should be similar to Figure 6–2.

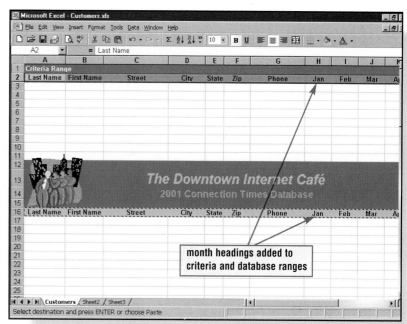

Figure 6–2

Next, you need to name the database and criteria ranges to define them for use. This will include the row of column labels you just entered as well as the row below it to allow for database record entry in the database range and for search condition entry in the criteria range.

3 ■ Select the cell range A16 through S17.

■ Click in the Name Box and type **Database**.

■ Press ⬅Enter.

■ Select A2 through S3 and name the range **Criteria**.

> Once you name a range of cells, you can select that range at any time just by choosing its name from the Name box drop-down list.

Your screen should be similar to Figure 6–3.

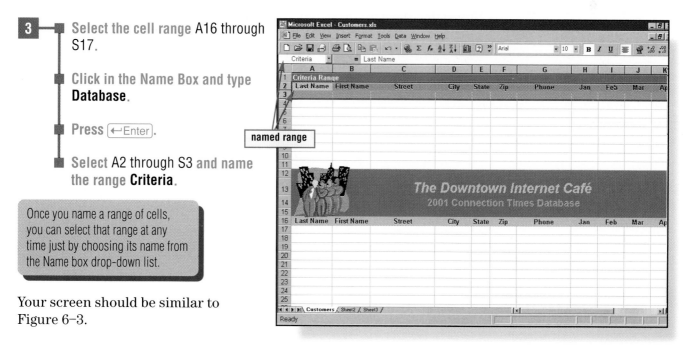

Figure 6–3

You have the customer information and connection time data for the first three months of the year and want to enter this information into the database range. Although you can enter the record information by typing it directly in the cells, Excel includes a special form, called a **data form,** that makes it easy to enter database records. To use the data form to enter the first record,

4 ── ■ Move to cell A17.

■ Choose **D**ata/**F**orm.

Your screen should be similar to Figure 6–4.

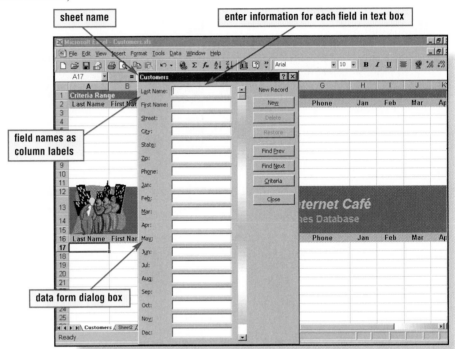

Figure 6–4

Notice that the data form dialog box has the name of your worksheet as its title and the column labels as its field names. In the box to the right of each label, you enter the record information for that field. When the field entry is complete, move to the next field by clicking in the next box or pressing [Tab ⇆].

5 Enter the information shown below for the first record.

Last Name	Dryer
First Name	Jack
Street	21 N. Navesink River Dr.
City	Red Bank
State	NJ
Zip	07730
Phone	(732) 555-0202
Jan	120
Feb	210
Mar	150

Connection time is recorded in minutes.

Your screen should be similar to Figure 6-5.

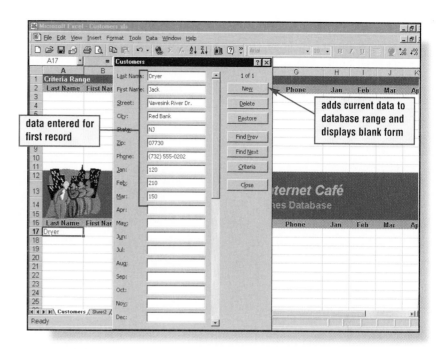

Figure 6-5

The data for the first record is complete. To add it to the database and display another blank entry form,

6 Click  New .

Enter the information shown below for the next two records.

	Record 1	Record 2
Last Name	Hamlin	Brown
First Name	Rose	Sara
Street	7 Church St.	1005 First Ave.
City	Dayton	Albany
State	Ohio	NY
Zip	73094	20203
Phone	(937) 555-7982	(518) 555-1234
Jan	270	299.5
Feb	210	330
Mar	240	239.5

These are the only records you want to enter for now. To close the data form and return to the worksheet,

7 ■ Click [Close] .

■ Best fit the Street column width so that the entire data entry is visible.

Your screen should look similar to Figure 6–6.

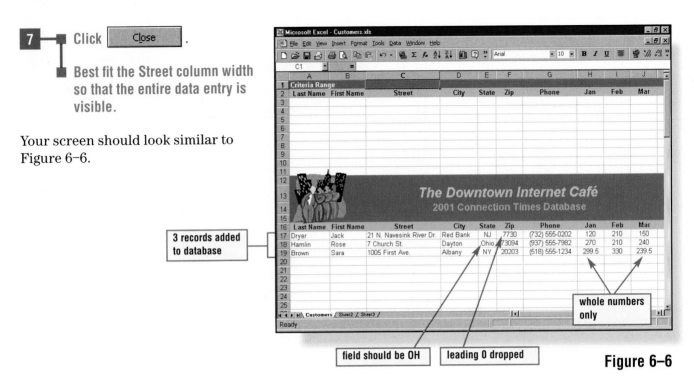

3 records added to database

field should be OH   leading 0 dropped

Figure 6–6

Notice that the zip code for the first record does not display the leading zero (07739). This is because Excel drops leading zeros for numeric data. Since this field will not be used in calculations, you can change the format for the field to Text so that numeric entries will appear as entered. Since you will be adding many more records to the database, you will extend the format for this field beyond the records that are currently entered.

8 ■ Select the range F17 through F100.

■ Choose F**o**rmat/C**e**lls.

■ Select Text from the Category list of the Number tab.

■ Click [OK] .

■ Change the entry in cell F17 to **07730**.

Adding Data Validation

After looking at the records you just entered, you see that you also made several other data entry mistakes. When you enter data in a record, it should be entered accurately and consistently. The data you enter in a field should be typed exactly as you want it to appear. This is important because any printouts of the data will display the information exactly as entered. It is also important to enter data in a consistent form. For example, if you decide to abbreviate the word "Street" as "St." in the Street field, then it should be abbreviated the same way in every record where it appears. Also be careful not to enter a blank space before or after a field entry. This can cause problems when you are using the table to locate information.

Certain database fields are meant to contain data of certain types or lengths. For example, in the Customer database, the State field uses the two-letter state abbreviations. Also, the connection times should always be whole numbers. You can ensure that these rules are met by adding data validation to these fields.

Concept ② Data Validation

Data validation defines the type or types of entries that are acceptable for a particular cell or range of cells. Data validation can be applied to standard worksheet cells as well as cells that are part of a database range in a database worksheet.

Excel provides a list of valid **data settings** from which you can choose:

Validation	Restricts to
Any value	Any entry, text or number
Whole number	Whole numbers only
Decimal	Decimal numbers only
List	Entry from a defined list
Date	Date entries only
Time	Time entries only
Text length	Number of characters specified
Custom	Custom specifications you set

You can attach an **input message** to a validation cell that appears when the cell is selected and tells the user what the valid entry for that cell is. You can also include an **error alert**, which appears when the user enters the wrong type of data and explains what the correct data entry type is.

The first field to which you will apply data validation is the State field. You want to restrict this field to a two-character text entry. You also want to include an input message that gives the user an example of a valid entry as well as an error alert if the user makes an incorrect entry in this field. To add data validation, you first select the range of cells you want to restrict.

EXCEL 2000

1 Select the cell range E17 through E100.

Choose **D**ata/Va**l**idation.

If necessary, open the Settings tab.

Your screen should be similar to Figure 6–7.

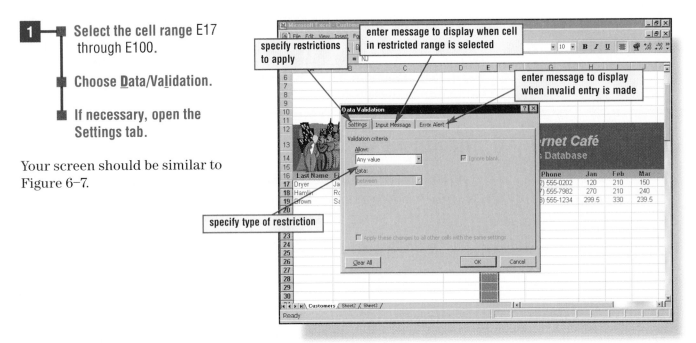

Figure 6–7

The Data Validation dialog box contains three folders that are used to define the validation settings and messages. First you will define the validation rules in the Settings tab. You want to limit the number of characters you can enter in the State field to 2.

2 From the Allow drop-down list, select Text length.

> As you make selections, additional options are displayed to complete the procedure.

From the Data drop-down list, select equal to.

Type **2** in the Length text box.

Next you will enter an input message that will appear when the user selects a cell in the State column on the worksheet.

3 Open the Input Message tab.

Type **State** in the Title text box.

Type **Enter the 2-letter state abbreviation (e.g., NJ for New Jersey)** in the Input message box.

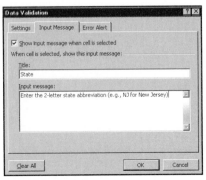

Finally, you'll include an error alert that will appear if the user enters invalid data in a restricted cell.

4 ■ Open the Error Alert tab.

■ Type **State** in the Title text box.

■ Type **The only valid entry is a 2-letter state abbreviation.** in the Error message box.

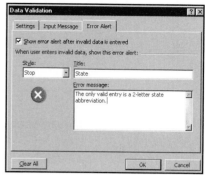

You are finished specifying the validation rules and messages for the State field. To apply this validation to the selected cell range and close the Data Validation dialog box,

5 ■ Click  .

Your screen should be similar to Figure 6–8.

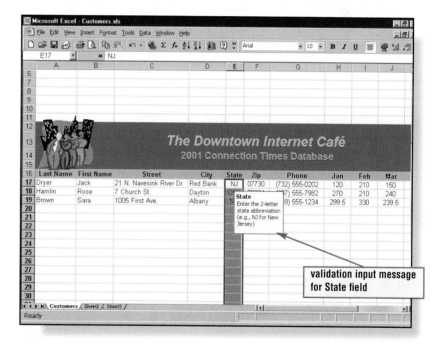

Figure 6–8

The validation input message is displayed because the cell range to which you applied the data validation is still selected. This message will appear whenever a cell in this range is selected.

You also want to restrict the monthly connection time fields to whole numbers only. To add data validation to these fields,

6 — Select the cell range H17 through S100.

— Choose Data/Validation.

— From the Allow drop-down list in the Settings tab, select Whole number.

— From the Data drop-down list, select Greater than.

— Type **0** (zero) in the Minimum text box.

— Enter **Connection Time** as the input message Title and **Enter the number of minutes the customer has been connected this month.** as the Input message text.

— Enter **Connection Time** as the Title for the error alert and **Only whole numbers (no fractions or decimals) can be entered in this field.** as the Error message text.

— Click [OK] .

Your screen should be similar to Figure 6–9.

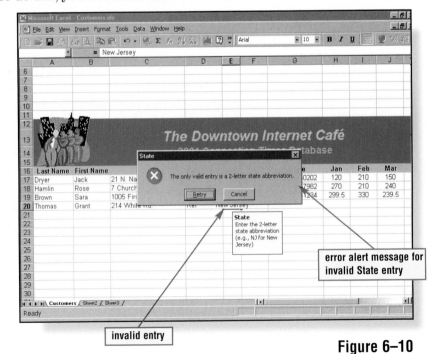

Figure 6–9

You know that the input messages for your validated cells are displaying correctly, but you would like to make sure the validation rules will be applied to them. To do this, you will enter incorrect data for another new record.

7 — Move to A20.

— Enter the following information directly in the cells of the worksheet:

Last Name	**Thomas**
First Name	**Grant**
Street	**214 White Rd.**
City	**Red Bank**
State	**New Jersey**

Your screen should be similar to Figure 6–10.

Figure 6–10

Additional Information

Data validation error messages only appear when data are typed directly into cells.

The error alert is displayed, letting users know that they have made an incorrect entry and allowing them to retry.

8 Click  Retry .

Type **NJ**.

Press Tab.

Continue entering the following data for this record.

Zip	**07730**
Phone	**(732) 555-0893**
Jan	**190**
Feb	**118**
Mar	**148.5**

Your screen should be similar to Figure 6–11.

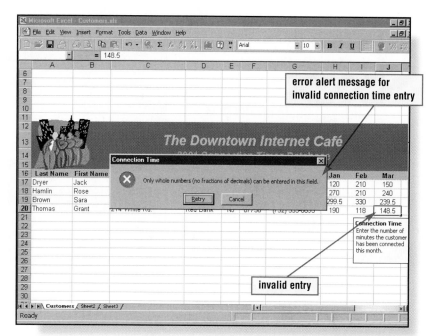

Figure 6–11

The Connection Time error alert message box lets you know that the entry you made is incorrect.

9 Click 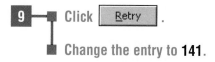 Retry .

Change the entry to **141**.

Identifying Invalid Data

Although the error message appears when you enter data directly in a cell, if the data form is used or values were copied or filled in cells, it does not display. Therefore, it is still possible to enter incorrect information. To help locate incorrect data, you can use the auditing feature to identify those cells with invalid entries.

1 • Use **T**ools/A**u**diting/**S**how Auditing Toolbar.

• Click 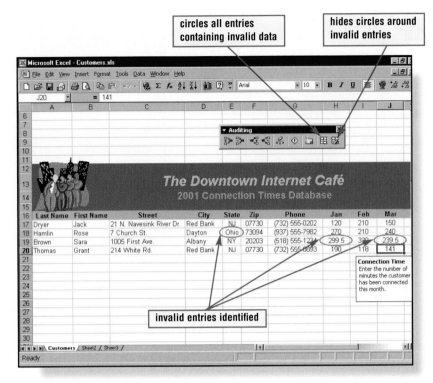 Circle Invalid Data.

Click ▣ Clear Validation Circles to hide the circles around invalid data entries.

Your screen should be similar to Figure 6–12.

Figure 6–12

All cells containing invalid entries are identified.

Additional Information

Up to 255 cells containing invalid data can be identified at one time. As you correct the entries, use ▦ again to identify any additional invalid entries.

2 • Make the corrections to the invalid entries as appropriate, rounding any decimals to the nearest whole.

• Close the Auditing toolbar.

• Save the workbook as **Internet Customers**.

• Close the file.

Using the Find Command

You have continued to work on the customer database by adding additional records. To see the additional records,

1 Open the workbook file Café Customers.

Use the data form to add your name as record 50. Enter connection times of **210**, **270**, and **240** for Jan, Feb, and Mar fields. All other information can be fictitious.

Scroll the worksheet to display row 12 at the top of the work-space, and move to cell A17.

Your screen should be similar to Figure 6–13.

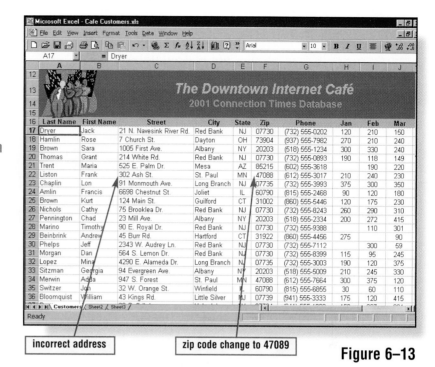

incorrect address

zip code change to 47089

Figure 6–13

As you look over the records in the list and check the information against the customer registration information, you notice that the address for one of the café's customers, Frank Liston, was entered incorrectly. The street address should be 3021 Ash St. instead of 302. You have also been notified of a zip code change; 47088 is now 47089. Also, the January connection time for Jill Brown should be 135, not 235.

You could correct the data just by changing the appropriate cells directly on the worksheet. However, the larger your database becomes, the more unwieldy it will be to find the data you want to modify. Therefore, you'll practice using the other data location and modification methods to make the necessary changes.

Concept ③ Find and Replace

The **Find and Replace** feature helps you quickly find specific information and automatically replace it with new information. The Find command will locate all specified values in a worksheet, and the Replace command will both find a value and automatically replace it with another. For example, in a list containing supplier and item prices, you may need to increase the price of all items supplied by one manufacturer.

To quickly locate these items, you would use the Find command to locate all records with the name of the manufacturer and then update the price appropriately. Alternatively, you could use the Replace command if you knew that all items priced at $9.95 were increasing to $11.89. This command would locate all values matching the original price and replace them with the new price. Finding and replacing data is fast and accurate, but you need to be careful when replacing not to replace unintended matches.

First you will locate and correct the incorrect data using the Find command. This command can be used to locate data on any type of worksheet, not just a database.

2 ■■ Choose <u>E</u>dit/<u>F</u>ind.

> The keyboard shortcut is Ctrl + F.

Your screen should be similar to Figure 6–14.

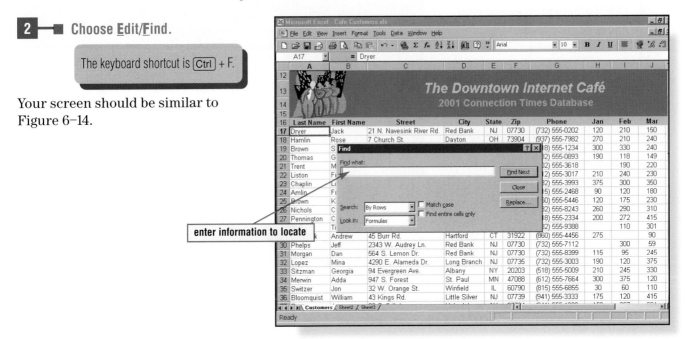

Figure 6–14

In the Find dialog box, you can enter the information you want to locate in the Find What text box. It must be entered exactly as it appears in the worksheet. You can also use the **wildcard characters;** a question mark (?) will match any single character, and an asterisk (*) will match any string of characters. For example, Smit? locates Smitt and Smith, but not Smithers and *ford locates Guilford, and Milford but does not locate Fordham.

The additional options in the Find dialog box can be combined in many ways to help you locate information. They are described in the table below.

Option	Effect
Search	Specifies the direction to search in the worksheet: By Columns searches down through columns, and By Rows searches to the right across rows.
Look in	Looks for a match in the specified worksheet element; formulas, values, comments.
Match case	Finds words that have the same pattern of uppercase letters as entered in the Find What text box. Using this option makes the search **case sensitive.**
Find entire cells only	Looks for an exact and complete match of the characters specified in the Find What text box.

To enter the address to find, and to search using the default options,

3 ▪ Type **302 ash** in the Find What box.

> Because the Match Case option is not selected, Find will look for an exact match regardless of whether the characters are uppercase or lowercase.

▪ Click [**Find Next**].

> If necessary, move the dialog box so you can see the located entry.

Your screen should be similar to Figure 6–15.

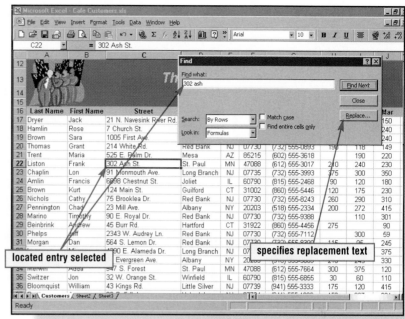

located entry selected   specifies replacement text

Figure 6–15

Excel locates and selects the specified data. To replace the selected data,

4 ▪ Click [Replace...].

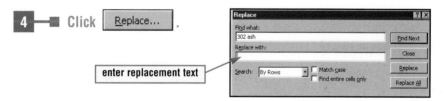

enter replacement text

The Find dialog box has changed to a Replace dialog box, with the selected data displayed in the Find What box. You can now enter what you want to replace the selected data with.

5 ▪ Type **3021 Ash** in the Replace With box.

> The replacement text must be entered exactly as you want it to appear.

▪ Click [Replace...].

▪ Click [Close].

Your screen should be similar to Figure 6–16.

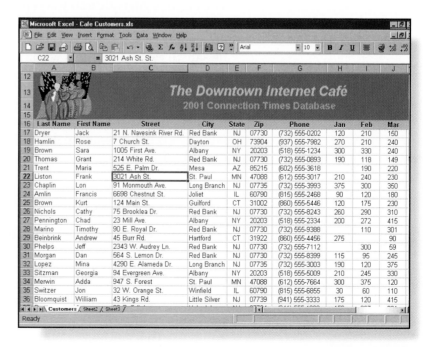

Figure 6–16

Excel has replaced the original data with the new text.

Using the Replace Command

Next, you'll use the Replace command to change the incorrect zip code. Once again, this command can be used on any type of worksheet to change cell data.

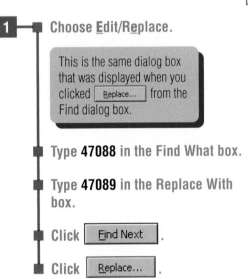

The keyboard shortcut for the Replace command is Ctrl + H.

1 ▪ Choose **Edit/Replace**.

This is the same dialog box that was displayed when you clicked Replace... from the Find dialog box.

▪ Type **47088** in the Find What box.

▪ Type **47089** in the Replace With box.

▪ Click **Find Next** .

▪ Click **Replace...** .

Your screen should be similar to Figure 6–17.

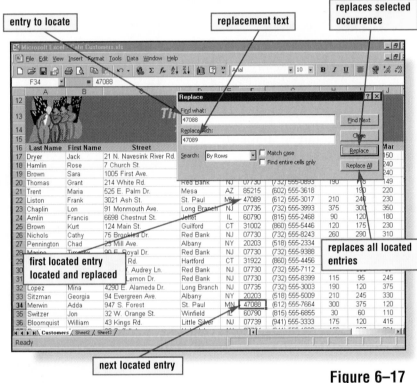

Figure 6–17

The original zip code entry is replaced with the new zip code. The program immediately continues searching and locates a second occurrence of the entry. You decide the program is locating the values accurately, and it will be safe to replace all finds with the replacement value. To do this,

2 ▪ Click **Replace All** .

All matches are replaced with the replacement text, and the dialog box is closed. It is much faster to use Replace All than to confirm each match separately. However, exercise care when using Replace All, because the search text you specify might be part of another word and you may accidentally replace text you want to keep.

Using the Data Form to Locate and Change Data

Since the data you are working with have been defined as a database range, you can also use another method to find and modify them. You can open the Data Form dialog box for the database again, use the  button to locate the record you want to change, and edit it as desired. You'll use this method to make the final change to your data, correcting the connection time for Jill Brown.

1 Choose <u>D</u>ata/F<u>o</u>rm.

Click <u>C</u>riteria .

A blank data form is displayed in which you can enter any field data unique to a record in order to locate and display that record. In this case, you'll enter the customer's last name, Brown, to locate and display the record for Jill Brown.

2 Type **Brown** in the Last Name field text box.

Click Find <u>N</u>ext .

Your screen should be similar to Figure 6–18.

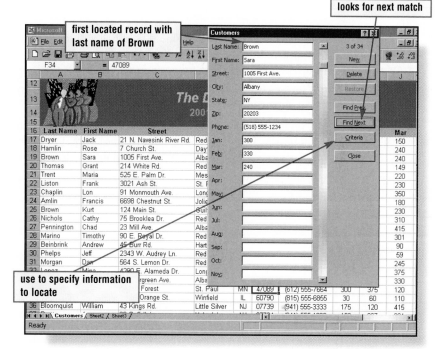

Figure 6–18

The first located record with a last name of Brown, Sara Brown, is displayed in the data form. You want to find the record for Jill Brown.

3 Click Find <u>N</u>ext two more times until Jill Brown's record is displayed.

Double-click the Jan field text box to highlight the current value, 235.

Type **135**.

Click C<u>l</u>ose .

The record for Jill Brown is updated and now contains the correct value, 135, in the January connection time field.

Now that your data entries are error-free, you're ready to move on to sorting the data in a logical order.

Sorting Data

Currently, the database records are in the order in which you entered them. However, you feel that they would be easier to work with if they were displayed in alphabetical order by last name. To do this you can sort the records in the list.

Concept ④ Sort

You can **sort** data in a specified sequence, alphabetically, numerically, or by date. Sorting data often helps you find specific information quickly. The data in a worksheet can be sorted into ascending (A to Z, 1 to 9, earliest date to most recent date) or descending (Z to A, 9 to 1, most recent date to earliest date) order. When you sort, Excel rearranges the rows, columns, fields, or individual cells according to the sort order you specify.

A single sort operation can be based on up to three columns or fields of data. When a sort is done on more than one column or field, it is called a **multilevel sort.** For example, if you wanted to rearrange a list of employee data to begin with those who have worked for the company the longest, you could sort it in ascending order by date and then by name.

For the first sort, you want the records arranged in ascending alphabetical order by last name.

1 ■ Move to cell **A17**.

■ Click 🔼 **Sort Ascending**.

> The menu equivalent is **D**ata/**S**ort.

Your screen should be similar to Figure 6–19.

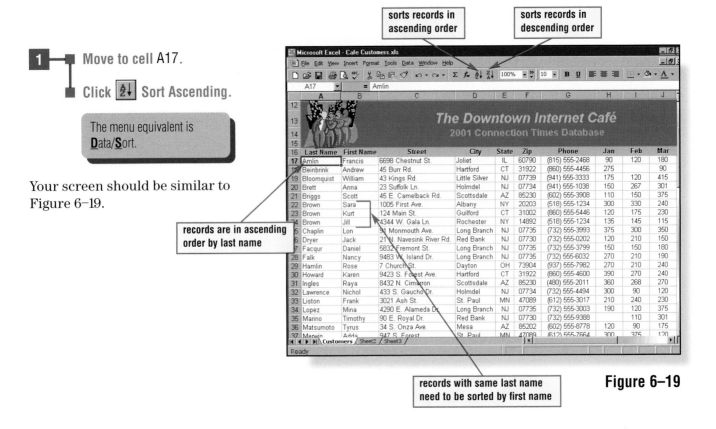

sorts records in ascending order

sorts records in descending order

records are in ascending order by last name

records with same last name need to be sorted by first name

Figure 6–19

The records in the database range are rearranged to display in ascending alphabetical order by last name. However, notice that although the records for Sara, Kurt, and Jill Brown are sorted correctly by last name, they are not sorted correctly by first name. You want the records that have the same last name to be further sorted by first name. To do this, you will perform a multilevel sort.

2 ■ Choose **D**ata/**S**ort.

Your screen should be similar to Figure 6–20.

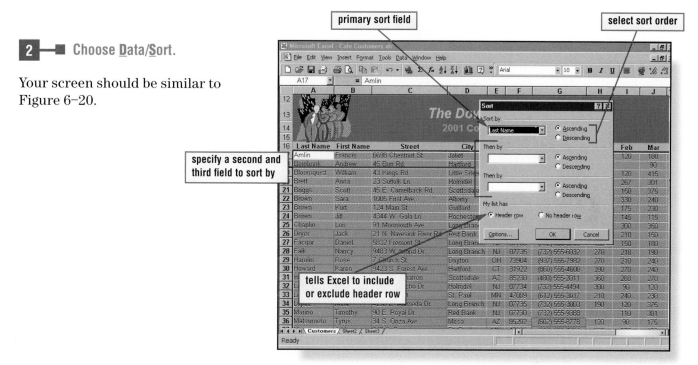

Figure 6–20

A multilevel sort uses the first field name selected in the Sort By section of the dialog box as the primary sort field; all other fields are sorted in order after the primary sort is performed. The Sort By text box correctly displays the name of the field on which the primary sort will be performed. Additionally, because the default setting is Ascending sort order, this option does not need to be changed. You need to specify the secondary sort field as the First Name field.

3 ■ Select First Name from the first Then By drop-down list.

When a sort is performed, Excel assumes that you want all data except the uppermost row contained in contiguous rows and columns surrounding the selected cell to be sorted. The first row is not included in the sort range because the default setting assumes that the first row contains column labels or field names that you do not want included in the sort. If your data did not include a column label or field name as the first row in the range, you would need to choose the No Header Row option to change the setting to include this row in the sort. Since this worksheet includes field names in the first row, the Header Row option is correctly specified already.

4 — Click OK .

Your screen should be similar to Figure 6–21.

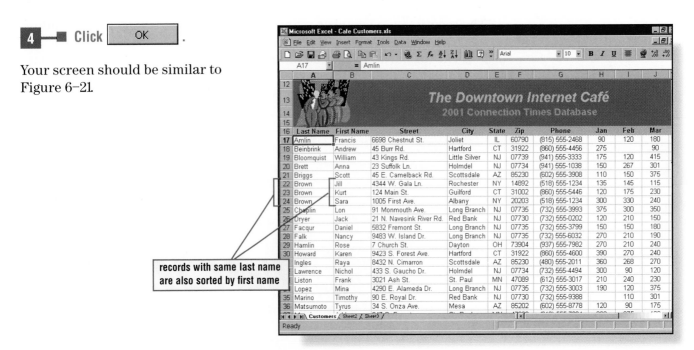

records with same last name are also sorted by first name

Figure 6–21

The records are now in sorted order first by last name and second by first name within same last names. As you can see, sorting is a fast, useful tool. The original sort order remains in effect until you replace it with a new sort order. If the order in which you enter records in a list is important, include a field for a unique record number. Then you can return to the entry order by sorting on the number field.

Adding Automatic Subtotals

Next, Evan has asked you to find out how much of the total Internet connection time is attributed to local residents as opposed to out-of-state customers. This will not only illustrate any seasonal usage trends (for example, if the computers are being used more or less during a holiday season because of more or fewer out-of state visitors) but will also alert Evan to any upward or downward slides so he can take appropriate action (such as launching a marketing campaign to attract out-of-towners). To provide this information for him, you will add automatic subtotals to the worksheet.

Concept ⑤ Automatic Subtotal

The **automatic subtotal** feature calculates and displays a running subtotal for selected numeric columns or fields in a list. To use automatic subtotals, you must first sort your list by the column or field on which you want the subtotals to be based. For example, to subtotal all sales in a specific region, you would sort the list by the region column or field, and request a subtotal for the sales column or field. The subtotals for each region are shown below that region's row, and the grand total of all sales is shown in a new row at the bottom of the list.

There are several subtotal functions that can be used:

Function	Calculates
Sum	Sum of the values in a list. This is the default subtotal function for numeric data.
Count	Number of items in a list. This is the default subtotal function for nonnumeric data.
Average	Average of the values in a list.
Min	Smallest value in a list.
Max	Largest value in a list.
Product	Result of multiplying all values in a list.
Count Nums	Number of records or rows in a list that contain numeric data.
StdDev	The standard estimated deviation of a population using the list as the sample.
StDevp	Standard deviation of a population using the list as the entire population.
Var	The estimated variance of a population using the list as the sample.
Varp	Variance of a population using the list as the entire population.

Of these functions, the first five (Sum, Count, Average, Min, and Max) are the most commonly used.

Since your database is currently sorted by last name, you need to resort it by state. You can then calculate the monthly usage subtotals for each state.

1 ■ Move to cell E16.

■ Click ⬆ Sort Ascending.

■ Choose **D**ata/Su**b**totals.

Your screen should be similar to
Figure 6–22.

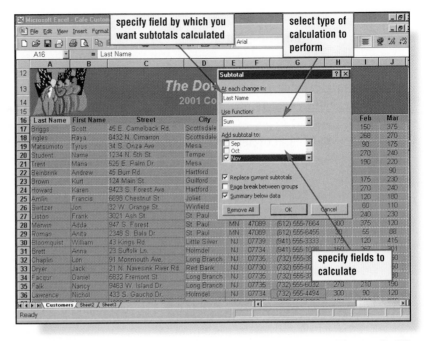

Figure 6–22

The database range (or list) is highlighted on the worksheet, and the
Subtotal dialog box is displayed. In the "At each change" box you need to
specify the field by which you want subtotal values calculated. In this
case, you want a subtotal displayed for each new value in the State field.

From the Use Function list box, you can specify the calculation to be
performed. Since you want to add all the connection times for each state,
the default of Sum is correct.

From the Add Subtotal to list box, you can select the fields on which
you want the subtotals to be calculated. For this database, you want the
subtotals calculated for the first three months of connection time data.

2 ■ Select **State** from the At Each
Change In drop-down list box.

■ Click the boxes for the **Jan**, **Feb**,
and **Mar** fields in the Add
Subtotal to list box to select
them. If necessary, clear any
others.

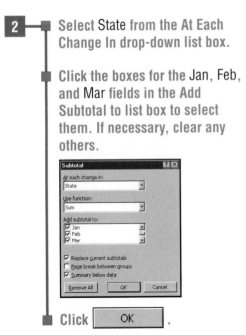

■ Click ▢ OK ▢.

Your screen should be similar to
Figure 6–23.

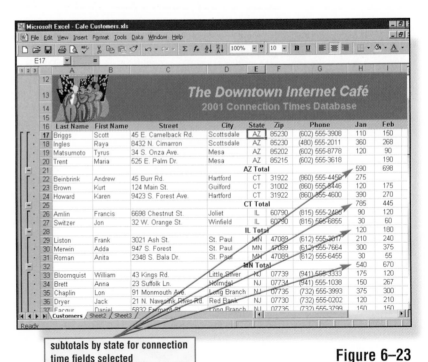

subtotals by state for connection
time fields selected

Figure 6–23

Excel has inserted new rows for each state's monthly subtotals and a row at the end of the list containing the total connection time for each month. If you change the connection time for any of the records, the corresponding subtotal and total will be automatically recalculated. To test this automatic recalculation function,

3 ■ Change the Jan connection time for Scott Briggs to **200**.

> You can move the Connection Time message out of the way.

Your screen should be similar to Figure 6–24.

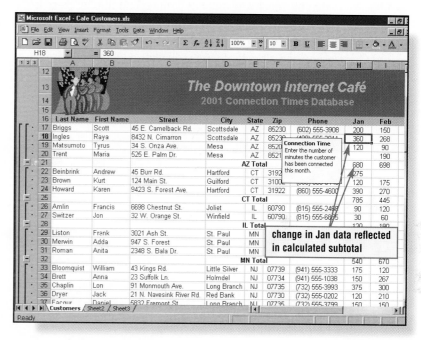

Figure 6–24

The new total connection time for Arizona is 680. After seeing how the subtotals look on the database worksheet, you decide that you would rather create a separate worksheet that summarizes all the data, including the connection time subtotals and totals. You will do this with the Pivot Table tool later, but for now you'll just remove the subtotal and total rows and re-sort the worksheet data.

> You can also remove the subtotals and totals by redisplaying the Subtotal dialog box and clicking 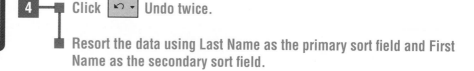 Remove All .

4 ■ Click ↶ ▾ Undo twice.

■ Resort the data using Last Name as the primary sort field and First Name as the secondary sort field.

Filtering Data

Evan has informed you that he is sending out "valued customer" notes to in-state customers who have been using the computers at the café since the beginning of the year. He has asked you for a printout of the connection times and contact information for those customers. Rather than creating a separate worksheet, you can filter the database range in the current worksheet to show only the requested records.

Concept 6 Filter

A **filter** is a restriction you place on records in the list to quickly isolate and display a subset of records. A filter is created by specifying a set of limiting conditions, or **criteria,** you want records to meet in order to be displayed. A filter is ideal when you want to display the subset for only a brief time and then return immediately to the full set of records. You can print the filtered records as you would any worksheet. A filter is only temporary, and all records are redisplayed when you remove the filter.

Unlike the Sort feature, the Filter feature does not rearrange a list. It just temporarily hides rows that do not meet the specified criteria. Data in a filtered list can be edited, formatted, charted, or printed.

To filter the database range,

1 ■ Move to any cell in the database range.

■ Choose **D**ata/**F**ilter/Auto**F**ilter.

Your screen should be similar to Figure 6–25.

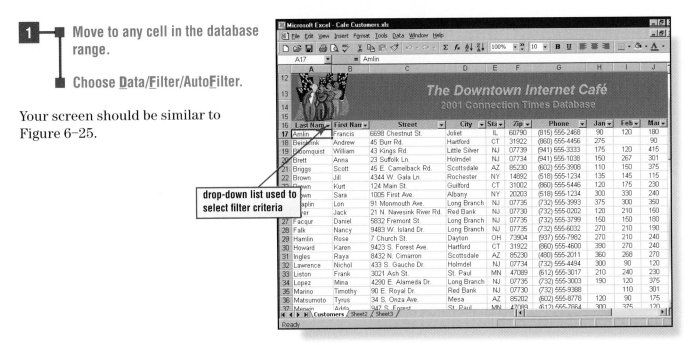

Figure 6–25

Drop-down list arrows appear next to each field name. These enable you to select the field or fields and field criteria you want to use to filter the list. The first criterion you want the records in your database range to meet is in the State field.

2 ■ Open the State drop-down list.

The drop-down list contains the current values in the field. In addition you can select from these options:

Option	Effect
(All)	Displays all records regardless of the value in this field
(Top 10)	Displays the records with the highest values in this field
(Custom)	Used to specify ranges of values that a record must meet to be displayed
(Blanks)	Displays only those records that do not contain a value in this field
(NonBlanks)	Displays only those records that contain a value in this field

To specify that only records that have a state value of NY are displayed,

3 ■ Select NY from the drop-down list.

Your screen should be similar to Figure 6–26.

filter displays only those records with a State field of NY

number of filtered records

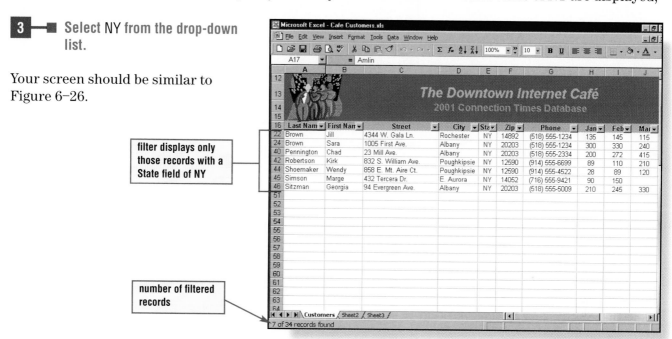

Figure 6–26

Only those records for customers in New York are displayed. However, not all of these customers have been online at the café since January. Therefore, you want to specify further criteria to accept only "nonblanks" in the month field for March.

4 — ■ Open the Mar drop-down list.

■ Select (NonBlanks).

Your screen should be similar to
Figure 6–27.

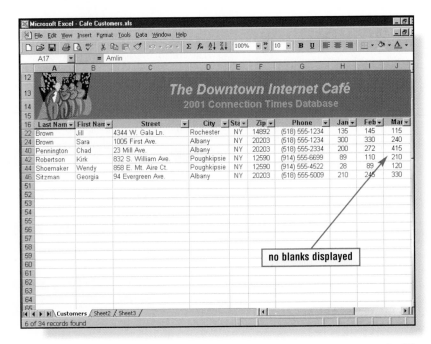

Figure 6–27

Only the six records that meet all criteria are displayed. To get the information for the other out-of-state customers, you could change the State criteria and print each filter result. However, a faster way is to create a custom filter for the State field.

5 — ■ From the State drop-down list,
select Custom.

Your screen should be similar to
Figure 6–28.

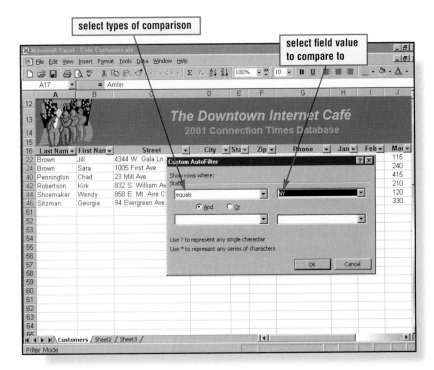

Figure 6–28

The Custom AutoFilter dialog box is used to specify a filtering operation that makes comparisons between two values. The type of comparison to make is specified in the box on the left, and the value to compare to is specified in the box on the right. You can include a second set of criteria by selecting And or Or and specifying the settings in the lower row of boxes. The AND and OR operators are used to specify multiple conditions that must be met for the records to display in the filtered list. The AND operator narrows the search, because a record must meet both conditions to be included. The OR operator broadens the search, because any record meeting either condition is included in the output.

You want to display records for all states except New Jersey. To do this,

6 ■ Select Does Not Equal from the list of operations on the left.

■ Select NJ from the list of field values in the State field on the right.

■ Click [OK] .

> Your record may appear in the filtered list if your state field entry is not NJ.

Now the filtered list displays records for all states except New Jersey that have connection time usage in all three months.

7 ■ Set the filter for the Jan and Feb connection time fields to display nonblanks only.

Your screen should be similar to Figure 6–29.

no blanks displayed

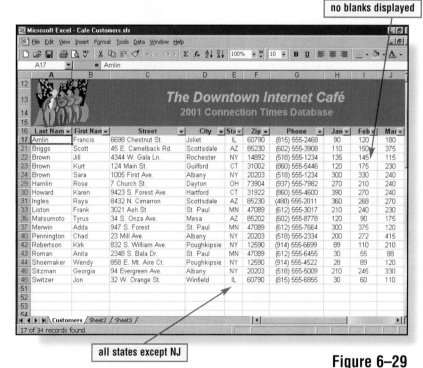

all states except NJ

Figure 6–29

Setting, Printing, and Clearing a Print Area

You are finished filtering the data, and you've got the information Evan requested. However, you do not want the worksheet printout to include the months that do not yet have any connection data in them, so you will set a print area that includes only the database list fields through March. To define a print area, you first select the cell range that you want to print and then choose the Print Area command from the File menu.

You may need to use the directional keys to select cell A12 (and not the graphic) or begin your selection from the bottom right corner of the range.

1 ■ Select the cell range beginning with cell A12 through column J of the last row of displayed records.

■ Choose **F**ile/**Prin**t Area/**S**et Print Area.

A dotted line surrounds the selected print area and a page break line shows where the selected range will print on a second page. You need to change the orientation to landscape so that the range will print on one page.

2 ■ Click 🔍 Print Preview.

■ Click Setup... .

■ From the Page tab, select Landscape.

■ Add a footer that displays your name and the current date.

■ Click OK .

■ If necessary, set the zoom to full-page view.

Your screen should be similar to Figure 6–30.

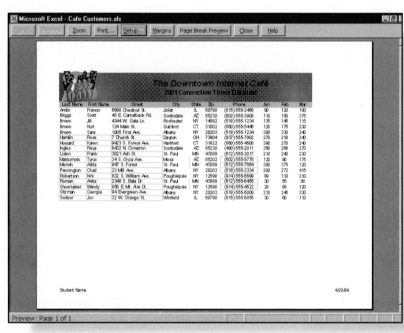

Figure 6–30

To remove a Print Area use **F**ile/**Prin**t Area/**C**lear Print Area.

When you send this worksheet to the printer, only the selected area will be printed. The defined print area is saved with the worksheet and will be used automatically whenever you print the worksheet.

3 ■ Print the worksheet.

Evan has his printout. You can now remove the AutoFilter from the database range and continue working on it. To remove the filter,

4 ■ Choose **D**ata/**F**ilter/**AutoF**ilter.

The filter is removed and all records are again displayed.

Additional Information

You can also select a range to print and use the Selection option in the Print dialog box to specify a temporary print area.

Using the Criteria Range

Although you could continue to manipulate the database range using sorting and filtering, you will use the criteria range to specify more complex filtering criteria. Evan also wants to know more about the connection time usage of the in-state customers. He is particularly interested in finding out which customers have connection times of 150 minutes or more in each of the first three months.

First, you will enter the criteria the records must meet in order to be displayed in the blank row below the field names in the criteria range.

1 Enter **NJ** in cell E3.

Enter **>=150** in cells H3, I3, and J3.

Additional Information

The comparison operators symbols are = (equal to) <> (not equal to), <(less than), > (greater than), <= (less than or equal to), and >= (greater than or equal to).

Your screen should be similar to Figure 6–31.

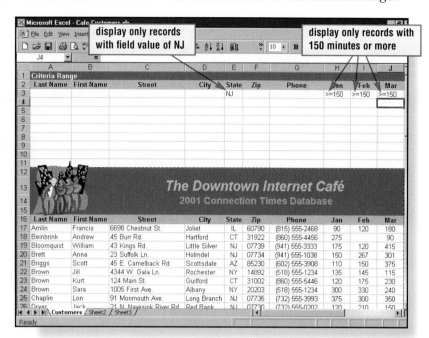

Figure 6–31

Next, you use the Advanced Filter feature to apply the specified criteria in the criteria range to the records in the database range.

2 Move to cell **A17**.

Choose **Data/Filter/Advanced Filter**.

Your screen should be similar to Figure 6–32.

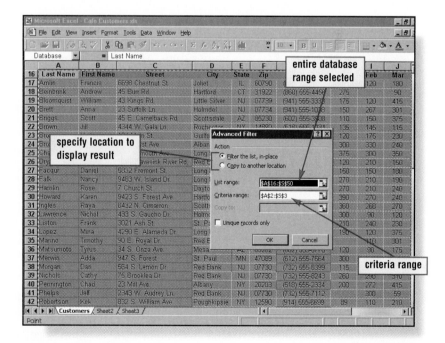

Figure 6–32

The database range is selected and the Advanced Filter dialog box is displayed. The Action area of the dialog box has the option "Filter the list, in place" selected. This means that the filtered list will appear in the database range. If you select "Copy to another location," the filtered list will be displayed in a blank portion of the worksheet, leaving the original database range list as is. You decide to accept the default and view the filtered list in the database range.

Notice that the List Range box automatically displays the database range and the Criteria Range box automatically displays the criteria range. So all you need to do now is apply the filter.

3 ■ Click [OK] .

Your screen should be similar to Figure 6–33.

records that meet criteria

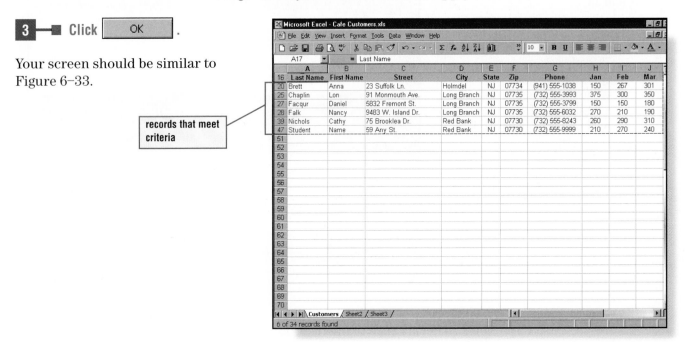

Figure 6–33

Only those records that meet all of the criteria are displayed in the database range. After providing this information to Evan, you want to remove the filter so you can continue to work with the entire database range.

> If your record's State field is NJ, your record will appear in the filtered output.

4 ■ Choose **D**ata/**F**ilter/**S**how All.

All the records are redisplayed.

Creating a Pivot Table

Next, you will create a pivot table to analyze your worksheet data from different viewpoints.

Concept ⑦ Pivot Table

A **pivot table** is an interactive table that can be used to summarize and manipulate worksheet data. When a PivotTable report is created, Excel automatically sorts, subtotals, and totals the data. You can then rotate the report to see different data summaries, filter the data, or display details about the data.

A pivot table is most useful for comparing related totals in a data list, especially when the list you're summarizing is quite lengthy and contains many values.

To create a PivotTable report for the database,

1 ■ Move to cell A17.

■ Choose **D**ata/**P**ivotTable and PivotChart Report.

Your screen should be similar to Figure 6–34.

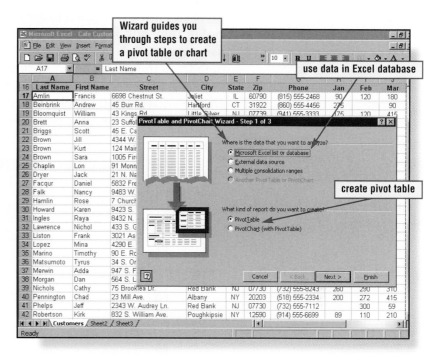

Figure 6–34

Excel automatically activates the PivotTable and PivotChart Wizard, which guides you through each step of creating a pivot table or pivot chart. In the first step, you select the data you want to analyze and the type of report you want to create. The default data selection is the current list or database, which is what you want to analyze. Because you are creating a pivot table, the second selection is also acceptable. To proceed to the next step,

2 ■ Click  .

The second step is to select the range that contains the data you want analyzed. The range named "Database" is automatically selected, so you do not need to change it.

3 ■ Click  .

In the third step, you specify whether you want the pivot table to be located on an existing worksheet or a different worksheet. The  Layout... and Options... buttons are used to arrange the layout of the table in a dialog box rather than on the worksheet itself. This may be necessary when you are using external data sources, but is not recommended when you are using data from the current worksheet. Whenever possible, you should lay out the PivotTable report directly on the sheet so that you can view the data while you arrange the fields. You decide to place the pivot table on a separate worksheet, which is the default.

4 ── Click [Finish] .

Your screen should be similar to Figure 6–35.

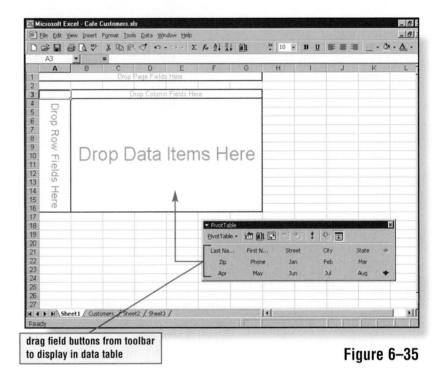

drag field buttons from toolbar
to display in data table

Figure 6–35

A blank pivot table form is displayed in a new sheet. In addition, the PivotTable toolbar is displayed. It consists of buttons (identified below) as well as the field names from the database.

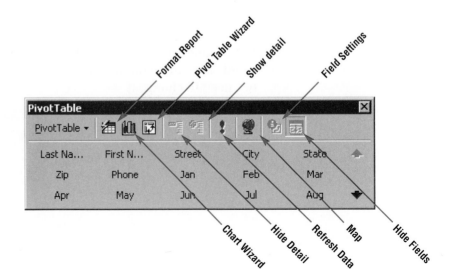

You can use the displayed form to construct the pivot table. Instructions for using each area of this form are displayed in gray, and field buttons that correspond to the fields in your database are displayed in the PivotTable toolbar. You can drag the fields you want to display along the left side of the table to the Row area, the fields you want to display at the top of the table in the Column area, and the fields containing the values you want to calculate to the Data area.

You would like this table to summarize monthly connection times by city and state. To set up this table layout,

> You can use the Page area when you want to display only one record at a time.

5 — Drag the State field button and drop it in the Row area.

Drag the City field button and drop it in the Column area.

Drag the Jan, Feb, and Mar field buttons and drop them in the Data area.

Your screen should be similar to Figure 6–36.

calculated as a count

count of number of connection times by city and state

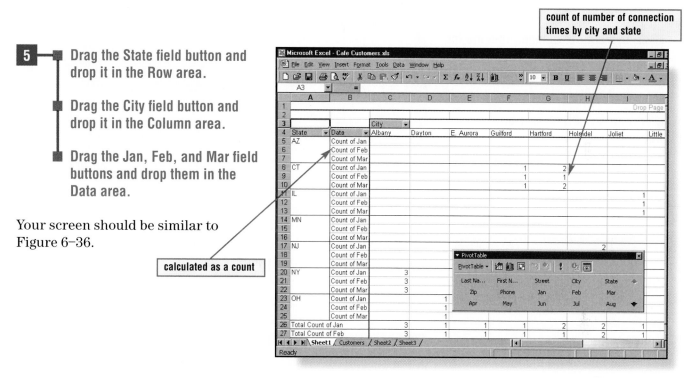

Figure 6–36

The pivot table displays a count of the number of connection times in each month for each city within the state. You want the table to display a sum of the usage times rather than a count. You would also like to change the label to simply display the month. To make these changes,

6 ■ Click on any cell containing the label Count of Jan.

■ Click [icon] Field Settings in the Pivot Table toolbar.

■ In the Name field type **January**.

■ Select Sum from the Summarize by List box.

■ Click [OK].

■ In a similar manner, rename the February and March data fields, and change the field function to a sum.

Your screen should be similar to Figure 6–37.

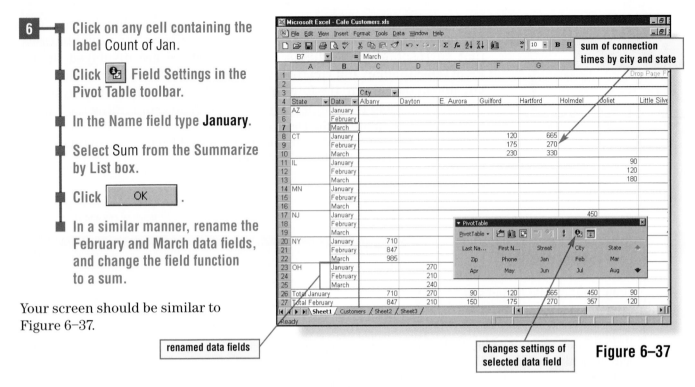

Figure 6–37

Rows 5 through 28 of the table show the connection times for each city in each month as well as the grand total of their connection times (column T). Rows 29 through 31 show the connection time totals for each city, along with the grand total of the monthly subtotals.

You decide that the data would be more meaningful without the city breakdown.

7 ■ Drag the City field button back to the PivotTable toolbar.

Your screen should be similar to Figure 6–38.

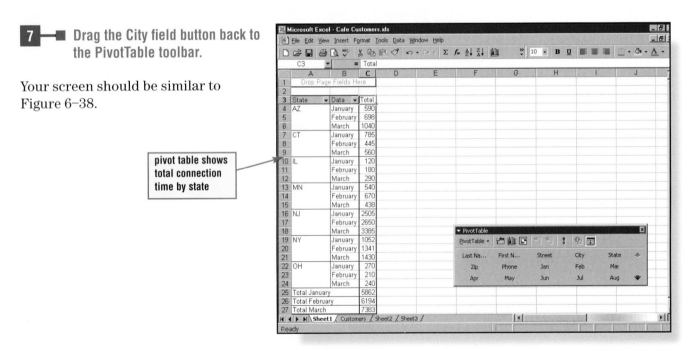

Figure 6–38

The table now simply shows a summary of connection usage for each month by state. You are satisfied with the pivot table, so you are going to name and move the worksheet.

 ■ Name the worksheet **Pivot Table**.

■ Move the Pivot Table worksheet so it follows the Customers worksheet.

Creating a Pivot Chart

You want to see the state and connection time data graphed on a chart. To do this, you will create a pivot chart using the pivot table you just created as the data source.

Concept ⑧ Pivot Chart

A **pivot chart** is an interactive chart that can be used to view and rearrange data. A pivot chart is most useful when you need to quickly change data views to see comparisons and trends in different ways.

A PivotChart report must have an associated PivotTable report in the same workbook. Both of these reports contain the same source data and, as in the PivotTable report, you can rearrange the data to see different views and display details.

You can use the PivotTable and PivotChart Wizard to create a pivot chart as well as an associated pivot table, or you can create a pivot chart based on an existing pivot table. When you make changes to a pivot table (such as removing a field from it), the associated pivot chart also changes, and vice versa.

To create a pivot chart,

1 — Click 🔲 Chart Wizard on the
PivotTable toolbar.

— If necessary, dock the Chart toolbar below the Standard toolbar.

Your screen should be similar to
Figure 6–39.

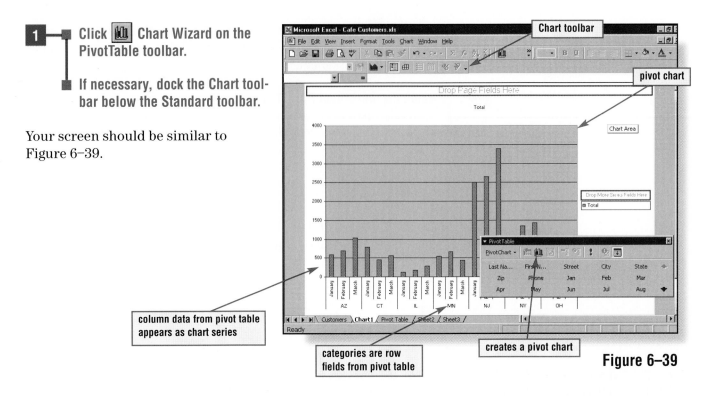

Figure 6–39

The pivot chart has been automatically created using the pivot table data.
The row fields in the table become the category fields in the chart, and the
column fields in the table become the series fields in the chart. As with the
pivot table, you can manipulate and reformat the chart to view the data in
different ways. But remember, anything you do to the chart fields will affect the associated table fields. For example, to show the State field as a
legend, you move its Field Name button up to the Series Field drop-down
box on the right side of the chart.

2 — Drag the State field name button
into the Series box.

Your screen should be similar to
Figure 6–40.

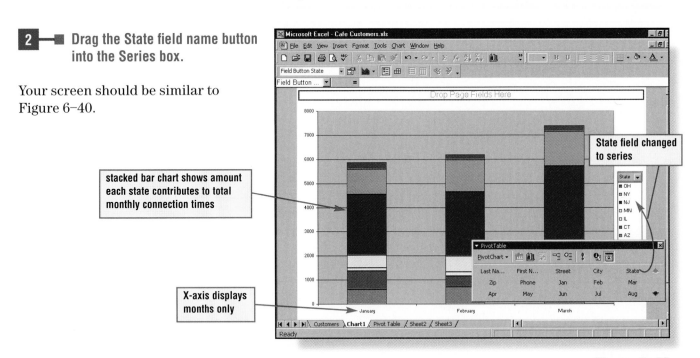

Figure 6–40

A legend has been created with the state names, and color has been added to the bars on the chart to coincide with the legend. To see the effect the changes you made to the chart have had on the table,

3 ■ Make the Pivot Table sheet active.

Your screen should be similar to Figure 6–41.

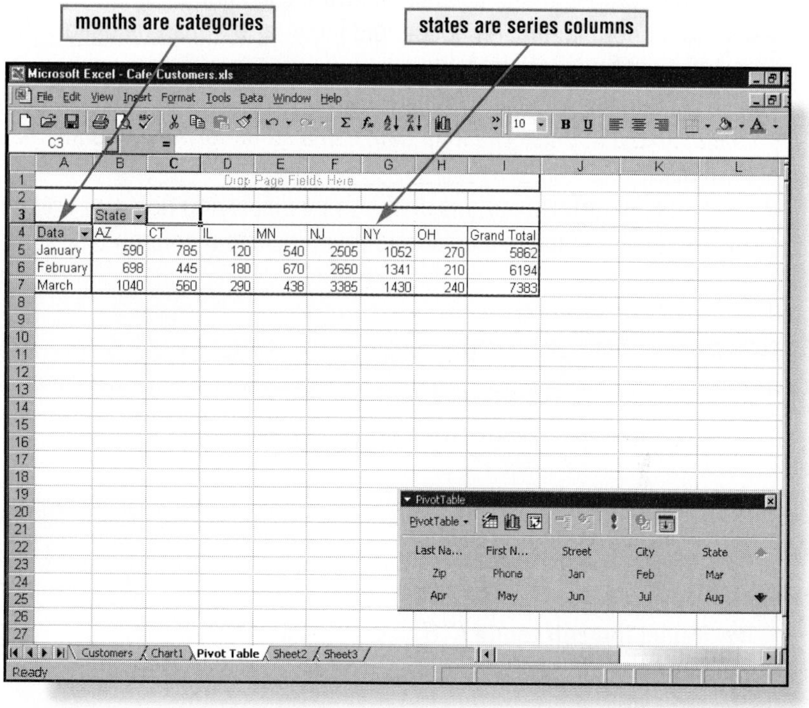

Figure 6–41

> The pivot table may also include another state field for the state you entered in your personal record.

The pivot table now displays the states as the columns and the months as the rows. You will now rename and move the chart worksheet as you did with the pivot table worksheet.

4 ■ Rename the Chart1 sheet **Pivot Chart**.

■ Move the Pivot Chart sheet so it follows the Pivot Table sheet.

Creating a Data Map

Note: The Data Map is an additional Excel tool that must be installed. If it is not available, you will not be able to complete this section.

One final way you want to view the customer database is geographically. To do this, you'll use Excel's data map feature. By creating a data map, you can graphically illustrate the diversity of the Downtown Internet Café's customer base. This data map can also be enhanced to serve as an attractive marketing tool.

Concept ⑨ Data Map

The **data map** feature is used to illustrate and analyze data by geographic region. It includes demographic data (e.g., population and household income) that can be used with worksheet data to recognize trends and perform analyses in a map.

A data map of any location in the world can be embedded in a worksheet. It can then be formatted with labels, text, and pins. The map data can also be formatted, such as changing the dot density or graduated symbols.

You can perform various analyses by displaying different columns of worksheet data on the map. Data that are analyzed using a data map must include a column that contains geographic data, such as country or state names.

To create the data map,

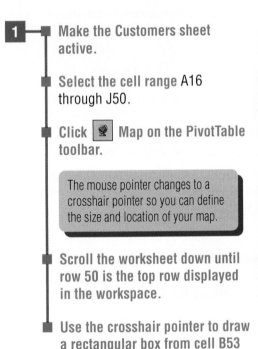

1 ● Make the Customers sheet active.

● Select the cell range A16 through J50.

● Click 🌐 Map on the PivotTable toolbar.

> The mouse pointer changes to a crosshair pointer so you can define the size and location of your map.

● Scroll the worksheet down until row 50 is the top row displayed in the workspace.

● Use the crosshair pointer to draw a rectangular box from cell B53 to cell I72.

Your screen should be similar to Figure 6–42.

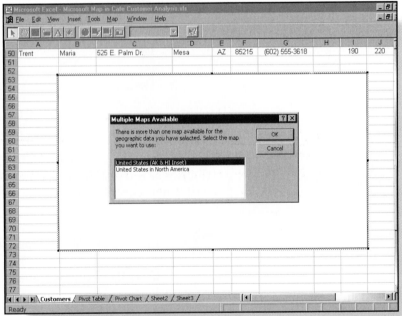

Figure 6–42

The Multiple Maps Available dialog box is displayed with a selection of maps that fit the data you selected. For example, if your data comprise only states in the United States, Excel displays the North American maps available; if your data include European countries, you are given a selection of world maps. To specify the map you want to use,

2 ■ Select United States (AK & HI Inset).

■ Click [OK] .

■ If necessary, move the dialog box to the bottom left corner of the screen.

Your screen should be similar to Figure 6–43.

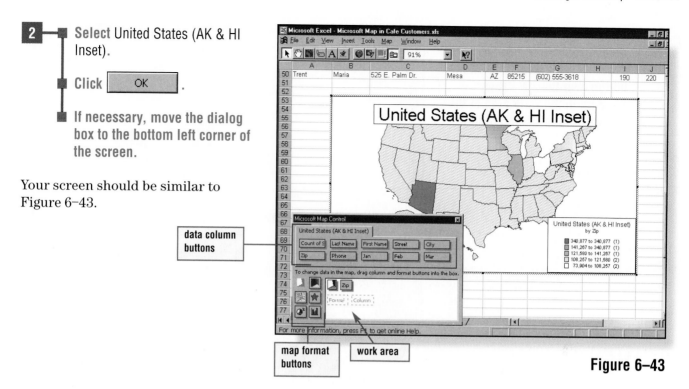

data column buttons

map format buttons

work area

Figure 6–43

A map of North America is drawn on your screen, with the seven "home states" of the café customers delineated by different shades of gray. In addition, the Microsoft Map menu and toolbar have replaced the Excel menu and toolbars at the top of the screen, and the Microsoft Map Control dialog box is displayed.

The Microsoft Map Control dialog box is used to rearrange the map data and format the map. The data column buttons are at the top of the dialog box, the map format buttons are on the left side, and the work area, which shows the current data and format selections, is in middle.

The first thing you would like to do is hide the chart title and display the states in color.

3 ▪ Choose <u>V</u>iew/Ti<u>t</u>le.

▪ Drag the ▨ Category Shading button over the ▨ Value Shading in the work area of the Microsoft Map Control dialog box.

Your screen should be similar to Figure 6–44.

displays map categories in different colors

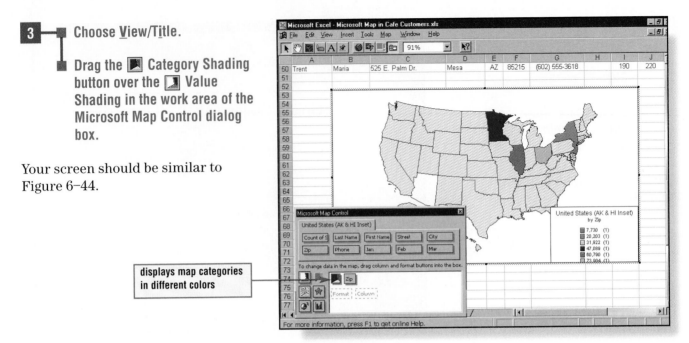

Figure 6–44

The states are now shown in color on the map. Next you want to change the data in the legend (called the column chart) and on the map to display the cities rather than the zip codes. To change the column chart,

4 ▪ Drag the City button over the Zip button in the work area of the Microsoft Map Control dialog box.

> You can also add another column of data by dragging a column button from the top to the Column box in the work area.

Your screen should be similar to Figure 6–45.

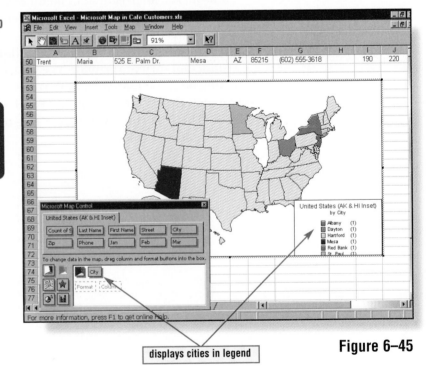

displays cities in legend

Figure 6–45

The legend lists the cities and applies different colors to them. In order for the entire legend to be seen, you will increase the size of the data map. You also decide that you don't want any of the cities displayed in white, so you need to change the color applied to Winfield.

5 Increase the size of the data map object to fully display the legend.

Choose **M**ap/Ca**t**egory Shading Options.

Your screen should be similar to Figure 6–46.

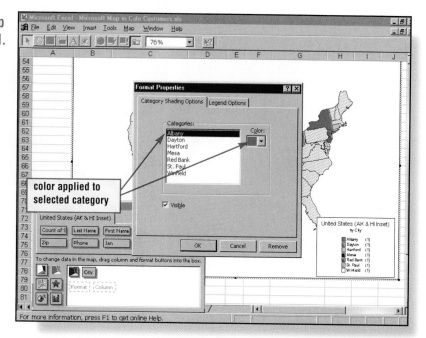

Figure 6–46

The Category Shading dialog box enables you to change the colors used to depict the data on the map as well as change the legend text. You will change the color of a category and the legend title and subtitle as well.

6 ■ Select Winfield in the Categories list.

■ Select dark green from the Color drop-down menu.

> You may need to scroll upward in the Color list to find the color you want.

■ Open the Legend Options tab.

■ Enter **Café Customers** as the new title.

■ Click   OK   .

■ Drag the legend to the lower right corner of the data map.

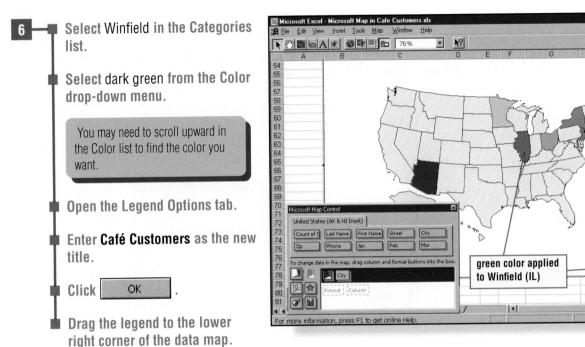

Figure 6–47

Your screen should be similar to Figure 6–47.

Additional Information

There are other map formatting operations you can use, such as using **M**ap/**A**dd **F**eature to add lakes, rivers, major cities, zip code centers, and major highways to the map. You can also display a custom pin map with **M**ap/**O**pen Custom Pin Map.

The legend's title and subtitle have been changed, and Winfield, and thus the state of Illinois, is now displayed in dark green. You like the way the map looks now, so you can exit the mapping feature and return to the Excel worksheet.

7 Close the Microsoft Map Control dialog box.

Click outside the data map to de-select it and turn off the Microsoft Map feature.

Close the PivotTable toolbar.

Your screen should be similar to Figure 6–48.

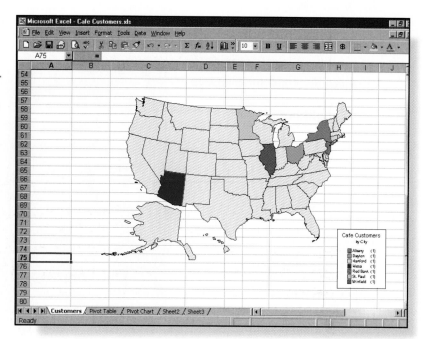

Figure 6–48

The Excel menus and toolbars are redisplayed, and the map is an embedded object in the Customers worksheet.

Defining Print Page Breaks

Your database workbook is finished and ready to be printed.

1 Extend the print area to include the data map.

Preview the worksheet.

You want the records to print on the first page and the map on the second. Excel automatically divides a worksheet into multiple pages for printing by inserting automatic page breaks based upon the page setup settings. You can change where these page breaks occur by inserting manual page breaks using Page Break Preview.

2 ■ Click Page Break Preview .

■ If necessary, click OK to close the Welcome message.

Your screen should be similar to Figure 6–49.

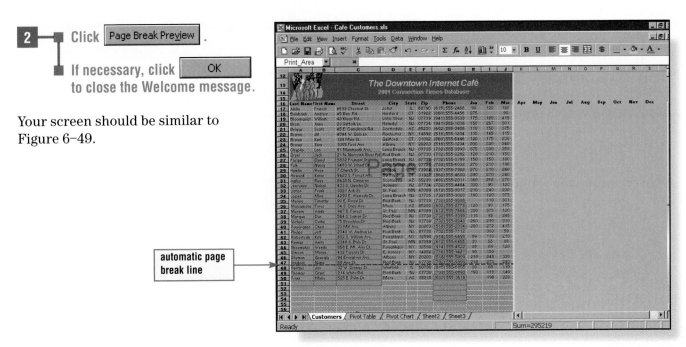

automatic page break line →

Figure 6–49

Additional Information

To remove a manual page break, move to a cell below or to the right of the page break and use Remove Page Break on the **I**nsert menu. In Page **B**reak Preview, you can use Reset All Page Breaks from a cell: short-cut menu to clear all manual page breaks or drag the page break line outside the print area to remove them individually.

In Page Break Preview you can insert and move page breaks before printing a worksheet as well as adjust a defined print area. Dashed lines show where an automatic page break occurs and solid lines show where a manual page break occurs. If the cells you want to add are adjacent to the current print area, merely drag the thick blue horizontal or vertical border to include the cells. To include nonadjacent cells, select the cells you want to add, right-click a cell in the selection, and then choose Add to Print Area on the shortcut menu. You want to adjust the location of the automatic page break to include all the database records on the first printed page. Excel will automatically reduce the font size to fit the data on the page.

3 ■ Click and drag the dashed blue page-break line to below the last record.

■ Click ⌷ Print Preview to see how your change looks.

■ Print the sheet.

■ Click Normal View to display the worksheet again.

You can also use **V**iew/**P**age Break Preview to change Page Break Preview and the use **V**iew/**N**ormal to return to the standard worksheet view again.

Your printed output should look like the Case Study illustrations at the beginning of this tutorial.

Saving to a New Folder

Since this workbook will be used mostly for marketing purposes, you decide to save it in a separate folder from the rest of the café's spreadsheet workbooks. You also want the cell pointer in cell A17 and row 11 at the top of the window when the file opens.

1 With the cell selector in cell A17 and row 11 at the top of the window, choose File/Save As.

■ Type **Café Customer Analysis** as the File name.

■ If necessary, change the location to the drive containing your data disk.

■ Click  Create New Folder in the Save As dialog box.

Your screen should be similar to Figure 6–50.

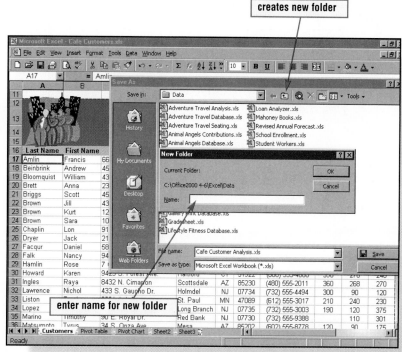

creates new folder

enter name for new folder

Figure 6–50

The New Folder dialog box enables you to create and name a new folder.

2 Type **Marketing** in the Name text box.

■ Click OK.

The Save As dialog box is redisplayed, with the new folder name in the Save In text box.

3 Click  Save.

Your Café Customer Analysis workbook is saved in the Marketing folder.

4 Exit Excel.

Concept Summary

Tutorial 6: Creating and Using an Excel Database

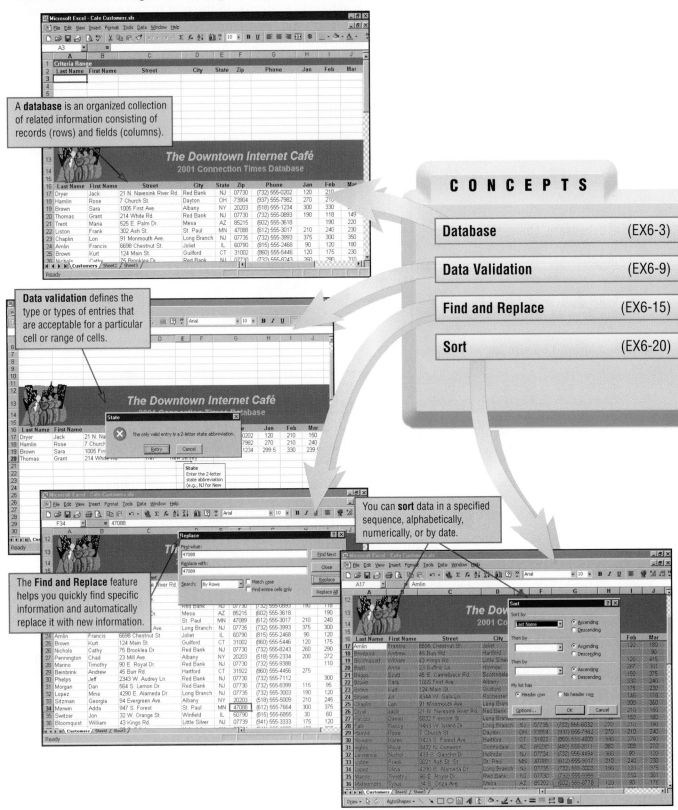

A **database** is an organized collection of related information consisting of records (rows) and fields (columns).

Data validation defines the type or types of entries that are acceptable for a particular cell or range of cells.

The **Find and Replace** feature helps you quickly find specific information and automatically replace it with new information.

You can **sort** data in a specified sequence, alphabetically, numerically, or by date.

CONCEPTS

Database	(EX6-3)
Data Validation	(EX6-9)
Find and Replace	(EX6-15)
Sort	(EX6-20)

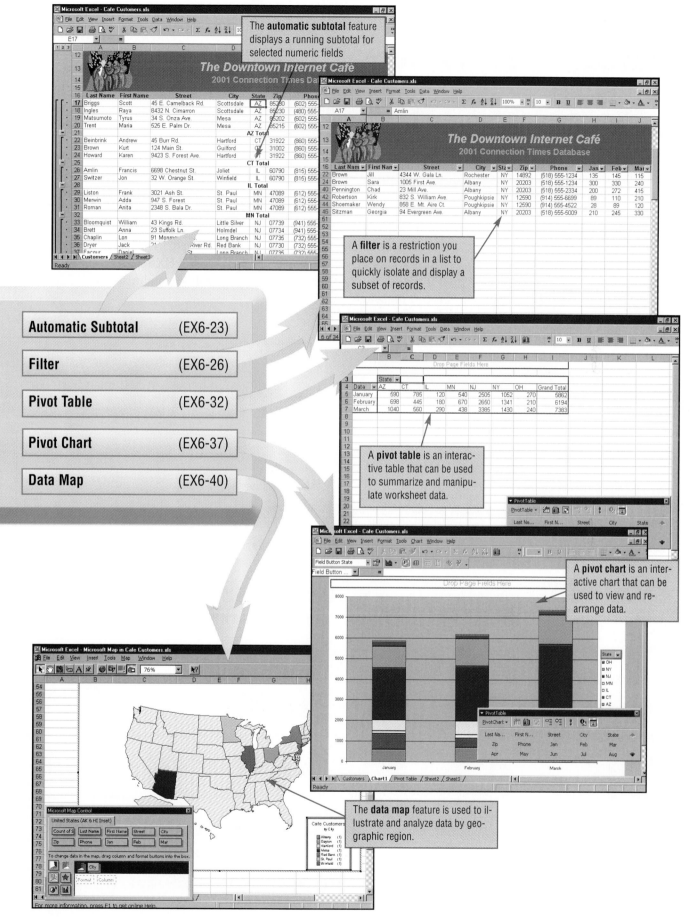

The **automatic subtotal** feature displays a running subtotal for selected numeric fields

Automatic Subtotal   (EX6-23)

Filter   (EX6-26)

Pivot Table   (EX6-32)

Pivot Chart   (EX6-37)

Data Map   (EX6-40)

A **filter** is a restriction you place on records in a list to quickly isolate and display a subset of records.

A **pivot table** is an interactive table that can be used to summarize and manipulate worksheet data.

A **pivot chart** is an interactive chart that can be used to view and re-arrange data.

The **data map** feature is used to illustrate and analyze data by geographic region.

Tutorial Review

Key Terms

automatic subtotal   EX6-23

case sensitive   EX6-16

criteria   EX6-26

criteria range   EX6-3

database   EX6-3

database range   EX6-3

data form   EX6-6

data map   EX6-40

data settings   EX6-9

data validation   EX6-9

error alert   EX6-9

field   EX6-3

field name   EX6-3

filter   EX6-26

Find and Replace   EX6-15

input message   EX6-9

list   EX6-3

multilevel sort   EX6-20

pivot chart   EX6-37

pivot table   EX6-32

record   EX6-3

sort   EX6-20

wildcard characters   EX6-16

Command Summary

Command	Shortcut Key	Button	Action
File/Prin**t** Area/**S**et Print Area			Sets area of worksheet to be printed
File/Prin**t** Area/**C**lear Print Area			Clears print area
Edit/**F**ind	Ctrl + F		Searches selected cells for a specified value
Edit/R**e**place	Ctrl + H		Searches for a specified value and replaces it with another specified value
View/**N**ormal			Displays standard worksheet view
View/**P**age Break Preview			Displays worksheet in Page Break view
F**o**rmat/C**e**lls/**C**ategory/Text			Treats all entries, including numbers, as text
Tools/A**u**diting/**S**how Auditing Toolbar			Displays auditing toolbar
Data/**S**ort		⟨↓⟩	Arranges selected data alphabetically, numerically, or by date
Data/**F**ilter/Auto**F**ilter			Displays items based on selections in a list or database range
Data/**F**ilter/**S**how All			Redisplays all records after a filter operation has been performed
Data/**F**ilter/**A**dvanced Filter			Displays items based on the criteria range of a database worksheet
Data/**F**orm			Displays a data form dialog box for record entry and modification
Data/Su**b**totals			Calculates subtotals and grand totals for selected columns or fields
Data/Va**l**idation			Defines valid data for a cell or cell range
Data/**P**ivotTable and PivotChart Report			Starts the PivotTable and PivotChart Wizard to create or modify a PivotTable or PivotChart report

Command	Shortcut Key	Button	Action
Microsoft Map			
View/T**i**tle			Displays/hides map title
Map/**A**dd Features			Adds features such as lakes and cities to map
Map/**O**pen Custom Pin Map			Creates a custom pin map
Map/Cat**e**gory Shading Options			Sets color and label options for series

Screen Identification

In the following worksheet, several items are identified by letters. Enter the correct term for each item in the spaces that follow.

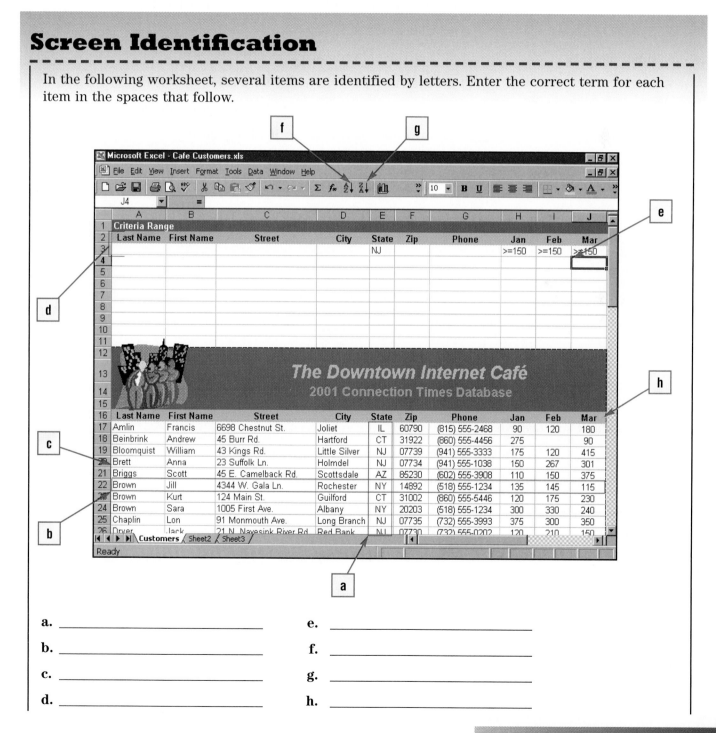

a. _____

b. _____

c. _____

d. _____

e. _____

f. _____

g. _____

h. _____

Matching

Match the numbered item with the correct lettered description.

1. criteria range _____   **a.** a database column

2. field _____   **b.** displays a subset of list data according to specified criteria

3. database _____   **c.** defines acceptable entries for a cell or cells

4. filter _____   **d.** used to enter complex criteria to filter records

5. database range _____   **e.** a database row

6. input message _____   **f.** used to enter database records

7. sort _____   **g.** describes the valid entry for a cell

8. record _____   **h.** where database fields and records are entered

9. data form _____   **i.** organizes data in a specified sequence

10. data validation _____   **j.** a list of related worksheet information

Fill-In

Complete the following statements by filling in the blanks with the correct terms.

a. You define a database range in the _____ at the top of the worksheet.

b. A _____ is used to enter records into a database.

c. _____ adds drop-down lists to the field names in a database.

d. To move from field to field in a data form, press _____.

e. The default sort order is _____.

f. The _____ subtotal function calculates the smallest value in a list.

g. The two types of filter functions are _____ and _____.

h. A _____ is an interactive chart used to view and rearrange data.

i. You use a _____ to illustrate and analyze data by geographic region.

j. If a user makes an incorrect entry in a validated cell, a(n) _____ appears.

Multiple-Choice

Circle the correct response to the questions below.

1. A _____ summarizes data and can be manipulated to show different views of the data.

   a. data map

   b. pivot table

   c. data list

   d. database range

2. Excel automatically displays the _____ from the database range as the field names in a data form.

   a. row names

   b. records

   c. column labels

   d. cell references

3. The sort feature lets you sort up to _____ fields in a database at a time.

   a. 2

   b. 1

   c. 3

   d. 4

4. The _____ option in a filter field drop-down list enables you to specify ranges of values that the record must meet to be displayed.

   a. Options

   b. Range

   c. Values

   d. Custom

5. The quickest way to locate a record in the data form for a large database is to click _____.

   a. Find Prev

   b. Criteria

   c. Find Next

   d. ⇨ Find

6. A sort that is performed on more than one column or field is called a _____.

   a. multiple sort

   b. advanced sort

   c. multilevel sort

   d. selective sort

7. To enter a new record using the data form, you click _____.

   a. | New |

   b. | Add... |

   c. | Next > |

   d. | OK |

8. The "Filter the list, in place" option in the Advanced Filter dialog box means that the filtered list will appear in the _____.

   a. specified worksheet

   b. database range

   c. specified column

   d. criteria range

9. To locate and correct data in a database range, you use the _____.

   a. Find command

   b. Replace command

   c. Data form

   d. All of the above

10. To remove a filter from a database range and redisplay all records, you use the _____ command.

    a. Undo

    b. Remove Filter

    c. Show All

    d. None of the above

True/False

Circle the correct answer to the following questions.

1. You can erase any changes you made to a record in the data form by clicking ⟳ ▾, as long as you do it before proceeding to the next record or closing the dialog box. True False

2. If there are no blank rows below a database range, Excel cannot add the new records. True False

3. You can select a named cell range from the Name box drop-down list. True False

4. Excel includes a special form, called a database form, that makes it easy to enter database records. True False

5. To use automatic subtotals, you must sort the database range by the field that the subtotals will be based on. True False

6. A filter operation rearranges data according to the criteria you specify. True False

7. A pivot table modifies a database in order to summarize the data. True False

8. Data that is analyzed using a data map must include a column that contains geographic data. True False

9. The Count Subtotal function adds the numeric values in a list. True False

10. You must first create a new folder in Windows Explorer before you can save a workbook in it. True False

Discussion Questions

1. Discuss different ways that an Excel database can be used. Why would you create a database worksheet as opposed to a standard worksheet?

2. Discuss the differences between the AutoFilter function and the Advanced Filter function. When would you use AutoFilter? When would Advanced Filter be more appropriate?

3. Discuss how a pivot table can be used to analyze data. When would you want to create a combined PivotTable and PivotChart report?

4. Discuss how a data map can be used to recognize trends and serve as a marketing tool. What types of data would you include?

Hands-On Practice Exercises

- -

Step by Step

Rating System   ☆ Easy
☆☆ Moderate
☆☆☆ Difficult

1. The Adventure Travel Tours company maintains records on each travel agent's tour bookings during the year. This information is used to determine the agents' commission as well as to track how successful they are in promoting different tours. You want to use Excel to create a database to record and analyze this information. Your completed database will be similar to the one shown here.

a. Open the file Adventure Travel Database on your data disk.

b. Enter the following information into the database.

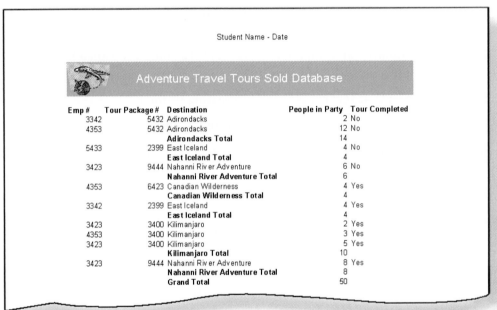

Employee Number	Tour Package Number	Destination	People in Party	Tour Completed
3423	3400	Kilimanjaro	2	Yes
5433	2399	East Iceland	4	No
3342	2399	East Iceland	4	Yes
4353	3400	Kilimanjaro	3	Yes
3423	9444	Nahanni River Adventure	6	No
3342	5432	Adirondacks	2	No
4353	5432	Adirondacks	12	No
3423	3400	Kilimanjaro	5	Yes
4353	6423	Canadian Wilderness	4	Yes
3423	9444	Nahanni River Adventure	8	Yes

c. Adjust the widths of the columns to fully display the data.

d. Add appropriate data validation settings.

e. Define the database range. Create and define a criteria range.

f. Use the criteria range to display only those tours booked with five or more people in the party. Redisplay all records.

g. Sort the database by Tour Completed and Destination.

h. Subtotal the worksheet data by every change in destination, and sum the People in Party field.

i. Adjust the Destination column width to fully display the subtotal labels.

j. Enter your name and the current date in the header of the worksheet. Save the worksheet. Print the database range of the worksheet only.

☆

2. Starting in January, the Animal Angels animal rescue agency has been using an Excel database to keep track of the animals that have been adopted. They have asked you to do some analysis on the data so they can better see trends and make any needed adjustments. Your completed analysis of the database will be similar to the one shown here.

Student Name
4/26/01

Animal Angels
Animal Adoptions Database

Date	Category	Animal Age	Adoptee	Phone	Adoption Fee
2/9/01	Dog	2 Years	Harvey, Sara	555-1243	$55.00
1/4/01	Dog	4 Months	Jones, April	555-3443	$55.00
1/6/01	Dog	4 Years	Sierra, Judy	555-7464	$55.00
1/6/01	Dog	6 Months	Kelly, William	555-7674	$55.00

a. Open the Animal Angels Database on your data disk.

b. Define the database range.

c. Using the data form, enter three new records into the database. Use your name as the Adoptee name in the last record.

d. Sort the database on Category.

e. Enter your name in the header of the worksheet. Print the sorted database.

f. Create a criteria range and use it to display only the dogs in the database.

g. Print the database title and filtered output only.

h. Remove the filter and save the worksheet as Animal Angels Database Updated.

3. The Lifestyle Fitness Club maintains an Excel database of employee information. You are responsible for updating and using the database. You have been asked to provide an analysis of jobs and pay rates. Your completed analysis will be similar to the one shown here.

Lifestyle Fitness Club
Employee Database

Employee ID	Hire Date	Last Name	First Name	Location	Job Title	Pay Rate	Hours	Weekly Pay
1329	3/8/00	Delucchi	Bill	Fort Myers	Aerobics Director	$12.00	40	$480.00
1345	4/15/00	Helfand	Eric	Fort Myers	Aerobics Instructor	$9.75	18	$175.50
1341	4/15/00	Lembi	Damon	Fort Myers	Child Care Provider	$6.75	20	$135.00
0021	2/1/95	Schiff	Marc	Fort Myers	Greeter	$6.00	25	$150.00
2209	10/15/00	Fromthart	Lisa	Fort Myers	Greeter	$6.00	25	$150.00
0234	4/12/98	Delano	Gordon	Fort Myers	Instructor	$8.50	25	$212.50
0061	7/8/95	Nichols	Cathy	Fort Myers	Office Manager	Salary		
0322	5/1/96	Morgan	Dan	Fort Myers	Sales Associate	$10.00	35	$350.00
0090	12/12/95	Pennington	Chad	Fort Myers	Sales Associate	$10.50	35	$367.50
9999	5/24/01	Student	Name	Fort Myers	Sales Associate	$10.00	20	$200.00

a. Open the file Lifestyle Fitness Database on your data disk.

b. Define the database range.

c. Using the data form, enter a new record into the database. Use your name as the employee name. Enter **9999** as your employee number, the current date as the Hire Date, **Fort Myers** as your Location, **Sales Associate** as your job title, **10.00** as your pay rate and **20** as your Hours.

d. Sort the database on job title and subtotal the report. Subtotal the pay rate, and weekly pay columns on changes in job title. Best fit the job title field column.

e. Print the database range, including the title. Remove the subtotals.

f. Create a criteria range above the database table, and use an advanced filter to display just the employees who work in the Fort Myers location. Best fit the job title column again.

g. Hide columns E through K. Print the database area of the worksheet including the title using landscape orientation and displaying the worksheet gridlines. Save the workbook.

4. Mahoney Book Store has asked you to help with the inventory database it maintains of books on hand. The store manager would also like you to analyze the data. Your completed analysis of the database will be similar to the one shown here.

Student Name   4/26/99

Mahoney Books

ISBN	Author	Title	Age Group	Wholesale Price	Retail Price	On Hand
839-29-383	Marc Tolon Brown	Arthur Goes to Camp	Childrens	$2.95	$4.76	4
883-39-333	Marc Tolon Brown	Arthur Accused	Childrens	$2.95	$4.76	4
938-28-848	Marc Tolon Brown	Arthur's Valentine	Childrens	$2.95	$4.76	5
					$4.76 Total	13
899-332-38	Judy Serra	Counting Crocodiles	Childrens	$4.89	$6.99	5
					$6.99 Total	5
849-343-38	Maurice Sendak	Where the Wild Things Are	Childrens	$5.57	$7.95	3
					$7.95 Total	3
003-383-38	Michael Roizen	Real Age: Are You As Young As You Can Be?	Adults	$6.60	$11.00	3
					$11.00 Total	3
899-483-38	John Grisham	The Testament	Adults	$10.50	$15.00	4
999-393-38	Kevin Henkes	Lilly's Purple Plastic Purse	Childrens	$11.20	$15.00	6
899-383-38	Bernhard Schlink	The Reader	Childrens	$10.50	$15.00	3
					$15.00 Total	13
768-389-77	David Macaulay	The New Way Things Work	Adults	$11.87	$16.00	1
					$16.00 Total	1
958-484-82	Laurence Yep	Child of the Owl	Childrens	$11.87	$16.95	2
					$16.95 Total	2
873-944-33	Laurence Yep	The Butterfly Boy	Childrens	$14.89	$18.00	8
					$18.00 Total	8
007-383-38	Suze Orman	The 9 Steps to Financial Freedom	Adults	$13.77	$23.00	4
559-383-56	Sam McBratney	Guess How Much I Love You	Childrens	$14.97	$23.00	1
559-383-38	Margaret Wise Brown	Goodnight Moon	Childrens	$16.10	$23.00	4
					$23.00 Total	9
549-383-22	J K Rowling	Harry Potter and the Sorcerer's Stone	Childrens	$17.50	$25.00	8
					$25.00 Total	8
009-383-66	Tami Hoag	Ashes to Ashes	Adults	$19.57	$27.95	5
					$27.95 Total	5
899-383-34	Robert B. Parker	Hush Money	Adults	$24.50	$35.00	6

a. Open the file Mahoney Books on your data disk.

b. Define the database range.

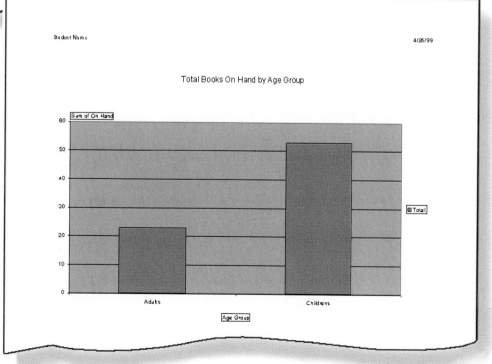

c. Using the data form, enter the following records into the database.

ISBN	Author	Title	Age Group	Wholesale Price	Retail Price	Quantity On Hand
549-383-22	J. K. Rowling	Harry Potter and the Sorcerer's Stone	Childrens	$17.50	$25.00	8
958-484-82	Laurence Yep	Child of the Owl	Childrens	$11.87	$16.95	2
938-28-848	Marc Tolon Brown	Arthur's Valentine	Childrens	$2.95	$4.76	5

d. Create a criteria range and use it to display only those records with fewer than four books on hand. Redisplay all records.

e. Sort the records in ascending order by retail price.

f. Display subtotals for each change in retail price. Use the sum function for the number of books on hand at each price.

g. Preview the worksheet. Add a header that displays your name and the current date. Print the database range, including the title, in landscape orientation on one page.

h. Remove the subtotals from the worksheet.

i. Create a pivot table in a new worksheet that displays the age group as the rows and the sum of the quantity on hand as the column. Name the sheet appropriately.

j. Create a pivot chart from the pivot table. Add an appropriate chart title. Name the sheet appropriately.

k. Create a custom header for the pivot chart worksheet that contains your name and the current date. Print the pivot chart in landscape orientation. Save the workbook.

5. The Gallery Print Distribution Co. is a print supplier to retail art stores. The company keeps track of the suppliers of the prints it sells in an Excel database. The manager has asked you to help with the analysis of the information. Your completed analysis of the database will be similar to that shown here.

a. Open the file Gallery Print Database on your data disk.

b. Name the database range.

c. Using the data form, enter three new records into the database. Use your name as the artist in the last record.

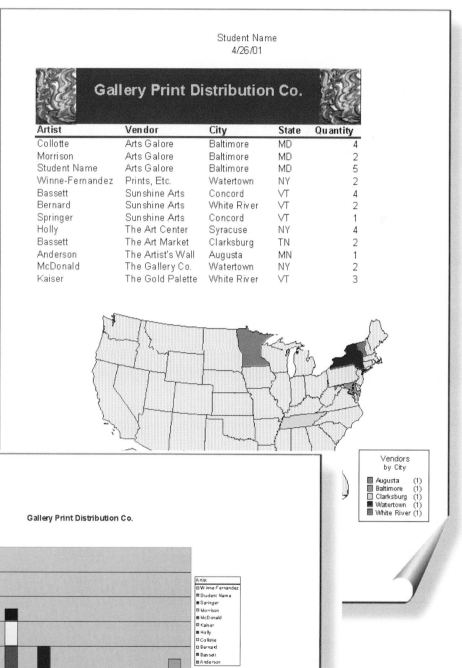

d. Filter the database to display only those records with a state of NY or VT. Redisplay all records.

e. Sort the database by vendor and artist. Create a subtotal on the vendor field and sum the quantity.

f. Print the database showing subtotals, then remove the subtotals.

g. Create a pivot table in a new worksheet that displays the vendor as the rows and the artists as the columns. Use quantity as the data. Create a pivot chart from the pivot table. Add an appropriate chart title.

h. In the database worksheet, create a data map below the database. Remove the map title. Add color to the map. Change the legend so that it displays cities and change the legend title appropriately. If necessary, move the legend box so it does not cover the map.

i. Rename the sheet tabs to describe the type of data displayed.

j. Add a header to all the worksheets that contains your name and the current date. Create a footer that displays the sheet tab name centered. Print the database sheet and the pivot chart sheet. Save the workbook.

On Your Own

6. The Kids Express Toy Company needs help with its inventory. Create a worksheet that has 15 database records to hold the inventory. The records should contain a product identification number, description, wholesale distributor, wholesale price, retail price, and quantity on hand. Sort the records by distributor. Add a subtotal to the records based on retail price. Create a pivot table and pivot chart that clarify the data. Enter your name and the current date as a header to the worksheets. Print the worksheets.

7. Jones Mail Order Office Supply needs a database to hold records of the suppliers it buys inventory from. Create a database with the appropriate fields. Enter 15 records into the database. Sort the database by the state in which the distributor resides. Subtotal the data on the categories to which the inventory belongs. For example, résumé paper and wrapping paper would be in the paper category. Create a pivot table and pivot chart that clarify the data. Enter your name and the current date as a header to the worksheets. Print the worksheets.

8. You work for the city recreation department. As part of your responsibilities, you maintain records for the enrollments in the summer baseball league. The league consists of six teams. The enrollments have just started for this summer's program, and you want to create a database of players who have signed up so far for the various teams. Create a database that lists the players' names, address, phone number, age, and team name. Enter 30 records into the database. Enter your name as one of the records. Sort the database by teams, last name, and first name, in that order. Create a pivot table and pivot chart that clarify the data. Enter your name and the current date as a header to the worksheets. Print the worksheets.

9. Desert Cleaning Company has been growing rapidly and wants to keep track of its customers with an Excel worksheet database. Create a worksheet database that includes each customer's ID number, cleaning address with suite or apartment number, contact name, phone number, square footage, and hourly rate. Enter 15 records into the database. Enter your name as the contact for the first record. Sort the database by square footage. Create a pivot table and pivot chart that clarify the data. Enter your name and the current date as a header to the worksheets. Print the worksheets.

10. The Work at Home Office Supply Company is finding its current method of maintaining employee information on file cards to be cumbersome. The management has asked you to create a worksheet database using Excel that includes all the information that would be required for payroll. Include fields for hours worked each week. Enter 15 records into the database. Enter your name as the first record. Sort the database by employee first name within last name. Create a pivot table and pivot chart that clarify the data. Enter your name and the current date as a header to the worksheet. Print the worksheet.

Working Together 2: Creating Hyperlinks and Web Pages; E-Mailing and Embedding

Case Study   You have two workbooks set up with data pertaining to the Downtown Internet Café customers. To make it easier to work with the two workbooks you will create a hyperlink in one workbook to open the other workbook.

In addition, Evan has requested that you e-mail a copy of the pivot chart sheet to him. As for the data map, Evan would like you to convert it to a Web page so he can see if it would be a good marketing tool to add to the café Web site.

One last thing Evan would like to see is the five-year forecast with the scenarios you created for it. You will embed the workbook in a cover memo created in Word to be sent to Evan via e-mail. Your completed document will look like the one shown below.

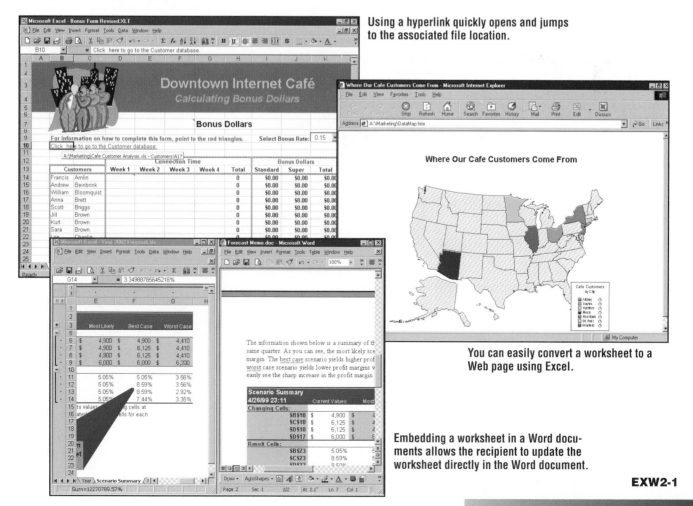

Using a hyperlink quickly opens and jumps to the associated file location.

You can easily convert a worksheet to a Web page using Excel.

Embedding a worksheet in a Word documents allows the recipient to update the worksheet directly in the Word document.

EXW2-1

Note: This tutorial assumes that you already know how to use Word 2000 and that you have completed Tutorial 6 of Excel. You will need the Café Customer Analysis data file you created in that tutorial.

Creating a Hyperlink between Workbooks

As you continue to work on the bonus form worksheet, you have decided to add a **hyperlink** from the bonus form to the Café Customer Analysis database worksheet. A hyperlink creates a shortcut or jump to another location in the same or different workbook, or to a document in a different application or to a document on a Web site. Adding this hyperlink will make it easy to switch to the Customers database and copy the customers' total monthly connection times from the form into the database. You will also be able to copy the customer names from the database into the form each month as new customers are added and others deleted.

1 Load Excel and open the workbook template file Bonus Form Revised on your data disk.

You want to display the hyperlink in cell B10. To create the hyperlink,

2 If necessary, move to B10.

Choose **I**nsert/**H**yper**l**ink.

You can also access the Insert Hyperlink dialog box by selecting **H**yperlink from a cell's shortcut menu or using the keyboard shortcut Ctrl + K.

Your screen should be similar to Figure 1.

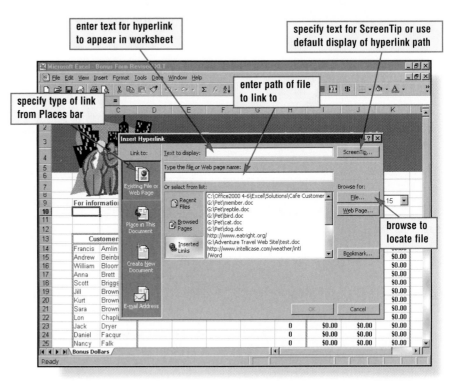

Figure 1

From the Insert Hyperlink dialog box, you first need to specify the type of link from the Places bar. The four options are described below.

Option	Effect
Existing File or Web Page	Creates a link in an existing Web page or file
Place in This Document	Creates a link to a place in the active file
Create New Document	Creates a link to a file that you have not created yet
E-mail Address	Creates a link that allows users to create an e-mail message with the correct address in the To line

You want to create a link to a location in another workbook file. Then you need to select the location in the document to which the link will jump.

3 ■ If necessary, select E**x**isting File or Web Page from the Places bar.

■ In the Type the File or Web Page Name text box, enter the location of the Café Customer Analysis workbook (e.g., **A:\Excel Student Files\Marketing\Café Customer Analysis**).

> You can also click ☐ File... ☐ and browse to locate and select the file from a series of dialog boxes.

Next you want to enter the text that the hyperlink will display in the worksheet. If you do not enter anything in the "Text to Display" box, the hyperlink automatically displays the name of the linked file.

4 ■ Replace the entry in the Text to Display text box with **Click here to go to the Customer database**.

> If you would rather put instructions in a comment box that will be displayed only when the pointer is over the hyperlink cell, you can click ☐ ScreenTip... ☐ and enter the instructional text.

Your screen should be similar to Figure 2.

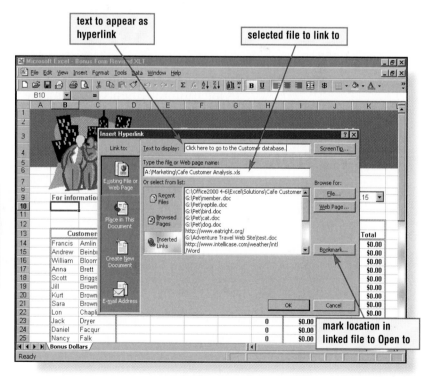

text to appear as hyperlink

selected file to link to

mark location in linked file to Open to

Figure 2

Because the Café Customer Analysis workbook contains several worksheets, you want to make sure the user is taken directly to the worksheet containing the database information. To do this, you create a bookmark to that location in the linked workbook file.

Click

Your screen should be similar to Figure 3.

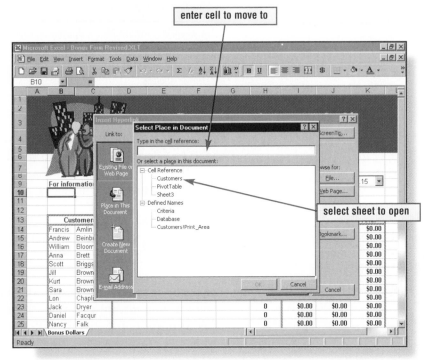

Figure 3

The Select Place in Document dialog box enables you to select a specific location to which you want the user to be taken in the linked document. The list box displays a tree diagram showing the outline of the information in the workbook and named ranges. From the outline you select the location to which you want to link. You also want the cell pointer positioned on the first cell in the Customers list (A17).

6 ■ Select Customers in the Cell Reference list.

■ In the Type in the Cell Reference text box, enter **A17**.

■ Click [OK] to close the Select Place in Document dialog box.

■ Click [OK] to close the Insert Hyperlink dialog box.

■ Point to cell B10.

Your screen should be similar to Figure 4.

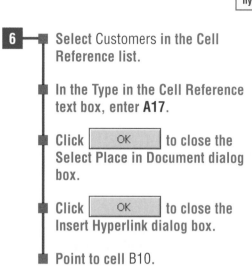
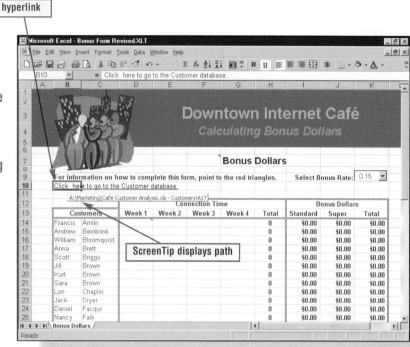

Figure 4

Use **I**nsert/**H**yperlink or **H**yperlink/Edit **H**yperlink on the shortcut menu to edit an existing hyperlink and **H**yperlink/**R**emove Hyperlink to remove the hyperlink.

The default hyperlink color is blue for a link that has not been selected and purple for a followed link.

The text you entered for the hyperlink is displayed in the cell. It appears underlined and in the hyperlink colors associated with the worksheet. The ScreenTip displays the path to the linked document. To use the hyperlink, you click on it.

7 ■ Click on the hyperlink text.

Your screen should be similar to Figure 5.

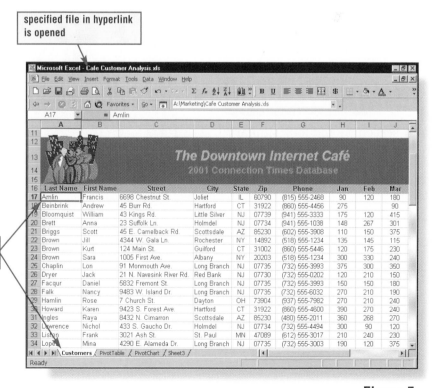

Figure 5

Once both workbooks are open, you can switch back and forth between them or tile the two workbooks so you can see them both simultaneously.

The Café Customer Analysis workbook is opened and the cell selector is in the location you specified as the bookmark. The user can now copy the customer names from the Customer database worksheet to the Bonus form, and copy the monthly Internet connection totals from the Bonus form to the Customers database worksheet.

8 ■ Save the revised bonus form as a template file named **Café Bonus2** on your data disk.

■ Close the Café Bonus2 workbook.

E-Mailing a Worksheet

Evan's next request was for you to e-mail him the pivot chart from the Café Customer Analysis workbook.

select how and what you want sent in the e-mail message

1 ■ Make the PivotChart sheet active.

■ Click 🖼 E-mail.

The menu equivalent is **F**ile/Sen**d** to/**M**ail Recipient.

If you do not have an e-mail program installed, the 🖼 button is not displayed and you will need to skip this section.

Your screen should look similar to Figure 6.

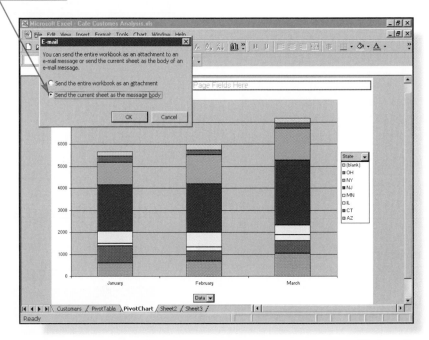

Figure 6

If the E-mail dialog box does not display, Excel automatically attaches the entire workbook file and the PivotChart will not appear in the message body as in Figure 7.

From the E-mail dialog box, you can choose whether to send the entire active workbook as an attachment to your e-mail message or the current worksheet as the body of the message. In this case, you want to send only the PivotChart sheet in the body of the message.

2 Select Send the current sheet as the message **b**ody.

Click [OK] .

Your screen should look similar to Figure 7.

E-mail toolbar

message header

PivotChart sheet is displayed as message contents

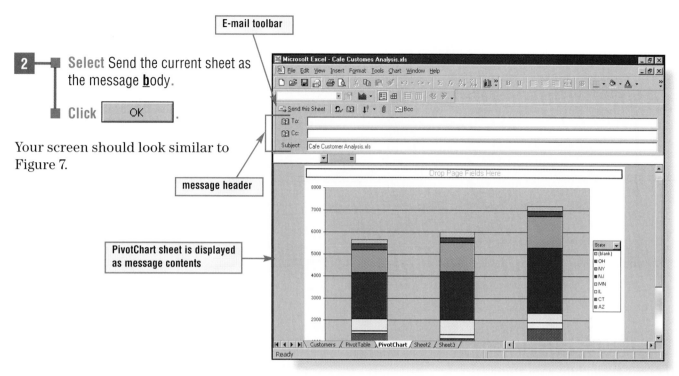

Figure 7

Additional Information

To send an e-mail message to multiple recipients, separate the e-mail addresses with semicolons.

An e-mail message box is displayed at the top of the worksheet. You use the message box to specify the recipient's e-mail address, the e-mail address of anyone you want to send a copy of this message to (cc:), and the subject of the message. You can also use the toolbar buttons to select recipient names from your e-mail address book, attach a file to the message, set the message priority (high, normal, or low), include a follow-up message flag, and set other e-mail options. The name of the worksheet appears in the Subject box by default. And, finally, you can use this message box to send the message.

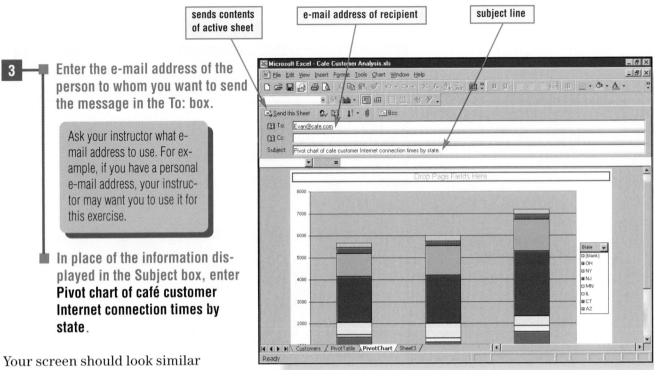

Figure 8

3 Enter the e-mail address of the person to whom you want to send the message in the To: box.

> Ask your instructor what e-mail address to use. For example, if you have a personal e-mail address, your instructor may want you to use it for this exercise.

Place of the information displayed in the Subject box, enter **Pivot chart of café customer Internet connection times by state**.

Your screen should look similar to Figure 8.

That is all the information that is required to send the e-mail message. You are now ready to send your e-mail message.

> If you do not have an Internet connection established, you will not be able to send this message. Click Cancel to cancel the connection message.

4 Click .

Your message is sent and the e-mail message box is removed from the screen.

Saving a Worksheet as Web Page

> This portion of the tutorial assumes that a Web browser application is installed on the computer you are using.

Evan has also asked you to create a Web page using the Data Map worksheet. A **Web page** is a document that can be used on the World Wide Web (WWW) and displayed in your browser application. A **browser** is a program that connects you to remote computers and displays the Web pages you request. You could use **F**ile/We**b** Page Preview to see what your current workbook would look like as a Web page before actually converting it. However, since you already know what you want the Web page to contain, you will go ahead and create it.

1 ■ Make the Customers sheet active.

■ Select the data map object and copy it to a blank sheet.

■ Use <u>I</u>nsert/<u>W</u>orksheet to insert a new blank sheet.

■ Paste the data map object into the new sheet.

■ Name the sheet **DataMap**.

■ If necessary, deselect the data map object.

■ Choose <u>F</u>ile/Save as Web Page.

Your screen should look similar to Figure 9.

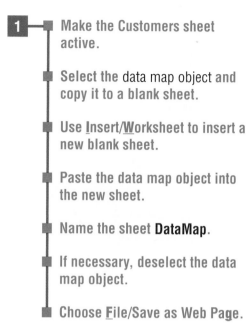

specify location to save file

enter name of file   Web page file extension

Figure 9

The Save As dialog box is used to name your Web page file, choose the location where you want the file saved, and specify whether you want to use the entire workbook or just the current selection as your Web page contents. The default file name is the same as the workbook file name with the Web page file extension of .htm. Excel converts a worksheet to a Web page by adding **hypertext markup language (HTML)** coding to the document. HTML is a programming language in which all Web pages are written. HTML commands are interpreted by the browser software you are using and control how the information on a page is displayed, such as font colors and size, and how an item, such as a form will be processed. HTML also allows users to click on highlighted text or images and jump to other locations on the same page, other pages in the same site, or to other sites and locations on the WWW altogether. You can also add a title to your Web page from this dialog box. First you will specify the current worksheet as the contents for the Web page.

2 ■ Select S<u>e</u>lection:Sheet.

Because the Web page will not include the entire workbook, the default file name has been changed to Page.htm. You want to rename this so it reflects the page contents.

3 ■ Change the file name to **DataMap**.

You also want to include a title that will appear over the sheet contents on the Web page and in the title bar of the browser.

4  Click Change Title... .

Your screen should look similar to Figure 10.

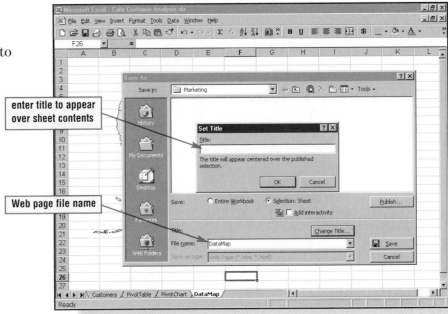

Figure 10

5 Type **Where Our Café Customers Come From**.

Click OK .

The title you specified is now displayed in the Save As dialog box. Next, you want the Web page displayed in the browser application so you can check how it looks.

6 Click Publish... .

Your screen should look similar to Figure 11.

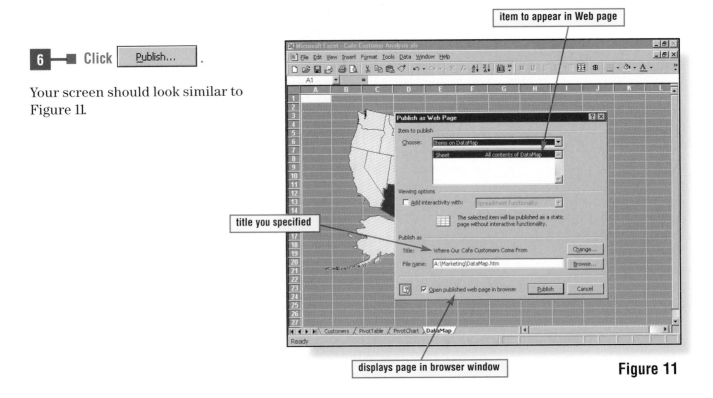

Figure 11

The Web page selections you have already made are displayed in the Publish As Web Page dialog box. The only thing you need to do here is specify that you want the page displayed in the browser.

7 ■ If necessary, select **O**pen published web page in browser.

■ Click Publish... .

■ If necessary, maximize your browser window.

Your screen should look similar to Figure 12.

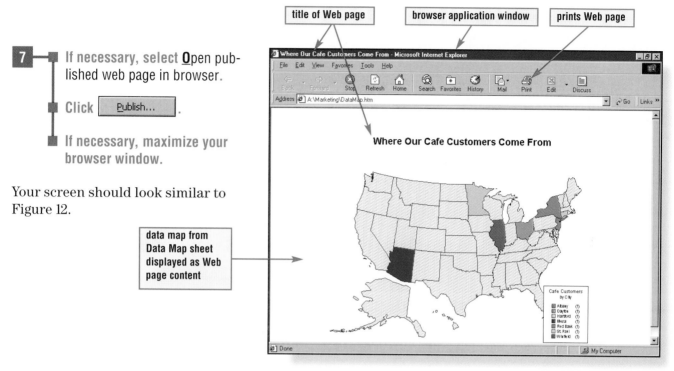

title of Web page

browser application window

prints Web page

data map from Data Map sheet displayed as Web page content

Where Our Cafe Customers Come From

Figure 12

The data map is displayed as a Web page in your Internet browser. You like the way this looks, so you can go ahead and print it and then close the browser and Customers workbook.

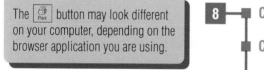

The ⊠ button may look different on your computer, depending on the browser application you are using.

8 ■ Click .

■ Close the browser application.

■ Close and save the Café Customer Analysis workbook.

Embedding an Object in Another Application

The last thing you need to send Evan is a memo that describes and shows the first-quarter 2002 forecast and scenarios. To do this, you'll open the memo already created for you in Word and, in the appropriate locations, **embed** the sections from the 2002 Forecast workbook that Evan wants. An object that is embedded in a document becomes part of that document, called the **destination document**. This means that you can modify it without affecting the **source document** where the original object resides.

1 Start Microsoft Word 2000 and open the file Forecast Memo on your data disk.

Inthe memo header, replace the Student Name with your name.

Move to the blank line below the first paragraph of the memo.

Your screen should be similar to Figure 13.

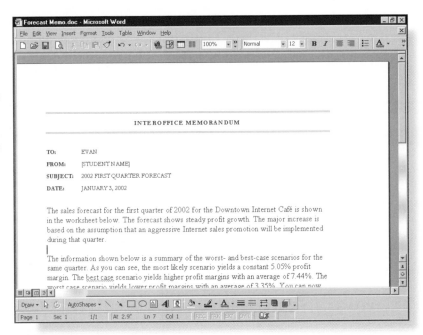

Figure 13

You will use two different methods to embed the worksheet objects into this document, Paste Special and drag-and-drop. First, you will embed the first-quarter 2002 forecast spreadsheet with Paste Special.

2 Switch to Excel and open the Year 2002 Forecast workbook file on your data disk. If you are asked whether you want to update the file, click No .

Make the First Quarter sheet active.

Copy the range A1 through F24.

Switch to Word.

Choose Edit/Paste Special.

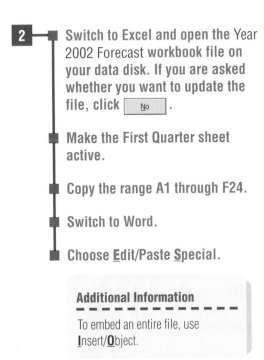

Additional Information

To embed an entire file, use Insert/Object.

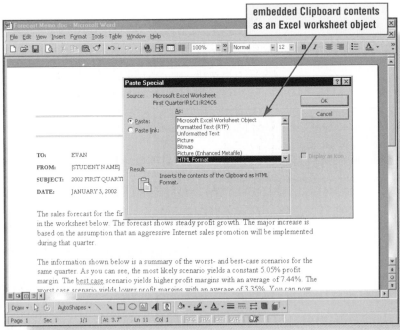

Figure 14

Your screen should be similar to Figure 14.

The Paste option inserts or embeds the Clipboard contents in the format you specify from the As list box. To embed the contents of the Clipboard into a document so it can be edited using the server application, select the option that displays the server name, in this case Excel.

3 ■ **Select** Microsoft Excel Worksheet Object.

■ **Click** [OK] .

Your screen should be similar to Figure 15.

worksheet selection embedded in memo

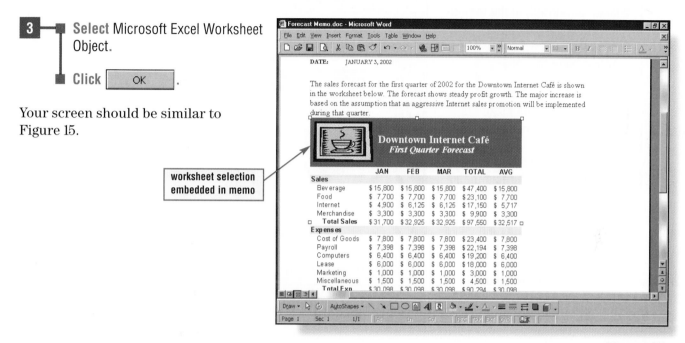

Figure 15

The selected portion of the worksheet is displayed in the memo at the location of the insertion point. When an object is embedded, the entire selection is pasted and displayed in the destination document as a single object.

As you can see, the object is a bit large. You will decrease the size and center it below the paragraph.

4 ■ **Decrease the size of the worksheet object and center it between the margins.**

Your screen should be similar to Figure 16.

embedded object sized and moved

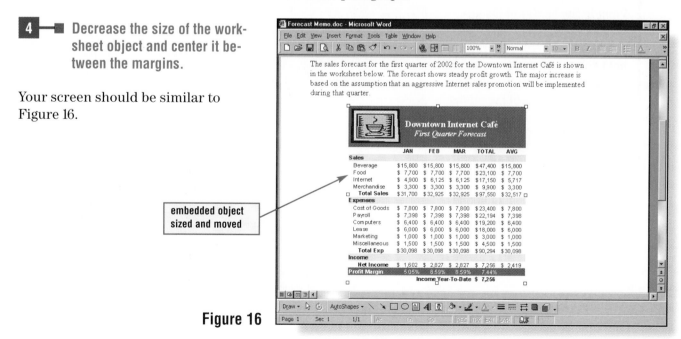

Figure 16

Next, you'll embed the second Excel object, the scenarios, using drag-and-drop.

5   Insert a page break before the second paragraph of the memo.

> Press Ctrl + ←Enter to quickly insert a page break.

Switch to Excel and make the Scenario Summary sheet active.

Choose Tile Windows **V**ertically from the taskbar shortcut menu.

Scroll the Word document to see the second paragraph in the window.

Your screen should be similar to Figure 17.

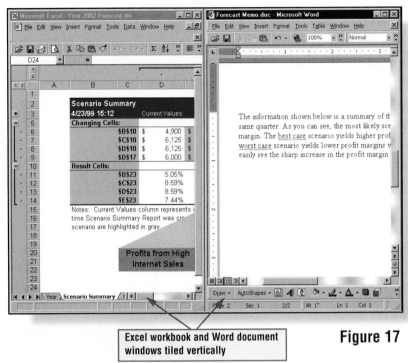

Excel workbook and Word document windows tiled vertically

Figure 17

The screen now displays both the Word and Excel windows. Now you can drag the object you want to embed from Excel into the Word document.

6   On the Excel Scenario Summary worksheet, select the range B2 through G14.

Point to the border of the selected range. When the mouse pointer appears as an arrow, hold down Ctrl while you drag the selected object to below the second paragraph of the memo.

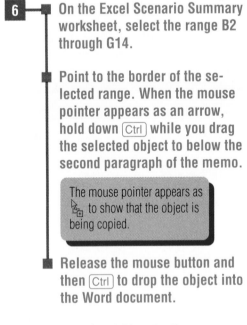

> The mouse pointer appears as to show that the object is being copied.

Release the mouse button and then Ctrl to drop the object into the Word document.

Your screen should be similar to Figure 18.

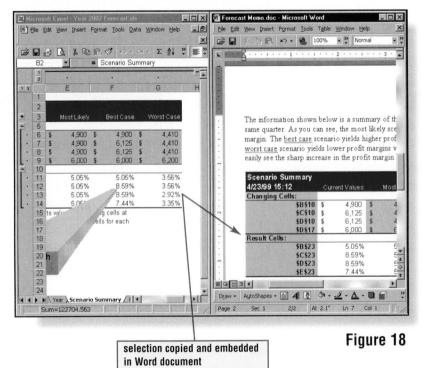

selection copied and embedded in Word document

Figure 18

7 ■ Choose <u>U</u>ndo Tile from the taskbar shortcut menu.

■ If necessary, maximize the Word window.

Your screen should be similar to Figure 19.

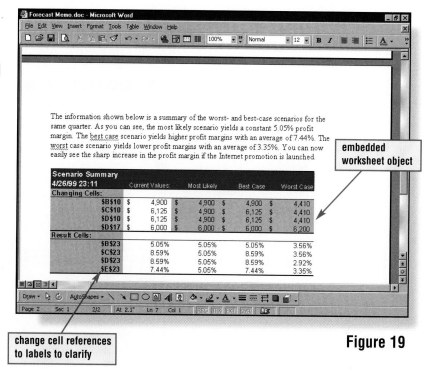

embedded worksheet object

change cell references to labels to clarify

Figure 19

Both Excel objects are now embedded in the Word document. However, you would like to make some changes to the second object.

Updating an Embedded Object

The cell references in the Scenario summary do not make much sense now because the column letters and row numbers are not shown. Therefore, you would like to change the references in the memo without changing the actual spreadsheet. This is possible because the object is embedded, not linked.

To demonstrate how an embedded object works, you will close the Excel source file and application and edit the worksheet from within the Word document.

1 ■ Switch to Excel, and if necessary, maximize the window.

■ Close the workbook without saving changes and exit Excel.

The server application is used to edit data in an embedded object. To open the server application and edit the worksheet, you double-click the embedded object.

2 ■ Double-click the Scenario Summary object.

Your screen should be similar to Figure 20.

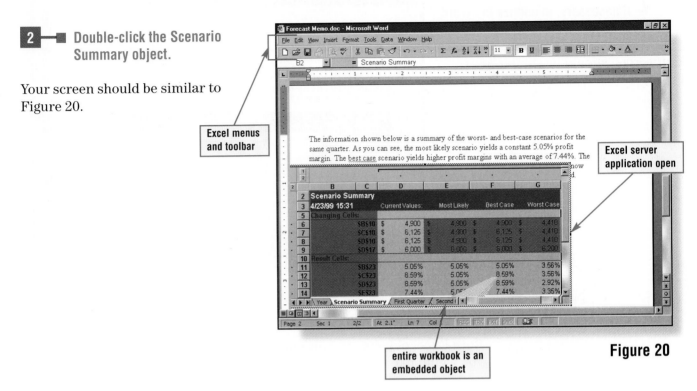

Excel menus and toolbar

Excel server application open

entire workbook is an embedded object

Figure 20

The server application, in this case Excel, is opened. The Excel menus and toolbars replace some of the menus and toolbars in the Word application window. The selected portion of the embedded object is displayed in an editing worksheet window. Now you can use the server commands to edit the object.

3 — ■ Make the following changes to the worksheet:

Cell	Entry	Cell	Entry
C5	**Internet Sales**	C10	**Profit Margin**
C6	**Jan**	C11	**Jan**
C7	**Feb**	C12	**Feb**
C8	**Mar**	C13	**Mar**
C9	**Total**	C14	**Total**

Additional Information

- - - - - - - - - - - - - - - -

You can also change numeric values in an embedded object. Any formulas that contain these values will be recalculated in the embedded object without affecting the source workbook.

■ Adjust the column width as needed to fully display the labels.

■ Delete the 3-D shape.

■ Position and size the object to display only that portion of the worksheet you want to appear in the memo.

■ Close the server application by clicking anywhere outside the object.

Your screen should be similar to Figure 21.

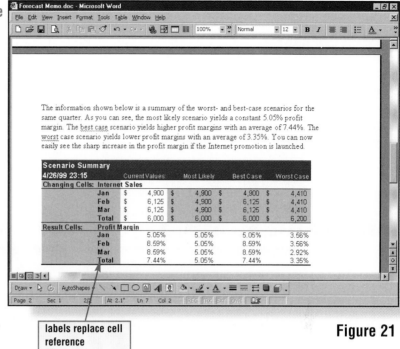

labels replace cell reference

Figure 21

The embedded object in the memo is updated to reflect the changes you made. You could now send the memo to Evan as an attachment in an e-mail message.

4 — ■ Save the memo as **2002 Forecast**.

■ Preview and print both pages of the memo.

■ Exit Word.

Deciding When to Link or Embed Objects

- -

Keep the following in mind when deciding whether to link or embed objects.

Linking was covered in the Working Together section following Tutorial 3.

Use Linking When:	Use Embedding When:
File size is important	File size is not important
Users have access to the source file and application	Users have access to the application but not to the source file
The information is updated frequently	The data changes infrequently

Key Terms

browser EXW2-8
destination document EXW2-11
embed EXW2-11
hyperlink EXW2-2

hypertext markup language (HTML) EXW2-9
source document EXW2-11
Web page EXW2-8

Command Summary

Command	Shortcut Key	Button	Action
File/Save as Web Page			Creates a Web page from the entire active workbook or the current worksheet selection
File/Web Page Preview			Displays the active workbook as a Web page in the browser without actually publishing it
File/Send to/Mail Recipient			Sends the active workbook as an attachment to an e-mail message or the current worksheet as the body of an e-mail message
Insert/Worksheet			Inserts a new blank sheet in the workbook
Insert/Object			Inserts an entire file as an embedded object
Insert/Hyperlink	Ctrl + K		Inserts a new hyperlink or modifies the selected hyperlink
Insert/Hyperlink/Remove Hyperlink			Removes hyperlink settings from selected cell

Hands-on Practice Exercises

Rating System   ☆ Easy
☆ ☆ Moderate
☆ ☆ ☆ Difficult

Step by Step

☆

1. To complete this problem you must have completed Problem 5 in Tutorial 4. Karen at Animal Angels has asked you to provide her with information about projected income for 2002. You want to create a memo to her and include a copy of the scenario summary you created in the memo. The completed memo is shown on the next page.

   a. Load Word and open the document Animal Angels Memo on your data disk.

   b. In the header, replace the From placeholder with your name.

   c. Load Excel and open the workbook file Animal Angels Contributions.

   d. Switch to the scenario summary page.

e. Select the range containing the Scenario Summary (without the Notes) and embed it below the first paragraph in the Word memo. Center the summary below the paragraph.

f. Double-click on the scenario summary in Word to edit the row labels in the Excel worksheet.

g. Change the following cell contents in Excel.

C6   **Annual Memberships**

C7   **Phone Solicitation**

C8   **Corporate Donations**

C9   **Raffle Tickets**

C10 **Pet Shows**

C11 **Other**

C13 **Total**

h. Save the Excel workbook as Animal Angels Income. Exit Excel.

i. If necessary adjust the size and placement of the summary in the memo. Save the Word document as Animal Angels Projected. Preview and print the document.

☆☆

2. Alice at the Gallery Print Distribution Co. has asked you to send her the database of vendors that buy from the distribution company. You would like to send it to her in an e-mail so that she can review it before the meeting in the morning.

a. Open the file Gallery Print Database (Problem 5, tutorial 6) on your data disk.

b. Select Send the current sheet as the message body after choosing the e-mail command.

c. Address the message to your instructor and carbon-copy yourself.

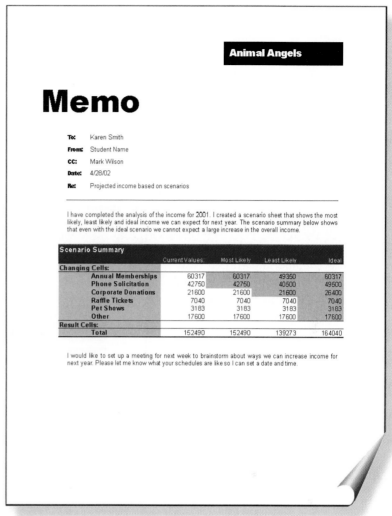

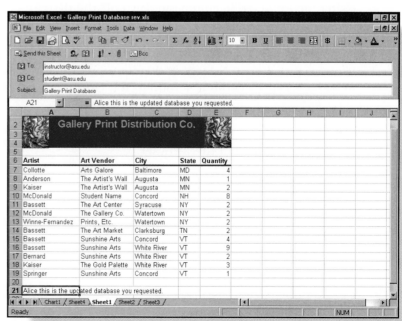

d. Edit the subject line to read **Gallery Print Database**.

e. Below the database data, enter the following message: **Alice this is the updated database you requested.**

f. If you are connected, send the sheet. Close the workbook.

g. Print the message when you receive it in your inbox.

3. You have been working on the Auto Loan worksheet to compare the loan amounts on three automobiles. You would like to add this worksheet to your Web site so that others can use it also.

a. Open the file Auto Loan Calculator you created in Problem 3 in Tutorial 5.

b. Enter the following text in cell A19: **Enter the Adjustable Variables to match the loan you are considering.** In cell A20 enter: **Replace the make and model information with three autos of your choice.**

c. Save the current sheet only as a Web page. Add the title **Compare Loans on Three Automobiles**.

d. Publish the sheet with the Add interactivity with spreadsheet functionality feature on.

e. Maximize the browser window.

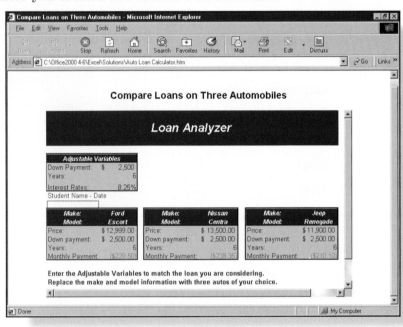

f. Open the Property Toolbox by right-clicking on the worksheet in the browser window.

g. Using the Show/Hide command, turn off the display of the toolbar, gridlines, column headers, and row headers. Close the Property toolbox.

h. Test the functionality of the Web page by changing the number of years for the loan to 6.

i. If necessary, adjust the text and column widths on the original worksheet to display the whole worksheet without scrolling. You can then republish the sheet after removing the existing sheet from your data disk.

j. Enter your name and the current date in a cell below the adjustable variables.

k. Print the Web page in the browser.

Glossary of Key Terms

3-D reference: A reference to the same cell or range on multiple sheets in the same workbook.

3-D shape: A line, AutoShape, or free-form drawing object that has a three-dimensional effect applied to it.

Absolute reference: A cell or range reference in a formula whose location remains the same (absolute) when copied. Indicated by a $ character entered before the column letter or row number or both.

Active cell: The cell displaying the cell selector that will be affected by the next entry or procedure.

Active pane: The pane that contains the cell selector.

Active sheet: A sheet that contains the cell selector and that will be affected by the next action.

Active workbook: The workbook that contains the cell selector and that will be affected by the next action.

Adjacent range: A rectangular block of adjoining cells.

Adjustable cells: In Solver, the cells whose values will be changed in order to attain the value set in the target cell.

Alignment: The vertical or horizontal placement and orientation of an entry in a cell.

Area chart: A chart that shows trends by emphasizing the area under the curve.

Argument: The data used in a function on which the calculation is performed.

Arrange Windows: A feature that displays all open workbook files in separate windows on the screen in a tiled, cascade, horizontal, or vertical arrangement.

Autofill: Feature that logically repeats and extends a series.

Autoformat: A built-in combination of formats that can be applied to a range.

Automatic recalculation: The recalculation of a formula within the worksheet whenever a value in a referenced cell in the formula changes.

Automatic subtotal: A feature that calculates and displays a running subtotal for selected numeric columns or fields in a list.

Browser: A program that connects you to the remote computers and displays the Web pages you request.

Cascade: The window arrangement that displays one workbook window on top of the other, cascading down from the top of the screen.

Case sensitive: The capability to distinguish between uppercase and lowercase characters.

Category-axis title: A label that describes the X axis.

Category name: Labels displayed along the X axis in a chart to identify the data being plotted.

Cell: The space created by the intersection of a vertical column and a horizontal row.

Cell selector: The heavy border surrounding a cell in the worksheet that identifies the active cell.

Chart: A visual representation of data in a worksheet.

Chart gridlines: Lines extending from the axis lines across the plot area that make it easier to read and evaluate the chart data.

Chart object: One type of graphic object that is created using charting features included in Excel 2000. A chart object can be inserted into a worksheet or into a special chart sheet.

Chart title: Appears at the top of a chart and is used to describe the contents of the chart.

ClipArt: A collection of graphics that is usually bundled with a software application.

Column: A vertical block of cells one cell wide in the worksheet.

Column chart: A chart that displays data as vertical columns.

Column letters: The border of letters across the top of the worksheet that identifies the columns in the worksheet.

Column-oriented: In a data table, the orientation of the data in a table down a column as opposed to across a row (row-oriented).

Combination chart: A chart type that includes mixed data markers, such as both columns and lines.

Comments: Notes attached to cells that can be used to help clarify the meaning of the data, provide documentation, or ask a question.

Constant: A value that does not change unless you change it directly by typing in another entry.

Controls: Graphic objects that are designed to automate the process of completing information in a worksheet.

Copy area: The cell or cells containing the data to be copied.

Criteria: A set of of limiting conditions entered in the criteria range that you want records to meet in order to be displayed.

Criteria range: A named range consisting of the field names from the database and at least one blank row where the search conditions are entered that are used to locate and analyze the information contained in a database.

Custom dictionary: An additional dictionary you create to supplement the main dictionary.

Database range: A named range consisting of the field names and records in a database where the database records are displayed.

Data form: A special form that makes it easy to enter database records.

Data labels: Labels for data points or bars that show the values being plotted on a chart.

Data map: A feature that identifies areas on a map used to illustrate and analyze data by geographic region.

Data marker: Represents a data series on a chart. It can be a symbol, color, or pattern, depending upon the type of chart.

Data series: The numbers to be charted.

Data settings: The data validation restrictions you place on a field.

Data table: A type of what-if analysis where one or more variables are changed to see the effect on the formula or formulas that include these variables.

Data validation: Restrictions placed on a cell or range of cells that defines the type or types of entries that are acceptable.

Database: An organized collection of related information consisting of fields and records. Also called a *list* in Excel.

Date numbers: The integers assigned to the days from January 1, 1900, through December 31, 2099, that allow dates to be used in calculations.

Dependent cell: The cell that receives linked data.

Dependent workbook: The workbook file that receives the linked data.

Destination: The cell or range of cells that receives the data from the copy area or source.

Destination document: The workbook file in which a linked object is inserted.

Destination file: A document in which a linked object is inserted.

Drawing object: Object consisting of shapes such as lines and boxes that can be created using features on the Drawing toolbar.

Embed: To insert information into a destination file of another application that becomes part of this file but can be edited within the destination file using the server application.

Embedded chart: A chart that is inserted into another file.

Embedded object: Information inserted into a destination file of another application that becomes part of this file but can be edited within the destination file using the server application.

Error alert: A message that appears when a validation rule is violated and reminds the user of what the correct data entry type is.

Explode: To separate a wedge of a pie chart slightly from the other wedges in the pie.

External reference formula: A formula that creates a link between workbooks.

Field: A single category of data in a list, the values of which appear in a column of a worksheet.

Field name: A label used to identify the data stored in a field.

Find and Replace: A feature that allows users to find specific information and replace it with new information.

Fill handle: A small black square located in the lower-right corner of the selection that is used to create a series or copy to adjacent cells with a mouse.

Filter: A restriction placed on records in a database to temporarily isolate a subset of records.

Form: A formatted worksheet that is designed to be completed by filling in data in the blank spaces.

Font: The typeface, type size, and style associated with a worksheet entry that can be selected to improve the appearance of the worksheet.

Footer: A line (or several lines) of text that appears at the bottom of each page just above the bottom margin.

Format: Formats are settings that affect the display of entries in a worksheet.

Formatting toolbar: A toolbar that contains buttons used to change the format of a worksheet.

Formula: An entry that performs a calculation.

Formula bar: The bar near the top of the Excel window that displays the cell contents.

Freeze: To fix in place on the screen specified rows or columns or both when scrolling.

Function: A prewritten formula that performs certain types of calculations automatically.

Goal Seek: Tool used to find the value needed in one cell to attain a result you want in another cell.

Graphic: A non-text element or object, such as a drawing or picture that can be added to a document.

Group: An object that contains other objects.

Header: A line (or several lines) of text that appears at the top of each page just below the top margin.

Heading: Row and column entries that are used to create the structure of the worksheet and describe other worksheet entries.

Horizontal: The window arrangement that displays one open workbook window above the other.

Hyperlink: A special type of link that provides a shortcut or jump to another location in the same or different workbook, to a document in a different application, or to a document on a Web site.

Hypertext markup language (HTML): A programming language whose commands are interpreted by the browser software you are using and control how the information on a Web page is displayed.

IF function: A function that checks to see if certain conditions are met and then takes action based upon the results of the check.

Input cell: A cell in which a list of values is substituted to see the resulting effect on the related formulas. Input values can be listed down a column (column-oriented) or across a row (row-oriented).

Input message: A message attached to a validation cell that appears when the cell is selected and tells the user what the valid entry for that cell is.

Landscape: The orientation of the printed document so that it prints sideways across the length of the page.

Legend: A brief description of the symbols used in a chart that represent the data ranges.

Line chart: A chart that represents data as a set of points along a line.

Link: A relationship created between files that allows data in the destination file to be updated automatically when changes occur in the source file.

Linked object: Information created in a source file from one application and inserted into a destination file of another application while maintaining a link between files.

List: An organized collection of related information consisting of fields and records. Also called a **database**.

Live link: A linked object that automatically reflects in the destination document any changes made in the source document when the destination document is opened.

Logical operators: Symbols used in formulas that compare values in two or more cells.

Macro: A stored series of keystrokes and commands. When the macro is executed or run, the stored actions are performed automatically.

Macro Recorder: A tool used to create a macro by recording a series of actions as macro statements as they are performed.

Main dictionary: The dictionary included with Office 2000.

Merged cell: A cell made up of several selected cells combined into one.

Minimal recalculation: The recalculation of only the formulas in a worksheet that are affected by a change of data.

Mixed reference: A cell address that is part absolute and part relative.

Multilevel sort: A sort on more than one column or field.

Name box: The area located on the left side of the formula bar that provides information about the selected item such as the reference of the active cell.

Nested function: A second argument in a function that is enclosed within its own set of parentheses.

Nonadjacent range: Cells or ranges that are not adjacent but are included in the same selection.

Nper: In the PMT function, the nper argument is the total number of payments for the loan.

Number: A cell entry that contains any of the digits 0 to 9 and any of the special characters + = ( ) , . / $ % E e.

Number formats: Affect how numbers look onscreen and when printed.

Object: An element such as a text box that can be added to a workbook and that can be selected, sized, and moved. In Visual Basic, the object is the item that the statement will affect (such as a cell, cell range, worksheet, or workbook). The object is enclosed in parentheses and surrounded by quotes.

One-variable data table: A data table that can contain one or more formulas and in which each formula refers to one input cell.

Operand: A value on which a numeric formula performs a calculation.

Order of precedence: Order in which calculations are performed and can be overridden by the use of parentheses.

Pane: A division of the worksheet window, either horizontal or vertical, through which different areas of the worksheet can be viewed at the same time.

Password: A secret code that prevents unauthorized users from turning off protection.

Paste area: The cells or range of cells that receive the data from the copy area or source.

Picture: An illustration such as a scanned photograph.

Pie chart: A chart that compares parts to the whole. Each value in the data range is a wedge of the pie (circle).

Pivot chart: An interactive chart that can be used to view and rearrange data.

Pivot table: An interactive table that can be used to summarize and manipulate worksheet data in an easy-to-read, row-and-column format.

Plot area: The area of the chart bounded by the axes.

Portrait: The orientation of the printed document so that it prints across the width of the page.

Principal: In the PMT function, the principal, or **pv**, argument is the amount of the loan.

Property: In Visual Basic Editor, the property is what you want to do to the object. The property consists of reserved words that have special meaning and direct Excel to perform the specified action.

Protection: A feature that prevents unauthorized users from changing a worksheet's contents by protecting the entire worksheet or specified areas of it.

Pv: See **Principle**.

Range: A selection consisting of two or more cells in a worksheet.

Range name: A descriptive name assigned to a cell or range of cells.

Rate: In the PMT function, the rate argument is the interest rate of the loan.

Record: A row of a database or list consisting of a group of related fields.

Reference: The column letter and row number of a cell.

Relative reference: A cell or range reference that automatically adjusts to the new location in the worksheet when the formula is copied.

Row: A horizontal block of cells one cell high in the worksheet.

Row numbers: The border of numbers along the left side of the worksheet that identifies the rows in the worksheet.

Row-oriented: In a data table, the orientation of the data in a table across a row as opposed to down a column (column-oriented).

Run: To execute the commands stored in the macro.

Sans serif font: A font, such as Arial or Helvetica, that does not have a flair at the base of each letter.

Scenario: A named set of input values that you can substitute in a worksheet to see the effects of a possible alternative course of action.

Selection handles: Small boxes surrounding a selected object that are used to size the object.

Selection rectangle: Border around selected object indicating it can be sized or moved.

Series formula: A formula that links a chart object to the source worksheet.

Serif font: A font, such as Times New Roman, that has a flair at the base of each letter.

Sheet reference: Used in references to other worksheets and consists of the name of the sheet enclosed in quotes and is separated from the cell reference by an exclamation point.

Sheet tab: On the bottom of the workbook window, the tabs where the sheet names appear.

Sizing handle: Box used to size a selected object.

Solver: A tool that is used to perform what-if analyses to determine the effect of changing values in two more cells, called the adjustable cells, on another cell, called the target cell.

Sort: To rearrange the records in a list in ascending or descending alphabetical order.

Source: The cell or range of cells containing the data you want to copy.

Source cell: The cell or range of cells containing the data you want to copy.

Source document: The document that stores the data for the linked object.

Source file: The document that stores the data for the linked object.

Source workbook: The workbook file that supplies linked data.

Spell-checking: Feature that locates misspelled words and proposes correction.

Spreadsheet: A rectangular grid of rows and columns used to enter data.

Stack: The order in which objects are added in layers to the worksheet.

Stacked-column chart: A chart that displays the data values as columns stacked upon each other.

Standard toolbar: A toolbar that contains buttons used to complete the most frequently used menu commands.

Statement: Information you enter into the Visual Basic Editor.

Style: A named combination of formats that can be applied to a selection.

Sub procedure: In Visual Basic Editor, a Sub procedure begins with a statement that starts the macro and ends with one that closes the macro (an End Sub statement). Sub procedures can also include remarks about the macro (such as its name and purpose) and functions (such as returning values to the procedure).

Syntax: Rules of structure for entering all Visual Basic statements.

Tab scroll buttons: Located to the left of the sheet tabs, they are used to scroll sheet tabs right or left.

Target cell: In Solver, the cell you set to the value that you want to be attained.

Template: A workbook file that contains predesigned worksheets that can be used as a pattern for creating other similar sheets in new workbooks. It has an .xlt file extension.

Text: A cell entry that contains text, numbers, or any other special characters.

Text box: A rectangular object in which you type text.

Tiled: A window arrangement in which open workbook windows are displayed one after the other in succession, across and down the screen.

Title: In a chart, descriptive text that explains the contents of the chart.

Two-variable data table: A data table that uses only one formula that refers to two different input cells, one column-oriented and one row-oriented. The purpose of this table is to show the resulting effect on the formula when the values in both of these cells are changed.

Typeface: The appearance and shape of characters. Some common typefaces are Roman and Courier.

Value axis: Y axis of a chart that usually contains numerical values.

Value axis title: A label that describes the values on the Y axis.

Variable: The resulting value of a formula that changes if the data it depends on change.

Vertical: The window arrangement in which open workbook windows are displayed side-by-side.

Visual Basic Editor: A programming application used to write and edit macros attached to Excel workbooks.

Web page: A document that can be used on the World Wide Web (WWW) and displayed in your browser application.

What-if analysis: A technique used to evaluate what effect changing one or more values in formulas has on other values in the worksheet.

Wildcard characters: A question mark (?) used to match any single character or an asterisk (*) to match any string of characters.

Word wrap: Feature that automatically determines when to begin the next line of text.

Workbook: The file in which you work and store sheets created in Excel 2000.

Workbook window: A window that displays an open workbook file.

Worksheet: Similar to a financial spreadsheet in that it is a rectangular grid of rows and columns used to enter data.

Workspace: The area of the Excel 2000 application window where workbook windows are displayed.

X axis: The bottom boundary line of a chart.

Y axis: The left boundary line of a chart.

Z axis: The left boundary line of a 3-D chart.

Command Summary

Command	Shortcut Key	Button	Action
File/**O**pen <file name>	Ctrl + O	📂	Opens an existing workbook file
File/**C**lose		✖	Closes open workbook file
File/**S**ave <file name>	Ctrl + S	💾	Saves current file on disk using same file name
File/Save **A**s <file name>			Saves current file on disk using a new file name
File/Save as Web Pa**g**e			Creates a Web page from the entire active workbook or the current worksheet selection.
File/We**b** Page Preview			Displays the active workbook as a Web page in the browser without actually publishing it
File/Page Set**u**p/Header/Footer			Adds header and/or footer
File/Prin**t** Area/**S**et Print Area			Sets area of worksheet to be printed
File/Prin**t** Area/**C**lear Print Area			Clears print area
File/Print Pre**v**iew		🔍	Displays worksheet as it will appear when printed
File/**P**rint	Ctrl + P	🖨	Prints a worksheet
File/**P**rint/**E**ntire Workbook			Prints all the sheets in a workbook
File/Sen**d** to/**M**ail Recipient			Sends the active workbook as an attachment to an e-mail message or the current worksheet as the body of an e-mail message
File/Propert**i**es			Displays information about a file
File/E**x**it		✖	Exits Excel 2000
Edit/**U**ndo	Ctrl + Z	↺ ▾	Undoes last editing or formatting change
Edit/**R**edo	Ctrl + Y	↻ ▾	Restores changes after using Undo
Edit/**C**opy	Ctrl + C	📋	Copies selected data to Clipboard
Edit/**P**aste	Ctrl + V	📋	Pastes selections stored in Clipboard
Edit/Paste **S**pecial/Paste **L**ink			Creates a link to the source document
Edit/Edit Lin**k**s			Modifies selected link
Edit/Linked **O**bject/**E**dit Link			Modifies selected linked object

EXC-1

Command	Shortcut Key	Button	Action
Edit/**Fi**ll			Fills selected cells with contents of source cell
Edit/Cle**a**r/Co**mm**ents		🗑	Deletes comment in selected cell
Edit/Cle**a**r/**C**ontents	Delete		Clears cell contents
Edit/**D**elete/**R**ow			Deletes selected rows
Edit/**D**elete/**C**olumn			Deletes selected columns
Edit/D**e**lete Sheet			Deletes selected sheets from a workbook
Edit/**M**ove or Copy Sheet			Moves or copies selected sheet
Edit/**F**ind	Ctrl + F		Searches selected cells for a specified value
Edit/R**e**place	Ctrl + H		Searches for a specified value and replaces it with another specified value
View/**T**oolbars			Displays or hides selected toolbar
View/**N**ormal			Displays standard worksheet view
View/**P**age Break Preview			Displays worksheet in Page Break Preview
View/**C**omments		🗗	Displays all comments or hides all displayed comments
View/**Z**oom		100% ▾	Changes magnification of window
Insert/Copied C**e**lls			Inserts row and copies text from Clipboard
Insert/**R**ows			Inserts a blank row
Insert/**C**olumns			Inserts a blank column
Insert/**W**orksheet			Inserts a new worksheet in a workbook
Insert/**Ch**art		📊	Inserts chart into worksheet
Insert/**F**unction	⇧Shift + F3	f_x	Inserts a function
Insert/**N**ame/**D**efine			Assigns a name you specify to a cell or range of cells
Insert/**N**ame/**P**aste			Places the selected cell or cell range name in the formula bar or lists names in the worksheet
Insert/**N**ame/**C**reate			Creates a range name using the text in cells
Insert/Co**mm**ent		🗨	Inserts a new comment in selected cell
Insert/**E**dit Comment		🗨	Edits comment in selected cell
Insert/**P**icture/**F**rom File			Inserts picture at insertion point from disk
Insert/**O**bject			Inserts an entire file as an embedded object
Insert/Hyperl**i**nk	Ctrl + K		Inserts a new hyperlink or modifies the selected hyperlink

Command	Shortcut Key	Button	Action
Insert/Hyper**l**ink/**R**emove Hyperlink			Removes hyperlink settings from selected cell
F**o**rmat/C**e**lls/Number/**C**ategory Currency		$	Applies Currency format to selection
F**o**rmat/C**e**lls/Number/**C**ategory Accounting			Applies Accounting format to selection
F**o**rmat/C**e**lls/Number/**C**ategory Date			Applies Date format to selection
F**o**rmat/C**e**lls/Number/**C**ategory Percent			Applies Percent format to selection
F**o**rmat/C**e**lls/Number/**C**ategory Decimal places		.00 / .0	Increases or decreases the number of decimal places associated with a number value
F**o**rmat/C**e**lls/Alignment/**H**orizontal/Left (Indent)		≡	Left-aligns entry in cell space
F**o**rmat/C**e**lls/Alignment/**H**orizontal/Center		≡	Center-aligns entry in cell space
F**o**rmat/C**e**lls/Alignment/**H**orizontal/Right		≡	Right-aligns entry in cell space
F**o**rmat/C**e**lls/Alignment/**H**orizontal/Left (Indent)/1		≣	Left-aligns and indents cell entry one space
F**o**rmat/C**e**lls/Alignment/**H**orizontal/Center Across Selection			Centers cell contents across selected cells
F**o**rmat/C**e**lls/**F**ont			Changes font and attributes of cell contents
F**o**rmat/C**e**lls/Font/F**o**nt Style/Bold	Ctrl + B	**B**	Bolds selected text
F**o**rmat/C**e**lls/Font/F**o**nt Style/Italic	Ctrl + I	*I*	Italicizes selected text
F**o**rmat/C**e**lls/Font/**U**nderline/Single	Ctrl + U	U	Underlines selected text
F**o**rmat/C**e**lls/Font/**C**olor		A ▾	Adds color to text
F**o**rmat/C**e**lls/Patterns/**C**olor		◇ ▾	Adds color to cell background
F**o**rmat/**R**ow/H**e**ight			Changes height of selected row
F**o**rmat/**R**ow/**H**ide			Hides selected rows
F**o**rmat/**R**ow/**U**nhide			Displays rows that were previously hidden
F**o**rmat/**C**olumn/**W**idth			Changes width of columns
F**o**rmat/**C**olumn/**A**utofit Selection			Changes column width to match widest cell entry
F**o**rmat/S**h**eet/**R**ename			Renames sheet
F**o**rmat/**A**utoformat			Applies one of 16 built-in table formats to the worksheet range
F**o**rmat/**S**tyle/**S**tyle name/Currency		$	Applies currency style to selection
F**o**rmat/**S**tyle/**S**tyle name/Percent		%	Changes cell style to display percentage
F**o**rmat/S**e**lected Data Series	Ctrl + 1	▣	Changes format of selected data series
F**o**rmat/S**e**lected Data Series/Data Labels	Ctrl + 1		Inserts data labels into chart

Command	Shortcut Key	Button	Action
F**o**rmat/S**e**lected Legend	Ctrl + 1		Changes format of legend
F**o**rmat/S**e**lected Chart Title	Ctrl + 1		Changes format of selected chart title
F**o**rmat/S**e**lected Object			Changes format of embedded objects
Tools/**S**pelling	F7		Spell-checks worksheet
Tools/**P**rotection/**P**rotect Sheet			Prevents unauthorized users from changing a sheet's contents
Tools/**G**oal Seek			Adjusts value in specified cell until a formula dependent on that cell reaches specified result
Tools/Sc**e**narios			Creates and saves sets of data used to perform what-if analyses
Tools/A**u**diting/**S**how Auditing Toolbar			Displays auditing toolbar
Tools/Sol**v**er			Calculates a formula to achieve a given value by changing one of the variables that affects formulas
Tools/**M**acro/**M**acros	Alt + F8		Runs, edits or deletes selected macro
Tools/**M**acro/**R**ecord New Macro			Records a series of actions as a macro
Tools/**M**acro/Stop **R**ecording			Stops the recording of a macro
Chart/Chart **T**ype			Changes type of chart
Chart/Chart **O**ptions			Adds options to chart
Chart/**L**ocation			Moves chart from worksheet to chart sheet
Data/**S**ort			Arranges selected data alphabetically, numerically, or by date
Data/**F**ilter/Auto**F**ilter			Displays items based on selections in a list or database range
Data/**F**ilter/**S**how All			Redisplays all records after a filter operation has been performed
Data/**F**ilter/**A**dvanced Filter			Displays items based on the criteria range of a database worksheet
Data/**F**orm			Displays a data form dialog box for record entry and modification
Data/Su**b**totals			Calculates subtotals and grand totals for selected columns or fields
Data/Va**l**idation			Defines valid data for a cell or cell range
Data/**T**able			Creates a data table based on specified input values and formulas
Data/**P**ivotTable and PivotChart Report			Starts the PivotTable and PivotChart Wizard to create or modify a PivotTable or PivotChart report

Command	Shortcut Key	Button	Action
Window/**A**rrange			Arranges open windows side-by-side, vertically, horizontally, or tiled.
Window/Un**f**reeze			Unfreezes window panes
Window/**F**reeze Panes			Freezes top and/or leftmost panes
Window/**S**plit			Divides window into four panes at active cell
Window/Remove **S**plit			Removes split bar from active worksheet
Visual Basic Editor			
File/**C**lose and Return to Microsoft Excel			Closes the Visual Basic Editor window and returns to the active Excel worksheet
Microsoft Map			
Map/Cat**e**gory Shading Options			Adds color shading to map
View/Ti**t**le			Displays/hides map title

Index

Notes